# Bertolt Brecht: Plays, Poetry and Prose

*Edited by* JOHN WILLETT, RALPH MANHEIM and TOM KUHN

## The Collected Plays

*Volume Four*

# Bertolt Brecht Collected Plays

Volume Four

Edited by Tom Kuhn and John Willett

Round Heads and Pointed Heads
*translated by Tom Kuhn*

Fear and Misery of the Third Reich
*translated by John Willett*

Señora Carrar's Rifles
*translated by Wolfgang Sauerländer*

Dansen
*translated by Rose and Martin Kastner*

How Much Is Your Iron?
*translated by Rose and Martin Kastner*

The Trial of Lucullus
*translated by H.R. Hays*

Methuen

10 9 8 7 6 5 4 3 2 1

First published in Great Britain in 2001
by Methuen Publishing Ltd
215 Vauxhall Bridge Road, London SW1V 1EJ
by arrangement with Suhrkamp Verlag, Frankfurt am Main

A CIP catalogue record for this book is available from the British Library

ISBN 0 413 47230 2

Typeset by Deltatype Ltd, Birkenhead, Wirral
Printed in Great Britain by St Edmundsbury Press, Bury St Edmunds,
Suffolk.

# Contents

# Introduction

1932/33 TO 1939: ANTI-FASCIST EXILE

This volume contains Brecht's important anti-Fascist plays from the 1930s, and indeed nearly all of his dramatic output from the years 1932 to 1939, the year of both *The Trial of Lucullus* (in the first version which we publish here) and *Mother Courage and Her Children* (in volume 5 of the series). These are the works that were conceived and written at the time of Brecht's flight from Germany in February 1933, immediately after the Reichstag Fire, and during his and the family's stay near Svendborg, a small town on the southern tip of the Danish island of Fyn. At the time of the conception and first version of *Round Heads and Pointed Heads* Brecht was still working in the seething atmosphere of artistic experiment and collaboration of Berlin in the late Weimar Republic, the political world and the artistic society which provided the context for the great *Lehrstück* experiments (of volume 3). For most of the thirties, however, Brecht and his colleagues were living and working in exile. The change in circumstances for a dramatic artist could scarcely be more stark. In Berlin he knew the theatres, the directors, the actors, and indeed the audiences. He could work closely with them, trying to evolve a new political avant-garde in the theatre. In exile he struggled to maintain links with other exiled artists, he travelled around, to Paris, to London, to Moscow, to New York, seeking out opportunities, making contacts, trying to stay up to date with political developments and aesthetic debates, and his diaries, letters and poems are full of worries about his isolation and the absence or inaccessibility of a public. The plays likewise document his concerns, and they signal a shift in his conception of a political literature: towards more immediate, accessible and practical contributions to the political struggles of a Europe threatened by the rising tide of Fascism.

Although they are more directly concerned with contemporary politics than most of Brecht's other works, so that one might expect them to have dated more, several of these pieces retain an important place in the repertoire of the German theatre. *Fear and Misery of the*

*Third Reich* especially is regularly performed, with various frameworks, new settings and combinations of scenes. The scene cycle has also inspired several imitations, in various languages, commenting in similar style on the miseries of the current political scene (most notably the East German Heiner Müller's scenes from Germany, *Die Schlacht*, 1974, and two cycles by the Bavarian playwright Franz Xaver Kroetz: *Furcht und Hoffnung der BRD*, 1983, and *Ich bin das Volk*, 1993). There is clearly material here for the living theatre; as there is also in *Round Heads and Pointed Heads* – the racial politics of which is devastatingly familiar in modern Eastern Europe, Africa, Indonesia and elsewhere – and in the great anti-war piece *The Trial of Lucullus*.

It is worth remarking also that this was the period of Brecht's first formulation of the notions of 'Verfremdung' ('alienation') and 'Gestus' in essays of 1935–38 on Chinese acting, on music, and on lyric poetry (see *Brecht on Theatre*, Methuen, 1964, pp. 91–120) and in the notes on the first production of *Round Heads and Pointed Heads* in 1936 (see also below, pp. 306–16). One might go so far as to say that it was only now, in exile, that Brecht fully formulated his theory of epic theatre. The 'Street Scene: A Basic Model for an Epic Theatre' also dates from 1938. And these are the years too in which Brecht wrote some of his most important essays on realism. The choice of forms for his political exile dramas was, it is clear, by no means merely an unreflected response to his reliance on amateur actors, ill-resourced theatres, and a public unversed in the experimental theatre of the Weimar Republic. On the contrary, it was perhaps the challenge of this change in circumstances, Fascism and exile, which provoked Brecht to some of his most important writings on aesthetics and the theatre.

\* \* \*

In November 1931 the theatre and film director Ludwig Berger asked Brecht if he would like to collaborate to adapt Shakespeare's *Measure for Measure* for a production with the Young Actors' Group at the Berlin Volksbühne. The première was planned for January 1932. It is not surprising that Brecht accepted. Although his head must have been full of competing projects at the time this was attractive work. He had already adapted *Macbeth* (1927) and *Hamlet* (1930/31) for radio, and he had a lifelong fascination and enthusiasm for the Elizabethan theatre. Besides, as he put it rather later, at the time of the Danish première in 1936:

Many people think that *Measure for Measure* is the most philosophical of all Shakespeare's works, and it is certainly his most progressive. It demands from those in positions of authority that they shouldn't measure others by standards different from those by which they themselves would be judged. It demonstrates that they ought not to demand of their subjects a moral stance which they cannot adopt themselves. (see p. 304)

The original plan was simply to retell Shakespeare's play in a more modern and somewhat ironised tone. Above all, the return of the Duke and his enlightened unravelling of the plot in the final scene were to be called into question.

It seems, however, that Brecht was soon distracted by the possibility of incorporating a strand of more contemporary political satire into the work, which consequently began to expand in all directions. The adaptation could no longer be completed as an efficient, and potentially money-making, commission, and Brecht went back to *The Mother*, which went into rehearsal in December 1931. He returned to the project in 1932, involving several of his closer co-workers, and the text went through a whole series of transformations, the most striking of which are described in the notes to the play in this volume. At this stage the director Heinz Hilpert hoped to secure a production at the Volksbühne, but the political climate was fast deteriorating and the plan was abandoned.

With the rise of Nazism Brecht had begun to exploit the work as a vehicle by which to respond to political developments in Germany. He now took a copy of the proofs of the first completed version into exile with him on 28 February 1933, and made concerted efforts to find a stage for the play. He sent it to the Soviet writer Sergei Tretiakov in Moscow, he talked to Ernst Josef Aufricht in Paris, and he and Elisabeth Hauptmann tried to interest theatres in Paris, London, New York and Prague. In 1934 the play was reworked and translated into Danish, with a view to a production directed by Per Knutzon in Copenhagen, but this collapsed amidst fears of censorship. Erwin Piscator contemplated a production in Moscow, or else in the Ukraine, on more than one occasion (letters to and from Brecht, September to December 1935, and again July 1936), but he ultimately left the Soviet Union in autumn 1936, never to return. There was a contract for a Russian film, which likewise came to nothing. Throughout 1934 Brecht continued to adapt the play, with input from a wide variety of collaborators and associates, including Hanns Eisler, who eventually produced some splendid music for the *Round Heads and Pointed Heads* songs. At this stage Brecht clearly thought of that play as a potential passport to the European theatre. And he had hopes of the Russian. He described it as 'unlike *The*

*Mother*, addressed to a "wide" public and taking account of purely entertainment considerations' ('On the Use of Music in an Epic Theatre', 1935, *Brecht on Theatre*, p. 89). He returned to the play again in 1936, and, after the première, continued to retouch it and added the notes. It was finally published in German in Herzfelde's Malik-Verlag (now in London) in 1938. Earlier versions had already appeared by this time in Russian (provoking heated debates about realism and epic theatre with Communist critics such as Julius Hay) and in English.

Brecht had had next to nothing performed in the theatre (only *The Mother* in New York and isolated scenes and readings in clubs and the like) between 1933 and November 1936, when *Round Heads and Pointed Heads* was eventually premièred, under the Danish director Per Knutzon, in his small Riddersalen Theatre in Copenhagen. The set was by Svend Johansen, incorporating ideas by Mordecai Gorelik (see below p. 304ff), and the role of Nanna was taken by Lulu Ziegler, a popular actress and Knutzon's wife. According to Margarete Steffin, Brecht thought it 'one of his best productions' (letter to Walter Benjamin, November 1936), but to Arnold Zweig the playwright was more cautious, describing it merely as 'a very interesting experiment' (letter of 18 February 1937). The play was not very well received, and it did not reach a wide public. It did, however, cause a storm of protest from local Fascists. It ran for twenty-one performances, and remained for some time the only one of Brecht's plays to have achieved a full-scale production (setting aside the low-profile stagings of *Señora Carrar* and *Fear and Misery*, see below). In June 1940 he was still complaining in his journal: 'it is impossible to finish a play without a stage. the proof of the pudding ... apart from MOTHER and ROUND HEADS everything i have written since JOAN is untested.'

Brecht was seldom one to plan his plays right through to the end, and a great many of his works go through several important stages and versions. Nevertheless, the fragmentary and non-programmatic way in which a fluid political satire entered *Round Heads and Pointed Heads* over the years from 1932 to 1938 has left the reader, and the theatres, with a problem. It seems clear that the play was not originally concerned with Nazism at all, but it became Brecht's first anti-Fascist play. Ultimately, however, the bones of Shakespeare could not provide a very satisfactory framework for a parable on Fascism, and the play was not as flexible a vehicle for the exile theatre as the scenes of *Fear and Misery*. That may be why, after 1938, despite the enormous amount of work that had gone into *Round Heads and Pointed Heads*, Brecht was never to return to it. Besides, the grotesque and fantastic approach to contemporary politics had not gone down well with the ordinary theatre-going public. As war approached and then engulfed Europe, and as Brecht moved on out of Denmark (April 1939), and eventually to the United States (July 1941), he may have despaired of ever refashioning the material to the even greater changes in circumstances, in politics and in the theatre.

*Round Heads and Pointed Heads* is certainly long and complex, and it perhaps needs another firm hand, to impose some discipline and to rescue what remains of its political insights. We underestimate the play, however, if we read it just as a botched satire on Nazism. The elements of more abstract and polyvalent political parable remain far more interesting, and indeed frighteningly contemporary. The portrait of a change in government as a betrayal of the people, the gulf between its programme and social reality, the empty promises of populist reformism, the strange mixtures of political conviction and cynicism, political demagogy and its confused echo amongst the people, all strike familiar chords. Embedded in Brecht's play are interesting commentaries on the relationship between economics and morality, between political representation and sub-stance, and, as in *Arturo Ui*, between the aspirations implicit in a high-flown verse dialogue, and the sordid reality of men's deeds. The analysis of racial politics, although it may in retrospect seem inadequate to Nazism, has a great deal of relevance to later twentieth-century conflicts on several continents. The use of racist politics, or even war, as a calculated distraction from social and economic problems is depressingly familiar. And we should not ignore Brecht's own efforts to generalise his text and, after 1934, to steer it away from explicit reference to Hitler and to Nazism. He was studious in his avoidance of obvious pointers to Nazi anti-Semitism, for example, and the non-specific setting of Yahoo with its Hispanic names and agrarian society can spark off a whole set of associations which have nothing to do with Germany.

The fact that this was one of the very few of his works to be staged at all in the period after 1933 gives *Round Heads and Pointed Heads* a peculiar prominence in Brecht's theoretical and practical reflections on acting, 'Verfremdung' and the epic theatre. It is often mentioned in the *Schriften*, simply as the only available example of practice, it features in the *Messingkauf Dialogues* and again and again in Brecht's letters. The programme of the Copenhagen première took up Brecht's essay from the *New York Times*, 'The German Drama: pre-Hitler' (1935, *Brecht on Theatre*, pp. 77–81), under the new title 'Episk teater'. As well as its intrinsic literary and political interest,

*Round Heads and Pointed Heads* becomes an important experiment in the development of Brecht's ideas about the theatre.

The play received its German première in Dresden in 1948. It was revived in several cities in both East and West in the 1960s, but with scant success. Evidently, despite its importance, it was still hard to get the play across. In most other European countries it remains unperformed, or at best briefly mangled by amateurs. On the other hand, the 1990s saw a relative upturn in its fortunes. Manfred Karge directed a widely debated production at the Akademietheater in Vienna in 1993, and in 1998 the Berliner Ensemble staged its first major production of the work. Perhaps its time has now come.

\* \* \*

At the beginning of the 1930s, while both *Saint Joan of the Stockyards* and *Round Heads and Pointed Heads* were written for the orthodox theatre, the didactic *Lehrstücke*, with all their formal originality, were written for left-wing German audiences and professional performers. But by the middle of the decade the political thrust of Brecht's theatre had begun to alter. *Fear and Misery of the Third Reich* and the Spanish Civil War play *Señora Carrar's Rifles*, both of which were premièred in Paris with the Bulgarian Slatan Dudow as director and Helene Weigel as principal actress, were intended for untrained performers and makeshift theatres; and the same applied also to the two minor satires on Scandinavian neutrality *Dansen* and *How Much Is Your Iron?* Themes were contemporary, the scale small, the approach realistic; even empathy was admitted; and only the aleatory, montage-like sequence of scenes was formally new.

These playlets were influenced by the wider scene of Fascism and its European impact, as diagnosed by the Third International, the Moscow-based Comintern. During Brecht's first year as an exile in Denmark, close to Nazi Germany but cut off from that country's theatre, publishers and cinema, Moscow's International Organisation of Revolutionary Theatres (or MORT) was broadened and put under an exiled German director, Erwin Piscator, the Communist who had been Brecht's major theatrical ally since setting up his Berlin company in 1927. MORT now became part of a whole Comintern arts apparatus, the MORP for writers, the MBRKh for artists, Mezhrabpom, the international workers' film production organisation, and the International Music Bureau for composers. Hanns Eisler, who had been Brecht's main musical collaborator since 1930, now became the bureau's president, and sent his son to the Comintern's Karl-Liebknecht School in Moscow.

When Piscator invited Brecht to a meeting of progressive theatre directors in that city in spring 1935 he found old and new friends there, not to mention new ideas such as 'Verfremdung'. Among them were two members of the Comintern Executive who were impressed by the 'Brecht Evening' given on 15 May by the VEGAAR or Foreign Workers' Publishing House. They were Bela Kun and Vilis Knorin, who are thought to have spoken to him about the need for short sketches of Nazi life that could be performed cheaply and independently of any professional stage. Piscator also knew these people, and during the summer of 1935 he developed the idea of producing a whole series of anti-Nazi propaganda films, which could be made separately in different studios. They never materialised, but the idea also appealed to Brecht, who had already started writing poems based on real-life reports from the new Germany – some of them for the anti-Nazi 'Freedom Radio'. Now he started two years of intermittently writing short scenes that could be strung together and played by political groups opposed to Hitler and his aims. This was the time of the Popular Front movements in France and Spain – the Blum government of spring 1936 and Franco's rebellion that led to the Spanish Civil War – and it was they that most engaged Brecht on his return from Moscow with a new sense of mission.

But his new toe-hold in Russia was less firm than it had seemed in 1935. With the help of Margarete Steffin, who had been convalescing in the USSR and knew the language, he had renewed his links with Tretiakov, Eisenstein and others of the theatrical avant-garde; his 'Epic Dramas' had been published in Russian; Semyon Kirsanov was his translator; he became a lifelong friend of Bernhard Reich and his wife Asya Lacis. But it was not till July 1936 that he got any kind of recognised position, when he became one of the three editors (with Feuchtwanger and Willi Bredel) of a new Moscow literary magazine, published in German by Mikhail Koltsov under his Jurgaz imprint. Called *Das Wort*, while undoubtedly on the Comintern line, it differed from that body's magazine *Internationale Literatur* by the fact that Feuchtwanger and Brecht were both living abroad, while its model was the *Neue Deutsche Blätter* of Wieland Herzfelde's Prague-based Malik-Verlag. Brecht was approached about this by Koltsov's partner Maria Osten, who under her real name of Gresshöner had worked as Herzfelde's assistant. It did not outlast the fall of Republican Spain, when its last issue included Brecht's scene of 'The Jewish wife'. Koltsov returned from Spain (where he is said to have been the model for the journalist Karkov in *For Whom the Bell Tolls*) only to be arrested, charged with spying for Britain and shot. And Brecht had started talking about what he called 'the dark times'.

Partly this was because of the new Soviet reaction against the modern movement in the arts, which became crippling early in 1936 with *Pravda*'s denunciations of Shostakovitch, Eisenstein and other outstanding 'formalists', followed by the closing of Meyerhold's theatre in 1938: denunciations echoed for the German emigration by Georg Lukács's critical articles, with their schoolmasterly dismissal of reportage, montage and other departures from nineteenth-century naturalism. Partly it was due to the dissolution on security grounds of such internationally staffed organisations as MORT and Mezhrab-pom-Film, which led to the abandonment of all Piscator's plans and to Piscator's decision to move to Paris. Partly it was due to the wave of arrests consequent on the Great Purge, which began seriously affecting the Moscow Germans and their friends in the second half of 1936.

So whatever stimulus Brecht had found in the USSR, his hopes of gaining a rewarding new outlet for his work and ideas, and a new platform for the acting talents of his wife, had been knocked on the head. Any chance of a Soviet production of *Round Heads and Pointed Heads*, or of work on Piscator's film plans, or of the establishment of a major German émigré theatre in the Ukraine, now disappeared. As for his commission with Eisler for a Lenin Requiem on the twentieth anniversary of the Revolution, it was reputedly handed in in time but was neither published nor performed.

While the Soviet climate was thus changing, the hopes of the European Left were turning towards France and Spain. In France the new Popular Front policy gained an absolute majority in the May 1936 elections, sweeping Léon Blum into power and helping inspire the renaissance of the French cinema; in Spain the Franco revolt against a rather similar Communist-approved government led to the outbreak of the civil war that July. At least for a time it looked as if the task of bodies like MORT would be taken over by organisations based in Paris, and at first this, along with the impending World Exhibition in that city and the mounting movement against war and Fascism, formed the centre of Piscator's new concerns. Among the Paris theatre groups to be activated as a result was the émigré cabaret called Die Laterne, which was now strengthened by the arrival of Slatan Dudow, the Bulgarian director of *Kuhle Wampe* and *The Mother*, whom Brecht had more than once tried to help find permanent work. With Hitler and Mussolini soon giving signs of their intention to intervene in the Spanish war, Dudow wrote to Brecht in Denmark that September to ask for a short play in support of the Republican cause. This now took priority over the *Fear and Misery* concept, and Brecht instantly started collecting reports and pictures of the fighting, particularly on the northern front. For the moment admittedly he was caught up in the preparations for the Copenhagen première of *Round Heads and Pointed Heads*, but early in the New Year he got down to the writing, modelling his story on Synge's *Riders to the Sea*.

*Generals over Bilbao*, the new play's earliest title, became out of date after June 1937 when Franco took that city; so Brecht shifted its locale to the Mediterranean and renamed it *Señora Carrar's Rifles*. It was agreed that Helene Weigel would come from Denmark to act with the group, and Brecht also wanted the production coordinated with that of *The Threepenny Opera*, which Aufricht was once again planning to present in Paris. 'I imagine it being performed in a very simple style,' he wrote to Dudow.

> Three-dimensional figures against limewashed walls, with the various groupings very carefully composed as in a painting ... just calm, considered realism.

It was just this comparatively conventional form of presentation that most satisfied the critic of the local émigré paper *Deutsche Volkszeitung* and, along with the play's topicality, allowed it to be taken up by Communist or Popular Front theatre groups in several countries. In addition there was the deep impression made by Weigel's performance in the title part, which led Brecht to hope that she might be invited to play it in Zurich and other professional German-language theatres. Thanks to this combination of factors, *Carrar* was a success, and Dudow's stock went up.

Thus it was Dudow to whom Brecht communicated the start of work on *Fear and Misery*, even before the *Carrar* rehearsals had begun. 'At present,' he told him in July 1937,

> I'm writing a series of little (ten-minute) plays 'Spiritual Upsurge of the German People Under the Nazi Regime'; these and the Spain play would fill an evening. Minimal cast. As you see, in this way I too am turning to small-scale forms.

In the event the *Carrar* evening was to be filled out by some Brecht songs performed by Weigel, along with a showing of René Clair's film *Le Dernier Milliardaire*. But Brecht saw the new scenes as the best possible way of developing 'epic' acting further after his wife's *Carrar* performance, and he continued to turn them out during the months that followed. By October the series consisted of five – 'The spy', 'The Jewish wife', 'Justice', 'Occupational disease' and 'The chalk cross' – under the overall title *Angst*; in November there were seven; by the following spring nineteen, now to be presented under the *Fear and Misery* title, with *German March-Past* as a possible alternative; finally six more by the end of April 1938, when Brecht said that he was stopping at the grand total of twenty-five. By then it was understood that Dudow would stage some of them with a cast including Helene Weigel. Brecht's main concern at this point was that the actors should not simply be drawn from Die Laterne, whose level seemed to him amateurish, but should if possible include Ernst Busch and Felix Bressart. Dudow's was rather that the play's cumulative effect was too depressing, to which Brecht replied that 'it's not for us to preach the need to fight back, we show the fight going on. The final "*no*" seems enough to me.'

As staged in the Salle d'Iéna on 21 May 1938 the play consisted of eight scenes only, presented under the title 99% – an ironic reference to the popular support for Hitler at the elections of March 1936 – and ending (as in our text) with the plebiscite that had followed the annexation of Austria a bare two months before the première. The prologue ('The German march-past') and the introductory verses to each scene were set to music by Paul Dessau; this setting, which has apparently not survived, represents Dessau's first involvement with Brecht. The simple scenery was by *Carrar*'s designer Heinz Lohmar, this time with costumes by Sylta Busse, who had previously been with one of the German theatre groups in the USSR. Brecht himself received no royalties, nor does the play's run appear to have exceeded the two performances originally planned. Nevertheless the production was greeted as a success, and not only because of what was generally agreed to be another outstanding performance by Helene Weigel. Thus Walter Benjamin, who at that time was close to Brecht and had a special understanding of his work, wrote in *Die Neue Weltbühne* that Brecht had turned aside from his experiments in 'epic theatre' out of consideration for such émigré groups and their audiences. These needed no specific aids to 'alienate' them from the events shown: the alienation was already there, thanks to their political experience, and this made the new balance of the artistic and the political in the new scenes epic indeed. Soaked in current actuality, he said, this unique play would be an enduring testimony for generations to come.

*Carrar* meanwhile was being widely performed throughout 1938 – not only in Copenhagen (as reflected in our notes pp. 356–62) but also in Stockholm, Prague, New York (by the People's Theater in April) and San Francisco; likewise by Unity Theatre in London and other British cities. And it continued to be played by similar left-wing groups even after the fall of the Spanish Republic in March 1939, which prompted Brecht to provide the new prologue and epilogue printed on pp. 360–2. The *Fear and Misery* scenes were not so popular, though Pierre Abraham staged his own translation in various French cities and finally, following the German invasion of Poland, in Paris itself with settings by Frans Masereel. Berthold Viertel too included 'The spy' in a mixed programme for the Free German League of Culture in London in May 1939, just when John Lehmann published it in *New Writing* along with an article on film by Viertel himself. Both Viertel and Abraham however were friends of Brecht's, and no doubt the problem for other potential directors was that, unlike *Carrar*, the play as a whole remained unpublished until the middle of the Second World War. Though several scenes appeared in *Das Wort* (winning somewhat patronising praise from Lukács, to Brecht's considerable irritation) and elsewhere, the complete work's expected appearance as part of the collected Malik edition – under the title *Germany – an Atrocity Story* – was blocked when that edition's Czech printers were taken over by the Nazis. However, Brecht's own interest, to judge from his correspondence of the time, lay rather in the possibility of a production in New York, where Eisler had been working since January 1938 and Piscator went at the end of that year. Even before the première Brecht was writing to Piscator to this effect, and from then on he kept the idea in his friend's mind. There is no sign that he even considered trying for a Soviet production.

*   *   *

The story of *Fear and Misery of the Third Reich* in America is one of multiple refunctioning and transformation with a view to the major production which never occurred. It begins with the visit of Brecht's American friend Ferdinand Reyher some five months after the Paris première, when the former, now wholly immersed in that profoundly different play *Life of Galileo*, met him in Copenhagen. This was just when Brecht had made up his mind to follow Eisler's and Piscator's examples and put in for an American visa himself, and as a result he and Reyher now began looking at his recent plays to see how far these could be used to establish him in the US. *Galileo* was certainly the most important, but the most promising in Reyher's eyes was *Fear and Misery*, which he persuaded Brecht to let him adapt with a view to what he termed 'an honest commercial production' based on his own skills as a Hollywood rewriter. This meant in the first place tying the original scenes together in a conventional three-act plot. To quote James K. Lyon's account, Reyher

constructed a frame story involving a young man from the working class named Eric. As the play opens on the night of January 30, 1933, this young worker has been beaten by the SA. He is helped from the scene by the daughter of a Jew, and the two fall in love. They reappear together or individually in a number of scenes. Their relationship has the effect of tying together otherwise unrelated action and events . . .

A mutual friend with whom Reyher discussed his adaptation told Brecht that it 'has a good chance of being a "hit" on Broadway':

> The scene that he read to me was so American, and the plan for the play has been worked out in such a way that the most sentimental viewer would listen and be captivated.

Among the suggested titles for this version were *The Devil's Opera* and *The Devil's Sunday*. It was never produced, possibly because Brecht failed to sign the contract which Reyher sent him.

Once war had broken out in Europe nothing more was heard of this scheme, and the play then lay on the shelf until Brecht and his family arrived in California in July 1941. By then the Russians too were at war and criticism of the Nazis was no longer denied them by the Soviet–German pact. Promptly the former published a thirteen-scene version of the play under the *Germany – an Atrocity Story* title, followed in 1942 by an English translation called (for the first time in public) *Fear and Misery of the Third Reich*. That same year, at Alma-Ata, Pudovkin filmed *The Murderers Are on Their Way*, based on 'One big family', 'Winter aid', 'The chalk cross', 'The spy' and 'Job creation'; though the result was never released, on the grounds (says Jay Leyda) that its depiction of the Germans was not savage enough. Brecht for his part straightway began once again trying to promote the play in the United States. To H.R. Hays, his first wholly American translator, he wrote that he should try to get hold of a script, since this seemed to offer the best prospects of all his work. To Piscator he proposed it as a teaching exercise for his expected attachment (never realised) to his old ally's Dramatic Workshop at the New School. His letter concluded: 'Of course it would require collaboration. You yourself would have to collaborate. Please write me what you think.'

It was not till the summer of 1942 that any such schemes began to look serious. Then Berthold Viertel staged four of the original *Angst* scenes for an anti-Nazi group called Die Tribüne in the Fraternal Clubhouse in New York, while Max Reinhardt himself also thought of producing the play. This stimulated Brecht to devise a new wartime framework for the scenes, which he described in his journal as a kind of PRIVATE LIFE OF THE MASTER RACE. one could put on stage the classic blitzkrieg lorry containing the third reich's soldiers in their steel helmets bringing europe the new order, which the scenes proper would show operating in germany. the lorry would be treated in ballad style, to a barbaric horst-wessel march [the Nazi anthem] simultaneously sentimental and disgusting.

Though Reinhardt's interest petered out along with his scheme to take over a New York theatre, Brecht completed the framework and evidently passed the result on to Piscator. For in the winter of 1942/ 43 Piscator was already making plans to stage this version at the Dramatic Workshop's semi-professional Studio Theatre, in a translation which Hays was commissioned to make. Once again the project fell through, this time because Brecht allowed Eric Bentley simultaneously to translate the play in apparent competition with Hays. Hays cried off and Bentley went ahead.

Then in the spring of 1945, with the war on the point of ending, Piscator made what on the face of it should have been the most serious of the various proposals for an American staging of the play. This was for a production off Broadway under the sponsorship of the CIO unions. Brecht, who had already licensed a first performance of the new version by the university theatre at Berkeley, was prepared to agree, this time specifying his conditions as 'a *very* good cast' and an 'excellent performance'. The translation in both cases was to be Bentley's, now equipped with a new scene, the 'Peat-bog soldiers', written in New York largely by Elisabeth Hauptmann (who was to get 17 per cent of the royalties). Eisler too was drawn in to compose the framework choruses, the original interscene verses having been cut; these were restored in the published version that same year. The '*very* good cast' consisted of what Brecht described as émigrés and Piscator pupils, the former including most notably the Bassermanns, an elderly couple of great eminence in the German theatre who however had never established themselves on the English-language stage and were not to do so now. Three weeks before the opening Brecht himself arrived from California, immediately rejected the introductory scene which Piscator wanted to add – a quasi-informal discussion of dictatorship and democracy in the light of the German surrender on 7/8 May – and threatened to withdraw the rights. Piscator thereupon resigned and was replaced by Berthold Viertel, who had also been in the market for the play earlier. The performance was beyond rescue – according to Brecht the budget had only been $6000 – and it was devastatingly panned by George Jean

Nathan and other critics. 'A terrible failure', Eisler later called it. 'Brecht wasn't unhappy, but he was embarrassed.'

Somewhat confusingly, American critics even today refer to the original play by the title of this wartime adaptation, which was already outdated by the time of its performance. This is probably because for nearly forty years it was the only published text available in English. In fact the play's whole history, as outlined so far, has meant that Brecht in effect provided us with two distinct works reflecting his relationships – both theatrical and political – with two very different parts of the world. For we now have on the one hand *The Private Life of the Master Race*, a quite closely woven sequence of scenes in three acts presenting the early years of the Nazi regime from the imagined point of view of a victorious army which has been turned back at Stalingrad. This, though far less crassly commercial than Reyher's *The Devil's Sunday*, was certainly devised with American professional production in view and following discussion with Clifford Odets and other Hollywood friends; the title itself smacks of American journalism, and even though Brecht himself may have devised it he virtually never used it in German. And then on the other hand we have the loose assortment of scenes designed for German émigré performance – part professional, part amateur – often on the most cheese-paring scale, from which the American version was itself adapted. This do-it-yourself theatrical kit, whose German text – the standard one in that language – was the source of 99%, *The Murderers Are on Their Way* and other topical selections, evolved more or less directly from Comintern policy, vintage 1935, and was aimed mainly at politically sympathetic audiences. While it may be remoter from ourselves than *The Private Life*, both chronologically and in terms of theatrical tradition, it is more modern in form and very much closer to the events portrayed.

\*    \*    \*

If the play's ambiguous career makes *Fear and Misery* something of a puzzle for the modern director, particularly in the English-speaking world, this is only secondary to the ambiguity of its original form. Particularly in Eastern Europe, critics have tended to link it with *Carrar* as constituting Brecht's most 'Socialist Realist' works in the old Stalinist sense: that is to say, naturalistic in form and immediately political in content. *Carrar* indeed, in the twenty years following Brecht's return to Europe after the war, was his most effective passport to acceptability in the Communist theatre; during that time, as Claude Hill has pointed out, it had more than twice as many performances in East Germany as any other of his plays, while that country's cheap Reclam edition, starting with a printing of 50,000 copies in 1961, had reprinted sixteen times by 1977. But with *Fear and Misery of the Third Reich* the position – reflected in its much less frequent production – is rather different, because although the individual scenes are often naturalistic they are generally much terser and more sketch-like, while the overall construction is not naturalistic at all. Hence Brecht's comments when Lukács welcomed 'The spy' on its publication in *Das Wort* 'as though I were a sinner entering the bosom of the Salvation Army':

> he has failed to notice the montage of 27 scenes and the fact that it is just a table of gests: the gest of keeping silent, of looking over one's shoulder, of being frightened and so on: gestics under dictatorship.... the montage which he so decries originated in dudow's letters asking for something for the little proletarian company in paris. it shows how it is the proletarian exiled theatre that keeps theatre going, at a time when in moscow the former leader of a berlin agitprop group, maxim vallentin, has gone over to the bourgeois theatre

– which is Brecht's heretical way of describing the officially-approved Stanislavsky method.

The 'epic' aspect of this play, in other words, can be seen not only in the coolness of the writing (by comparison with that of *Carrar*) but first and foremost in the stringing-together of the scenes on a long processional ballad, itself comparable with several other characteristic Brecht poems, ranging from 'The Legend of the Dead Soldier' (1918) to 'The Anachronistic Procession' (1947). The actual order of those scenes as printed is not conceived in terms of 'acts' or 'parts' but simply chronological: what moves them relentlessly past us, in any order one chooses, is the regular rhythm of the linking stanzas. Brecht himself suggested to Piscator in 1938 that he might stage them by interspersing documentary material – presumably projections – 'in the style of Goya's etchings on the Civil War'; but really the analogy with *The Disasters of War* is much closer than that, because it is the scenes themselves that are the terrible images, which the stanzas seem to caption much as do Goya's chillingly laconic titles. 'The whole thing must be played straight through,' he wrote on another occasion, 'possibly beneath a forest of illuminated swastika flags, with a ballad interspersed.' Max Reinhardt for his part was reminded of Büchner's *Woyzeck*, evidently by the brevity of the scenes. Benjamin saw them as providing 'an entire repertoire for the stage' and thought that when published – something that he never lived to see – they would read like Karl Kraus's *The Last Days of*

*Mankind,* that enormous film-like panorama of Austria in the First World War.

Unfortunately Brecht for some reason never directed a production himself, and it was only after his death that the Berliner Ensemble presented some half-dozen scenes in a slow-moving production by five of the younger directors. Since returning from America he seems to have seen the play no longer as a work to be staged in its own right but more as a necessary prelude to any performance of *The Resistible Rise of Arturo Ui* – that other, much more oblique and superficial critique of the Nazis which, unlike *Fear and Misery*, really had been written for the American stage and conceived in largely American terms, yet never was seen by an American audience while he lived. It was almost as if he felt that the earlier play presented the facts of Nazism while the latter could only offer a mocking commentary unintelligible to those who had not yet faced them; and meanwhile was hesitant to produce either till more time had elapsed. Having seen neither Ernst Ginsberg's production of January 1947 (on a red platform with a minimal setting by Caspar Neher) nor the (East) Berlin production at the Deutsches Theater a year later, he was still perhaps inhibited by the failure of *The Private Life*, and after that had made no further attempt to update the original play. Yet there is a powerful account of the Basel production by the then thirty-five-year-old Max Frisch, who contrasted Brecht's reticent, low-level view of the Third Reich in the 1930s with Carl Zuckmayer's far more successful *The Devil's General* 'which has relieved so many of us. Brecht doesn't give this relief.'

> A friend told me he felt that everything Brecht shows us here is more or less harmless by comparison with what came later. Perhaps this is its greatest strength: we know the results, what we are looking for is the beginnings.

Written several months before Frisch met Brecht, this is an extraordinarily perceptive verdict for the time. And it is even more clearly true today. For by now we have been stunned into insensibility by the continued fictional and semi-fictional regurgitation of 'the results', to a point where pornography starts to take over and neo-Fascists become almost flattered by the scale of the Nazi crimes. With the normal imagination no longer able to relate such things to our common humanity, use of the word 'Fascism' has largely degenerated into nonsense, while dangerously few are able to distinguish symptoms of real Fascism when they occur. We are in short in a situation where some understanding of 'the beginnings' of the great German tragedy are urgently needed if the all-important links between petty everyday actions and outsize human atrocities are not to escape our grasp. What Brecht can do for us here is to take us back to the pre-Auschwitz phase of Hitler's reign, when many in the West considered that the German dictator was leading his country out of chaos, and viewed any incidental excesses as excusable in the fight against Communism. This is a case where the wisdom of hindsight vastly strengthens a play, because unlike the audience of 1938 we *know* what all the small-scale sneaking, lying and creeping eventually led to; we have looked at the end of the story, just as Brecht's notion of epic theatre demands that we should. And so there is no suspense, only inexorable demonstration.

Today this can grip audiences as the contrived wartime version could not. All that perhaps needs changing in the original conception of the play is the prologue with its image of 'The German march-past', the parade of a nation going to war, and the title with its allusion to a Third Reich now barely known except to those steeped in the historical background. As for the earlier objections by Dudow and others that Brecht's picture of low-level Nazi life is too depressing and not 'positive' enough, they can now be seen to be very wide of the mark, so wide indeed that the optimistic 'No!' of the final scene sounds to us like wishful thinking, inconsistent with Brecht's ruthlessly critical approach. It is this approach above all that has to be maintained, whatever the selection of scenes chosen, and it depends (as Brecht said) on the sharpness of the portrayal, which in turn is a function of the actors' abilities, and the momentum with which the scenes follow one another. Once this tightness and drive can be achieved the scenes will have the same qualities as Frisch saw in them; that is, they will seem not like reportage but like carefully observed and purposefully formed extracts from life; what the Swiss writer termed 'a revue for the memory'.

> If mankind had a memory surely things would start to improve? We would either shoot ourselves or change. Brecht hopes the latter. Hence the sober way in which he speaks to us, without ever being carried away or taking refuge in that vagueness which often masquerades as poetry; his poetry is his seriousness, his love of mankind. And his beauty, I'd say, lies in the dignity of his approach.

It can be no minor or secondary work that inspires such a tribute as this from a fellow-artist. Nor can it be ephemeral so long as the death camps haunt our mind.

\* \* \*

*The Trial of Lucullus* has a mixed ancestry. It was written soon after

*Mother Courage* in the first weeks of the Second World War, and it showed the common people judging a successful military commander who was overweeningly confident of his great reputation. (We too got to know some of these.) But Brecht did not situate his characters in his own world, where Hitler had at last launched his expected assault on his neighbours after making a pact with the Russians who had been trusted to oppose him. Rather he went back to classical times, and particularly to the Roman history which he had been studying. His unfinished play about Julius Caesar had developed around 1937 into an equally unfinished novel about Caesar's business affairs on which he was still working; his story 'Lucullus's Trophies', which we include in our notes, was written some six months before the war, and points the way interestingly towards the Lucretian (hexameter) version of the Communist Manifesto which he would complete in 1945. Now he made Lucullus the centre of a 'Hörspiel' or radio play somewhat in the tradition of the 'Lehrstücke' of his last Berlin years. And in making an opera for a very different Germany after the war it would suffer a sea-change more notorious than any other transformation of his often variable works.

The radio play was intended to be performed by Stockholm radio with music by Hilding Rosenberg. It was accepted, but the plan fell through. Then it simmered in silence until the spring of 1940, when the Brechts moved from Sweden to Finland as the German pressure on the former increased. Curt Reiss, the Swiss publisher who represented Brecht, had placed the work with the Swiss radio Beromünster, who broadcast it from their Berne studio on 12 May under the title *Lucullus vor Gericht*; it had no music. This was two days after the invasion of Belgium and Holland, and the family spent another year with Finnish friends before managing to leave via the USSR and catch one of the last boats from Vladivostok to California. During that time *Mother Courage*, written in 1939 but not performed, had its première at the Zurich Schauspielhaus (19 April 1941, two months before the German invasion of Russia). Away in the United States the poet Hofmann Hays read *Lucullus*, probably at Hanns Eisler's suggestion, and made a good translation.

Brecht had been invited by Piscator to teach at the New School in New York, where Eisler was directing the Rockefeller Film Music Project. However, on arriving in Los Angeles, where some of his guarantors and other friends were working, he chose to settle within the possibly lucrative (and frequently German-speaking) orbit of Hollywood. It was on a visit to New York in spring 1943, at a 'Brecht evening' with performers like Bergner and Peter Lorre, that he heard Paul Dessau sing a setting from *St Joan of the Stockyards* and decided to get him out to LA. This was the start of a new collaboration to supplement those with Weill and Eisler, both of whom were now too much in demand for other commissions. From Brecht's point of view the main results were the music for *Mother Courage* and the *German Miserere*, but quite early on it seemed that Dessau was hoping also to compose an opera. Brecht and he certainly discussed *The Trial of Lucullus*, as well as a new project for an opera on the theme of Brecht's 'Marie Sanders' song (October 1944). But the primary composer Brecht had in mind for *Lucullus* was Stravinsky, and Dessau's role had to be that of an intermediary. He was, noted Brecht in his journal for 6 November 1944,

> much less developed than eisler, and seems tied up in routine. modern music converts texts into prose, even verse texts, and then poeticises that prose. it poeticises it and at the same time makes it psychological. the rhythm is dissolved. (except with stravinsky and bartok.) for the epic theatre this is useless.

Stravinsky was in California, but too busy; Brecht never worked with him. And for the rest of his time in America Dessau had to abandon his operatic hopes.

There was however a first English-language production of the work at Berkeley in California, where Roger Sessions was the resident composer. In September 1946 Heinrich Schnitzler, the Austrian playwright's son, producer at the university theatre, had asked Brecht for another children's play like *He Says Yes* which might make a double-bill with Stravinsky's *Soldier's Tale* for performance in the spring of 1947. He was sent Hays's translation of *The Trial of Lucullus* and the original German texts, but Brecht never seems to have taken any interest in the project, which overlapped with his plans for Laughton's *Galileo* and his family's return to Europe in the autumn. It is regarded by Sessions's biographer Andrea Olmstead as his 'most successful dramatic work', while David Drew, reviewing a later production in New York, calls it 'an opera that towers above the American operas favoured by the Met'. Yet it has seldom been performed even in the US, and this was at least for a time due to the reluctance of the copyright holders, who ensured that the subsequent Dessau opera was far better known. Until 1989, in fact, the original broadcast text, well translated by Hays and set by Sessions, remained virtually unpublished among Brecht's works. Consciously or not, the changes made in the 1951 *Trial* version were camouflaged.

*   *   *

The new phase in this story began when both Brecht and Dessau were back in Berlin, just before Christmas 1948, for rehearsals of the historic opening production of *Mother Courage*. It seems that they were in the Möwe café, where Brecht was talking to R.A. Stemmle from the North-West German radio. Suddenly Brecht called across the room to Dessau that he could get him a commission for an opera; Stemmle was looking for a radio opera version of *The Trial of Lucullus*, and there would be a sizeable advance. This appealed to Dessau, who (he said) had no money and no substantial tasks; he would get a contract soon. Unfortunately no contract materialised, but clearly this set the composer thinking, and from 1949 till 1951, the date of the work's first publication in the *Versuche* series, he was consulting Brecht about the change of scale and content which seemed to be called for by the ten-year-old radio play. What bothered him was partly the change of medium, but he also felt that the Nuremberg Trials, the Hiroshima bomb and (from June 1950) the Korean War invalidated the original open-minded ending of the 1940 Hörspiel script, whose pacifism would be contrary to the policy of the new (East) German Democratic Republic. Brecht at that time had other and larger problems: notably the establishment of the Berliner Ensemble and its programme, the attempt to get a footing in Salzburg where he had hoped that Von Einem would compose a *Lucullus* opera and his own position as a leading GDR writer. Nevertheless over the next months he agreed with Dessau to make the required changes in the script.

In 1949 the newly established Suhrkamp publishing house in West Berlin began to revive the grey-bound *Versuche* series of Brecht's more recent works, with Elisabeth Hauptmann, newly returned from America, in her pre-Hitler role as its editor. Formerly Brecht's chief collaboratrix, she was for a time Dessau's wife. In 1951 *Versuche 11*, the third of the new issues, included the Hörspiel *The Trial of Lucullus*, whose 1940 version had remained unpublished since its appearance in the Moscow *Internationale Literatur*. Already a fair amount of extra material had found its way into the new text, and this was followed by five pages of 'Notes to the opera *The Condemnation of Lucullus*' signed 'Brecht. Dessau'. These started:

The 'Hörspiel' *The Trial of Lucullus* was the basis for the opera *The Condemnation of Lucullus*. The former work ended with the verses

The court
Withdraws for consultation.

'The Judgement' (scene 14) was borrowed from the latter. It kept its title, however, the better to distinguish it from this.

The same notes also include the changed passages in scene 9 ('The Hearing') where the king whom Lucullus had defeated was applauded for his defence of his own country, and a brief reference to the final damnation of the great general for waging an aggressive war. From then until the first publication of the 1939/40 text in the Berlin and Frankfurt edition of 1989 the 1951 *Versuche* version was generally taken to be the Hörspiel text, and theatres abroad were not allowed to use the previous ending.

A first project for the opera was ready by February 1950, when the East Berlin State Opera director Ernst Legal, an old friend of Brecht's, sent a script to the Ministry for Education. His interest had been stimulated by Brecht's designer Caspar Neher, an Austrian subject who was independent of the Communist-led GDR, and for the Ministry Kurt Bork agreed. It would open in March 1951. The conductor would be Hermann Scherchen from Switzerland, an admirer of Brecht and outstanding proponent of modern music; the producer, the Opera's own Wolfgang Völker. At first all seemed to be well. The piano score was finished, even though the latest textual changes had still to be worked in. The Education Minister was Paul Wandel, who had appointed Brecht to the Academy of Arts under Arnold Zweig's presidency. But following the Soviet campaign against the international modern movement in the arts, the Central Committee made the new crime of 'Formalism' the main topic of its Fifth Conference. This too was scheduled for March 1951, when rehearsals for the opera were far advanced. Then in June the first meeting of the CIA-sponsored Congress for Cultural Freedom was held in West Berlin.

The material for a major controversy was now there; the Party called for reports, not always from the best-qualified judges; the verdict of Dessau's fellow-composers was bad; it was difficult, dissonant music, with lavish use of percussion, and not helped by a full trial rehearsal on 13 March to piano accompaniment, which made Wandel say he had been right to propose rejecting the work. The ensuing discussion was at the Opera, and was carried on the same evening at the Möwe club, with Georg Knepler and Ernst Hermann Meyer as the main critics. Scherchen too was there, but could not show the final, damning 'Judgement' which had not yet been rehearsed. Publicly, the production was cancelled, but the first night on the 17th now took place before an officially recruited audience drawn from good, firm comrades and friends who could be counted on for a healthy reaction to this formalistic music. All departments had been told what this discussion was about.

So said Maria Rentmeister of the Ministry, noting that some 200 tickets had been commandeered by Brecht, Dessau, Scherchen and Legal. The total audience expected must have been at least 1,500, and their reaction was most enthusiastic. Scherchen is reputed to have said he had never known a modern work to score such a success.

President Pieck was in the audience, as was Walter Ulbricht, the Party Secretary, and now the former took a hand, holding a meeting at his own house a week after the première with Brecht, Dessau, Grotewohl, Wandel and other politicians. Brecht insisted on his contract with Legal. So *The Condemnation of Lucullus* would remain off the repertoire for the present, but would be performed normally in the 1951/2 season; and during the next few months the two collaborators would work to improve it. Meanwhile there were some organisational changes. Wandel's Education Ministry lost its responsibility for the arts in favour of a new Committee for Art Affairs, an Office for Literature and other organs poorly thought of by Brecht. Legal resigned from the State Opera and his other functions; he had just passed seventy. What certainly did not change was the official policy of discouraging modern or difficult art under the label of 'formalism', and giving priority to the 'Kulturerbe' or national heritage. Among the consequences was the denunciation and eventual stifling of Hanns Eisler's opera *Johann Faustus*, whose music was never written.

An interesting story, but for us an upsetting one. How could the very existence of the first and best version of Brecht's play have been hidden from our view for so many years? It must above all have been because of something intolerable, the cultural Cold War. The Soviet orthodoxy of the 1930s on the one hand, the counter-propaganda of the Congress for Cultural Freedom on the other – their friction for so many years has given a news value to a case like that of Dessau's opera which acquired an interest over and above its merits. We have not denied it, but the fusion of some of its elements with the ambiguous 'radio play' of 1951 (e.g. in the *Versuche* edition) will never produce a satisfactory work. What we have done in this volume therefore is to start with the more spontaneous text of 1939/40, list and identify the infiltrated additions or alternatives of the intervening decade, then give the full opera text of 1951, the year of its controversial performance. The objective must be to bring the first of these three versions out of the cupboard and get it played as it deserves.

THE EDITORS

# Round Heads and Pointed Heads

or
Money Calls to Money

*A tale of horror*

*Collaborators*: HANNS EISLER, EMIL HESSE-BURRI,
ELISABETH HAUPTMANN, MARGARETE STEFFIN

*Translator*: TOM KUHN; *songs by* TOM KUHN, RALPH
MANHEIM *and* JOHN WILLETT

*Characters*:

THEATRE DIRECTOR

*Zaks (Round Heads)*:

THE VICEROY
MISSENA, *his Privy
  Councillor*
ANGELO IBERIN
CALLAS, *a tenant farmer*
NANNA, *his daughter, a
  waitress in Madame
  Cornamontis's coffeehouse*
MRS CALLAS and her four
  small children
PARR, *a tenant farmer*
MOTHER SUPERIOR OF SAN
  BARABAS
ABBOT OF SAN STEFANO
ALFONSO SAZ, *landowner*
JUAN DUARTE, *landowner*

SEBASTIAN DE HOZ,
  *landowner*
MADAME CORNAMONTIS,
  *proprietress of a
  coffeehouse*
ATTORNEY OF THE DE
  GUZMAN FAMILY
HIGH COURT JUDGE
INSPECTOR
CALLAMASSI, *a landlord*
PALMOSA, *a tobacconist*
FAT WOMAN
CLERK, THREE HATSOS,
  TWO NUNS, IBERIN
  SOLDIERS, PEASANTS,
  CITIZENS

*Ziks (Pointed Heads)*:

EMANUELE DE GUZMAN,
  *landowner*
ISABELLA, *his sister*
LOPEZ, *a tenant farmer*
MRS LOPEZ and her three
  small children

IGNATIO PERUINER,
  *landowner*
SECOND ATTORNEY,
  DOCTOR, GROCER,
  PEASANTS, CITIZENS

The population of the town of Luma, in which the play takes
place, comprises Zaks and Ziks, two races, of whom the first
have *round* and the second *pointed* heads. The pointed heads
should be at least 15 cm higher than the round ones. But the
round heads must be no less abnormal than the pointed ones.

*Seven actors step in front of a low curtain: the director of the theatre, Governor Iberin, the rebellious tenant farmer, the landowner, his sister, Farmer Callas and his daughter. The last four are in their shirts. The Governor, in costume but without make-up, is holding a scale with two pointed and two round skulls; the rebel farmer is holding a scale with two fine and two scruffy outfits; he too is in costume but not made-up.*

THEATRE DIRECTOR:
  Ladies and gentlemen, welcome to the show!
  Bert Brecht, who wrote it, as I guess you know,
  Travelled the wide world – if only as a refugee,
  And what he witnessed on the way shocked even me.
  This play's about the things he saw:
  *Strife and conflict, even war.*
  He saw a white man wrestling with a black,
  An angry yellow giant with a yellow midget on his back.
  A Finn took up a stone and flung it at a Swede,
  And someone with a snub nose punched a hook-nosed man
      and made him bleed.
  Our playwright stopped to ask the cause, and heard
  That in these parts a spectre is abroad:
  The great distributor of skulls is on his rounds again,
  A quack with snake oil in his pack for every man.
  He keeps a stock of noses and bags of coloured skin
  With which he stirs the folk against their kith and kin.
  Far and wide you'll hear it said
  That all that matters these days are the contours of your
      head,
  And where the skull-man goes
  People look more closely at your hair and skin and nose.

Most likely you'll be beaten up or raped
If your head's a bit irregularly shaped.
Our playwright was cross-questioned on occasion
Whether he cared if someone's face was Slav or Jew or
    Asian,
Or were such things of little consequence?
And he replied: Of course, some people take offence
At little things, yet what impresses me
Is more than physiognomy.
There's one thing matters more than all the rest
For it alone determines if you're cursed or blessed.
I'd better make myself quite clear:
It's rich and poor that really matters here.
And just in case you'd like some explanation
I've penned this parable in demonstration,
In which I prove beyond all doubt
That this is the difference to shout about.
So, dear audience, we'll play his little game,
We've built a set here of a distant land, Yahoo by name.
The skull-distributor will distribute his pates,
And some will hasten off to meet their fates.
Yet Mister Brecht will also make quite sure
That we can tell the rich from poor.
He'll share out costumes and rig the people out
According to their wealth and economic clout.
That's it now, close the doors!
His Excellency the skull-distributor. Applause!

THE GOVERNOR *comes forward and demonstrates his skull
scales to the accompaniment of stage thunder*:
I have two sorts of skulls here, as you see.
The difference isn't trivial, you'll agree:
This one is pointed, whereas this one here is round.
This one's sick and rotten. This one sound.
Wherever injustice and misery hold sway,
This one is never far away.
Where there's inequality, obesity or muscular degeneration –
Well, here's your explanation.
Use *my* scales, and all will be laid bare:
Right is on this side . . .

*He presses down with his finger on the scale with the round heads in it.*

                   ... wrong is over there.

DIRECTOR *introducing the rebel farmer:*
Now you, you outfitter, explain
Your scales and the clothes you use for weights
In order to determine men's estates.

REBEL FARMER *demonstrates his clothes scales:*
The differences, I think, are plain –
These here are the good ones, those the bad.
We needn't argue about that.
Walk around in this attire
And the level of respect you get will be appreciably higher
Than if you're dressed in clothes like those.
That's something everybody knows.
Use *my* scales, and all will be laid bare:
Who on this earth has the better share.
*He presses down with his finger on the scale with the fine clothes in it.*

DIRECTOR:
Our playwright, as you see, has scales with different norms.
With one he weighs the finery and the tatters,
And, with the other, skulls of different forms.
But then: he weighs the scales themselves, and that's what
    really matters.
*He has picked up the scales, one after the other, and weighed them in his hands. Now he gives them back and turns to his actors.*
You act out the parable, it's up to you
To choose your skulls and clothes in public view –
It's all determined right here in the play –
And if our writer's got it right
Your choice of clothes will seal your fate tonight
And not your head-shape. So no more delay!

FARMER *reaching for two round heads:*
We'll take the round heads, daughter dear, these two.

LANDOWNER:
Pointed for us.

LANDOWNER'S SISTER:
                    It's one of Brecht's 'effects'.
FARMER'S DAUGHTER:
  The daughter of a Round Head is a Round Head too.
  So I'm a Round Head of the weaker sex.
DIRECTOR:
  And now the costumes.
  *The actors choose their costumes.*
LANDOWNER:
  I own the land, I'm rich.
FARMER:
                    I pay the dues, I'm poor.
LANDOWNER'S SISTER:
  I am the landlord's sister.
FARMER'S DAUGHTER:
                    And me, I'm just a whore.
DIRECTOR *to the actors*:
  Is that clear? I trust you've understood?
ACTORS:
  Oh quite!
DIRECTOR *checking through once more*:
  Let's see: Round and Pointed Heads, that's good.
  Poor and posher clothes: that looks all right.
  And now the other props! As best we're able
  We'll show the world afresh, done up as fable!
  Our pantomime will demonstrate
  Which of these distinctions really carries weight.
  *They all withdraw behind the curtain.*

I

THE VICEROY'S PALACE

*The Viceroy of Yahoo and his privy councillor Missena have been up all night. They are sitting in the Viceroy's chamber surrounded by newspapers and sekt bottles. Missena is marking unpalatable sections of the newspapers with a big red pencil, for the attention of the Viceroy. Next door in the antechamber a shabby clerk is seated by a candle; a man stands with his back to the audience.*

VICEROY:
  Enough, Missena.
  The day is dawning: all our calculations,
  Creative twists, accounting sleights of hand
  Have demonstrated, each and every time,
  Precisely what we can't afford to know,
  And what, if we sat here till doomsday counting,
  Would always be the outcome: the economic
  Meltdown of the state. We're ...
MISSENA:
  No, don't say it!
VICEROY:
                                 ... bankrupt.
  A stronger hand than mine is needed now.
  *Missena does not answer.*
VICEROY *with a glance at the newspapers*:
  Perhaps your sums aren't right?
MISSENA:
                                 They're not that wrong!
VICEROY:
  From time to time I like to read the papers
  To see what state my country's really in.

MISSENA:

My lord, production surpluses consume us.
Our country, fair Yahoo, depends on grain;
It lives, and may perhaps now die, by grain.
We're sickening of a surfeit. Our prairies yield
Corn in such measure that the fortunate
Plough in their fortunes. Prices slump until
They scarcely justify the transport. The grain
Won't even pay the cost of harvest. Sire,
The corn has risen up against the people.
And surpluses give way to shortage. Farmers
Refuse to pay their tithes. The state and all
Its institutions start to tremble. Landowners
Demand the government enforce their dues,
And take firm measures. Meanwhile in the south
The peasants rally round a flag which bears
A giant sickle: emblem, dire threat
Of peasant revolution. The state's in crisis.
*The Viceroy sighs. Missena's words have struck a chord: he
himself is a landowner.*

VICEROY:

Suppose we raise a mortgage on the railways?

MISSENA:

We've done that, twice.

VICEROY:

                    The excise?

MISSENA:

                                        Done that too.

VICEROY:

The Big Five? Maybe they would guarantee
A preferential loan to help us out?
One third of all the profitable land
Belongs to them. They could, you know.

MISSENA:

                                        Except . . .
They'd first insist we smash the Sickle which
Endangers everybody's rents and dues.

VICEROY:

A fine thing that would be.

MISSENA:

>The Big Five now
Oppose our government. They feel betrayed.
We've been too lax about the rents, they say.

VICEROY:

You mean, they've lost their confidence in me.

MISSENA:

And yet, between ourselves: you are yourself
Our largest feudal lord.

*He has spoken the key word.*

VICEROY *rouses himself*:

>That's very true!
I own great tracts of land. And so my failures
In government are hurting my own class.
My sympathy's with those who now condemn me!

MISSENA:

There may be one solution, but of course
It could turn bloody ...

VICEROY:

>No, not that.
Don't say it!

MISSENA:

>No one can hear us here. War
Would furnish welcome markets for our wasted
Surpluses of grain, as well as sources
For the raw materials we lack.

VICEROY *shaking his head vehemently*:

>No.
If but a single tank disturbs the streets
Of Luma, there'll be such unrest that ...

MISSENA:

The enemy within prevents us marching
Against our ancient enemies abroad.
For shame! When soldiers slink away and hide
Like vermin! A general scarcely dares to show
His face upon the streets! The people treat
Our men as if they were but common thieves.
But for the Sickle, 'twould be a different tale.

VICEROY:

The Sickle's here to stay.

MISSENA:

They could be smashed.

VICEROY:

By whom? If you can find a man for that,
I swear I'll give you all the power you need
And delegate authority.

MISSENA:

I know
One man who'd only be too glad.

VICEROY *forcefully*:

Not him.
No. Once and for all, I won't have him.
*Pause.*
Besides, you overestimate the Sickle!

MISSENA:

I fear that I've upset you, sire. Perhaps
My lord would care to be alone awhile.
I'm sure you'll chance upon some course of action.

VICEROY:

Until tomorrow then ...

MISSENA *makes to go*:

I'll take my leave.

*To the audience*:
Good sense, it seems, cannot persuade my master,
I'll scare him with a sign that bodes disaster!
*He pauses by the door. Suddenly he takes a red pencil and
quickly draws something on the wall.*
But wait, what's this?

VICEROY:

What is it?

MISSENA:

Nothing.

VICEROY:

But ...
Why do you stare so?

MISSENA:

Me, stare?

VICEROY:

Yes, you.

You're trembling.
*He gets up.*
MISSENA:
                        Please, my lord, it's nothing really.
Nothing.
VICEROY:
            Stand aside!
MISSENA:
                        My lord, I can't
Imagine how this dreadful symbol got here!
*The Viceroy is devastated to see a huge sickle on the wall.*
VICEROY:
It's come to this. In my own palace chambers ...
*Pause.*
Perhaps I should withdraw a while to think,
To ponder on ... *Suddenly*: I'll delegate my powers.
MISSENA:
Oh careful, sire!
*Pause.*
                To whom?
VICEROY:
                            So you agree?
All right. To whom?
MISSENA:
                        It must be someone who
Can cow the peasants. While the Sickle still
Holds sway there's little chance of war, that's sure.
They're scum with no desire to pay their way.
But traders, craftsmen, servants of the state,
In other words: your upright citizens
Believe the peasants *can't* contribute more.
They're all for property, and yet they balk
At kicking naked hunger in the face.
The rebel spirit of the farmers can
Be broken only by a man who has
Little concern but to uphold the state,
A selfless soul – or known at least as such.
There's one ...

VICEROY *irritably*:

Just spit it out then: Iberin.

MISSENA:

The man is of the middle class himself,
He's neither landed gent nor tenant farmer,
Not rich nor poor. What's more, he's quite against
The very notion of a war between
The classes. To him both rich and poor are base
Materialists. And he demands, for rich
And poor alike, justice in equal measure.
It's his opinion that our sad decline
Is of the spirit.

VICEROY:

Uhuh. Of the spirit.

And what's with ... ?
*He gestures as if counting out money.*

MISSENA:

A side effect.

VICEROY:

I see.

And what, pray, has provoked this 'sad decline'?

MISSENA:

My lord, the cause of that is Iberin's
Great discovery!

VICEROY:

A true Columbus!

MISSENA:

Quite!

His explanation has two legs.

VICEROY:

Has what?

MISSENA:

Two legs. Iberin knows, the common people
Have little fondness for abstraction, and
Are eager to discover blame for our
Financial woes in some familiar cause,
With mouth and ears and arms and legs, in short
A person we might meet on any street.

VICEROY:

And has your man discovered such a scapegoat?

MISSENA:

He has.

VICEROY:

And we're not it?

MISSENA:

Indeed we're not.

The man's discovered that Yahoo has two
Quite separate races, living side by side,
Who even outwardly are quite distinct.
The key is in the shape of people's skulls:
One race has rounded heads, the others pointed,
And each head has a corresponding soul:
The blunt bespeaks blunt wholesome honesty,
The pointed points to sharp and cunning minds
Inclined to calculation and deceit.
The one race, with the rounded skulls, are called,
Says Iberin, the Zaks, and they have been
A part of Yahoo's healthy blood and soil
Right from the dawn of immemorial time.
The others – those with pointed heads, you follow –
Are foreign interlopers in our land,
They're called the Ziks, they have no proper home.
It's Zikkish spirit, so says Iberin,
That bears the blame for all this country's ills.
And that, my lord, is Iberin's whole theory.

VICEROY:

A pretty tale. But tell me, what's the point?

MISSENA:

Instead of class war cleaving rich from poor
There's war between the Zaks and Ziks.

VICEROY:

Ahah.

Not bad.

MISSENA:

Justice for all, that's Iberin's
Proud slogan, regardless whether rich or poor.
He'll gladly castigate the rich as well,
If they should dare step out of line. Why then
He speaks of 'Zikkish impudence'.

VICEROY:
>Really,

Zikkish impudence! ... But seriously,
What does he have to say about the rents?

MISSENA:

He doesn't talk about such things. Or only
Vaguely. Yet he's keen in his defence
Of 'Zakkish pride in property'.
*The Viceroy smiles. Missena smiles too.*

VICEROY:
>That's good!

Step out of line – and you're a Zik, take pride
In what is yours – a Zak! And who's behind him?

MISSENA:

His main support is petty bourgeoisie,
The little businessmen, the guilds, officials,
The lower folk with higher education,
The pensioners. In short: the middle class.
They're all behind his Iberin Alliance
Which, by the way, is said to be well armed.
If anyone can smash the Sickle, he can.

VICEROY:

We'd better keep the army out of this.
No tanks or soldiers ever won us votes.

MISSENA:

Iberin doesn't need the army.

VICEROY:
>That's good.

I'll delegate authority at once.
The night is passed and jocund day is dawning,
And we're resolved: we'll test his mettle, see
What he can do – for us. Go fetch the man.

MISSENA *rings*:

He's here already, he's been waiting hours
Across the hall.

VICEROY *startled*:
>Of course, I should have known

Your skill and foresight. Wait! The Big Five!
Are they behind him? Without them he's lost.

MISSENA:

'Twas one of them who brought him here. What's more
They fund him secretly.

VICEROY *signs the decree, puts on hat and coat, takes up his
stick*:

Then I must needs
Be off, retreat a while from worldly cares,
With just some traveller's cheques for sustenance.
Perhaps I'll take a book or two, there's some
I've waited years to read. I'll drift a bit,
And mingle with the careless bustling throng,
I'll contemplate the patchwork of the streets,
Enjoy the spectacle of life. And as
I rest my weary legs I'll witness all
The silent changes of this moon.

MISSENA:

Meanwhile,
Either the Sickle triumphs here in Luma,
Or else . . .
*With a grand gesture towards the door:*
Señor Iberin!
*At a signal from the shabby clerk, the man waiting in the
antechamber has risen. As he steps through the portals he
takes a deep bow.*


2

A BACKSTREET IN THE OLD TOWN

*Outside Madame Cornamontis's coffeehouse the girls are
raising a large white flag with a portrait of Iberin. Down
below Madame Cornamontis is directing operations. With her
are a police inspector and a court clerk, both barefoot and in
rags. A grocer's shop on the left still has its shutters down. In
front of the tobacco shop stands the tobacconist Palmosa
reading the newspaper. In an upstairs window of the house a
man is shaving: the landlord Callamassi. In front of another
grocery store, on the right, stand a fat woman and a soldier of
Iberin's militia, wearing a white armband and a large straw*

*hat and armed to the teeth. They are all watching the raising
of the flag. In the distance the sound of marching troops can
just be heard, and the newspaper sellers' cries: 'Get your copies
here, the new Governor's proclamation!'*

MADAME CORNAMONTIS: Push the pole out a bit further, so
the wind can catch the cloth. And a little more to the side!
*She demonstrates with large gestures how the flag should
hang.*

NANNA: More to the left, more to the right, you're the boss!

POLICE INSPECTOR: So Madame Cornamontis, you're a
businesswoman, what do you think about this latest turn?

CORNAMONTIS: I'm flying the flag aren't I, that says it all.
And you can depend on it, I shan't be employing any more
Zikkish girls here. *She sits herself down on a wicker chair in
front of her house and begins to read the newspaper, like
everybody else.*

CALLAMASSI *shaving himself in the window*: This day, the
eleventh of September, it'll go down in history! *He looks at
his flag.* It cost a tidy sum, that.

PALMOSA: Do you think it'll come to war? Our Gabriel has
just turned twenty.

IBERIN SOLDIER: Whatever gives you that idea? Nobody
wants war. Señor Iberin is a friend of peace, like he's a
friend of the people. Why, only this morning everything to
do with the military was pulled out of the city. On Señor
Iberin's express instructions. Do you see any tin-hats?
They've left the streets to us, completely, the Iberin Militia.

PALMOSA: It says here in the newspaper, Iberin, who's such a
good friend of the people, only seized power in order to
call a halt to the increasing oppression of the poorer
elements in our society.

SOLDIER: Yes, and that's a fact.

FAT WOMAN, *the owner of the grocery store on the right*: Well
then he should look to it first that there aren't two grocers
right next door on such a little street, where there's scarcely
business for one. To my mind that shop over there is quite
superfluous.

CLERK: Believe me, Inspector, if the new government can't

provide some relief for us civil servants I shan't dare show my face at home on the first of the month.

INSPECTOR: My truncheon's so rotten, one good blow to a pointy head and it would crumble to pieces. And as for my whistle, which I might always need to summon reinforcements if I'm in a corner, well, it's been rusted up for months. *He tries to whistle.* Do you hear anything?

CLERK *shakes his head*: Yesterday I was forced to requisition some whitewash from a worker's bucket over at the building site, just so as I could whiten my collar. So Inspector, do you really think we'll get paid next month?

INSPECTOR: I'm so sure of it, this morning I'm going to treat myself to a cigar from Señor Palmosa.

*They both go into the tobacco shop.*

CALLAMASSI *gestures at the clerk and inspector*: The best thing is, now the civil service will get pruned a bit. There are far too many of them, and they get paid too well.

CORNAMONTIS: That's a fine thing to say to your tenants! That you want to 'prune' their last remaining customers.

SOLDIER: What do you say to my new boots? These are standard issue now! *He reads out to the landlord and the fat woman:* 'The very manner of Iberin's seizure of power tells us much about the man. In the middle of the night, when Government House was sleeping, he forced his way in with a handful of fearless companions and demanded at pistol point to speak to the Viceroy. According to reliable sources, there was a short exchange, after which he simply deposed him. The Viceroy himself is believed to be on the run.'

FAT WOMAN: In that case it's all the more surprising that here in this street, where all the houses are showing the flag, there's just the one house where they haven't bothered. *She points to the grocer's opposite.*

SOLDIER *shocked*: You're right, he hasn't got a flag. *He looks at them, one by one. They all shake their heads.* Perhaps we should offer a little help, what do you say?

FAT WOMAN: The man's got no use for it. He's a Zik, you know.

SOLDIER: The cheek of it! In that case, Mrs Tomaso, we'll

teach the bastard how to celebrate Iberin's inauguration. Here come some of my colleagues. These are the Hatsos, the dreaded Hats-Off Brigade, run by Zazarante the Bloody, Commander of the Holy Cross. But don't you worry! They'll take a look under your hats, but as long as they don't find a pointed head they can be real gentlemen. *There are cries of: 'Hats off! Head Inspection!' The three Hatsos come into the street. They knock the hat off a passer-by.*

FIRST HATSO: I do declare, sir, you've lost your hat.

SECOND HATSO: Quite a wind today, eh?

PASSER-BY: I'm terribly sorry.

HATSOS: Don't mention it!

FAT WOMAN: Gentlemen! Officer Head Inspector, sir! If you want to see a real Pointed Head, I mean a really nasty sharp one, just knock on the door of the grocer's over there!

SOLDIER *reporting*: A Zikkish grocer, sir. Shows his disrespect for the Iberin Government by refusal to show the flag.
*A Zik, very pale, comes out of the shop with a ladder and a flag. They all watch him.*

FIRST HATSO: I don't believe it. He's hanging out a flag!

SECOND HATSO: The Iberin flag in the greasy paws of a full-blooded Zik!
*The Hatso looks at them one by one. They all shake their heads.*

SOLDIER: It's a pointed insult!
*The three Hatsos go up to the Pointed Head.*

THIRD HATSO: You Zikkish swine! Get back inside, at the double, and get your hat! D'you think we want to have to look at your pointy head?

FAT WOMAN: The poor Zik probably thinks Iberin's going to look after his kind too! If he flies the flag that must mean he's happy Iberin is in power. So he's insulting the Government by suggesting they're friends of the Ziks.
*The Zik turns to get his hat.*

FIRST HATSO *pointing*: Trying to escape!
*They beat him up and start to drag him off.*

FIRST HATSO: Resisting arrest too. I thump him in the eye and he lifts his arm. I think I'd better interpret that as premeditated provocation!

SECOND HATSO *still punching the Zik*: It's off to Protective Custody with him. That's where we protect his sort from the righteous anger of the people.

FAT WOMAN: Hail Iberin!

*The third Hatso hangs up a sign outside the left-hand grocery store: 'Zikkish Trader'.*

THIRD HATSO *to the fat woman, as he gets another notice out of his pocket*: So, Missus Race Comrade, you see how it pays to have it in black and white, your racial allegiance. The notice costs thirty pesos. But it'll pay dividends, three hundred per cent, and that's a promise!

FAT WOMAN: Can't you do it for ten? I don't sell much.

SOLDIER *threateningly*: Of course, there are some people who still have pointed heads in their hearts!

FAT WOMAN: Give it here! *She pays hurriedly.* Have you got change for a fifty? *She hangs up the sign: 'Zakkish Trader'.*

THIRD HATSO: Right you are. Twenty pesos change. Honest Juan, that's me. *He goes off without giving her her change.*

FAT WOMAN: He didn't give me my change! *The Iberin soldier looks at her threateningly.* Well at least the Zik had to clear out! Only a fortnight ago he was saying even Iberin wouldn't make the cabbages grow bigger.

CORNAMONTIS: There's a Zikkish attitude for you! A nation bestirs itself, and he talks about cabbages.

SOLDIER: The Ziks are entirely governed by, you know, base materialism. Only concerned with their own advantage, they'll deny their Fatherland as soon as look at you – and it's not even theirs anyway. Ziks don't even know who their own fathers are, or their mothers. You know, it's probably because they've got no sense of humour. You've just seen it for yourselves. These Ziks, they're possessed by a morbid sensuality, they're quite without scruples. The only thing that stands in the way of their lust is their greed. Zikkish materialism. You know.

PALMOSA *calls up to the first floor, where Landlord Calla-massi is shaving*: It's all over with materialism now! I expect you've gathered, Señor Callamassi, there'll be no more shop-rents now.

SOLDIER: That's right!

CALLAMASSI: On the contrary, my dear fellow! Government bailiffs will help us collect the rents from now on. Do you hear the battalions marching? Those are the Stormtroops of the Iberin Alliance. Marching off to put down the rebel farmers who don't want to pay their dues! Think about it, Mr Palmosa, while you think about not paying your rent!

SOLDIER: And you can't say fairer than that.

PALMOSA: Perhaps you've forgotten, Señor Callamassi, my son is with those troops! *To the fat woman*: I told him just this morning, as he took his leave to march south: Son, I said, make sure you bring me back a captured Sickle flag, and I'll let you start smoking! They say the banks are going to take over the debts of the bankrupt craftsmen and shopkeepers, and they'll grant new credit, especially to all the small businesses in difficulties.

SOLDIER: Hoorah for Iberin!

FAT WOMAN *to her shopowner, Madame Cornamontis*: Have you heard? They're going to lower the rents!

SOLDIER: Yes, that's right.

CORNAMONTIS: My dear, I'm told they're going to raise them.

SOLDIER: Yes, that's true too.

FAT WOMAN: That can't be true. Maybe they're just putting up the rent for Ziks. Whatever, I shan't be in too much of a hurry to pay.

CORNAMONTIS: Oh yes you will, Mrs Tomaso, you will! And a higher rent at that! *To the Iberin soldier*: These simple folk have no idea about politics.

FAT WOMAN: Even higher rents?

SOLDIER *interrupts*: The big thing today is the Zik pogroms. *He reads out from the newspaper*: Iberin has announced, our only goal is: To flush out the Ziks, wherever they're hiding!

*The marching troops get louder. Singing.*

SOLDIER: Stand to attention now! The Iberin Chorale! Everybody sing along! Spontaneously mind!

*They all sing, led by the Iberin soldier:*

HYMN, YAHOO AWAKES

1
Bid Señor Iberin grant us a big rent reduction!
At the same time
He should allow rents to climb
Lest landlords suffer destruction!

2
May he grant farmers a corn price which rises up steeply!
At the same time
Townsfolk believe it a crime
If they can't have their bread cheaply!

3
May he relieve the small traders from debts that oppress
     them!
At the same time
For those who don't have a dime
Help the cut-price stores and bless them!

4
Praise to the Leader who's rallied our glorious nation!
Roused from our sleep
We stand in line just like sheep
Hoping he'll bring us salvation!

CORNAMONTIS *to the Iberin soldier*: Come along, let's go and
     watch our glorious warriors, they'll soon root out those
     clodhoppers and their Sickle!
*She and the Iberin soldier exit.*
FAT WOMAN *and* PALMOSA *together*: I can't leave my shop.
     What if a customer came by?
*They go back into their shops.*
NANNA CALLAS *comes out of Madame Cornamontis's coffee-
     house with a letter*: Just a moment ago Señor de Guzman
     came down the street. He's going for his little walk before
     lunch, he'll be back any minute. I must have a word with
     him. My mother has written to me about my father, he's a
     tenant farmer and he's got in with a bad crowd because he

can't pay the dues. He's joined the Sickle League and they're planning a violent uprising of all the peasants. I'd better ask Señor de Guzman if we can have a rent rebate! With a bit of luck he still feels enough for me at least to listen to my request. It's been three years now since he had something with me. He was the first man I went with, and really the only reason why I, a simple peasant's daughter, came to the prosperous house of Madame Cornamontis. He was very good to my family then. I don't like having to ask him for another favour now. But at least it's quickly over. *She sings*:

NANNA'S SONG

There was I, with sixteen summers
Prenticed to the trade of love
Ready to take on all comers.
Nasty things occurred
Frequently, I'd heard
Even so I found it rather rough.
(After all, I'm not an animal, you know.)
   Thank the Lord the whole thing's quickly over
   All the loving and the sorrow, my dear.
   Where are the teardrops you wept last evening?
   Where are the snows of yesteryear?

Certainly the passing summers
Simplify the trade of love
Let you take increasing numbers:
First it may feel nice
But you turn to ice
If you don't withhold yourself enough.
(After all, stocks can't last for ever, can they?)
   Thank the Lord the whole thing's quickly over
   All the loving and the sorrow, my dear.
   Where are the teardrops you wept last evening?
   Where are the snows of yesteryear?

Even once you've got the measure
Of the ways how love is sold
Making money out of pleasure

Isn't all that fun.
Well, it has been done
But it can't prevent you getting old.
(After all, you don't go on being sixteen always, do you?)
    Thank the Lord the whole thing's quickly over
    All the loving and the sorrow, my dear.
    Where are the teardrops you wept last evening?
    Where are the snows of yesteryear?

NANNA: Here he comes now. But there are three other men with him, including that rich Señor Peruiner. How can I talk to him now? *She beckons to Señor de Guzman, and he comes over. His three friends stand waiting.*

DE GUZMAN: Good morning, Nanna.

NANNA: I must have a word with you. Step into this doorway here. *They do so.* My father has written again to say he can't pay the rent.

DE GUZMAN: Well, this time he must, I'm afraid. My sister is entering the Convent of San Barabas and she needs her novice's dowry.

NANNA: Surely you don't want my parents to starve because of that.

DE GUZMAN: My dear Nanna, my sister is about to dedicate herself to a life of virtue and renunciation with the Needy Sisters of San Barabas. You have to respect that. Even if it is not necessary for all girls to live chaste lives, at least you should think more highly of those who do.

NANNA: If you'd just offer the poor girl a lover for a husband, instead of some landed gent, it wouldn't cross her mind to enter a nunnery. But your sort doesn't marry people, you marry property.

DE GUZMAN: You seem to have changed, Nanna, much for the worse, I hardly recognise you.

NANNA: So it's no use telling you that my folks can't pay the rent any more, and they've simply got to get a horse. The village is too far from the railway station.

DE GUZMAN: They can borrow a horse from the estate.

NANNA: But that costs money.

DE GUZMAN: That's the way of the world. I have to pay for my horses too.

NANNA: Don't you love me any more, Emanuele!

DE GUZMAN: It has nothing to do with us. I'll come and visit you this very afternoon. Then you'll see how fond of you I still am.

NANNA: Wait a moment. Here are some people who might pick on you for being a Zik.

*The three Hatsos come back down the street.*

FIRST HATSO: A while back, wherever we went we kept treading on them. And now, far and wide, not a Zik to be seen.

SECOND HATSO: Never give up hope, that's what I say!

NANNA: You know, Emanuele, when I think about it, you always treated me like a dog. Perhaps you'd like to think it over, and repay me for the liberties you've taken!

DE GUZMAN: For Christ's sake, keep quiet!

NANNA: So you won't pay, is that it?

THIRD HATSO: I think I hear something.

NANNA: If I were to appeal to these gentlemen here, I'm sure they'd side with me. I'm only asking what's my due.

FIRST HATSO: There's someone talking.

NANNA: Gentlemen, what do you say, can't a poor girl expect the man who's led her astray at least to show his appreciation a bit? Or is that too much to ask?

DE GUZMAN: I must say, I'm astonished at you, Nanna!

NANNA: That's your problem.

*The three Hatsos approach.*

FIRST HATSO: Now here's a pretty specimen, and what a fine outfit!

SECOND HATSO: Oh, I do like your hat, sir! I'd love to have one like that. Go on, show me the *inside* so I can see the maker's name.

*He knocks off the hat and points at de Guzman's pointed head. The three Hatsos shriek and bay.*

THE THREE HATSOS: A Zik!

FIRST HATSO: Thump him on his pointy head! Mind he doesn't get away!

SEÑOR SAZ: We must intervene. Our friend de Guzman is in trouble.

SEÑOR PERUINER *holds him back*: Don't let's attract attention, I'm a Zik myself!
*The three landowners hurry away.*
THIRD HATSO: I thought as much, all along I thought I could smell a Zik.
SECOND HATSO: A Zik! Let's take him to the tribunal!
*Two Hatsos drag off de Guzman. The third stays at Nanna's side.*
THIRD HATSO: Didn't you say something about money he owes you, miss?
NANNA *sulkily*: That's right, he won't pay.
THIRD HATSO: They're like that, these Ziks!
*The third Hatso leaves. Nanna goes slowly back into Madame Cornamontis's coffeeshop. Hearing the noise, Landlord Callamassi has appeared at the window, and the fat woman has come to the door of her shop. The tobacconist reappears at his shopdoor.*
CALLAMASSI: What's all the commotion?
FAT WOMAN: They've just rounded up a very wealthy-looking Zik gentleman who was talking to one of the waitresses at Madame Cornamontis's.
PALMOSA: Well now, is that illegal?
FAT WOMAN: They say the girl was a Zak. But the gentleman, it seems, was one of the Big Five.
CALLAMASSI: You don't say!
PALMOSA *going back into his shop*: Inspector! They've just assaulted one of the Big Five and dragged him off!
INSPECTOR *walks off with the clerk*: That's no business for the police.
FAT WOMAN: The rich are getting their come-uppance now!
CALLAMASSI: You think so?
PALMOSA: The landowners won't have much to celebrate!
CALLAMASSI: But they're starting a campaign against the farmers who won't pay their rent too!
PALMOSA: In the newspaper this morning it said: Today is the beginning of a new age!

INTERLUDE

*A street in the Old Town, painted on a large sheet of cardboard. The Iberin soldiers come running with pots and pails of whitewash. With long-handled brushes and short-handled brushes they paint over the cracks and crevices in the houses.*

WHITEWASH SONG

When the rot sets in, when walls and roof start dripping
Something must be done at any price.
Now the mortar's crumbling, bricks are slipping.
If somebody comes it won't be nice.
But whitewash will do it, fresh whitewash will do it.
When the place caves in 'twill be too late.
Give us whitewash, boys, then we'll go to it
With our brushes till we fix things up first-rate.
Now, here's a fresh disaster
This damp patch on the plaster!
That isn't nice. (No, not nice.)
Look, the chimney's falling!
Really, it's appalling!
Something must be done at any price.
Oh, if only things would look up!
This abominable fuck-up
Isn't nice. (No, not nice.)
But whitewash will do it, lots of white will do it.
When the place caves in 'twill be too late.
Give us whitewash, boys, then we'll go to it
And we'll whitewash till we've got it all first-rate.
Here's the whitewash, let's not get upset!
Day and night we've got the stuff on hand.
This old shack will be a palace yet.
You'll get your new age, just as planned.

3

AT A VILLAGE WELL

Coming fishing?
Said the fisherman to the worm.

*The round-headed Farmer Callas, his wife and children, and
the pointed-headed Farmer Lopez, his wife and children, are
drawing water.*

FARMERS CALLAS *and* LOPEZ:
 We sweat and we slave under feudal rule.
 Our master won't give us horses to work
 So we have to be our own pack-mule.
MRS LOPEZ: Do you hear that noise? It's people from our
 village going over to join the Sickle.
 *The clatter of many wooden clogs. A round-headed farmer
 enters with two shotguns under his arm.*
THIRD FARMER: In these terrible circumstances, which we
 have suffered ever since the corn prices collapsed, we, the
 tenant farmers of Yahoo – clog-wearers one and all – have
 come together, at first in secret and now in open assembly,
 and are resolved to take up arms and to fight under the
 banner of the Sickle, rather than to go on paying our rents
 and dues. The time has come, Callas, Lopez, here are your
 guns. *He hands over the shotguns and exits.*
LOPEZ: You were going to wait, weren't you, Callas, in case
 you heard better news from your daughter in the city.
CALLAS: But help never comes. I'm ready to fight alongside
 you.
LOPEZ: Give me your hand, Callas, and you too, take each
 other's hands, children too! Today, the eleventh of September, is a day to remember. For today we farmers have taken
 up arms, prepared to fight to shake off the yoke of
 oppression – or else to die.
 *They all take hands and sing the Song of the Sickle.*

THE SONG OF THE SICKLE

Peasants arise!
Open your eyes!
Don't let life pass you by
One day you all must die.

Your chains will only be broken
When you yourselves have spoken.
Open your eyes!
Peasants arise!

EVERYONE: The Sickle! Hurrah!
*The bells start to ring out.*
MRS LOPEZ: Listen. What are those bells?
MRS CALLAS *calls out towards backstage*: What's up, Paolo?
VOICE FROM OFFSTAGE: We've just heard the news from the
city: a new People's Government has come to power.
MRS CALLAS: I'll go and find out what's really going on.
*She exits. The others wait. The radio broadcasts the
'Proclamation of the new Governor to the People of the
Land'.*
VOICE OF IBERIN:

My Zakkish countrymen! For many a year
Yahoo has been beset and ravaged by
A foreign spirit alien to our blood:
A ghost of greed which threatens rich and poor.
My Zakkish countrymen, who live in fear,
Oppressed, exploited and in misery,
A fearsome foe lurks in our pleasant land,
Silently working his evil ways: the Zik!
'Tis he who bears the blame for all our ills.
'Tis he whom you must fight with all your strength.
I hear you ask how you may recognise
The fiend. His head! His pointed head betrays him!
So I, Angelo Iberin, hereby
Decree: the people shall henceforth be split
In two: the Round Heads and the Pointed Heads.
And all that's Zakkish shall unite against
The threat of all that's Zikkish! Henceforth Zaks
Shall know no rivalry! All Zaks unite
And stand together 'gainst your pointed foe
Beneath Iberin's proud white fluttering flag!
*During the proclamation the listening farmers have, more or
less openly, been feeling their heads. The round-headed
children point grinning at the Pointed Heads.*

LOPEZ: It's just talk again! They're always coming up with something new. What I want to know is, what are they going to do about the landlords.

CALLAS: That's right.

*Mrs Callas has returned. She doesn't look at Lopez, and she gathers her children closer around her.*

LOPEZ: Good news, Mrs Callas?

MRS CALLAS: They've arrested our landlord Señor de Guzman.

LOPEZ: Why?

CALLAS: Lopez, I hardly think we need ask why. It's clear. He's been arrested for rack-renting.

MRS LOPEZ: Mrs Callas, then we're saved.

CALLAS: That's better, eh Lopez? Children, our days of misery are at an end! *He leans his gun against the well.*

MRS LOPEZ: This is a great day!

MRS CALLAS: Don't get too excited, Mrs Lopez! I'm afraid the news isn't quite so good for you. Angelo Iberin has taken over the government, and you're Ziks! They say that in the capital Luma there have already been great pogroms against the Ziks. Señor de Guzman himself was arrested because he's a Zik.

LOPEZ: This is bad news, and a great misfortune.

CALLAS: I don't know, it's not that much of a misfortune, at least not for everybody. It's no misfortune for us.

MRS CALLAS: No, only for you!

CALLAS: For us Zaks you could even say it's rather good news.

MRS CALLAS: In this hour, Mr Lopez, we are inspired by a hope which you can't grasp. Perhaps you're just a different sort of human being, I'm not saying an inferior sort, necessarily.

LOPEZ: Up to now, Callas, my head has never been too sharp for you.

*Callas is silent. The two families have drawn apart, on the one side stand the Pointed Heads, on the other the Round Heads.*

LOPEZ: We always paid the same dues. And only five minutes

ago you wanted to fight with us under the banner of the
Sickle, to abolish rents; and you were right, force is the only
way. Here, wife, take up his gun.

*Mrs Lopez hesitatingly takes the gun.*

CALLAS: But the prospect is so grim! If there were a hope of
success, of course that would be best. But there is no hope.

LOPEZ: Why talk about the grim prospects if it's the only
way?

CALLAS: Maybe for me it isn't the only way.

MRS CALLAS: Of course, we reckon we'll be let off the rent
now.

LOPEZ: I understand, you'll clutch at any straw. But you'll be
disappointed, believe me. Whoever heard of any of these
people handing out free gifts just on account of the shape of
someone's head.

CALLAS: That's enough, Lopez. I have no reason to doubt the
integrity of this government. They've only been in power
five hours, and my landlord is already under arrest.

MRS CALLAS: They're saying in the village that there's no
point joining the Sickle now.

*Five farmers, including Farmer Parr, enter in some excite-
ment. They are all Round Heads. One of them is carrying a
flag bearing the Sickle, all of them carry shotguns.*

FARMER PARR: What are you going to do? We were going to
join the Sickle this evening, as we'd all agreed. But then we
heard the Proclamation and the news of the arrest of the
landlords. Should we still fight?

CALLAS: I'm going to Luma to see Iberin. If he can get me
horses to draw my plough, and if he gets me off the rent,
then I've no need of fighting. De Guzman is a Zik, he'll
have no say.

FIRST FARMER: That's well and good, your landlord is a Zik,
but ours is a Round Head!

PARR: But perhaps ours will relax the rent too when the Ziks
are out of the way. He's got debts with a Zikkish bank and
they'll be cancelled now.

LOPEZ: Even if his debts are cancelled, he'll still want the rent.

THIRD FARMER: After all, it's the landlords who are behind
Iberin.

PARR: From what I've heard, that's not true. They say he lives quite modestly, doesn't drink, doesn't smoke, and he's the son of a tenant farmer himself. He's a selfless soul, that's what it says in the newspaper. He says the Parliament is useless too, and that's true.

FIRST FARMER: Yes, that's true.

*Silence.*

THIRD FARMER: So the farmers shouldn't do anything against the landlords now?

PARR: Of course they should: the Zakkish farmers against the Zikkish landlords.

LOPEZ: And what about the Zikkish farmers, what should they do about the Zakkish landlords?

PARR: There aren't that many Zikkish farmers. Ziks don't like hard work.

FIFTH FARMER: But there are plenty of Zakkish landlords.

PARR: Zak against Zak, that sort of squabbling has got to stop now.

LOPEZ: The rain still comes through our roofs, and that's got to stop too.

CALLAS: Our Zik has already been arrested.

FOURTH FARMER: But the rain comes through my roof too, and my landlord is a Zak.

THIRD FARMER: This is nonsense! What I want to know is: will your Iberin get rid of the landlords, all of them?

PARR: He'll get rid of the Zikkish landlords all right, and then he'll force the Zaks to let up a bit.

THIRD FARMER: That's no good: Zak or Zik, a landlord's a landlord! We've got to get rid of them all. I'm off to join the Sickle. I don't see why I should have faith in anyone but myself. If you want to get out of this misery, you'll come with me and join the Sickle. This Iberin is just another fraud. *To the public*:
Lord and tenant should unite, they're saying,
And what's the reason? 'Cause our heads are round!
But *he* collects the rent, while *I* must pay it!
You've got to see, the reasoning's not sound!
With all this 'Zakkish' talk the man derides us;

If we're such friends, why not abolish rent!
A gulf of cold and hunger still divides us,
That's not a thing we'll lightly circumvent!

CALLAS: Say what you like: I'm going to try my luck with Iberin!

FARMERS: Join us, Lopez!
Round or pointed heads, that's not our lore!
For us there's only one thing: rich or poor!
*They hold out their hands to him, and exit.*

MRS LOPEZ: I think we'd better go home now.

MRS CALLAS: But you won't be able to do that, Mrs Lopez. As I came past the village pond a moment ago I heard people saying that it was time to settle with the Lopez family. And when I looked up in the direction of your house I saw a red glow.

MRS LOPEZ: Oh God!

LOPEZ: Please, Callas, give my family shelter at your place – until this first wave of persecution has blown over.
*Silence.*

CALLAS: I'd rather you were not found under my roof, tonight or any night ...

LOPEZ: Can't you just take my children into hiding, at least for the first few days?

CALLAS: Maybe I could. But as you're with the Sickle, it would be dangerous for my own family if you were associated with us in any way.

LOPEZ: We'll be leaving then, Callas.
*Callas is silent.*

THE TWO WOMEN:
We used to be united by our woes
But now our different head shapes make us bitter foes.
*The Lopez family exit slowly.*

MRS CALLAS: Now, husband, you must get on your way to Luma as quickly as you can, and make the most of this opportunity! Don't pay the rent, and make sure you get a written assurance that you don't have to pay!

CALLAS: Right. I won't be back until I've got it in writing!

4

THE VICEROY'S PALACE

*At court a trial is in progress. The parties are the Mother Superior of San Barabas and the Abbot of San Stefano. A news flash projection reads: 'The Sickle advances on the Imperial capital.'*

JUDGE: In the trial of the Barefoot Mendicants of San Stefano against the Needy Sisters of San Barabas the Barefoot Mendicants have set their claim for damages at seven million. On what do the Brothers base their claim for a sum of such magnitude?

ABBOT OF SAN STEFANO: On the building of a new church of pilgrimage by the Convent of San Barabas, which is draining away the devout congregation from our own parish.

MOTHER SUPERIOR OF SAN BARABAS: We submit that the court inspect the accounts of the new pilgrims' chapel of San Sebastian, which is the cause of this dispute; Your Honour will establish that the revenue is not seven million, as the Brothers claim, but scarcely four million.

ABBOT: Naturally, in the books! I should merely like to point out that the Needy Sisters of San Barabas have appeared before this High Court once before, when there was a little question of tax evasion to the tune of one and a half million; on that occasion too the Sisters based their defence on their accounts.

*They shake their fists at each other. A court clerk appears.*

JUDGE: What is it? I don't wish to be disturbed in the conduct of a trial where such large sums are at stake.

CLERK: Your Honour, there's a crowd on its way to the courthouse, they've got Señor de Guzman. The people are saying he raped a Zakkish girl.

JUDGE: Ridiculous. Señor de Guzman is one of the country's five biggest landowners. He was released from false arrest just three days ago.

*The crowd forces its way into the courtroom. De Guzman is shoved in front of the judge. Madame Cornamontis and Nanna are pushed forward too. The judge rings his bell agitatedly. Meanwhile de Guzman is jostled and spat on by the crowd.*

VOICES: Look at that suit. A family of six could live for a month off the price of that. – Look at his soft hands, he's never held a spade in his life. – We'll have to hang this one on a silk rope.

*The Hatsos begin to throw dice for de Guzman's rings.*

A MAN: Mr Judge, sir, the people of Yahoo demand that this man is punished for his crimes.

JUDGE: Good people, the matter will be properly investigated. At present we're right in the middle of another case of great urgency.

ABBOT *who has been conferring with the Mother Superior, in some agitation*: We don't think it's necessary to discuss our little local difficulties in front of all these people. We should be happy to accept an adjournment.

SHOUTS: No more postponements! – We said right from the start we should set fire to the whole damn place! – Hang the judge too! – String up the whole lot of 'em, without a trial!

A MAN *to the crowds outside*:

Here you see real justice for our times:

Compassion for the victims, but tough on those who commit the crimes!

Here's pity for the virtuous and meek,

But ruthlessness for those who persecute the weak.

ANOTHER MAN: Even the lawcourts have to learn: this is a new age for Yahoo, and a new justice!

*Projection: 'In his address to the teachers the Governor describes the unrest in the South as the struggle of Right against Wrong.'*

THE CROWD: Sit down everybody, we'll stay put until justice is done and the landlord is hanged!

*They all sit down, smoke, open up their newspapers, spit and chat.*

THE INSPECTOR *comes and talks to the judge*: The Governor has given instructions that you should let the crowd have its way, and let the trial proceed. The court is no longer to restrict itself to the dry letter of the law, but must let itself be guided by the people's natural sense of justice. The conflict in the South is looking very bad for the government, and the capital is getting more restless by the minute.

JUDGE *to the audience*: These excitements are all too much for me. I'm no longer up to it, simply physically. It's been two months since we last got paid. The situation is quite uncertain, and I have to think of my family. This morning I had just a cup of weak tea and a stale roll for breakfast. You can't mete out justice on an empty stomach. People have no confidence in a man who hasn't had his breakfast, he's got no energy, no conviction. The law loses all its lustre.

*The de Guzman attorneys burst into the antechamber with their robes flying, followed by a number of landowners.*

ZAKKISH ATTORNEY *in the antechamber to his colleague*: You stay in the common room. It'll be better for you, as a Zik, if you don't show yourself in here.

ZIKKISH ATTORNEY: Just make sure you get him behind bars for the next week or so. I wish I was in prison myself.

*The Zakkish attorney and the landowners enter the court.*

CRIES: Get a move on! – It's almost too dark already if we want to hang the man!

JUDGE: Everybody at least sit down properly. We must discover the facts first. We must have a bit of order. *To Madame Cornamontis*: Who are you?

MADAME CORNAMONTIS: Madame Cornamontis, Emma. Proprietress of the coffeehouse El Paradiso, Estrada number 5.

JUDGE: And what do you want?

CORNAMONTIS: I don't want anything.

JUDGE: Then why are you here?

CORNAMONTIS: About half an hour ago people gathered in front of my house and demanded that one of my waitresses, this girl here, accompany them to court. I refused to let her go, and so I was made to come along too. I'm as innocent in this affair as Pontius Pilate in the creed.

JUDGE: And you are the girl? Sit down here in the dock.

*Catcalls from the crowd.*

CRIES: Hey, that's where the other guys belong.

*Projection: 'Government troops offer fierce resistance to the Sickle.'*

JUDGE: I'll decide who belongs in the dock. *To Nanna*: You solicited the gentleman quite openly in the street. You know, you can get three weeks' hard labour for that. *Nanna is silent, so he turns to de Guzman, and bows*: I beg you, approach the bench, Señor de Guzman. Do I have the facts aright?

DE GUZMAN: Indeed, Your Honour. The young thing importuned me as I took my morning constitutional. She's the daughter of one of my tenants, and she asked me to release her father from his financial obligations. *Quietly*: Please, put me in custody, I'm a Zik.

ATTORNEY: I am the de Guzman family attorney. If I may represent my client ...

JUDGE: Do you have witnesses?

ATTORNEY: Here are the gentlemen, Señores Saz, Duarte and de Hoz.

CRIES: Fine folk as witnesses against the poor!
*Whistles.*

JUDGE: Silence! *To the witnesses*: What have you to say? I must remind you that perjury is a serious offence.

CRIES: That's more like it!

SAZ: Señor de Guzman was accosted by this young girl on the street.

ATTORNEY: The social standing of my client, surely, is enough to vouch for the truth of his statement, which is disputed only by a waitress from a common coffeehouse.

VOICE FROM ABOVE: Ohoh! Quite the reverse, I'd say! Take off your cap a moment, dear fellow! Let's see the shape of your head! With opinions like that!

SECOND VOICE FROM ABOVE: Off with his cap!

ATTORNEY *takes off his cap*: It's just as round as yours, you see!

VOICE FROM ABOVE: Why don't you ask your client who it is who demands so much rent from the father that his daughter has to sell herself?

SECOND VOICE FROM ABOVE: Start from the beginning!

JUDGE *to Nanna*: You take your place in the dock now, so we can get started!

VOICE FROM ABOVE: Don't sit there! We've come here to see you get justice, not to put you in the dock.

ATTORNEY: We can't conduct these matters like some street brawl. There are subtle legal issues here. We must use our heads.

VOICE FROM ABOVE: We get the point.

*Laughter.*

SECOND VOICE FROM ABOVE: We should get Iberin to settle this.

VOICES: Who do we want in the dock: the racketeer landlord, the pimping madam, and the shyster lawyer.

VOICE FROM ABOVE: And let's get Iberin. Or is he too good for this?

VOICES: Iberin! Iberin! Iberin!

*Iberin has already entered, unnoticed, and now sits to one side behind the judge's bench.*

OTHER VOICES: Look, there's Iberin!

MORE CRIES: Hail Iberin!

JUDGE *to Iberin*: Excellency, I'm relying on statements by some of the leading landowners in the country.

IBERIN: You'd do better to pay attention to the news from the front!

*Projection: 'Inadequate equipment a serious setback for loyal Government troops! Ammunition shortages and poor provisions erode the fighting spirit of our soldiers.' There is a disturbance. In a crowd of other people, Farmer Callas enters the court.*

VOICE: Here's the girl's father.

NANNA: Oh dear, my father! I'd better hide so he doesn't see me. This time I've really done it! And it'll be the folks back home who suffer.

JUDGE *to Callas*: What do you want here?

VOICE FROM ABOVE: He wants justice!

CALLAS'S COMPANIONS: We met this man on the street. He asked us when and where the de Guzman case was being tried. We told him, right now, he had only to follow the crowds, everyone is coming here.

CALLAS: That's a fact. I've come here from my farm to bear

witness against my landlord, who's on trial for rack-renting.

JUDGE: This court is not concerned with rack-renting.

CALLAS: Oh yes it is! I can prove that the rent was exorbitant. The land is marshy and the fields are too far apart, the tools are primitive and we have to use the cow to pull the cart. The whole summer through we worked from three o'clock in the morning, the children helped as well. And the price of corn is not in our hands, it's been different every year, but the rent is always the same. The landlord doesn't lift a finger, he just pockets the money. So I ask that the rent be written off, once and for all, and that the price of corn be set so that we can make a living from our work.

VOICE FROM ABOVE: Quite right!

*Applause.*

THE MAN *stands up and addresses the crowds in the street behind*: The father of the girl who was molested, he's a tenant farmer of the accused, he demands the abolition of the rents and fair corn prices.

*Loud applause from a great crowd backstage.*

JUDGE *to Iberin*: Excellency, how do you wish me to proceed in this case?

IBERIN: You must do what you think right.

*Projection: 'Reports from all regions of the South: unlawful land appropriation by the peasants.'*

JUDGE: According to the provisions of the law, only the girl has committed an offence. It is illegal for her to address any gentleman outside the establishment in which she works.

IBERIN: Is that all you have to say for yourself? It's not a lot.

VOICE FROM ABOVE: Bravo! You hear how the Governor puts the judge in his place? That's not a lot, says he.

THE MAN *addressing the street behind*: The Governor has intervened. He's already reprimanded the judge, and told him he doesn't know enough about the law. There's more to come.

IBERIN: Cross-question the girl's father more carefully! That way you'll get to the heart of the matter.

JUDGE: So you maintain that your landlord exceeded his legal rights when he set your rents?

CALLAS: There's no way we could pay the rent, not in a hundred years. We had to live on crab-apples and roots, we had to send all the corn to the city. Our children run around naked most of the year. We can't afford repairs, so the house is falling in over our heads. The taxes are much too high too. So I have another request, that people who can't pay their taxes shouldn't have to.
*General applause.*

THE MAN *addressing the street behind*: The farmer demands the abolition of taxes for all those who can't pay them! But there's more.
*Tremendous applause backstage.*

JUDGE: How high are the dues? How high are the taxes?

IBERIN *gets up so energetically that he knocks the chair over*: Can't you think of anything more important to ask? Have you no inner voice to tell you what the people really need?

CALLAS: Horses! Give us horses!

IBERIN *sternly*: Silence! What are horses? There's more at stake here! *To the judge*: You can go. Leave the office which you are unfit to fill. I shall conduct this case.
*The judge gathers up his papers and leaves the bench and the courtroom in dismay.*

THE MAN *addressing the street behind*: The Governor has dismissed the Chief Justice and has taken over the case himself. The judge is leaving the hall. Hail Iberin!

CALLAS: Did you hear that: What are horses? There's more at stake!

THE MAN *at the back*: Now we've driven out the greatest racketeer of all, the Viceroy, why shouldn't we redistribute the land?
*Applause. Projection: 'New reports from the Northern regions: minor incidents with rebel peasants.'*

IBERIN: As the court seems incapable of getting to the heart of this affair, I shall conduct the case myself. In the name of the Zakkish people.
So let this case now serve as an example
Of honest Zakkish justice. An evil spirit
Is at work here. And, as we rely
Upon our troops to curb the rebellious peasants,

So must this court take the unbridled landlords
Firmly in the grip of Zakkish justice.
It's not a question here of rich or poor:
But equal sentences on all who step outside the law.
Into the dock: the landlord de Guzman and – *pointing at Madame Cornamontis* – this person here, and on the plaintiffs' bench: this young woman and her father.

THE MAN *addressing the street behind*: The Governor's giving us an example of Zakkish justice. He's brought discipline to the proceedings. And he's set the accused and plaintiffs in their proper places.

IBERIN *to Callas*: Step forward! Look at your daughter!

CALLAS: Oh, you're here too, Nanna?

IBERIN: You recognise her?

CALLAS: Of course.

IBERIN: I ask you, because surely she must have changed?

CALLAS: Not specially.

IBERIN: Are those the clothes you bought her?

CALLAS: No, of course not.

IBERIN: Indeed, those are not the clothes a simple farmer, who works the land with his calloused hands, would buy his daughter.

CALLAS: I couldn't possibly, given the dues I have to pay.

IBERIN: And you wouldn't, even if you could? Such tawdry rags offend your simple, upright taste. How is it your daughter is able to buy clothes like these?

CALLAS: She earns pretty good money.

IBERIN *sharply*: A terrible response! I'll ask again: Do you recognise in this modishly dressed young thing the carefree child who once skipped across the fields by your side? *Callas gawps, uncomprehending.* Could you ever imagine that your daughter would have an unlawful relationship with your landlord at the tender age of sixteen?

CALLAS: Certainly, but the advantages for us weren't that significant. A couple of times we were allowed to use the horses to cart wood. But – *he addresses the assembled crowd* – if you have to pay rents which are ten times too high, then it doesn't help that much if you're just let off a little bit every now and again. Even then we couldn't rely on it! What I need are horses of my own.

IBERIN: So the landlord abused his economic power, and plunged your daughter into misfortune?

CALLAS: Misfortune? It was the girl who had all the benefits! At least she got to wear decent clothes! She never had to work. But we did! You just try ploughing without horses!

IBERIN: Are you aware, things got so bad your daughter moved into Madame Cornamontis's house?

CALLAS: Yes of course. Good day to you, Madame Cornamontis.

IBERIN: Are you aware what manner of establishment that is?

CALLAS: Yes of course. And I'd like to add, by the way, we had to pay for using the estate's horses. Through the nose. And we weren't permitted to use any other horses anyway.

IBERIN *to Nanna*: How did you come to be at this establishment?

NANNA: I didn't fancy working on the fields any more. By the time they're twenty-five farm-girls all look like they're forty.

IBERIN: The life of ease with which your seducer tempted you alienated you from the simple life of your parental home. And was the lord of the estate your first lover?

NANNA: Yes.

IBERIN: Describe the life in the coffeehouse into which you came.

NANNA: I've no complaints. The laundry bills are a bit high, and we don't get to keep the tips, but otherwise ... We all have big debts with Madame, so I have to work late into the night.

IBERIN: But you say you have no complaints about the work. We all have to work. But aren't there other things you have to complain about?

NANNA: Well ... there are other bars where the staff are permitted to serve their favourite customers.

IBERIN: Ahah! So in this establishment you were forced to endure the embraces of any paying customer?

NANNA: That's right.

IBERIN: That's enough. *To Callas*: What are the charges you
wish to press against the defendant?

CALLAS: Rack-renting.

IBERIN: You have reason enough to press for more.

CALLAS: That's enough to be getting on with.

IBERIN: You have suffered a more terrible wrong than just
high rents. Don't you see that?

CALLAS: Oh yes.

IBERIN: So what injustice have you suffered? *Callas is silent.
Iberin to de Guzman*: Do you confess that you abused your
position of economic power when you seduced the daughter of your own tenant?

DE GUZMAN: I had the impression that she was not unflat-
tered by my attentions.

IBERIN *to Nanna*: What do you say to that? *Nanna is silent.
Iberin to the inspector*: Take the accused away! *De Guzman is
led away. Iberin to Nanna*: Now, what do you wish to say
about how you felt about de Guzman's 'attentions'.

NANNA *reluctantly*: I don't remember.

IBERIN: An appalling response!

ATTORNEY *to Nanna*:

Was it love perhaps?

Sir, mysterious are the ways of men.

We can't account for all we do ourselves,

How should we speak for others? The sharpest eye

Can't penetrate the mists of human nature.

Before you here there stands a man accused

That he seduced a girl – and that he paid:

Gave filthy money for her priceless treasure.

If this be so, then blame must lie with both in equal
measure,

For if he bought, then she most surely sold.

So let me ask you this: is that dark, sweet, eternal

Play 'twixt man and woman to be understood

As trade merely, commerce? May it not be love as well,

Or love alone? I would submit that in this case,

My lord, 'tis love that here stands trial.

*Sits down.* There.

IBERIN *to the inspector*: Go and fetch him back in again!

*De Guzman is led back in.*
If it was love, well then, this man inspired it!
*General laughter.*

ATTORNEY:
Sir, what is love? Why do we humans love?
One man may make a chance encounter
And fall in love. Another wants to love
And searches till he finds a willing soul.
One loves thus the beloved, the other
Loves but love. The first we might call fate,
The other lust. Perhaps this case before us now
Is nothing more than base and carnal lust?

CORNAMONTIS *stands up*: I should like to make a statement.
*Iberin nods.* You ought to know, Nanna Callas is one of my
most respectable girls. She saves up and sends money home.

IBERIN *to the attorney*: You can go. A just cause is its own
defence.
*The attorney gathers up his papers and leaves the court-
room.*

IBERIN *to de Guzman*: Accused, why don't you admit that
you abused your economic power?
*De Guzman is silent. Iberin suddenly*: What are you?

DE GUZMAN: A landowner.

IBERIN: What are you?

DE GUZMAN: A member of the landed nobility.

IBERIN: I asked, what are you?

DE GUZMAN: A Catholic.

IBERIN *slowly*: What are you? *De Guzman is silent.* You're a
Zik, and you abused your economic position to seduce a
Zakkish girl. *To Madame Cornamontis*: And you, a Zak,
had the effrontery to sell this Zakkish girl to Ziks. That is
the crux of the matter. *To de Guzman*:
Look at the wretch there with his pointed head!
Discovered in the vile abuse of power!
For power itself is no disgrace, except
When it's abused. Oh you who seek to trade
In things which truly are beyond all price,
Who value only what you buy and sell,
And recognise material worth alone:

Should an oak-tree sell its growth or realise
Its leaves as assets? See how you've become
Alien to yourselves, and alien among us!
But now the scales have tipped: enough's enough!
*To the others*: Learn from this, and see how hard it is
To disentangle justice from the mess,
To recognise beneath all this confusion
A simple truth.

HATSO: Hail Iberin!

IBERIN: Now hear my verdict. The girl is acquitted of all
blame. Madame Cornamontis's coffeehouse, where a poor
Zakkish girl was procured for Ziks, I hereby declare
closed . . .

CORNAMONTIS *hushed*: That can't be right.

IBERIN: . . . to all Ziks. As for the Zikkish seducer, let him be
sentenced to death.

CALLAS: And the rents cancelled! Oh, Lopez, now what have
you to say against this great man!

IBERIN:

How can you talk of rent? That is the least
Of all your injuries, a paltry thing,
Raise up your head, man, aspire to more!
A Zakkish father! And his Zakkish daughter!
Oppressed by Ziks! Exploited! And now free!

CALLAS: Free! Do you hear that, Lopez?

IBERIN:

To you I give your daughter back, that once
Walked carefree by your side through Zakkish fields.
But hear me out: this here was Zakkish justice.
Just as we distinguish right from wrong,
So we divide our people in two parts,
The one we'll root out, that the other live
In peace and prosper. Our purpose is to raise
The healthy part, just like this farmer whom,
With his sweet girl, I've lifted from the mire.
And so I'll separate the Zik from Zak,
Abuse from proud tradition! White from black!

THE CROWD: Hail Iberin!

*They clap hysterically. And while Nanna is carried out shoulder high, the man reports to the street behind.*

THE MAN: The Governor has condemned the Zik de Guzman to death for corrupting a Zakkish girl. The girl's exonerated, she's being carried out of the courtroom on the shoulders of the crowd. Hail Iberin!

*The crowd takes up the cry. Iberin exits quickly.*

ABBOT OF SAN STEFANO *to the people around him*: This is a monstrous judgement: the de Guzman family is one of the most respected in all Yahoo. Yet they dare to sacrifice them to the mob! Just as the accused's sister was about to enter the convent.

*De Guzman is led away. He passes the group of rich landowners, who avert their eyes.*

DE GUZMAN:
Oh, Don Duarte, help me! You, my lords,
You must stand by me in my hour of need!
Remember how we dined as friends together.
Alfonso, speak for me, speak up! You're favoured
With a round head! That's what matters here.
Tell them: what I have done you've done as well!
Don't look away! I beg you! It's not right
To treat me thus! Look at my noble robes!
Abandon me ... it may be your turn soon!
Round heads may not protect you that much longer!

*The landowners continue to act as if they didn't know him. He is led off.*

IBERIN SOLDIERS *hitting him*: Dirty old racketeer! Seducing Zakkish girls! Hit him on his pointy head! And let's take a good look at his friends!

*The landowners make hurriedly to leave.*

CALLAS *pointing at de Guzman*: To think, that was once my landlord! Madame Cornamontis, my daughter's quitting! She'll have nothing more to do with an establishment like yours.

PALMOSA: Well I've never seen anything like it! This is the new age. They're actually hanging a landlord! The farmers are on their way up, Madame Cornamontis!

CORNAMONTIS: Mr Palmosa, I do love the sound of your voice: you still have all the innocence of a child.

CALLAMASSI: So, Madame Cornamontis, you don't believe that, once in a while, a poor man can triumph over a rich man?

CORNAMONTIS: I'll tell you what I think about that sort of thing. *Madame Cornamontis sings the 'Ballad of the Button'.*

BALLAD OF THE BUTTON

I

If a bent old man comes by
Dares to ask, although he's shy
If my prettiest girl could love him well
I reply, how can we ever tell?
Then I tear a button from his coat, and cry
Let's ask fortune, fortune cannot lie!
We'll soon know:
If this button comes up heads you
May be sure she never weds you
All you'll get is grief and woe.
So let's see if luck is on your side!
Then I toss it up, and say: 'fraid not dear.
If they get upset and say: these holes
Go right through! Say I: they're all you've got dear.
 And I tell 'em: luck deserted you at birth
 Yet there is a way, if you'll just try it:
 Loving ain't for free down here on earth
 If you must have love, you'll have to buy it.

2

If a foolish man comes by
Asks me, gazing at the sky
Will his brother ever pay his debt
I reply: I wouldn't care to bet.
Then I tear a button from his coat, and cry
Let's ask fortune, fortune cannot lie!
We'll soon know:
If this button comes up heads you
May be certain he forgets you
And he'll never pay what's owed.

So let's see if luck is on your side!
Then I toss it up, and say: 'fraid not dear.
If they get upset and say: these holes
Go right through! Say I: they're all you've got dear.
  And I tell 'em: luck deserted you at birth
  Still there is some hope of peace and quiet:
  If your only want is peace on earth
  Tell your brother you're prepared to buy it.

*She takes Farmer Callas by the arm and leads him towards
the front of the stage. Then she uses him as an illustration
for the third verse.*

3
If a poor man then comes by
Tells me, anger in his eye:
There's this rich man driving me to ruin
What's my chances if I try to sue him?
First I tear a button from his coat, then cry
Let's ask fortune, fortune cannot lie!
We'll soon know:
If this button comes up tails you
May be certain justice fails you
Better take your leave and go!
Well, let's see if luck is on your side!
Then I toss it up, and say: 'fraid not dear.
If you get upset and say:
SOME BYSTANDERS *bend down to pick up the button. They
look up and say:*
                    But these holes
Go right through!
CORNAMONTIS:
                    Say I: they're all you've got dear.
  And I tell 'im: luck deserted you at birth
  That's the truth, whichever way you try it.
  Friend, whatever you desire on earth
  Right or wrong, you're going to have to buy it!

CALLAS: You've got wax in your ears, good woman. The
  Governor told us loud and clear, the rent is just a paltry
  matter! All I need now are horses, and I'll be fine!

*Madame Cornamontis bursts out laughing and points at
Farmer Callas who is behaving exactly as if he had just been
struck blind. Projection: 'The conflict in the South continues
unabated.'*


5

THE CONVENT OF SAN BARABAS

*Sitting opposite each other in negotiations are: two nuns of the
Needy Sisters of San Barabas and Isabella de Guzman with
her Zakkish attorney.*

ATTORNEY: Before we begin negotiations about Señorita de
Guzman's entry into the convent the young lady would like
to ask a few questions.
ISABELLA *reading the questions from a sheet*: Is the convent a
strict one?
MOTHER SUPERIOR: The most strict there is, my child. *To the
attorney*: But also the most expensive.
ATTORNEY: We're well aware of that.
MOTHER SUPERIOR: And therefore the finest.
ISABELLA: Are there many fast days? And how many?
MOTHER SUPERIOR: Twice a week, for a whole week before
each of the four major feast days, and on the ember days.
ISABELLA: Are men really not permitted? And can one ever
receive dispensation to go outside the convent?
MOTHER SUPERIOR: Under no circumstances.
ISABELLA: Are the meals simple, the beds hard and the
spiritual exercises plentiful?
MOTHER SUPERIOR: The meals are simple, the beds are hard
and the spiritual exercises are plentiful, my child.
ISABELLA:
Oft as I have beheld the fleshly
Desires and shameless flirtation of maidens
My heart was sickened. Even my brother's gaze
Was clouded by base temptation. Behind closed doors
I'd hear the playful cries. How I hate that laughter.

Grant that my own bed be pure, and my shoulders
  untouched by caresses.
O chastity, O priceless treasure, exalted poverty!
May my cell be barren, my repast lowly
And silent the walls which enclose me.
Young though I be in years, yet have I seen
Pride enough and poverty borne without grace.
Wherefore I wish ever to remain chaste, humble and poor.

MOTHER SUPERIOR:

So we live here, my child, and so too will you
And as we are, so will you become.
*To the attorney*: But first, sir, we must agree the terms.
What does the young lady bring with her?

ATTORNEY: Well, you can't expect to strip us bare . . . Here's
  the list.

MOTHER SUPERIOR *reads*: Three dozen chemises. That won't
  do. Say five dozen.

ATTORNEY: Hang on, hang on. Four will be quite enough.

MOTHER SUPERIOR: And where's the linen?

ATTORNEY: What does she need linen for?

MOTHER SUPERIOR: What does she need linen for! God
  willing, the girl will live to be eighty in here. Fifty metres of
  linen. Hand woven. I trust the service is silver.

ATTORNEY: It's not going to be plate, is it!

MOTHER SUPERIOR: My dear Attorney, it's always better to
  ask first. And we don't like birchwood cupboards, we'd
  prefer cherry.

ATTORNEY: We needn't fall out over that. But now, Abbess,
  we come to the most important thing.

MOTHER SUPERIOR: Indeed we do.

ATTORNEY: Aha, so you agree there might be a problem!

MOTHER SUPERIOR: Unfortunately, yes.

ATTORNEY: Well, I'm afraid we can't deny the young lady's
  birth.

MOTHER SUPERIOR *relieved*: Oh, so that's what you meant?
  I meant something quite different. *She gets up, goes over to
  Isabella and runs her hand under her coiffure. She laughs.*
  You've got a point there, no denying it! But that doesn't
  matter. Outward appearance isn't a problem here. As long

as everything else is in order. So now, the most important thing: the monthly contribution ...

ATTORNEY: Well you know how much rent the de Guzman estates are worth.

MOTHER SUPERIOR: Indeed, the income doesn't amount to much. We'd need a fair proportion of that for our beloved convent. We were thinking at least a quarter.

ATTORNEY: Out of the question. The young lady's brother, Señor de Guzman, has to maintain the family's position, and he lives exclusively from the rents.

MOTHER SUPERIOR: As far as I am aware, Señor de Guzman is not really in a position to maintain very much at all at the moment.

ATTORNEY: The young lady will live very simply here, as we've just heard.

MOTHER SUPERIOR: Simply doesn't come cheaply.

ATTORNEY: Besides, there's now the possibility, with this new regime, that the rents will not only be guaranteed, but actually increased.

MOTHER SUPERIOR: Ah yes, but we can't rely on that. We need to be sure of at least eight thousand a month.

ATTORNEY: I don't know if we can squeeze that out of the tenants, they're under considerable pressure as it is. You may have to think twice about all this, Señorita de Guzman.

MOTHER SUPERIOR: Yes, think it over, dear child. That's how much it costs.

ISABELLA *to the attorney*: Is it really too expensive?
*The attorney takes the girl aside. As he does so, he asks the sisters again.*

ATTORNEY: Six thousand? *The sisters shake their heads and gaze into the middle distance. The attorney addresses Isabella*:
The life on which your heart is set
Will leave your family deep in debt.

ISABELLA *crying, because the beautiful life is so hard to attain*:
But I will have it. There's nothing wrong in it.

ATTORNEY *to the Superior*: You might bear in mind, the harvest was abundant this year, so the corn is worth next to nothing, even the landlords are having to cut back.

MOTHER SUPERIOR: We have farmland too. We suffer too.
And perhaps you might bear in mind that there's a very
good reason why the young lady wants to come here, the
family can expect all kinds of benefits. We've already
mentioned the little ethnic matter.

ATTORNEY: All right, all right. Just a few more questions. *He
reads from a sheet*: Could the estates pass nominally to the
convent? And would the Needy Sisters be prepared, as
necessary, to go to court to protect them? Would they sign
an undertaking to that effect here and now?

MOTHER SUPERIOR *who has nodded to each question*: That's
all fine. Your young lady is not the only case we've had like
this.

ATTORNEY: We're agreed then. Now we've only got to see to
it that we can get the money. And that's not easy in the
middle of a civil war. Here are the deeds to the de Guzman
estates.

*He passes them over. She locks them in the safe.*

MOTHER SUPERIOR: So, my dear young lady, we are
delighted to welcome you within our quiet walls. You will
live peacefully here. The storms of life outside cannot
disturb us here. *A stone smashes through the window.*
What's that? *She runs to open the other window.* What are
those people with armbands doing in our courtyard?
*She rings, a nun enters.*

NUN: Reverend Mother, in the courtyard ...

MOTHER SUPERIOR: Not now, dear. Have Señorita de
Guzman's coachman drive up.

NUN: Reverend Mother, there's been a terrible scene in the
courtyard. A man came to the convent with a whole mob of
people. There was a young painted woman with them too.
When he saw the horses he claimed they were his, he said
he was the farmer and he needed them for his plough. He
hit the coachman over the head, untied the horses and drove
them away. And then he said: Señor de Guzman could go
to the gallows on foot.

MOTHER SUPERIOR: This is terrible.

ATTORNEY: Mother Superior, under the circumstances perhaps I might ask you to take the young lady into your care

straight away. The streets are evidently no longer entirely safe.

*The Mother Superior exchanges glances with the other sisters.*

MOTHER SUPERIOR: I rather think the de Guzman estates are in greater danger than the family itself.

ATTORNEY: Are you denying asylum to the young lady?

MOTHER SUPERIOR: Sir, I am responsible for these quiet walls. I hope you understand the situation, don't make me say what I should prefer to leave unsaid.

ISABELLA: We had better leave.

ATTORNEY: And what is to become of our agreement about the de Guzman estates?

MOTHER SUPERIOR: We shall keep our word, as far as it lies within our power.

*The parties bow to each other. The attorney and Isabella exit.*

# 6

What you have you hold.

THE COFFEEHOUSE OF MADAME CORNAMONTIS

*Afternoon. The three wealthy landowners, Saz, de Hoz and Peruiner, are seated at a small table surrounded by large suitcases. In the background behind a newspaper, Landlord Callamassi. Behind the bar, Madame Cornamontis knitting and smoking a cigar.*

SAZ:
A good idea, let's just wait here until
Our train goes.

PERUINER:
If one ever goes at all.

DE HOZ:
At least we're unobtrusive here. And these days
That's what matters. How are the mighty fallen!

SAZ:
What news from the front? That's what really matters.

PERUINER:

The news is bad. Is this a time to travel?

DE HOZ:

The Viceroy's to blame for all this mess.

And Don Duarte, who sent for Iberin.

This talk of round and pointed heads will lure

The peasants from the Sickle, but at a price:

The cloggies threaten us in our backyard.

*Noises off.*

PERUINER:

What's all that noise?

SAZ *sarcastically*:

Behold, the people's hero!

Since yesterday the whole of Luma's full

Of Farmer Callas and his horses.

PERUINER:

Frightful.

SAZ:

It could be catching too.

PERUINER:

It could be, very!

*Farmer Callas and his daughter come down the street. He is leading two horses on a rope. With him are Farmer Parr, the three Hatsos and people from the street. He leads the horses into the coffeehouse and ties them up at the bar. The people shout, 'Hooray for Iberin!' and 'Hooray for Callas!'.*

HATSO: March on, Callas! Get in there, you old sinner!

ANOTHER HATSO: Ladies, gentlemen, you see before you 'Callas of the horses', a triumph of Zakkish justice.

MADAME CORNAMONTIS: Good day to you, Nanna. Let me welcome you as a customer in the coffeehouse where you used to work as a waitress.

CALLAS *introducing Parr*: This is my friend Parr, like me a farmer. – And yes, the horses! There I was, see, just two days ago, walking down the street with my daughter. The case was won, the landlord will hang. But, you see, I'd had no personal advantage from the affair. I was just as needy, so to speak, as ever, except for the honour, that is. They gave me my daughter back, that's all, and that's another mouth to feed. Then I see these horses, standing outside the gate of the good-for-nothing Sisters of San Barabas. Ahah, say I to my daughter, our horses! Didn't he promise you the horses, say I, when he seduced you? In actual fact he did, says my daughter. She was just a bit frightened no one would believe us. And why shouldn't they, say I, and untie the horses. I've had enough injustice.

PARR *admiring*: He didn't wait to see if the Governor would give him the horses or not.

CALLAS: No, I thought: what you have, you hold.
*He sings the 'What-You-Have-You-Hold Song'.*

THE WHAT-YOU-HAVE-YOU-HOLD SONG

1
There was a man of old
His life was hard and cold.
They said: Just keep on waiting!
He did as he was told.
It was debilitating.
  Hail Iberin! You say
  But
  What you have you hold!

2
The man had had enough
He started acting tough.
Before long they were quaking:
They promised loads of stuff
Like measures they'd be taking.
  Hail Iberin! You say
  But
  What you have you hold!

3
There was a man of old
He reckoned he'd been sold.
He grabbed what took his fancy.
He's getting bloody bold
He's got the upper hand, see.
  Hail Iberin! You say

But
What you have you hold!

SAZ: That's open rebellion!

HATSO: From a Zakkish standpoint it's one of the great heroic deeds. To be emulated.

*Madame Cornamontis is concerned to avoid a scene. She brings Nanna a cup of coffee.*

CORNAMONTIS: Perhaps you'd like a cup of coffee, Nanna?

NANNA: No thanks.

CORNAMONTIS: Go on, drink it.

NANNA: I didn't order it.

CORNAMONTIS: No no, it's on the house. *As she passes Saz, in a whisper*: Be careful!

SAZ *shrugs her off, to the Hatsos*: Do you really think that's in the spirit of Iberin?

HATSO: Yes indeed sir, it's exactly in the spirit of Iberin. I suppose you think someone who wears clogs isn't as good as you? Permit us to clarify matters by singing you our new Iberin song.

*The Hatsos sing 'The New Iberin Song'.*

THE NEW IBERIN SONG

I
The master muses day and night
Of things to tickle his whim
And when he's dreamt up a new delight
His peasants bring it him.
They fetch to his table
As much as they're able
Wine by the litre
And wurst by the metre.
Even in bed
He still gets fed
On fresh cream buns
While the bathwater runs.
If he'd like a puff
There's Virginia's best.
There's more than enough
At his behest.

And the rich man said: it's just our way
And that, God willing, is how it'll stay.

Finding themselves in this situation, dear friends, the
peasants went to their lord and master, Iberin, and Iberin
went to the landowner and took him down a peg or two.
And the landlord was suddenly so small that from that day
on he treated his tenants like brothers.

2

He fetches to their table
As much as he's able
Wine by the litre
And wurst by the metre.
Even in bed
They still get fed
On fresh cream buns
While the bathwater runs.
If they want a puff
There's Virginia's best.
There's more than enough
At their behest.
And the poor folk said: it's just our song
But that's how it should have been all along.
The peasants muse now day and night
Of things to tickle their whim
And when they've dreamt up a new delight
Their landlords bring it them.

*The Hatsos have been demonstrating the song with Farmer
Parr. In the first verse they made him bow down to the
landlords, but in the second they lift him up onto the table
and deck him out with Señor Saz's hat and the cigars and
glasses of de Hoz and Peruiner. Farmer Parr accompanies
the whole thing with a little clog dance.*

HATSO: Gentlemen, the redistribution of horses and farm
machinery to the tenant farmers will soon be implemented.
And the farmland too. What Callas has done with the
horses has just anticipated what's going to happen soon
anyway.

PARR *to Callas*: It's just the same as what the Sickle wants.

CALLAS: It's more. With the Sickle it's the village that gets the horses! But you listen: that's good, anticipate! You've heard what I did, my friend. And, all due respect to Señor Iberin – and I've got boundless respect for him you know – but if you can happen somehow in the next few days to get a hold of some horses, by chance you know, like me, it wouldn't be a bad thing. That way you can be certain.

PARR: I understand. Hail Iberin! But what you have, you hold! Callas, you've opened my eyes. Now I know what I've got to do. *He hurries off.*

HATSO: Anyway, I'd like to ask you all to lift your glasses and drink to the health of Mr Callas and his horses.

*The Hatsos stand up. The wealthy landowners, except for Señor Peruiner, stay seated.*

DE HOZ: *under his breath*: I'm not drinking to the health of a horse thief!

SAZ: Then we'd better leave right away.

*They pay, get up and leave.*

HATSO: I don't believe it! They didn't drink to your health Callas, I don't like that one bit. From the look of their clothes I'll bet they're Ziks.

CALLAS: I know them from somewhere. That's it, they're the ones who testified at the trial that my daughter had accosted a Zik. Those are de Guzman's friends, and his sort too!

HATSOS: Don't trouble yourself, Callas! We'll have a little talk about your affairs with these gentlemen.

*The Hatsos go after the landowners.*

CORNAMONTIS *running after the Hatsos*: For God's sake, don't go molesting the country's wealthiest landed gentlemen!

CALLAS *to Nanna*: You haven't got a bit of cash on you, have you? I'm ravenous.

NANNA: There's nothing I can do. For three days now Luma has been treating me like a bloody princess, the famous Zakkish maiden. People drink to my health and say how I've gone up in the world. For three days nobody's come near me. I can't earn a thing. Instead of lust, men look at me with respect. It's a disaster.

CALLAS: At least you don't have to go to the whorehouse

now. And I've got my draught horses. Without lifting a finger!

NANNA: If you ask me, you haven't got them yet.

*The two attorneys of the de Guzman family enter and approach Callas with open arms.*

ATTORNEYS: Ah here you are, my dear Mr Callas! We have a wonderful proposition for you. Everything is falling into place. *They sit down next to him.*

CALLAS: Uhuh.

ATTORNEYS: We are authorised to tell you that a certain family would be prepared, under certain circumstances, to come to an agreement about the two horses.

NANNA: What's the deal?

CALLAS: You're talking about a certain Zikkish family?

ATTORNEYS: You must be aware that the case we're talking about is to be reopened.

CALLAS: No, I didn't know that.

ATTORNEYS: Well ... you can imagine that, in certain quarters, everything possible will be set in motion to see that the judgement is overturned.

CALLAS: You mean, in Zikkish quarters.

ATTORNEYS *laughing*: In Zikkish quarters. We've come into possession of a sworn testimony, according to which your daughter – and we mean her no offence by this – had already had a relationship with a young man before she became acquainted with this particular – Zikkish – gentleman, so that the charge of corrupting a minor ceases to apply.

NANNA: That's not true.

ATTORNEYS: If you were to admit it, we could start talking about making a gift.

CALLAS: I've only one answer to that ...

NANNA: Hold on! *To the attorneys*: Let me talk to my father alone for a minute.

ATTORNEYS: To cut a long story short: you can get yourself two horses for free, if you're prepared to be sensible.

*The attorneys stroll over to the bar.*

CALLAS: We've got Iberin on our side, that's why they're

being so nice. We don't have to throw away the family's good name for a crust of bread. What do you think?

NANNA: I think we should take the horses. It's not a question of what Iberin wants. It all depends on the news from the front.

CALLAS: And what is the news from the front?

NANNA *leafing urgently through the newspaper*: This is all lies, but it's clear the Sickle forces keep advancing. Even here it says they've reached the gates of Mirasonnore. That's where the power station for the capital is. If they take that, they can turn off the lights.

CALLAS: Ah daughter dear, I drain my glass to the health of our good friend Lopez. He must be fighting like a lion. And the landowners are giving away horses. He should be here really: only what you have, you hold.

NANNA: The fortunes of war can change any minute. There are too few of them fighting for the Sickle, and too many like you, who've run away.

CALLAS: That's not how I see it. *He beckons the attorneys.* Gentlemen, here's my answer to the de Guzman family: No way! I don't need to make any accommodations. Read the newspapers. I don't have to lick your boots any longer!

ATTORNEYS: And the two horses?

CALLAS: I've got my horses. They're outside. And I wouldn't dream of throwing away the honour of my daughter.

ATTORNEYS: As you wish! *They exit.*

CALLAMASSI *who is sitting at the next table*: Trouble, Mr Callas?

CALLAS: Not a bit of it. These Ziks are a load of thickheads. Now they're trying to bribe me. But I've got the measure of them. They wanted to make me a gift of the horses. That's what it's come to. But they wanted me to dishonour myself too. Typical Ziks. They think you can deal with everything in base material terms. Oh yes, the Governor knew what he was talking about all right! Gentlemen, the days when I had to sell my honour are long gone. I can't think of these things in such base terms now. They'd better mark my words! See how stupid the Ziks are: now I've got my horses just for letting a Zik get his grubby hands on my daughter.

Not many people could pull off a trick like that. My daughter's no better looking than any girl her age, but just take a look at the horses! I've got them outside. And – between you and me – there was never really any talk of giving me the horses in exchange for the girl.

NANNA *sees that he's drunk*: We should be getting on our way now, Father.

CALLAS: It's a joke! Señor de Guzman just turned a blind eye when I used them. Who'd trade two horses like that for a girl? You should take a look at the horses, really!

CALLAMASSI: Mr Callas, it will be an honour to take a look at your horses.

*Nanna drags her father out by the coat-tails. Callamassi follows them. There is a radio announcement: 'The power station at Mirasonnore is under threat from the Sickle. Will the capital be without power tonight?' The wealthy land-owners Saz, de Hoz and Peruiner burst in through the back door. They are hurt. Madame Cornamontis enters after them.*

CORNAMONTIS: Oh dear, gentlemen, you would have done better to stand up and drink to the health of Mr Callas. After all, he's a folk hero now.

SAZ: Pull down the blinds, quickly! The Hatsos are after us!

PERUINER: Water and bandages!

*Madame Cornamontis brings them water and bandages and they start to bandage themselves.*

SAZ: Once the Sickle is crushed all these louts will hang.

PERUINER *to Madame Cornamontis*: My arm is quite limp. But you'd better bandage my head!

CORNAMONTIS: I don't see any hurt there, Señor.

PERUINER: But the point, my dear, the point!

*There is a knock. A man enters.*

THE MAN: You called for a doctor. I'm a doctor.

PERUINER *yells*: Off with your hat!

*The man takes off his hat. He has a pointed head.*

PERUINER: What are you? You're a Zik!

THE MAN *shouts*: I'm a doctor!

SAZ:
And if they find you here, it's us they'll kill.

*The man exits.*

DE HOZ *to Peruiner*:
    It's all because of you, 'cause you're a Zik.
    They'd never have pursued us else.

PERUINER:
                                    I wonder.
    I think it's what we're wearing. We look rich.
    We're at the mercy of the mob, I fear!
    And all because of the de Guzman judgement!
    It was folly that we landlords let
    One of our own fall to the angry mob.
    We thought we sacrificed a Zik, but they
    Sated their bloodlust on a landlord!

DE HOZ:
                                    What can we do?
    We'll never make it to the station now.
    *There is a knock. Madame Cornamontis opens the door
    cautiously. Enter Missena.*

MISSENA *eagerly*:
    Delighted to see you here!

SAZ:
                            Your humble servants.
    No really. Humbled, hounded, beaten up
    In broad daylight, by thugs employed by you!

DE HOZ:
    What news from the front?

MISSENA:
                            Not good.

SAZ:
                                    Just spit it out!

MISSENA:
    We're losing! Our troops are scattered and dispersed
    In headlong flight.

PERUINER:
                    And where's the fighting now?

MISSENA:
    They're fighting over Mirasonnore
    And for the power station.

SAZ:

By God! That's close!

MISSENA:

So now you see you have to act! We must
Have money! Money's what we need now! Money!

PERUINER:

Money! Money! Money! Money! Money!
All well and good. But what can it achieve?

SAZ:

It was Iberin's militia beat us up!

MISSENA:

There's little can be done, my friends, to help
If he can't give his men a decent meal.
Iberin's plan is this: to hire half
The country's poor, and pay them well, that they
Subdue the other half – with force of arms.
So please, let's all, both Zak and Zik, put up
As big a loan as you can muster. Or else
We're done for!
*The lights flicker and go out.*

SAZ:

Hey, what's happened to the lights?

MISSENA *solemnly*:

Mirasonnore has fallen, friends!

CORNAMONTIS *brings a candle*: For God's sake, what on
earth will become of us now, gentlemen? If it goes on like
this the Sickle will be in Luma tomorrow.

DE HOZ:

So what's the answer?

MISSENA:

Money.

SAZ:

Money, huh!
There's only finance where there's confidence.
It's not that I'm complaining of our beating.
So long as property's protected, let
Them thump me on the head from time to time.
The question is: what happens to our rents?

MISSENA:
  Rent is property and so it's sacred.
PERUINER:
  And what about this Callas and his horses?
MISSENA:
  What do you want?
SAZ:
      To see your conquering hero
  Arraigned! At once and publicly! The horses
  Taken from him! At once and publicly!
MISSENA:
  All right: you pay – we'll put him back on trial.
  I know that Iberin gets quite upset
  About the petty greed amongst the peasants.
  But stop complaining. Till the Sickle's smashed
  There's no way we can stop him taking horses,
  And anyone can grab whate'er they please.
  But if you help us smash the Sickle, then
  De Guzman's might will be restored, along with his horses.
  We won't even need to execute poor Callas!
  His horses are at issue, not his life.
  His life depends on them, not they on him!
  Let's go to Iberin! Just one more thing though:
  Tread softly when the subject turns to money!
  Iberin's lofty soul can scarce endure
  To lower itself to base material things.
  The Zakkish spirit on its own should vanquish
  Any foe. Just offer him your finance
  Which, as we know, is sorely needed – gently,
  Unselfishly, enthusiastically ...
  And he'll accept a gift that's freely made!
PERUINER:
  I guess a head like mine ...
  *He taps his pointed head.*
      ... will not be welcome.
MISSENA:
  Oh, in his hour of need he'll learn to like it.
PERUINER:
  He'll take no finance from a Zik.

MISSENA:

He will,
I'll wager that he will. But let's make haste!

### 7

THE VICEROY'S PALACE

*Again there is a trial in progress. But the court is much
changed. A large chandelier, a carpet, new uniforms for the
officials, all indicate a new wealth. The old judge is wearing a
new robe and smoking a fat cigar. The inspector is no longer
barefoot. While the officials, under Missena's supervision, are
constructing the courtroom, the judge sings the 'Song of the
Stimulating Impact of Cash' to a quiet musical accompaniment.*

#### SONG OF THE STIMULATING EFFECT OF CASH

I

People keep on saying cash is sordid
Yet this world's a cold place if you're short.
Not so once you can afford it
And have ample cash support.
No need then to feel you've been defrauded
Everything is bathed in rosy light
Warming all you set your eyes on
Giving each what's his by right.
Sunshine spreads to the horizon.
Just watch the smoke; the fire's alight.
    Then things soon become as different as they can.
    Longer views are taken. Hearts beat harder.
    Proper food to eat. Looking much smarter.
    And your man is quite a different man.

2

O you're all so hopelessly mistaken
If you think cash flow has no effect.
Fertile farms produce no bacon
When the water-pump's been wrecked.
Now men grab as much as they can collect.
Once they'd standards they used not to flout.

If your belly's full you don't start shooting.
Now there's so much violence about.
Father, mother, brothers put the boot in.
Look, no more smoke now: the fire's gone out.
  Everything explodes, incendiaries are hurled
  Smash-and-grab's the rule; it's a disaster.
  Every little servant thinks he's master
  And the world's a very bitter world.

3
That's the fate of all that's noble and splendid
People quickly write it off as trash
Since with empty stomach and unmended
Footwear nobody's equipped to cut a dash.
They don't want what's good, they want the cash
And their instinct's to be mean and tight.
But when Right has got the cash to back it
It's got what it takes to see it right.
Never mind your dirty little racket
Just watch the smoke now: the fire's alight.
  Then you start believing in humanity once more:
  Everyone's a saint, as white as plaster.
  Principles grow stronger. Just like before.
  Wider views are taken. Hearts beat faster.
  You can tell the servant from the master.
  So the law is once again the law.

*The inspector writes up on a blackboard in large letters:
'The Convent of San Barabas versus Farmer Callas. At
issue: 2 horses.' Projection: 'Government troops send reinforcements in counter-attack against the Sickle.' Iberin
comes out of the palace.*

IBERIN:
What news from the front?

MISSENA:
                    A mighty change of fortune.
The advancing Sickle troops were held last night
And in the early dawn our troops, refreshed
With all their reinforcements, countered boldly:
Now Mirasonnore will be decisive.

Around the power station at this moment,
Which fell in Sickle hands three days ago,
The present battle rages. – Will you, Señor,
Conduct this trial?

IBERIN:

Nothing is decided.
When we're victorious, then I'll give my verdict,
And not before.

MISSENA:

Well let the trial begin.

IBERIN:

As you think best.
*He goes back inside the palace.*

MISSENA:

As ever undecided!
But let's begin.
Your Honour, a word in your ear if I may!
*He takes the judge aside and talks quietly to him until the
parties enter. Then he exits.*

INSPECTOR: The Convent of San Barabas versus Farmer
Callas. At issue: two horses.
*Farmer Callas and his daughter, Isabella de Guzman, the
Mother Superior of San Barabas and the attorneys are
admitted to the courtroom.*

CALLAS: I'll show him how his great ideas get put into
practice. He'll soon say whether a Zik has the right to take
away the horses a Zak needs to plough his fields.

NANNA: But that way you could just take any horse that
happened to be standing around.

CALLAS: Any Zikkish horse.

ZAKKISH ATTORNEY *loudly*:
What news from the front?

MOTHER SUPERIOR:

This morning's news is good.

ATTORNEY:
That's excellent. It all depends on that.

ISABELLA:
Oh Reverend Mother, how I wish this row
About mere worldly goods might soon be over!

NANNA: Pointy head, better off dead. *Pause.* Pious cow! Mind you, she's got a backside like a princess. She's well-fed, she could handle the trade. But of course her sort don't need to work. *To Callas*: And you're the one who pays for it.

CALLAS: Me? I don't pay for anything. *To the women*: You'll get nothing more out of me.

MOTHER SUPERIOR: Dear child, it will be a good thing when you can come and live within our quiet walls.

NANNA: Yes, that'll do her good. The silly cow needs a rest from doing nothing.

CALLAS: Zikkish scum!

NANNA: It's the old judge again. That's bad.

CALLAS: The only bad thing is that there's no one here this time. But we'll soon see who gets justice today.

MOTHER SUPERIOR: Yes indeed, my good man, we shall soon see.

NANNA: At least darling brother will swing for it.
*Isabella comes over faint.*

NANNA *shouting*: She'll need the two horses, to shlep all her fancy stuff into the nunnery.

MOTHER SUPERIOR: You be quiet. *She goes over to Callas.* You think you're something special, I suppose, because you have a round head? You think that means you won't have to pay? Well, today you'll learn who it is you'll have to pay.

CALLAS: Not a Zik, whatever happens.
*The Mother Superior takes his hand and lays it on her own head.*

NANNA: What's that supposed to mean?

MOTHER SUPERIOR: You'll see. In any case, our heads are as round as yours.

NANNA *to her father*: It's looking bad for the Sickle. And here things look very different from last week. They've got new money. That's not good.

CALLAS: I put my trust in Iberin.
*Projection: 'Recent death sentence for wealthy landowner impresses the farmers. Many abandon the Sickle and return to their farms.'*

JUDGE: Señor Iberin is very busy, nevertheless he insists on passing judgement himself in this case – which is the talk of the capital, and which raises the fundamental issue of property.

CALLAS: I'd like to make it clear, my case rests on a statement by our Governor himself, that the rent in future is a paltry matter. Then there's his other statement: 'What are horses!' And anyway, I've been dealt an injustice.

JUDGE: All in good time, my friend. First we shall hear the attorney of the de Guzman family.

ZAKKISH ATTORNEY: The man has not the slightest claim to the horses.

NANNA: Whereas the young lady does have a claim: she prays on horseback, I suppose.

JUDGE: Silence! – Now, explain why you took the horses.

CALLAS: When my daughter was abused by the landlord it was agreed that I should get the horses.

ZAKKISH ATTORNEY:
It was a deal then, I suppose?
*Callas is silent.*
                                        A deal:
We said: Give us your daughter, farmer,
And we will give you horses. Laughable!
You'd never sell your daughter's honour, would you
For just two horses. Or perhaps you would?

CALLAS:
It wasn't a deal.

ZAKKISH ATTORNEY:
                        What then?

CALLAS *to Nanna:*
                        Now what's he want?

NANNA: Say you received the horses as a gift.

ZAKKISH ATTORNEY:
Then when?

CALLAS:
                What is this, when?

ZAKKISH ATTORNEY:
                        Before or after?

CALLAS: I don't see why I should answer to Ziks. *He looks around expecting applause, but sees only stony faces.* M'lord, this is a trick, I'm sure. These pointed questions could only come from a pointed head.

JUDGE:
If you received a prior promise, then –
I could insist you answer this – that means
That you're your daughter's pimp. The court presumes
It took place afterwards: your landlord gave
You horses, in exchange you promised silence.
The horses were a sop, because he'd wronged you.

CALLAS: Yes, it was afterwards. Yes, they were a sop. Because the landlord wronged me he gave me the horses as a sop.

*Projection: 'Advances on the Southern front. The Sickle on the defensive.'*

ZIKKISH ATTORNEY *aside to his colleague*:
No talk of Zak and Zik from the bench today!

ZAKKISH ATTORNEY *replies*: I've noticed. *He turns to the court*: Your Honour, ladies and gentlemen, we too are of the opinion that this case is of vital interest to the whole nation. One might think: why should two horses more or less matter to one of the largest landowners on the island? But that is not the issue.
If we give *these* two horses to *that* farmer
Then every farmer will take every horse.

NANNA: And the silly cow won't be able to go to the nunnery to take a rest from doing nothing.

MOTHER SUPERIOR *loudly*:
The peasants in the Southern shires drive
Our horses from our stables, steal our ploughs,
And scream that they've been dealt injustice, then
They squat on our land and dare to argue that
They're outraged land and livestock were not theirs already!

ZAKKISH ATTORNEY: Your Honour, there's a man who's been in prison since yesterday, he's also a farmer. I should like to call him.

*The judge nods.*

INSPECTOR *calls*: Call Farmer Parr!

NANNA: What do they want with Parr?

CALLAS: It doesn't mean a thing, these are just tricks.

*Parr is led in in heavy chains.*

ZAKKISH ATTORNEY: I believe you were with Mr Callas when he arrived with the horses at the coffeehouse of Madame Cornamontis?

PARR: Yes sir.

ZAKKISH ATTORNEY: And you are also a tenant farmer of the de Guzman family?

PARR: Yes sir.

ZIKKISH ATTORNEY: When you left the coffeehouse you walked the five hours back to your homestead, and drove away two horses from the de Guzman family estate?

PARR: Yes sir.

ZIKKISH ATTORNEY: What was your reason?

*Farmer Parr is silent.*

ZAKKISH ATTORNEY: You have no daughter, Mr Parr?

PARR: No sir.

ZAKKISH ATTORNEY: So this was not a gift from the de Guzman family?

*Farmer Parr is silent.*

ZAKKISH ATTORNEY: Why did you expropriate the horses?

PARR: Because I needed them.

*The attorneys smile at one another.*

JUDGE: But God in heaven, man, that's no reason!

PARR: Perhaps not for you, but it is for me! My field is just a bog, and I've got to have horses to plough it, anyone can see that.

ZIKKISH ATTORNEY: Mr Callas, is your field also a bog?

*Farmer Callas is silent.*

PARR: It's just the same.

ZAKKISH ATTORNEY: Mr Callas, did you also need the horses?

CALLAS: Yes sir, I mean no. I mean, I didn't take them because I needed them, but because they were given to me.

ZAKKISH ATTORNEY: So you don't approve of your friend's action?

CALLAS: No, I don't. *To Parr:* How can you just help yourself to horses? You didn't have the slightest claim to them.

PARR: You don't have a claim either.

ZAKKISH ATTORNEY: And why not? Why does Mr Callas have no claim?

PARR: Because the horses weren't a gift to him either.

CALLAS: You don't know that! How can you say that?

PARR: De Guzman would have to have an awful lot of horses if he were to give away two for every girl he's had.

ZAKKISH ATTORNEY: Your Honour! In his simple manner Farmer Parr has expounded the view which the tenant farmers themselves hold in this question, namely whether gifts of such considerable size are customary in a case like that of Nanna Callas. Your Honour, I should like now to call a witness whose testimony will surprise you. This witness will testify as to Mr Callas's own opinion about whether landlords part readily with their horses.

NANNA: Who have they drummed up now? You talked a lot of rubbish in the coffeehouse, you know.

CALLAS: It's all wrong! And it's that idiot Parr to blame. He's ruined it for me.

*Enter Señor Callamassi.*

ZAKKISH ATTORNEY: Please, could you repeat what Callas said to you in the coffeehouse?

NANNA: You'd better object now, straight away.

CALLAS: This witness doesn't count, Your Honour! What I may have said then was private.

ZAKKISH ATTORNEY: And what did Callas say?

CALLAMASSI *in one breath*: Mr Callas said: And – between you and me – there was never really any talk of giving me the horses in exchange for the girl. It's a joke! Señor de Guzman just turned a blind eye when I used them. Who'd trade two horses like that for a girl? You should take a look at the horses, really.

JUDGE *to Callas*: Did you say that?

NANNA: No

CALLAS: Yes, I mean no, I was drunk, Your Honour, everyone was buying me drinks because of winning the case against my landlord, and all the time nobody gave me anything to eat.

JUDGE: That doesn't sound good at all, Mr Callas. Perhaps, in

view of this testimony, you should think about renouncing
your claim to the horses of your own free will?

NANNA: Don't do that, whatever you do!

CALLAS: Never, Your Honour, I'm not in a position to do
that. *Loudly*: I request that the Governor himself pass
judgement, as it's not a matter of any ordinary horses,
they're Zikkish horses. Yes, that's it, it's a matter of Zikkish
horses!

*Projection: 'Latest Reports: Governor receives favourable
despatches from the Front.' Iberin comes out of the Palace.*

JUDGE: Our Governor, good sir, Farmer Callas demands your
judgement in the case of the San Barabas convent horses.

IBERIN *steps forward just a little way*:
What more d'you want, man? Have I not granted
Everything you could desire? Restored
Your honour? Condemned to death the man who dared
Offend you? Disregarding all his wealth
And all your poverty! I raised you up
To such great heights. And how do you respond?
I know your misdemeanours, man: be warned!

CALLAS: I'd like to point out that the horses in question,
which I need for my plough, were in Zikkish hands.

MOTHER SUPERIOR: And I should like to point out that they
are now in Zakkish hands. Good sir:
The horses here at issue are now ours.
And we're of Zakkish stock. But even if
They had been Zikkish horses, property
Is property, and needs must be respected!
You see two horses: check them over, check
Their mouths and count their teeth – there's nothing here
That's Zikkish, sir. For what, sir, is a horse?
A Zikkish or a Zakkish thing? Of course
It's neither! A horse is just a thing, a trifle
That's worth one hundred pesos, give or take.
It might as well be cheese or boots or bread!
In short, those things, those creatures over there
That paw the dust, are just one hundred pesos!
One hundred convent pesos! It so happens
These cash bags wear a horse's hide;

And as a hide befits a horse, 'tis fitting
They should have a rightful owner too:
These, sir, are convent horses.

ZAKKISH ATTORNEY: Because by deed of gift one half of all the livestock, goods and chattels of the de Guzman estate, from which these horses come, has passed to the convent.

CALLAS: When I took the horses they didn't belong to any convent.

ISABELLA *suddenly enraged*: But they didn't belong to you either, you pig! And take your cap off when you talk to us!

NANNA: You keep out of it.

CALLAS: There's not one of the clan even knows how to saddle up a horse.

ISABELLA: Take off your cap! Those are our horses! Off with the cap!

CALLAS: I refer to the Governor's own statement: It's not a question here of rich or poor!

ISABELLA: Well, so do we! Take off your cap!

IBERIN:
Yes, take it off!
*Callas takes off his cap.*
                    It's time to close this case!
I've heard there's talk in Luma that, because
I once condemned a Zikkish landlord, I
Must be the landlords' enemy. Not true.
My judgement wasn't aimed at property
But just at its abuse. And you, farmer,
You've only understood the meanest part
Of what inspires and swells a Zakkish chest!
Would you exchange your honour for a horse?
As if it were a decent trade. For shame!

ZAKKISH ATTORNEY *sharply*: Governor! Your Honour, ladies and gentlemen! My client, the Convent of San Barabas, can offer proof that this Callas is a subversive.

ZIKKISH ATTORNEY: A moment ago Mr Callas vigorously condemned the horse thievery committed by his friend Parr. *To the witness Callamassi*: In the coffeehouse I understand that Mr Callas sang a certain song, which caused some excitement amongst his audience?

CALLAMASSI: Yes sir. It was the outlawed 'What-You-Have-You-Hold Song'.

NANNA *to her father*: Now you're done for.

ZAKKISH ATTORNEY: I move that the defendant Callas repeat his song for the benefit of the court.

IBERIN *to Callas*: Did you sing this song?

CALLAS: No, I mean yes. I was drunk, Your Honour, everyone was buying me drinks and all the time nobody gave me anything to eat.

IBERIN: Repeat the song!

CALLAS: It's not really a song at all, it's just a couple of verses.

IBERIN: Sing them!

CALLAS: Yes sir. *He is silent.*

IBERIN: You're to sing!

CALLAS *sullenly*: I'm hoarse.

ZAKKISH ATTORNEY: We're not expecting an aria.

IBERIN: Sing!

CALLAS: I only heard it once, I'm not sure I can remember it. It went something like this. *He repeats the song, emphasising only the words 'Hail Iberin!'.*

THE WHAT-YOU-HAVE-YOU-HOLD SONG

1

There was a man of old
His life was hard and cold.
They said: Just keep on waiting!
He did as he was told.
It was debilitating.
  Hail Iberin! You say
  But
  What you have you hold!

2

The man had had enough
He started acting tough.
Before long they were quaking:
They promised loads of stuff
Like measures they'd be taking.
  Hail Iberin! You say
  But
  What you have you hold!

3
There was a man of old
He reckoned he'd been sold.
He grabbed what took his fancy.
He's getting bloody bold
He's got the upper hand, see.
   Hail Iberin! You say
   But
   What you have you hold!

MOTHER SUPERIOR *loudly*: That's open rebellion!

JUDGE: One could say this song represents a blatant affront to the Government.

IBERIN: The horses are to be taken away from him.

JUDGE: The horses are to be taken away from you. *He leaves.*

CALLAS: Sir, does that mean I don't get the horses?

IBERIN: That's right. The law is the law. For you and everyone else.

CALLAS: Then let me tell you something: I spit on your law, if I can't get the horses I need for ploughing! That's no law! That's no justice for me, if I don't get the horses I need! That's the justice of the landowners! I'm going to join the Sickle! They'll get me my horses!
*Suddenly the bells begin to toll. From afar the noise of an enormous crowd.*

VOICE BACKSTAGE: The Sickle has been smashed!

ZAKKISH ATTORNEY: We've won!
*Enter Missena with a microphone.*

MISSENA:
   Señor Iberin, the peasants' revolt has been
   With God's assistance bloodily put down!

MOTHER SUPERIOR *clapping quietly*: Bravo!

IBERIN *takes the microphone*:
   The peasants' Sickle has been smashed! Rejoice!
   We've smitten off the greedy hand that robbed
   And desecrated! For that is Zakkish law
   And ancient custom: property is sacred.
   A Zak would rather starve in poverty

Than steal his meat from someone else's table.
The mob that sponges on the state with pleas
Of 'God have mercy' and 'We're not to blame',
'There's no work to be had, don't let us starve',
We'll let them have their crust, but mark my words,
For me a leeching Zak's no Zak at all:
Let him be fed, and let him be despised.
And should he dare demand what's not his right,
Or lay claim to the land just 'cause he ploughs it,
Take horses, tools or stock, because he needs them –
In short, should he commit a crime of any sort
'Gainst property: let him be ripped apart!
For such a man can only bring us strife!
The sin of greed has forced a fearful wedge,
A rift between the healthy parts of our
Dear island race! Our land was riven by mistrust
Until this Sickle flag was trodden in the dust.
*At this moment the lights of the chandelier come on.*

VOICE BACKSTAGE: Mirasonnore has been relieved! Government troops have recaptured the power station! Hooray for Iberin!

IBERIN: And there was light! *To Callas, covering the microphone with his hand*:
As for you, farmer, go home to your plough
And leave affairs of state to those who know
What's what! When sometimes ends won't meet,
    remember:
It's you who're insufficient, only you!
We need your honest work, not idle plaints!
You think your land is lacking? – You're the lack!
And when your harvest fails, then you have failed!
Go home to sweat and toil, not to shirk,
And we shall honour you for all your honest work!
*He turns away and strides back into the palace, followed by Missena. Exeunt, except Callas and Nanna. Projection: 'Sickle in complete disarray. Peasants abandon occupied farms.'*

CALLAS: Did you hear that, the bastard has sentenced me to death.

NANNA: That I didn't hear. But he has taken your horses away.

CALLAS: It's the same thing.

*The bells go on tolling.*


8

A BACKSTREET IN THE OLD TOWN

*The bells are still tolling. The tobacconist stands at his shop door. The door of the grocer's on the right opens and the fat woman appears loaded down with boxes and suitcases.*

FAT WOMAN: Why are the bells ringing, Mr Palmosa?

TOBACCONIST PALMOSA: They're ringing for victory, Mrs Tomaso! The peasants from the Sickle have been bloodily put down, with God's assistance. It's a great victory!

FAT WOMAN: Whatever you say. Unfortunately I have to move out, I can't pay the rent.

PALMOSA: Couldn't you just hold on until the great projects of this new government have been realised?

FAT WOMAN: No. *She sits down for a moment on her suitcases.* Thirty-five years, that's how long I've lived here!

PALMOSA: I expect I'll have to move out soon too. Thank heaven at least my son's with the Zakkish legion, he'll get properly paid now.

FAT WOMAN: This Señor Iberin has been a great disappointment. He seemed so energetic at first.

PALMOSA: Reconstruction is a slow and painful business! Perhaps your little sacrifice was necessary, Mrs Tomaso, to nurture those delicate green shoots of recovery in Yahoo.

FAT WOMAN: The only thing he's done is get that Zik opposite put away!

*A man with a very timid manner and wearing a big hat has come down the street. He opens up the shop door of the grocer's on the left. It's the Zikkish shopkeeper.*

FAT WOMAN *exits with her suitcases*: Well I never! I don't understand the world any more!

*More bells. The Zikkish shopkeeper comes out of the grocer's on the left. He was only fetching his suitcase, now he exits too: he too has had to close down. Landlord Callamassi comes down the street.*

CALLAMASSI: I've just come from the trial. Hot news: Callas has had the horses taken away from him.

PALMOSA: You don't say! And the landlord?

CALLAMASSI: The landlord wasn't mentioned.

PALMOSA: Do you think he'll get off? That would be a thing.

CALLAMASSI: Is that some sort of criticism of the government, Mr Palmosa?

PALMOSA: Señor Callamassi, it's my job to sell cigars, not to criticise the government.

CALLAMASSI *going into the house*: Just watch what you say, Mr Palmosa! The Governor has had some serious things to say about malcontents. Besides, I still haven't had your rent.

*The tobacconist runs over to the coffeehouse and rings until Madame Cornamontis appears.*

PALMOSA *looking at Madame Cornamontis meaningfully*: Madame Cornamontis, Callas has had the horses taken away from him.

MADAME CORNAMONTIS: So I'll be expecting visitors soon. *She goes back inside.*

PALMOSA *goes back into his shop*: How times change. *Down the street come Farmer Callas and his daughter, she is carrying a suitcase.*

NANNA: Back where we started. This is the house. This where the people stood and said, what's a nice Zakkish girl like you doing in a house like this! It's shameful, they cried. But you can't eat fancy words. Now I'd be thankful if they'd take me back.

CALLAS: They'll be happy enough to have you back.

NANNA: I'm not so sure about that.

CALLAS: I hope none of those Iberin people sees us. Otherwise they'll lock me up for not behaving proper, like a real people's hero.
*They ring.*
Why does nobody answer?

NANNA: Perhaps they shut the place down after all.

CALLAS: Now we've had it! If I have to feed you all through the winter!

CORNAMONTIS *comes to the door*: Oh, Nanna.

NANNA: Good morning, Madame Cornamontis!

CALLAS: Good morning, Madame Cornamontis!

NANNA: Madame Cornamontis, the great expectations which my father had with regard to my future have not quite worked out, unfortunately. I could have told him right away. But some rather unusual legal proceedings, which we were at the centre of, got his hopes up, you know. Anyway, my father requests that you take me back into your house.

CORNAMONTIS: I'm not sure that's such a good idea.

NANNA: Ah, Madame Cornamontis, the ways of the world are strange. Two days ago the people carried me on their shoulders out of the courtroom – and ruined a brand-new pair of silk stockings while they were at it. But I can still count myself lucky, these things normally turn out even worse. All the little people who've been making such a to-do in recent days, they'll soon come to their senses again. They earn eight pesos, and they make enough racket for eighty, it won't end well.

CORNAMONTIS: Someone has to come out on top. *She looks Nanna up and down.* Only been gone a few days, and you're in a state! I'll have to start your education all over again. Why do I waste all that good money on make-up, if it only takes three days and all your sophistication's down the drain? Your stockings are a mess! And what have you been eating! That complexion is not a pretty sight! Pity you can't simply wipe away that new grin you've found. This girl used to have a smile like Aphrodite, and now she just grins. And the way you waggle your hips, like a common prostitute! I'll have to think about it. The only thing in your favour is that the gentlemen always go for a girl who, oh so recently, seemed quite unattainable. Perhaps I'll try it one more time. *She goes inside.*

CALLAS: So Nanna my dear, it's time for us to part again. I'm pleased we met up. I was able to see for myself that things aren't going all that badly for you, better than for your poor parents anyway! If you happen to have something to

spare these next months, we'd be grateful. At least your
dear mother and I gave you the wherewithal to make your
living here. Let's not forget that.

NANNA: Goodbye, Father dear. We've had a nice few days
together anyway. But don't get up to anything stupid now,
you just go straight home. *She goes inside.*

PALMOSA *comes out of the shop, where he's been listening*:
Aren't you that 'Callas of the horses'?

CALLAS: 'Callas of the horses', yes, that's what they used to
call me. But the horses were a three-day dream. In those
days the Sickle was still on the way up. Then everything
started to go wrong.

PALMOSA: But you had quite a coup in your trial with de
Guzman, didn't you, you know, when you moved that the
rents should be abolished.

CALLAS *startled*: The rents? That's right! In all the fuss and
bother nobody mentioned them again. I've got to find out.
Right away! Heavens!

PALMOSA: But how? Where can you find out?

CALLAS: Where?

PALMOSA: You'd best to go straight to Señor Iberin.

CALLAS: Iberin? I'm not going to him again, my friend. But I
must find out somehow. *He walks off, his walk turning to a
run.*

PALMOSA: Where are you running to?

*He goes back into his shop, shaking his head. Isabella de
Guzman, the Abbess of San Barabas and the attorneys are
on their way back from the trial.*

MOTHER SUPERIOR
I think the worst is past for us. Just now
Old Peruiner whispered in my ear
To give his greetings to your brother. So
We're back on course. Oh yes, and Señor Saz
Said when our loyal troops come marching home
And back into the capital, they'll bring
A small surprise for Señor Iberin.
And he laughed.

ZAKKISH ATTORNEY:
It all looks very healthy.

*Down the street come the inspector and a Hatso with Emanuele de Guzman in chains. De Guzman has a large cardboard sign around his neck, which reads: 'I'm a Zik, I raped a Zakkish girl, so I'm condemned to die.'*

ISABELLA:
What's this?

ZAKKISH ATTORNEY: Señor de Guzman! Señor de Guzman, congratulations! Everything's back under control.

MOTHER SUPERIOR:
The peasant's had his horses confiscated.

ZIKKISH ATTORNEY:
Which means that your estates are once again
Secure.

DE GUZMAN:
          And me?

ZAKKISH ATTORNEY:
                    We'll soon have that in hand.
Although it wasn't actually discussed.

ISABELLA:
Emanuele, why so silent?
Why so pale? What's wrong? And why these chains
And why this sign?

MOTHER SUPERIOR:
                    It's all for show, I'm sure!

ISABELLA:
Dear brother, speak! Where are you bound?
Speak to us please!

DE GUZMAN:
                    I'm done for, sister, finished!
I'm destined for the Holy Cross.

ISABELLA:
Oh no!

ZAKKISH ATTORNEY *to the inspector*: Is this true?

INSPECTOR: It's true Señor, it doesn't look at all promising. No one has ever come out of the Prison of the Holy Cross alive.

DE GUZMAN:
God help me, I won't take another step!
*He sits down on the ground.*

ISABELLA:
　　Oh Reverend Mother, now it all comes back,
　　And I recall what 'twas that troubled me.
　　In all the fuss and bother that we've had
　　About the horses, we forgot the man.
　　We saved the horses for him. But he
　　Is lost to us.

DE GUZMAN:
　　　　　　　I'll hang, for sure.

ZAKKISH ATTORNEY:
　　　　　　　　　　Nonsense.
　　It's been a victory!

MOTHER SUPERIOR:
　　　　　　　　You hear those bells,
　　My son? They ring for you!

ISABELLA:
　　　　　　　　　But don't you see?
　　It isn't right. And now it all comes back:
　　A man approached me in the celebrations
　　And said I wasn't to forget my brother.
　　The law, he said, could sometimes take its course
　　Relentlessly. And then he said he'd help.

ZAKKISH ATTORNEY:
　　What sort of man was this?

ISABELLA:
　　　　　　　　　An awful man,
　　An animal.

ZAKKISH ATTORNEY:
　　　　　　I'll wager that must be
　　Zazarante, Iberin's lieutenant.

INSPECTOR:
　　Commander of the Holy Cross!

ZAKKISH ATTORNEY:
　　　　　　　　　　But what
　　Exactly did he say? How help? And when?

ISABELLA:
　　He bade me to him when the clock strikes five.
　　*Pause.*

DE GUZMAN:
  Dear sister, this is my salvation!
ISABELLA:
                    Brother ...
DE GUZMAN:
  He ... likes you. It's, well it's a proposition.
  To talk things over, at five o'clock! I know
  That talk. I used to have my 'chats' at five –
  About the rents ... and such ... You'll have to go.
ISABELLA:
  But brother!
DE GUZMAN:
              Don't think of it, don't contradict!
MOTHER SUPERIOR:
  Señor de Guzman, let's not exaggerate.
  They'll never hang a wealthy gentleman.
  Reflect on what you are.
DE GUZMAN:
                    A Zik, that's what.
ZIKKISH ATTORNEY:
  Of course, a proposition, an attempt
  At blackmail, while the Sickle threatened still.
  Until that time they had the means to try it.
  But now the Sickle's finished, sir, with that
  The situation's changed!
ISABELLA:
                    I still don't follow.
MOTHER SUPERIOR:
  Well, yesterday they could still force their will
  Upon us, now they can't.
DE GUZMAN:
                        Oh yes they can!
  It's not so hard, dear sister: these people
  Would like me dead. Because, though I can't help it,
  I'm a Zik.
ISABELLA:
            That's it, we're Ziks. Just look,
  His pointed head won't vanish overnight!
DE GUZMAN:
  She understands!

ISABELLA:
                    I understand, I see.
DE GUZMAN:
   That I'm to hang!
ISABELLA:
                    They're going to hang my brother.
DE GUZMAN:
   We need a plan, what's more we need it quick:
   They want to hit us hard, and confiscate
   Or steal some precious part of our estate:
   We have to ask ourselves: what is the greater,
   What the lesser loss? Perhaps instead
   Of offering my head, we might divest
   Ourselves of something else which we'd miss less,
   Although our enemies, for all we know,
   Might like it more. To sum it up: I'd like
   To keep my life, for nothing is more precious.
ISABELLA *looking at her brother in horror*:
   What are you saying, brother! That man I saw
   Was like an animal.
DE GUZMAN:
                    And what am I?
   A peasant wench – it seems so long ago –
   Perhaps thought much the same of me. Of course
   It isn't easy, nor was it for her.
   Look at my paunch. And she was young, like you.
ISABELLA:
   You forced yourself on some poor girl?
DE GUZMAN:
   I did.
ISABELLA:
   You call yourself my brother! You may try
   To force me but I'll never, never do it!
DE GUZMAN:
   I had my way! And, mark me, he'll have his!
   It's not just my affair, it's yours as well!
   For if I'm hanged the rents will soon run dry,
   And then, to pay your debts, you'll have to take
   Your precious maidenhead out on the streets.

So since, this way or that, it must be sold,
The question is: to whom, and at what price!

ISABELLA:
Dear brother, ask me anything but this!

DE GUZMAN:
Oh don't make such a fuss, you're not a saint!
They want me hanged, and I don't want to hang:
Not for a whore, nor either for a nun.

ISABELLA:
Such talk is just a token of despair!
*She runs off.*

DE GUZMAN *shouts after her:*
This close to death and everything is fair!

ZAKKISH ATTORNEY:
She'll never do it.

MOTHER SUPERIOR:
            I'll see what I can do.
*Exit.*

ZIKKISH ATTORNEY:
I'll talk to Peruiner. In the morning
We'll get the landlords up in town to pledge
Support. Remember, Guzman, you're a landlord!
*Exit.*

THE HATSO, *who has been sitting on de Guzman's ball and chain, stands up:* Get up! *To the inspector:* Kick him in the balls! I'm sick of this whole victory business; the minute they announced it we had our expenses cut.

INSPECTOR: We must get moving, Señor de Guzman.

DE GUZMAN *stands up:*
I'm lost.

ZAKKISH ATTORNEY *to the inspector:*
        The poor man's nerves are playing up.
*Exeunt.*

PALMOSA, *who has been listening again, runs back to the coffeehouse and rings until Madame Cornamontis and Nanna appear:* Miss Callas, you've just missed it. They just came by with that de Guzman. They're taking him to the Holy Cross. Now at least you have the satisfaction of knowing he'll be hanged.

NANNA: Will he?

PALMOSA: You don't seem very happy about it.

NANNA: You know, Mr Palmosa, I've seen our Señor Iberin in action. Yesterday it was the Viceroy who held court over us; today it's Señor Iberin. Today it's the Holy Mother of San Barabas who takes our horses; tomorrow it may well be Señor de Guzman again. *She sings the 'Ballad of the Waterwheel'.*

BALLAD OF THE WATERWHEEL

1

Take mankind's outstanding figures
Don't their legends sound enthralling?
First they shoot up like a comet
Then tail off like comets falling.
What a comfort, and how well worth knowing!
As for us who have to keep them going
How are we to tell just what the difference is –
Upsurge or collapse, who pays the expenses?
    For the waterwheel must keep on turning
    And so what's on top is bound to fall.
    All the time the water underneath is learning
    It has to drive the waterwheel.

2

Oh, we've had so many masters
We've had tigers and hyenas
We've had eagles, we've had warthogs:
Fed the lot of them between us.
People tell us that all men are brothers
But each jackboot felt like all the others
And it crushed us. Which should serve to show one
That it's not a different master that we need, but no one.
    For the waterwheel must keep on turning
    And so what's on top is bound to fall.
    All the time the water underneath is learning
    It has to drive the waterwheel.

3

And they'll batter one another senseless

For the booty.
Each one will claim he's poor and defenceless
Acting from a sense of duty.
Watch them rip each other's hands to bits to prise off
Their adornments. But the consternation
When we say we're going to cut supplies off!
Then there is a total reconciliation.
　For the waterwheel must keep on turning
　And so what's on top is bound to fall.
　All the time the water underneath is learning
　It has to drive the waterwheel.


9

IN THE COFFEEHOUSE OF MADAME CORNAMONTIS

*Isabella de Guzman is standing at the entrance.*

ISABELLA:
　Now that I know their purpose is to hang him
　I know I must not shirk this bitter cup.
　But let me ask of those who've oft times made
　This sorry journey: how they keep themselves
　Detached and unaffected by their sin.
　Besides, I need to know what I should wear.
　Should one behave as if one freely came,
　As if the vile seducer once had caught
　One's eye, or had appeared by night in dream?
　That way I might perhaps anaesthetise
　This agony of being bought and used.
　Or is it better one should have it known
　Quite openly that one's abused and can
　Do nothing for it, yet remain untouch-
　able and cold the while that one submits.
　Are deeds this base so much the custom that
　The men who thus abuse our honour think
　It all a harmless game, their bit of fun?
　Perhaps what's asked is thought so little that
　Too agonised a protest might increase

Our shame: righteous disgust but spreads the stain.
The girls who work in places such as this
So seldom are with child; they must know ways
By which they may evade the consequences
Of their sin. I have so much to learn.
*She rings.*

NANNA *opens the door*: What do you want here?

ISABELLA: Good day to you, Nanna, you know me of course, when we were little we often played together in the courtyard.

NANNA: Yes, and what can I do for you?

ISABELLA: I'm not disturbing you?

NANNA: Think nothing of it.

ISABELLA: Circumstances compel me to seek you out. The execution of my brother has been announced, tomorrow morning at five o'clock. There is a possibility that I may save him, but it requires an unusual sacrifice, and it puts me in a situation which, being inexperienced in these matters, I cannot handle on my own.

NANNA: Sit down.

ISABELLA *sits down*: May I have a glass of water? I'm not feeling very well. *Nanna fetches a glass of water.* A certain proposition has been made by the Commander of the Holy Cross, he wants me to abase myself utterly. Were I to concur, I should face difficulties I can scarcely imagine.

NANNA: I see.

ISABELLA: I know nothing of love.

NANNA: No.

ISABELLA: Please don't think me cynical, but my plight forces me to ask you questions of a sort which you, because of your profession, must needs be well equipped to answer.

NANNA: Ask away, but you'll have to pay Madame for my time.

ISABELLA: I'll pay for your time.

NANNA: I can imagine what you need to know, you'd better ask the boss as well. She's had an awful lot of experience.

ISABELLA: Is she discreet?

NANNA: It's her job.

ISABELLA: Good, that's agreed then.

*Nanna fetches Madame Cornamontis.*

NANNA *at the bar to Madame Cornamontis*: Make sure you milk the cow, she's loaded.

*They both enter the room.*

MADAME CORNAMONTIS: No need to tell me your name, my child, just ask as freely and frankly as if I were your Father Confessor.

ISABELLA: You need to know that the life of my brother depends on my going to a certain highly placed gentleman who, they tell me, has conceived a liking for me. I have no idea how to conduct myself, nor whether this fashion of granting and demanding love is usual.

CORNAMONTIS: Entirely usual.

ISABELLA: Oh.

CORNAMONTIS: Go on.

ISABELLA: Is it not possible that a man who is disappointed by such an embrace will go back on his commitments and break the promises he has made?

NANNA: That's a definite possibility.

ISABELLA: And what can one do about it?

CORNAMONTIS: They all break their promises and there's nothing you can do about it. It's only the hope of future embraces that restrains them from the very worst brutalities.

ISABELLA: As so infinitely much depends on it: the clothes I am wearing are probably inappropriate.

CORNAMONTIS: On the contrary.

ISABELLA: It's a novice nun's habit.

CORNAMONTIS: Precisely.

ISABELLA: Forgive my confusion. All this cold linen?

CORNAMONTIS: The more linen the better. Linen is excellent.

ISABELLA: And shouldn't I adopt a rather less cold demeanour?

CORNAMONTIS: The colder the better.

ISABELLA: Oh! You're not afraid I might seem awkward?

CORNAMONTIS: Not at all.

ISABELLA: I know less of these things than you may presume.

CORNAMONTIS: There is less to know than you imagine, my child! That's the sad thing. It's not practice, but a natural disposition, a rare quality, that lends these matters a sort of charm. But have no fear: even without charm there can be enjoyment. For meagre gratification such as this almost anyone will do.

ISABELLA: So there's no reason why I should ask that this cup pass from me?

CORNAMONTIS: None at all. *Pause.* Yet. There is one thing.

ISABELLA: What is that? Speak! Tell me, please!

CORNAMONTIS: Your money, my dear! Indeed, it's a very strong reason. Why should you, in your position, lower yourself? Why should you do anything at all that you don't want to do? Wouldn't it be unseemly if you, for whom other, less sensitive souls sweat to create your wealth – if you were to do something which might set the common people gossiping? It would be most improper! What would you say, if one day the rain were to fall back up into the sky? You'd think it untoward, and rightly so. You shouldn't have to do a thing like this.

ISABELLA: But a certain highly placed person demands it.

CORNAMONTIS: And rightly so, my child, there's nothing to be said against that. Why should he not demand it, if he's highly placed? And why should he not receive what he demands? But what about you, what concern is this of yours, since you are highly placed too, and have the means to have your justice done in style? A certain *je ne sais quoi* . . .

ISABELLA: What are you suggesting?

CORNAMONTIS: My girls of course. Who else. We're so much better able to suffer abasement, base as we already are. Look at her sitting there, lazy slut, too idle to blink, and all the time we're talking about her employment prospects! Nanna, wait outside! *Nanna exits.* My best girl will go in your place.

ISABELLA: Impossible, you don't know who he is.

CORNAMONTIS: Whoever he is, he won't notice.

ISABELLA: The Commander of the Holy Cross!

CORNAMONTIS: So much the better. She'll go in your clothes, and she'll imitate your manner. But she'll be much better than you could ever be. Your brother will go free. And the

rain won't need to fall back up into the sky. And it'll cost
you a thousand pesos.

ISABELLA: She'd be willing to do it for money?

CORNAMONTIS: More than willing. Cash makes you randy.
*She sings Isabella a song.*

MADAM'S SONG

Oh, they say to see the red moon shining
On the waters causes girls to fall
And they'll talk about a woman pining
For some lovely man. But not at all!
  If you want to know what makes them swoon
  It's his chequebook, not the moon.
  Try to look at it in this light:
  Decent girls won't take to bed
  Any gent whose wad is tight
  But they can be very loving
  If a fellow sees them right.
  It's a fact: cash makes you randy
  As I've learnt night after night.

What's the use of all those red moons shining
On the waters once the money goes?
Beauty can provide no silver lining
When you're broke and everybody knows.
  If you want to know what makes them swoon
  It's the lining, not the moon.
  Try to look at it in this light:
  How can couples go to bed
  With the proper appetite
  If they've both got empty bellies?
  Better get the order right.
  Food is fuel, cash makes you randy.
  As I've learnt night after night.

CORNAMONTIS *shouts*: Nanna! *To Isabella*: The girl doesn't
have to know the price. *Nanna enters.* Nanna, swap clothes
with the young lady. You're going to the Commander in
her place.

NANNA: And what's in it for me?

CORNAMONTIS: Don't be cheeky. You'll get the normal rate. Now get yourself dressed.

ISABELLA: I should like a screen please.

NANNA: I shan't look.

ISABELLA: Nevertheless, I should like a screen.

*Nanna brings a screen. The girls swap clothes.*

CORNAMONTIS: So, Nanna, now you're wearing the right clothes, but will you know how to conduct yourself in them? I'll play the part of the important gentleman. How may I be of service, madam? Go on then, answer!

NANNA: I'm here once more on my brother's behalf, to ask you ...

CORNAMONTIS: To implore!

NANNA: To implore!

CORNAMONTIS *to Isabella*: Isn't that what you'd say?

ISABELLA: I should say nothing at all.

CORNAMONTIS: And let him work it out?

NANNA: And how's that supposed to work? It's not my style, these theatricals.

CORNAMONTIS: You be quiet! He may ask you about why you want to join the Needy Sisters of San Barabas. And what'll you say then?

NANNA: Well, I've got the money. If I don't stash it away here it may even get confiscated. On account of my pointed head. No marriage can help me out of that one. I don't want to marry a Pointed Head, he'd be no security in these times, and no Round Head would have me. I'll be comfortable with the Needy Sisters of San Barabas. Nothing to do all day, no physical work anyway, but lots to eat and I'll live in peace. No worries.

CORNAMONTIS: Is that right?

ISABELLA: Those are not my reasons. But why should it need to be true? I don't wish to tell you my reasons.

CORNAMONTIS: But *she* will have to tell *him*. And she'll tell it as you've just heard her, like some cowgirl, no refinement. You've got to tell her what to say.

*And so the landlord's sister instructs the tenant's daughter in the three chief virtues: abstinence, obedience and poverty.*

ISABELLA *quietly*:

Aah, I had always desired, that my childhood might never
end.

Wished that my days could be happy, and peaceful my
nights.

O to live in virtue, for ever safe from the greed and
brutality of men, that is what I have aspired to.

So that for me there'd only be the Lord

Whose love's a bounteous and sweet reward.

CORNAMONTIS *weeping*: You see what it is to be respectable,
you peasant trollop!

NANNA *cheekily*:

Aah, I had always desired, that my childhood might never
end.

*Aside:* The shit I put up with!

Wished that my days could be happy, and peaceful my
nights.

We should be so lucky!

O to live in virtue, safe from the greed and brutality of men,
that's what I'd like too!

For me there'd likewise be but one milord

Whose bounteous love would be my sweet reward.

CORNAMONTIS *angrily*: What are you on about, you slut!
Pull yourself together!

NANNA: I can see I'm going to have to do that.

CORNAMONTIS *to Isabella*: Please do continue! This is quite
an experience for me.

ISABELLA:

Of all the virtues obedience is the finest.

How should I know what is right? I know but this:

The dear Lord means me well, therefore I say:

Let not my will be done, but only His!

Transgression seeks forgiveness from above

And God rewards obedience with love.

CORNAMONTIS *to Nanna*: Now you say it, but get it right
this time!

NANNA *deadpan*:

Of all the virtues obedience is the finest.

How should I know what is right? I know but this:

The dear Lord means me well, therefore I say:

Let not my will be done, but only His!
  Transgression seeks forgiveness from above
  And God rewards obedience with love.

ISABELLA:
A life of poverty is our perpetual goal
For poverty cannot corrupt nor can it harm me.
Ask all You will of my body, my heart and my soul
I glory to serve and do battle in Jesus' Army.
  All worldly goods I do renounce, O Lord
  Your gracious love is all my rich reward.

NANNA:
A life of poverty is our perpetual goal
For poverty cannot corrupt nor can it harm me.
Ask all You will of my body, my heart and my soul
I glory to serve and do battle in Jesus' Army.
  All worldly goods I do renounce, O Lord
  I'm holding out for ten per cent reward.

CORNAMONTIS: Jesus, we've forgotten the most important thing!

NANNA: What's that?

CORNMONTIS: She's a Zak! She's got a round head! And our important gentleman has a particular interest in a Zik! You may look the same and move the same, and we'll manage the rest all right. The costume's fine. But the head is wrong! He just has to stroke her head and he'll find us out!

NANNA: Give me a hairpiece, I'll make sure he doesn't touch my head. Besides, I'm not so sure race has that much to do with this sort of thing.

*Nanna's hair is arranged so that her head looks like Isabella's.*

CORNAMONTIS: Well, whatever else the differences, class and wealth and so on: at least the head's the same now. *To Nanna*: Try to move a bit more woodenly, to go with all that refined talk. Forget everything you've learnt from me, act as if you hadn't learnt a thing, as if just being there was enough. Imagine how a plank of wood dispenses favours! Don't give him a thing, but act as if you were giving too much. Accept everything, but as if it was nothing. That way he'll get no gratification, but he'll still be indebted to you.

Now go upstairs and wash your hands again, and take some of my cologne, from on top of the cupboard; on second thoughts, that's too common; it's even more refined to smell of nothing. *Nanna goes upstairs. Madame Cornamontis to Isabella*: You'd better stay here until Nanna comes back, in a couple of hours you can go home in your own clothes.

*Madame Cornamontis leaves the room and goes back behind the bar. Enter Mrs Callas and her four little children.*

MRS CALLAS: Oh Madame Cornamontis, when we heard that a new age was dawning, my husband, the farmer, went into town to get his share of the new prosperity. We heard our landlord has been condemned to death. On account of he was rack-renting. But yesterday they came and took our cow away because we haven't paid our taxes. And my husband still hasn't come home. We've looked for him everywhere, the children are exhausted and hungry, but I've got no money to buy them gruel. In the old days Nanna used to help us sometimes, when we were hard up. We hear she's gone up in the world now and isn't working here any longer. In the long run a house like yours, Madame Cornamontis, wasn't the thing for our daughter. But perhaps you can tell us where she is now?

CORNAMONTIS: She's back here again, but she's not free right now. But you can have some soup all the same.

*Madame Cornamontis gives them soup. The family sits down on the steps and eats. Nanna enters. She pushes her way through the family sitting in the doorway, eating. They hold her back.*

MRS CALLAS: It's the young lady sister of our landlord! Say your piece!

THE CHILDREN:
Dear Señor de Guzman, you're a proper gent,
Dear Señor de Guzman, let us off the rent.

NANNA *behind her veil*: Don't get your hopes up! *To the audience*:
I'll set the world to rights by this old trick.
But it's not just a case of Zak for Zik:

For here the poor girl takes the rich girl's part
And where the nun should go, behold a tart!


10

A PRISON

*The gaoled tenant farmers, amongst them Lopez, are sitting in
a condemned cell. They are having their heads shaved by
Hatsos. In another cell, the landowner de Guzman. Outside a
gallows is being built.*

HATSO *to the farmer whom he's shaving*: So did you have to
  daub that sickle sign all over the place, was it that
  important?
FARMER: Yes.
HATSO: So who's going to help your women through the
  winter now?
FARMER: We don't know.
HATSO: And who's going to plough your fields in the spring
  if you're not there?
FARMER: We don't know that either.
HATSO: Will there be any fields left to plough by the spring?
FARMER: We don't even know that.
HATSO: But the Sickle will triumph in the end, you know
  that?
FARMER: Yes, that we do know.
THE INSPECTOR *enters with a measure and measures de
  Guzman's neck*: Personally, from a human standpoint, I
  find your case rather moving. They say there are lots of
  farmers in town, just waiting to see if a landlord is really
  going to hang. They say, on the first of the month they'll all
  refuse to pay their rents. How are we supposed to hang a
  man with all that going on! Neck sixteen inches, that's a
  drop of eight feet. Keep quiet in there! If I make a mistake
  there'll be such a stink! I remember the trouble the press
  made two years ago over the Colzoni case, when the
  guillotine didn't work, it was far worse than the trouble

they made when they found out the man was innocent all along.

*Enter the two attorneys.*

ZAKKISH ATTORNEY: Inspector, even as we speak the man's sister has in her hands the means to secure her brother's reprieve.

INSPECTOR *drily*: I've no doubt of it. Did you see the young lady in the veil who just went in to see the Commander?

*The attorneys breathe a sigh of relief.*

ZIKKISH ATTORNEY *to de Guzman who is too distressed to listen*: De Guzman, glad tidings! Your sister is with the Commander!

ZAKKISH ATTORNEY: At least we can be sure Zazarante won't be bothering us for a while.

INSPECTOR *as he leaves*: You'll still have to get started shaving him!

*The Hatso starts to shave the landowner.*

ZAKKISH ATTORNEY *to his colleague*: It's looking rather grim, you know. Even if the Commander turns a blind eye, we don't have a real solution. Even though our client is one of the biggest landowners in the country.

*De Guzman and his two attorneys sing the 'Song of a Big Shot'.*

SONG OF A BIG SHOT

I

DE GUZMAN:

In my cot I used to hear them sing
How I'd never have to toil or sweat
Willing arms would rush to take the strain
This was their habitual refrain:
I'm a big shot, there's no doubt of that!
In those days I only weighed four pounds, but I'm as big as the next man now!

ATTORNEYS:

So who helped you grow so big and strong?
Were you brought up by your gentle mother?

DE GUZMAN:

Gracious no, there was some nurse or other

Just some prole who, for a coin or two
Eagerly took on the household toil.
ATTORNEYS:
But of course, there's always someone who
Is so poor and wretched they'll be loyal!

2

DE GUZMAN:
When I inherited my stock and acres
I was still a carefree teenage brat
But I had no reason to complain
This was their habitual refrain:
I'm a big shot, there's no doubt of that!
You know, I never had the slightest interest in agriculture!
ATTORNEYS:
Who then ploughed and sowed and reaped your acres
Was it you who took on all that bother?
DE GUZMAN:
Gracious no, some labourers or other
Just some proles who, for a coin or two
Brought the harvest in, or dug the soil.
ATTORNEYS:
But of course, there's always someone who
Is so poor and wretched they'll be loyal!

3

ATTORNEYS:
Now they say our client's going to swing!
'Cause his head is pointed, where it should be flat!
This affair's turned out a sorry mess
Can you wonder that he's showing signs of stress?
He's a big shot, there's no doubt of that!
DE GUZMAN:
I'm a big shot, there's no doubt of that!
ATTORNEYS: What are the farmers to do if their landlord is
hanged?
DE GUZMAN:
What are we to do about this hanging?
ATTORNEYS:
The situation's looking rather bad!

Is there really no one to be had?
Just some prole who, for a coin or two
Would even shuffle off this mortal coil?
Surely, damn it, we'll find someone who
Is so poor and stupid they'll be loyal!

*Farmer Callas appears upstage at a gap in the wall, closed off with stout iron bars.*

FARMER CALLAS *waving*: Señor de Guzman! Señor de Guzman! Señor de Guzman, it's Farmer Callas! I still need to know what's going to happen about the rent!

ZAKKISH ATTORNEY: The rent is to be paid to the Convent of San Barabas, the Treasury, back court, right-hand side.

CALLAS: I'm not asking you! Señor de Guzman, you've got to let up on the rent!

ZIKKISH ATTORNEY: Come in, come in, we're not monsters you know! *Callas disappears from the window.* Señor de Guzman, I believe we've found you a replacement.

*Enter Farmer Callas.*

CALLAS *to the audience*:
When I went off and left my farm
I didn't really mean much harm,
I simply hoped to live rent free
And grow my barley just for me.
I came to Luma town 'ere long:
The bells were ringing: ding dang dong!
And everybody treated me
As if I were some V.I.P.
If any man did anything
To hurt me, I was told, he'd swing.
And so the frog crawled from his pond,
The fairy waved her magic wand.
But what that honour may have meant –
It didn't help to pay the rent.
Honour goes straight to your head
But it's no substitute for bread.
If all the food is in the pond
The frog will know that he's been conned.
They've talked of honour now for weeks,
But of my rent, nobody speaks!

They've tried to keep me in the dark.
I've got to make the landlord talk.
Whatever all their judgements meant,
I have to know: what's with the rent!
*As he walks past he sees his onetime friend Lopez in the condemned cell.*

CALLAS *yells at Lopez, who looks at him in silence*: You shut your mouth! *In front of de Guzman's cell*: Señor de Guzman, if you won't let me off the rent I'll take a rope and hang myself, to end this misery.

LOPEZ: And yet there was a time, Callas, when it was all going so well!

CALLAS *yells*: You just keep your mouth shut!

ZAKKISH ATTORNEY: Mr Callas, we have a proposition to make! *He pulls up a chair for Callas.*

ZIKKISH ATTORNEY: You're in luck! Señor de Guzman's pardon is as good as in the bag. The underlings here just don't know it yet. He's to be pardoned on the gallows, in celebration of the return of a certain great statesman who is due back in town tomorrow. But we're still a little worried, you see, about letting him walk to the gallows in the state he's in. He's been under so much stress. Why don't you go in his place, in return, say, for one year's rent relief? It's perfectly safe, as good as.

CALLAS: And I'm supposed to let myself be strung up for him?

ZIKKISH ATTORNEY: Nonsense! Nobody could ask that!

ZAKKISH ATTORNEY: You must decide, of course, it's entirely up to you. There's no serfdom in Yahoo. Nobody's forcing you to do anything. You know your financial situation, and you must be the judge, can you afford to ignore the offer of a year without rent?

ZIKKISH ATTORNEY: After all, just a moment ago, you said you were going to hang yourself anyway!

ZAKKISH ATTORNEY: You do understand, a wealthy man isn't up to this sort of exertion. All that luxury has made him soft, it's taking its toll. Between you and me, he's a sissy. But you peasants, you're made of sterner stuff. You take it all in your stride. *He beckons to an Iberin soldier who's just finished in the farmers' cell.* Hey, you! Give this man a shave too, Zazarante's orders!

CALLAS: But they'll hang me!

ZIKKISH ATTORNEY: You don't have to decide yet, just get yourself shaved, in case, otherwise it won't be all that much use to us when you do agree.

CALLAS: But I haven't said yes yet!
*On a chair next to the cell in which his landlord is being shaved, Farmer Callas is shaved too.*

THE HATSO *shaving the Sickle men*: By the way, what are you going to do with your shoes?

A FARMER: Why do you ask?

HATSO: Take a look at my boots! We got them free, although we still had to pay for the re-soling. But I don't enjoy kicking people any more, not with these boots. One guy even reckoned it was doing him good!

FARMER: You can have mine.

CALLAS *has been thinking, hesitantly*: Two years rent-free, at least! After all, I'm risking my neck.

ZIKKISH ATTORNEY: Señor de Guzman, your tenant Callas is prepared to take your place. You just have to come to an agreement about the rent.

THE HATSO *who is shaving Callas*: Callas, Callas! Don't turn Zikkish on me and start haggling!

CALLAS: The rents are too high.

DE GUZMAN *pricks up his ears*: What do you say about the rents?

CALLAS: They're too high. We don't have enough to live.

DE GUZMAN: And how am I supposed to live? You're a lazy, slovenly lot, otherwise you wouldn't have to beg.

CALLAS: If I'm lazy, what do you call yourself?

DE GUZMAN: Less of your cheek, otherwise there'll be no deal.

CALLAS: I'm not cheeky, I'm needy.

DE GUZMAN: The land is good.

CALLAS: It's good for you. But not because of the corn, because of the dues.

LOPEZ:
Landlord and peasant: always picking fights.

One's in the right, the other one has rights.

DE GUZMAN: You should be ashamed of yourself, always wanting something for nothing.

CALLAS: I don't want something for nothing, I just want something!

DE GUZMAN: You can go if you like, you're a free man!

CALLAS: Yes, I can go. But where can I go?

DE GUZMAN: I've heard enough. I'll keep what's mine.

CALLAS: Is that your last word? *To the Hatso*: Stop shaving!

ZAKKISH ATTORNEY *to Callas*: Señor de Guzman is simply confident that there's no risk involved, or very little. *To de Guzman*: Señor de Guzman, you've got to compromise. You can't be sure! One year's rent isn't a great deal.

CALLAS: Two years. I'm risking my neck!

DE GUZMAN *as if he's woken up*: Your neck? What's going on here?

ZIKKISH ATTORNEY: Callas will go to the gallows in your place, there being no danger, like we've been saying, you know.

DE GUZMAN: Yes, that's what you've been saying.

CALLAS: And I want two years rent-free. Since I may be hanged for it.

ZAKKISH ATTORNEY: One year.

CALLAS *to the Hatso*: Hold on!

INSPECTOR *calls from backstage*: Get them ready, the Commander wants to see all the condemned before they're taken away.

ZAKKISH ATTORNEY: All right, one and a half years, Callas! *Callas is silent.*

DE GUZMAN: Two years.

CALLAS: But I still haven't said I'll do it!

*In the meantime the four Sickle farmers have been led out.*

ZIKKISH ATTORNEY: You'll do it all right, Callas, you've got no choice.

CALLAS *to the audience*: But that would mean:
Zak for Zik? Injustice reaps all the reward.
The poor die for the rich, the serf dies for his lord!

ZIKKISH ATTORNEY *to his colleague*: Let's hope the Viceroy turns up on time! Otherwise he'll hang!

ZAKKISH ATTORNEY: Indeed, now he's got good reason to
pray to the Lord that they don't hang his master.

11

THE VICEROY'S PALACE

*It is early morning. A gibbet stands in the courtyard. On a
board with writing: 'Executions: 1 landowner and 200 peasants'. Between the inspector and a Hatso stands a man in
chains with a hood over his face. They are waiting. From
backstage the clatter of many wooden clogs.*

INSPECTOR *to the Hatso*: I just don't understand why we
haven't had the order for the hanging yet. Now the Sickle
people are here already.
HATSO: What makes you think they're the Sickle? Just the
clatter of clogs? Many of us Iberin soldiers have only got
wooden shoes now.
INSPECTOR: You keep your mouth shut, or there'll be
trouble. Get the gallows ready.
*The Hatso, grumbling, goes round the back and busies
himself.*
INSPECTOR *sighs, to the man in the hood*: That's what comes of
letting them hang whoever they want to. They get cheeky.
*Shouts to the Hatso*: What are you up to back there?
HATSO *coming back*: It's all ready to go. You can start
hanging them now.
*Into the courtyard comes the Governor, followed by
Missena and Señores Saz, Peruiner, de Hoz and Duarte. We
hear their protestations from afar.*
SAZ:
Are you completely mad? This man's a landlord
Not a Zik! And if he's hanged, they're sure
To say he must indeed have racked the rents.
PERUINER:
Not one estate that has a Zikkish lord
Has managed to collect the dues this month!
What's more, on neighbouring estates, where rents

Aren't lower after all, some Zakkish landlords
Say their tenants just refuse to pay.

IBERIN:

So what?

DUARTE:

That's all he has to say: So what!

MISSENA:

Just stop and think who 'tis you're hanging here:
A Zik, that's true, and p'raps he went astray,
But still: the man's a gentleman, like us.

IBERIN:

A man like us?

MISSENA:

Well yes, he lives from rent.

IBERIN:

I don't live from rent.

SAZ:

From what then, pray?

DUARTE:

What is it pays to keep this court? How were
Your gallows paid for, and – *pointing at the Hatso* – who
   pays for him?
What paid the army that destroyed the Sickle?

PERUINER:

It's rent, man, rent! And nothing else but rent!
But let's not get worked up about it, friends,
The man's stuck in a rut and we should help.
He's talked so much of Ziks and Zaks, perhaps
He's overdone it. Well, we understand.
And no offence to you! Your work was good.
You kept your promises: the peasantry
Are well and truly cowed. That's quite a feat!
And now we can proceed to other plans,
Bold plans that seemed, but recently, too bold.

IBERIN

What plans are these?

MISSENA *warning*:

Ahem.

PERUINER:

                          Well, other plans ...
But now it's time to compromise, be smart!

MISSENA:

The situation's awkward, so let's think:
Who could procure this Zik's acquittal?

IBERIN *obstinately*:

Not I.

MISSENA:

      Who could?

*Pause.*

                    The Viceroy could.

PERUINER:

                                    He could.
Let's just suspend the sentence, till he's back!

IBERIN:

Until he's back?

MISSENA:

                Well, Señor Iberin,
The Viceroy, our dear beloved and
Respected master, has resolved he should
Return to office – which, I have no doubt,
Gladdens your heart, just as it gladdens ours.

*Silence.*

IBERIN:

He's coming back?

MISSENA:

                    Indeed. Last night the troops
Joyfully received him, and requested that
He lead them back in triumph into Luma,
This very day.

IBERIN *after an embarrassing pause*:

                I see. So that's the plan.
And I was not consulted? I should have thought
I had deserved that much, that I be asked.

MISSENA:

All right, I'm asking.

IBERIN *after a difficult inner struggle*:

                      What if I agree
To free the Zik?

MISSENA:

You'd do that?

IBERIN:

Yes, I'd do that!

MISSENA *embarrassed*:
Most unexpected. What about your creed
Of Zaks and Ziks?

IBERIN *firmly*:

Don't let that trouble you,
That's my affair. About the victory march
And who should lead our troops back home to Luma,
I have a thing or two to say on that!
*The sound of drums and marching feet offstage.*

MISSENA *smiling*:
The army makes its entrance. At its head ...
*Enter the Viceroy, elegant and smiling, wearing a steel
helmet and a military overcoat over his dinner jacket. They
all bow.*

MISSENA *quietly to Iberin, who has not bowed*:
You ought to bow: this is your sovereign!
*Iberin bows.*

VICEROY:
Good day there, Iberin!

MISSENA:

You come on cue,
My lord! A thorny problem has engaged us.
And Señor Iberin, who's occupied
With an exemplary affair to show
The common people what is right and wrong,
Is rather in a rut.

VICEROY:

I know the case.
Dear Iberin, permit me to reveal
The fish that have so hopelessly enmeshed
Themselves within your closely knotted net.
I hear that you've condemned a wealthy man
To death, because he had his pleasure with
A peasant's daughter. Now he's to be hanged.
The man's a Zik and can't afford to err.

This man right here: is this the wealthy Zik?

INSPECTOR: This is the Zikkish landowner, Your Excellency!

VICEROY:

Can we be sure? Would he wear wooden shoes?
To clear up any lingering doubt I'll lift
His hood – of course there's no doubt really ...
*He tries to take off the hood, but the man pulls it down firmly.*

THE MAN: Leave it alone!

*The inspector removes the hood.*

MISSENA: Why, it's the Zakkish peasant!

VICEROY: And what brings you here?

FARMER CALLAS: I was going to get off two years' rent for this. They said no one would ever hang a landlord!

VICEROY:

Indeed, my friend, indeed. They spoke the truth!
Go fetch the other man!
*Exit the inspector.*

IBERIN *to Callas*:

Would you be hanged
For such a small advantage, wretch?

CALLAS: Not so small, for two years' rent.

VICEROY:

So Iberin: this farmer's daughter once,
For him, submitted to their Zikkish lord.
That lofty justice, which you preach, condemned
The lecherous landed gent to death. But then,
On his behalf – and this you don't yet know,
Although you must approve: it's oh, so just –
The landlord's Zikkish sister paid a visit,
Rather as the Zakkish daughter had,
And offered ... well, what only woman can.
A certain Zak was eager to enjoy
Her favours. Thus you caught a second fish:
The Zik lord's sister. Bring in the second catch!
*Nanna is led in in the clothes of Isabella de Guzman. The clothes are torn and she walks with difficulty, but she is still wearing the veil.*

THE RICH LANDOWNERS:

What's wrong with her? What ails the lady?

INSPECTOR: Your Excellency, we found her lying in the
corridor, with a gag in her mouth and badly beaten up.
According to her, after she'd left the Commander the
soldiers on sentry duty had their way with her.

VICEROY: Is this true?

*Nanna nods.*

THE RICH LANDOWNERS:
Oh shameful! This cries out for vengeance!
You'll pay for this, Iberin! A maiden,
A tender flower of this suffering land,
Of noble blood, and now reduced to this!
Renowned throughout the land for chastity,
A model of virtue, ravaged by the mob!

VICEROY:
That would be hard! Yet here as well you'll find
A kindly fate has saved us from the worst.
It was, no doubt, uncomfortable for her,
And yet discomfort of this sort's her trade.
For, Iberin, I think I know this fish.

*He lifts her veil.*

MISSENA:
The peasant's daughter!

THE RICH LANDOWNERS:
                              Ha, the Zakkish girl!
*They burst into wild laughter.*
A comic masterpiece, dear Iberin!
This is the pack you tried to elevate.
If you heap honour on degenerates
Just look, and learn, what then becomes of honour!
These creatures, for a little cash, will sell
Their Zakkish bodies, even for their own
Tormentors! To us you'll say: it's just a wench,
The daughter of a peasant! But you'd have
Your own supporters say she's just a Zik!
Restore the daughter to her Zakkish father
A second time! Here's your sweet lass, peasant!
In faith, it's too good to be true!

VICEROY:
                              Enough!

This is indeed his daughter. And with that:
Our order is restored. But these were Round Heads ...
*De Guzman is brought in. His sister accompanies him.*
Behold, here come our real Pointed Heads.
Now why, de Guzman, should we pardon you?
I'll tell you why: because your tenant farmer
Is so concerned to see that you don't hang
He'd rather go and face the noose himself.
What's more, we feel we must acquit you since
This farmer's girl would rather sell herself
And work the streets than see you hanged. In short,
We have to set you free: you're so well-loved!
The farmer likewise must of course go free
To pay the rent. *To Callas:* For that's what you must do,
Dear Callas! Set a good example, friend!
For as of now there's even more to pay.
We've had to put those horse-thieves in their place,
You see. And who's to pay for that but you?
Untie the landlord, and the farmer too!
Measure for measure! And freedom for them both!
Live and let live!
*To Iberin:*
           I trust that you agree?
*Iberin nods. Landlord and tenant are released from their chains.*

ISABELLA:
Emanuele! Really free?
DE GUZMAN *smiling*:
           Of course.
CALLAS:
And what about my two years' rent?
VICEROY:
                 Oh no!
That contract was unethical, and void.
ACTRESS PLAYING NANNA:
He's given both their life and liberty
And yet it's clear there's glaring inequality.
They're both alive. Yet this one eats, the while
The other sweats to keep him dining in such style.

The poor man's free to live in peace, and yet the rich
Is free to push him back into the ditch.
They both go free. It has a hopeful sound,
And yet you have to ask yourself where both are bound.

VICEROY:
One more thing, friend, while I bethink me of it.
We know you find life hard, so hark to this:
We didn't come back empty-handed, and
We've brought a little something from our travels:
Your hat is full of holes, so please take mine!
You need a coat, this one will suit you fine!
*He sets the steel helmet on Callas's head and puts the army*
*coat around his shoulders.*
Well, what d'you say to that? Of course, for now
We'd rather see you labour in the fields.
We'll call you when a nobler task is due,
Which may be soon. – Iberin's made a useful
Start, but greater things are called for now.
The kingdom you have started to establish
Needs room to grow, or else it soon may wither.
And, as you know, across the southern seas
Our old ancestral enemy resides,
A fearful nation, peopled with Square Heads,
A threat for which we need to be prepared.
Your task then, Iberin, it is to teach
All Callases about the foreign peril.
For we are on the brink and threshold of
A war of such ferocity we'll need
The services of every honest man.
But now, my friends, let's eat, let's drink and eat!
We'll take this table, which till now has served
The cause of justice, and lay out our feast.
For you, good farmer, there'll be soup at least.

CALLAS *to Nanna*: Did you hear that, they're planning a war?
*The table is brought and laid. The Viceroy, Missena,*
*Isabella and the rich landowners take their seats.*

VICEROY *serving out the soup with huge ladle*:
The farmer first, eh, Señor Iberin?
We'd better feed him well now he's our soldier.

Bring two more plates! And more? We're hungry too.

INSPECTOR: Your Excellency must excuse me, but the farmers from the Sickle who were condemned to death are still waiting to be executed. I suppose they're to be set free too now?

VICEROY: Whatever makes you think that?

INSPECTOR: So the general amnesty in celebration of Your Excellency's return doesn't apply to the Sickle farmers?

VICEROY:
Señor Iberin's judgement stands.
They're to be hanged, I think? But look to Callas
And give my loyal man a generous helping!
*The Hatso brings soup for Callas and his daughter. They sit down on the ground and eat. The Hatso goes to the board and uses his sleeve to wipe out the words 'I landlord and', so that it reads: 'Executions: . . . 200 peasants'. Then he goes and stands behind Callas.*

HATSO:
Eat up your soup Callas, don't be shy
You've just been smarter than the rest, that's why
You've got such rich rewards, you're bright,
And you'll have soup enough – at least tonight.
*The Sickle farmers, including Lopez, are led under the gallows. Drums.*

FARMER LOPEZ *calls to Callas from the gallows*:
Look up Callas, don't try to hide.
Once we stood together on the same side.
We laboured once together, but whereas we awoke
And rose up in rebellion, you still wear the yoke.
They break your neck if you don't bow your head:
The way you stoop you'll still be spooning soup when
   we're long dead.
And yet: we'd rather hear them kick away the stool
Than join with you, and beg for gruel.
When you became a Round Head, when you shut
The door on us and chased us from your hut,
Hung your gun away behind the door
To seek advantage in their courts of law,
You swallowed all their myths that racial health

Would solve the inequalities of wealth.
You stole two horses from your landlord's fief,
Behaving like a common thief.
You thought you'd solve your problems all alone,
At least you'd keep an eye out for your own.
A while they even let you keep the horses,
But only till they'd smashed our Sickle forces.
For you, a Zak, you thought Iberin would provide,
But that turned out an idle wish:
Here Round and Pointed Heads hang side by side,
While there they eat together from one dish.
The old division rears its ugly head:
There's poor, there's rich. And though you said
You'd be a fisherman – you're just the fish.
*During Farmer Lopez's speech Callas and Nanna have
stopped eating their soup. They stand up. The farmers under
the gallows sing 'The Song of the Sickle.'*

THE SONG OF THE SICKLE

Peasants arise!
Open your eyes!
Don't let life pass you by
One day you all must die.
Your chains will only be broken
When you yourselves have spoken.
Open your eyes!
Peasants arise!

THE TENANT FARMERS: Long live the Sickle!
*The drumbeat has got louder, now it drowns out everything
else. Callas has thrown down his and Nanna's soup, he lays
his steel helmet and coat on the ground.*
CALLAS *shouting*: Lopez, Lopez, I wish it could be the
eleventh of September a second time!
*Exit Callas and Nanna. A rosy dawn floods into the palace,
at the Viceroy's table round- and pointed-headed landowners dine together, while at the foot of his gallows
pointed- and round-headed farmers are prepared for execution.*

VICEROY:
  It but remains, dear Iberin, that I
  Assure you of our heartfelt satisfaction.
  For you have managed, by your doctrine
  Of round and pointed heads, to save the state
  From mortal peril, and to resurrect
  The precious order that we know and love.

IBERIN:
  My lord, I think we may be sure this Sickle,
  Once emblem of rebellion and unrest,
  Is now for ever banished from your land
  And from your capital.

VICEROY *smilingly wagging a finger at him*:
                              Quite right, my friend
  So no more Zik and Zak!

IBERIN:
                      Sire, as you wish.

MISSENA *stands up*:
  And yet there's much that has been learnt from this:
  We've learnt to live and feel and breathe as Zaks!
  From this day forwards let our maxim be:
  Peace and peace again, and once more peace.
  And if we must we'll even take up arms
  And fight for a muscular and Zakkish peace!
  If any man resist our peace, may he
  Be broken as the Sickle once was broken
  And smashed as they, with God's help, once were smashed.
  *During his speech a giant gun barrel has been lowered over*
  *the banqueting table.*

VICEROY *lifting his glass*:
  Drink, friends, drink! The status quo, I say!
  *The landowners smoke their cigars and rock together as they*
  *sing this round.*

CHORUS OF LANDED GENTRY

  Perhaps the years to come will just slip by us
  And all those nasty dreams start disappearing.
  Perhaps the rumours we're so sick of hearing
  Were never true, but only sent to try us.

  Perhaps men will forget us, as, if able

We'd all forget the names of those that harm us.
Then we perhaps can once more join the table.
Perhaps they'll let us even die in our pyjamas?

Perhaps they'll cease to curse our names and make them
    bywords?
Perhaps the dark will humanise our faces?
Perhaps our moon will now stay full, with no more phases?
Perhaps in future rain will start falling skywards ...

*When the song is over, the Hatso takes down a wooden
frame that has been leaning against a wall in the courtyard.
He needs it for the executions. Behind it, on the newly
whitewashed wall, a huge red Sickle is revealed. They all see
it, and freeze. The farmers, muted under their hoods, sing
'The Song of the Sickle'.*

THE SONG OF THE SICKLE

Peasants arise!
Open your eyes!
Don't let life pass you by
One day you all must die.
Your chains will only be broken
When you yourselves have spoken.
Open your eyes!
Peasants arise!

# Fear and Misery of the Third Reich

*24 scenes*

*Collaborator*: M. STEFFIN

*Translator*: JOHN WILLETT

*Characters*:

1 TWO SS OFFICERS
2 MAN
  WOMAN
3 SA MAN
  COOK
  MAIDSERVANT
  CHAUFFEUR
  WORKER
4 BRÜHL
  DIEVENBACH
  LOHMANN
  JEHOVAH'S WITNESS
  SS MAN
5 SS MAN
  DETAINEE
  SS OFFICER
6 JUDGE
  INSPECTOR
  PROSECUTOR
  USHER
  MAIDSERVANT
  SENIOR JUDGE
7 TWO PATIENTS
  SURGEON
  SISTER
  THREE ASSISTANTS
  NURSES
8 X AND Y, SCIENTISTS
9 WOMAN
  HUSBAND
10 MAIDSERVANT
  MAN
  WIFE
  BOY
11 DAUGHTER
  MOTHER
12 STUDENT
  YOUNG WORKER
  GROUP LEADER

13 ANNOUNCER
  TWO MALE WORKERS
  WOMAN WORKER
  GENTLEMAN
  SA MAN
14 WOMAN
  SA MEN
  CHILD
  WORKER
  YOUNG WOMAN
15 MAN
  WIFE
  RELEASED MAN
16 OLD WOMAN
  YOUNG WOMAN
  TWO SA MEN
17 TWO BAKERS
18 FARMER
  FARMER'S WIFE
19 PETIT-BOURGEOIS
  TWO WOMEN
  YOUNG FELLOW
  DAIRYWOMAN
  BUTCHER'S WIFE
20 DYING MAN
  WIFE
  SON
  PASTOR
21 FIVE BOYS
  SCHARFÜHRER
22 TWO BOYS
23 NEIGHBOUR
  MAN
  WIFE
24 WOMAN
  TWO WORKERS

## THE GERMAN MARCH-PAST

When He had ruled five years, and they informed us
That He who claimed to have been sent by God
Was ready for His promised war, the steelworks
Had forged tank, gun and warship, and there waited
Within His hangers aircraft in so great a number
That they, leaving the earth at His command
Would darken all the heavens, then we became determined
To see what sort of nation, formed from what sort of
        people
In what condition, what sort of thoughts thinking
He would be calling to His colours. We staged a march-
        past.

See, now they come towards us
A motley sight rewards us
Their banners go before.
To show how straight their course is
They carry crooked crosses
Which double-cross the poor.

Some march along like dummies
Others crawl on their tummies
Towards the war He's planned.
One hears no lamentation
No murmurs of vexation
One only hears the band.

With wives and kids arriving
Five years they've been surviving.
Five more is more than they'll last.
A ramshackle collection
They parade for our inspection
As they come marching past.

# One big family

> First the SS approaches.
> Blown up with beer and speeches .
> They're in a kind of daze.
> Their aim is a People imperious
> Respected and powerful and serious –
> Above all, one that obeys.

*The night of January 30th, 1933. Two SS officers lurching down the street.*

THE FIRST: Top dogs, that's us. That torchlight procession, impressive, what? Broke one moment, next day running the government. Rags to riches in a single day.
*They make water.*

THE SECOND: And now it'll be a united nation. I'm expecting the German people to have an unprecedented moral revival.

THE FIRST: Wait till we've coaxed German Man out from among all those filthy subhumans. Hey, what part of Berlin is this? Not a flag showing.

THE SECOND: We've come the wrong way.

THE FIRST: A horrible sight.

THE SECOND: Lot of crooks round here.

THE FIRST: Think it could be dangerous?

THE SECOND: Decent comrades don't live in such slums.

THE FIRST: Not a light to be seen either.

THE SECOND: Nobody at home.

THE FIRST: That lot are. Catch them coming along to watch the birth of the Third Reich. We'd best cover our rear.
*Staggering, they set off again, the first following the second.*

THE FIRST: Isn't this the bit by the canal?

THE SECOND: Don't ask me.

THE FIRST: Over by the corner's where we cleaned up a bunch of Marxists. Afterwards they said it was a Catholic youth club. Pack of lies. Not one of them was wearing a collar.

THE SECOND: Think he'll really make us a united nation?

THE FIRST: He'll make anything.

*He stops, freezes and listens. Somewhere a window has been opened.*

THE SECOND: Wozzat?

*He pushes forward the safety catch on his revolver. An old man in a nightshirt leans out of the window and is heard softly calling 'Emma, are you there?'*

THE SECOND: That's them!

*He rushes round like a maniac, and starts shooting in every direction.*

THE FIRST *bellows*: Help!

*Behind a window opposite the one where the old man is still standing a terrible cry is heard. Someone has been hit.*


**2**

# A case of betrayal

> The next to appear are the traitors
> Who've given away their neighbours.
> They know that people know.
> If only the street would forget them!
> They could sleep if their conscience would let them
> But there's so far still to go.

*Breslau 1933. Lower-middle-class flat. A man and a woman are standing by the door listening. They are very pale.*

THE WOMAN: They've got to the ground floor.

THE MAN: Not quite.

THE WOMAN: They've smashed the banisters. He'd already passed out when they dragged him out of his flat.

THE MAN: I simply said the sound of foreign broadcasts didn't come from here.

THE WOMAN: That wasn't all you said.

THE MAN: I said nothing more than that.

THE WOMAN: Don't look at me that way. If you said nothing more, then you said nothing more.

THE MAN: That's the point.

THE WOMAN: Why not go round to the police and make a statement saying nobody called there on Saturday?

*Pause.*

THE MAN: Catch me going to the police. It was inhuman, the way they were treating him.

THE WOMAN: He asked for it. What's he want to meddle in politics for?

THE MAN: They didn't have to rip his jacket though. Our sort isn't that well off for clothes.

THE WOMAN: What's a jacket more or less?

THE MAN: They didn't have to rip it.


# 3
# The chalk cross

Here come the brown storm troopers
That keen-eyed squad of snoopers
To check where each man stands
Their job's to put the boot in
Then hang around saluting
With bloodstained empty hands.

*Berlin 1933. Kitchen of a gentleman's house. The SA man, the cook, the maidservant, the chauffeur.*

THE MAIDSERVANT: Did they really only give you half an hour off?

THE SA MAN: Night exercise.

THE COOK: What are all these exercises about?

THE SA MAN: That's an official secret.

THE COOK: Is there a raid on?

THE SA MAN: Like to know, wouldn't you? None of you is going to find out from me. Wild horses wouldn't drag it from me.

THE MAIDSERVANT: So you got to go all the way out to Reinickendorf?

THE SA MAN: Reinickendorf or Rummelsburg or might be Lichtenfelde, why not eh?

THE MAIDSERVANT *somewhat confused*: Won't you have a bit to eat before going off?

THE SA MAN: If you twist my arm. Bring on the field kitchen. *The cook brings in a tray.*
No, you don't catch us talking. Always take the enemy by surprise. Zoom in from an unexpected direction. Look at the way the Führer prepares one of his coups. Like trying to see through a brick wall. No way of telling beforehand. For all I know he can't even tell himself. And then wham! – like that. It's amazing what happens. That's what makes people so frightened of us. *He has tucked in his napkin. With knife and fork poised he enquires*: How about if the gentry suddenly pop in, Anna? Me sitting here with a mouth full of sauce. *Exaggerating as though his mouth was full*: Heil Hitler!

THE MAIDSERVANT: Oh, they'll ring for the car first, won't they, Mr Francke?

THE CHAUFFEUR: What d'you say? Oh, of course.
*Pacified, the SA man starts turning his attention to the tray.*

THE MAIDSERVANT *sitting down beside him*: Don't you feel tired?

THE SA MAN: Bet your life.

THE MAIDSERVANT: But you've got Friday off, haven't you?

THE SA MAN *nods*: If nothing crops up.

THE MAIDSERVANT: Listen. Getting your watch mended was four marks fifty.

THE SA MAN: A bloody scandal.

THE MAIDSERVANT: The watch itself only cost 12 marks.

THE SA MAN: Is that assistant at the hardware shop still as saucy as ever?

THE MAIDSERVANT: Christ alive.

THE SA MAN: You only got to tell me.

THE MAIDSERVANT: I tell you everything anyway. Wearing
your new boots are you?

THE SA MAN *not interested*: Yes, what about it?

THE MAIDSERVANT: Minna, you seen Theo's new boots yet?

THE COOK: No.

THE MAIDSERVANT: Let's have a look, then. That's what
they're giving them now.

*The SA man, his mouth full, stretches out his leg to be
inspected.*

Lovely, aren't they?

*The SA man looks around, seeking something.*

THE COOK: Something missing?

THE SA MAN: Bit dry here.

THE MAIDSERVANT: Like some beer, love? I'll get it.

*She hurries out.*

THE COOK: She'd run her legs off for you, Herr Theo.

THE SA MAN: Yeh, I always do okay. Wham, like that.

THE COOK: You men take a lot for granted, don't you?

THE SA MAN: That's what women want. *Seeing the cook lift a
heavy pot.* What are you breaking your back for? Don't
you bother, that's my job. *He carries the pot for her.*

THE COOK: That's real good of you. You're always finding
things to do for me. Pity other people aren't so considerate.
*With a look at the chauffeur.*

THE SA MAN: Don't have to make a song and dance of it.
We're glad to help.

*There's a knock at the kitchen door.*

THE COOK: That'll be my brother. He's bringing a valve for
the wireless. *She admits her brother, a worker.* My brother.

THE SA MAN *and* THE CHAUFFEUR: Heil Hitler!

*The worker mumbles something that could be taken for
'Heil Hitler' at a pinch.*

THE COOK: Got the valve, have you?

THE WORKER: Yes.

THE COOK: Want to put it in right away?

*The two go out.*

THE SA MAN: What's that fellow do?

THE CHAUFFEUR: Out of a job.

THE SA MAN: Come here often?

THE CHAUFFEUR *shrugging his shoulders*: I'm not here that much.

THE SA MAN: Anyhow the old girl's a hundred per cent for Germany.

THE CHAUFFEUR: You bet.

THE SA MAN: But that wouldn't stop her brother being something quite different.

THE CHAUFFEUR: Got any definite reason to suspect him?

THE SA MAN: Me? No. Never. I never suspect anyone. You suspect somebody, see, and it's the same as being sure, almost. And then the fur will fly.

THE CHAUFFEUR *murmurs*: Wham, like that.

THE SA MAN: That's right. *Leaning back, with one eye shut*: Could you understand what he was mumbling? *He imitates the worker's greeting*: Might have been 'Heil Hitler'. Might not. Me and that lot's old pals.

*He gives a resounding laugh. The cook and the worker return. She sets food before him.*

THE COOK: My brother's that clever with the wireless. And yet he doesn't care a bit about listening to it. If I'd the time I'd always be putting it on. *To the worker*: And you've got more time than you know what to do with, Franz.

THE SA MAN: What's that? Got a wireless and never puts the thing on?

THE WORKER: Bit of music sometimes.

THE COOK: And to think he made himself that smashing set out of twice nothing.

THE SA MAN: How many valves you got then?

THE WORKER *with a challenging stare*: Four.

THE SA MAN: Well, well, no accounting for taste. *To chauffeur*: Is there?

*Maidservant comes back with the beer.*

THE MAIDSERVANT: Ice cold.

THE SA MAN *putting his hand on hers in a friendly way*: You're puffed, girl. No call to rush like that, I wouldn't have minded waiting.

*She pours the bottle out for him.*

THE MAIDSERVANT: Doesn't matter. *Shakes hands with the*

*worker*: Did you bring the valve? Fancy walking all that way here. *To the SA man*: He lives out in Moabit.

THE SA MAN: Hey, where's my beer got to? Somebody's drunk my beer. *To the chauffeur*: Was it you drunk my beer?

THE CHAUFFEUR: No, certainly not. What d'you say that for? Has your beer gone?

THE MAIDSERVANT: But I poured it out for you.

THE SA MAN *to the cook*: You swigged my beer, you did. *Gives a resounding laugh.* Keep your hair on. Little trick they teach you in our squad. How to knock back a beer without being seen or heard. *To the worker*: Did you want to say something?

THE WORKER: That trick's got whiskers.

THE SA MAN: Let's see how you do it then. *He pours him a beer from the bottle.*

THE WORKER: Right. Here I have one beer. *He raises his glass.* And now for the trick. *Calmly and appreciatively he drinks the beer.*

THE COOK: But we all saw you.

THE WORKER *wiping his mouth*: Did you? Then I must have done it wrong.

*The chauffeur laughs aloud.*

THE SA MAN: What's so funny about that?

THE WORKER: You couldn't have done it any different. How did you do it, then?

THE SA MAN: How can I show you when you've drunk up all my beer?

THE WORKER: Of course. That's right. You can't do that trick without beer. D'you know another trick? You people surely know more than one trick.

THE SA MAN: What d'you mean, 'you people'?

THE WORKER: You young fellows.

THE SA MAN: Oh.

THE MAIDSERVANT: But Theo, Mr Lincke was only joking.

THE WORKER *thinks he had better be conciliatory*: Don't mind, do you?

THE COOK: I'll get you another beer.

THE SA MAN: No call for that. I washed my food down all right.

THE COOK: Herr Theo can take a joke.

THE SA MAN *to the worker*: Why not sit down? We won't bite your head off.

*The worker sits down.*

Live and let live. And a joke now and then. Why not? Public opinion, that's the one thing we're really strict about.

THE COOK: A good thing you are.

THE WORKER: And how's public opinion these days?

THE SA MAN: Public opinion these days is fine. You with me there?

THE WORKER: Oh yes. It's just that nobody tells anyone what he thinks.

THE SA MAN: Nobody tells anyone? What d'you mean? They tell me all right.

THE WORKER: Really?

THE SA MAN: Well of course they're not going to come along and tell you all their thoughts. You go to them.

THE WORKER: Where?

THE SA MAN: To the public welfare for instance. In the mornings we'll be at the public welfare.

THE WORKER: That's right, now and again you hear some-body grumbling there.

THE SA MAN: You see?

THE WORKER: But that way all you can do is catch them once, then they know you. And after that they'll clam up again.

THE SA MAN: Why should they know me? Shall I show you why they don't? Interested in tricks, aren't you? No reason why I shouldn't show you one, we've got plenty. I always say if they only realised what a lot we've got up our sleeve, and how they'll never survive whatever happens, then perhaps they'd pack it in.

THE MAIDSERVANT: Go on, Theo, tell them how you do it.

THE SA MAN: Right. Let's suppose we're at the public welfare in the Münzstrasse. Let's say you – *looking at the worker* – are in the line ahead of me. But I got to make a few preparations first. *He goes out.*

THE WORKER *winking at the chauffeur*: So now we're getting a chance to see how they do it.

THE COOK: They're going to smell out all the Marxists because they got to be stopped disrupting everything.

THE WORKER: Is that it?

*The SA man comes back.*

THE SA MAN: I'd be in civvies of course. *To the worker*: Okay, start grumbling.

THE WORKER: What about?

THE SA MAN: Go on, you've got something on your chest. Your lot always have.

THE WORKER: Me? No.

THE SA MAN: You're a tough guy, aren't you? Don't tell me you think everything's a hundred per cent.

THE WORKER: Why not?

THE SA MAN: All right, let's call it off. If you won't play the whole thing's off.

THE WORKER: All right then. I'll shoot my mouth off for you. These buggers keep you hanging about as if we'd all the time in the world. Two hours it took me to get here from Rummelsburg.

THE SA MAN: What the hell. Don't tell me the distance from Rummelsburg to the Münzstrasse is any further under Hitler than it was under that racketeering Republic. Come on, you can do better than that.

THE COOK: It's only play acting, Franz, we all know what you say won't be your real opinions.

THE MAIDSERVANT: Don't you see you're just acting a grumbler? Theo won't take it amiss, you can depend on it. He just wants to show us something.

THE WORKER: Right. In that case I'll say. The SA looks very fine, but I think it's shit. Give me the Maxists and the Jews.

THE COOK: Franz! Really!

THE MAIDSERVANT: How can you say that, Mr Lincke?

THE SA MAN *laughing*: For Christ sake! I'd just turn you over to the nearest cop. Not got much imagination, have you? Look, you've got to say something you might be able to wriggle out of. Sort of thing you'd hear in real life.

THE WORKER: All right, then you'll have to give me a hand and provoke me.

THE SA MAN: That went out years ago. Suppose I said 'Our Führer's the greatest man there's ever been, greater than Jesus Christ and Napoleon rolled into one,' all you'd say was 'You bet he is.' So I'd best take the other road and say: 'They're a big-mouthed lot. You know the one about Goebbels and the two fleas? Well, the two fleas had a bet who could get from one side of his mouth to the other quickest. The winner was the one went round the back of his head. It wasn't so far that way.

THE CHAUFFEUR: Ha.

*All laugh.*

THE SA MAN *to the worker*: Now it's your turn to make a crack.

THE WORKER: I can't cap a story like that bang off. Telling the joke wouldn't stop you being an informer.

THE MAIDSERVANT: He's right, Theo.

THE SA MAN: You're a right bunch of turds. Make me sick, you do. Not a bloody soul got the guts to open his mouth.

THE WORKER: Is that what you really think, or is it what you say at the public welfare?

THE SA MAN: I say it at the public welfare too.

THE WORKER: In that case what I say at the public welfare is Look before you leap. I'm a coward. I don't carry a gun.

THE SA MAN: Right, brother, if you're going to be so careful about looking, let me tell you you can look and look, then all of a sudden you're in the voluntary labour service.

THE WORKER: And if you don't look?

THE SA MAN: Then you'll be in it just the same. Sure. It's voluntary, see? Voluntary's good, don't you think?

THE WORKER: That's where it might be possible for some daring fellow to make a joke or two about the Voluntary Labour Service, suppose both of you were standing at the Public Welfare and you gave him one of those looks with your blue eyes. I wonder what he could say. Maybe: another fifteen went off yesterday. Funny how they get them to do it, when you think it's all voluntary and folk are paid no more for doing something than for doing nothing though they must need to eat more. Then I heard the one about Dr Ley and the cat and of course I saw the whole thing. You know that story?

THE SA MAN: No, we don't.

THE WORKER: Well, Dr Ley went on this little Strength Through Joy trip, strictly on business, and he met one of those former Weimar party bosses – I'm not up in all their names, anyway it might have been in a concentration camp though Dr Ley's got much too much sense to visit one of those – and the old boss asked him how'd he get the workers to swallow all the things they usedn't to put up with at any price. Dr Ley pointed to a cat lying in the sun and said: suppose you wanted to give that cat a mouthful of mustard and make her swallow it whether she wanted or not. How would you do it? Boss takes the mustard and smears it over the cat's chops; of course it spits it back in his face, no question of swallowing, just a lot of bloody scratches. No, old boy, says Dr Ley in his endearing way, you got the wrong approach. Now watch me. He takes the mustard with a practised follow-through and sticks it abracadabra up the wretched beast's arsehole. *To the ladies*: Excuse my French, but that's part of the story. – Numbed and stunned by the frightful pain, cat instantly sets to licking out the lot. There you are, my dear fellow, says the triumphant Dr Ley, she's eating it. And voluntarily at that! *They laugh.*

THE WORKER: Yes, it's very funny.

THE SA MAN: That's got things going. Voluntary Labour Service, that's a favourite subject. Trouble is: nobody bothers to dig his toes in. Oh, they can make us eat shit and we'll still say thank you for it.

THE WORKER: I'm not so sure about that. There am I the other day on the Alexanderplatz wondering whether to volunteer for the Voluntary Labour Service spontaneous-like or wait till they shove me in. Over from the grocer's on the corner comes a skinny little woman, must be some proletarian's wife. Half a mo, says I, what are the proletarians doing in the Third Reich when we've got national unity and even Baron Thyssen is in it? No, says she, not when they've gone and put up the price of marge. From fifty pfennigs to one mark. You trying to tell me that's national unity? Better mind out, ma, says I, what you're saying to me, I'm patriotic to the backbone. All bones and no meat, says she, and chaff in the bread. She was that worked up. I just stand there mumbling: best get butter then. It's better for you. Mustn't skimp on your food, cause that saps the people's strength and we can't afford that what with so many enemies encircling us even in the top civil service ... we been warned. No, says she, we're all of us Nazis so long as we got breath in our bodies, what mayn't be long now in view of the war menace. Only the other day I got to offer my best sofa to the Winter Aid, says she, cause I hear Goering's having to sleep on the floor he's that worried about our raw materials, and in the office they say they'd rather have a piano – you know, for Strength Through Joy. And no proper flour to be had. I takes my sofa away from the Winter Aid People and goes to the second-hand dealer round the corner, I been meaning to buy half a pound of butter for some time. And at the dairy they tell me: no butter today, comrade, would you like some guns? I say, give me, says she. I say: come on what d'you want guns for, ma? On an empty stomach? No, says she, if I'm going to be hungry they should be shot, the whole lot of them starting with Hitler at the top ... Come on, says I, come on, exclaims I appalled ... With Hitler at the top we'll conquer France, says she. Now we're getting our petrol from wool. And the wool? says I. The wool, says she: these days that's made from petrol. Wool's another thing we need. Any time a bit of good stuff from the old days reaches the Winter Aid the lot that run the place grab it for themselves, says she. If Hitler only knew, says they, but he knows nothing the poor lamb, never went to secondary school they say. I was struck dumb by so much subversiveness. You just stay here, young lady, says I, I got to make a call at police headquarters. But when I come back with an officer what d'you you think, she's cleared off. *Stops play-acting.* What d'you say to that, eh?

THE SA MAN *still acting*: Me? What do I say? Well, I might

give a reproachful look. You went straight round to the police, I might say. Can't risk talking freely when you're around.

THE WORKER: I should think not. Not with me. You confide in me, you'll be done. I know my duty as a comrade: any time my own mother mutters something to me about the price of margarine or something I go straight to the local SA office. I'll denounce my own brother for grumbling about the Voluntary Labour Service. As for my girl, when she tells me 'Heil Hitler' she's got pregnant at a work camp then I have them bring her in: we can't have abortions because if we made exceptions for our nearest and dearest the Third Reich would run out of manpower, and the Third Reich's what we love best. – Was that more like it? Did I act all right?

THE SA MAN: I guess that'll do. *Goes on acting.* You'll be okay, go and draw your benefit, we've all understood, eh brothers? But you can count on me, my friend, 'nuff said, mum's the word. *He slaps him on the shoulder. No longer acting:* Right, then in you go into the office and they'll pick you up bang off.

THE WORKER: What, without you leaving the line and following me in?

THE SA MAN: Yeh.

THE WORKER: And without you giving someone a wink, which might look fishy?

THE SA MAN: Without me winking.

THE WORKER: How's it done then?

THE SA MAN: Ha, you'd like to know that trick. Well, stand up, and show us your back. *He turns him round by the shoulders, so that everyone can see his back. Then to the maidservant:* Seen it?

THE MAIDSERVANT: Look, he's got a white cross on it.

THE COOK: Right between his shoulders.

THE CHAUFFEUR: So he has.

THE SA MAN: And how did he get it? *Shows the palm of his hand.* See, just a little white chalk cross and there's its impression large as life.

*The worker takes off his jacket and looks at the cross.*

THE WORKER: Nice work.

THE SA MAN: Not bad, eh? I always have my chalk on me. Ah, you have to use your loaf, things don't always go according to the book. *With satisfaction*: Well, so it's off to Reinickendorf. *Corrects himself*: That's where my aunt lives, you know. You lot don't seem very enthusiastic. *To the maidservant*: What are you gawping like that for, Anna? Missed the whole point of the trick, I suppose?

THE MAIDSERVANT: Of course not. Think I'm silly or something?

THE SA MAN *as if the whole joke has gone sour, stretches his hand out to her*: Wipe it off.

*She washes his hand with a rag.*

THE COOK: You've got to use those sort of methods so long as they keep on trying to undermine everything our Führer has built up and what makes other people so envious of us.

THE CHAUFFEUR: What was that? Oh yes, quite so. *Looks at his watch*. Well, time to wash the car again. Heil Hitler! *Exit.*

THE SA MAN: What kind of a fellow's that?

THE MAIDSERVANT: Keeps himself to himself. Not a bit political.

THE WORKER: Well, Minna, I'd better be off. No hard feelings about the beer, eh? And let me say I'm surer than ever that no one's going to complain about the Third Reich and get away with it. That's set my mind at rest. Me, I don't ever come across that sort of subversive element. I'd gladly confront them if I did. Only I'm not quite so quick to the punch as you. *Clearly and distinctly*: All right, Minna, thanks a lot and Heil Hitler!

THE OTHERS: Heil Hitler!

THE SA MAN: Take a tip from me and don't be quite so innocent. It attracts attention. No call to have to watch your mouth with me, I can take a joke now and again. All right: Heil Hitler!

*The worker goes.*

THE SA MAN: Bit sudden the way those two cleared out. Something's put ants in their pants. I shouldn't have said that about Reinickendorf. They're waiting to pounce on that sort of thing.

THE MAIDSERVANT: There's something else I wanted to ask you, Theo.

THE SA MAN: Fire away, any time.

THE COOK: I'm off to put out the laundry. I was young once too. *Exit.*

THE SA MAN: What is it?

THE MAIDSERVANT: But I shan't ask unless I can see you won't mind; otherwise I'll say nothing.

THE SA MAN: Spit it out, then.

THE MAIDSERVANT: It's just that ... I don't like saying ... well, I need 20 marks from your account.

THE SA MAN: Twenty marks?

THE MAIDSERVANT: There you are, you *do* mind.

THE SA MAN: Twenty marks out of our savings account, can't expect me to give three cheers. What do you want it for?

THE MAIDSERVANT: I'd rather not say.

THE SA MAN: So. You're not saying. That's a laugh.

THE MAIDSERVANT: I know you won't agree with me, Theo, so I'd sooner not give my reasons yet awhile.

THE SA MAN: Well, if you don't trust me ...

THE MAIDSERVANT: Of course I trust you.

THE SA MAN: So you want to give up having a joint savings account?

THE MAIDSERVANT: How can you say that? If I take out twenty marks I'll still have ninety-seven marks left.

THE SA MAN: No need to do sums for my benefit. I know how much there is. I just think you're wanting to break it off, probably because you're flirting with someone else. Perhaps you'll be wanting to check our statement too.

THE MAIDSERVANT: I'm not flirting with anyone else.

THE SA MAN: Then tell me what it's for.

THE MAIDSERVANT: You don't want to let me have it.

THE SA MAN: How am I to tell it isn't for something wrong?

THE MAIDSERVANT: It's not anything wrong, and if I didn't need it I wouldn't call for it, you must know that.

THE SA MAN: I don't know nothing. All I know is the whole business strikes me as rather fishy. Why should you suddenly need twenty marks? It's quite a bit of money. You pregnant?

THE MAIDSERVANT: No.

THE SA MAN: Sure?

THE MAIDSERVANT: Yes.

THE SA MAN: If I thought for a minute you were planning anything illegal, if I caught a whiff of that kind of thing, I'd be down like a ton of bricks, let me tell you. You might just have heard that any interference with our burgeoning fruit is the worst crime you can commit. If the German people stopped multiplying itself it would be all up with our historic mission.

THE MAIDSERVANT: But Theo, I don't know what you're talking about. It's nothing like that, I'd have told you if it was because you'd be involved too. But if that's what you're thinking then let me tell you. It's just I want to help Frieda buy a winter coat.

THE SA MAN: And why can't your sister buy her coats for herself?

THE MAIDSERVANT: How could she on her disability pension, it's twenty-six marks eighty a month.

THE SA MAN: What about our Winter Aid? But that's just it, you've no confidence in our National Socialist state. I can tell that anyway from the sort of conversations that go on in this kitchen. Do you think I didn't see what a long face you pulled at my experiment?

THE MAIDSERVANT: What do you mean by a long face?

THE SA MAN: You pulled one all right. Just like our friends who cleared out so suddenly.

THE MAIDSERVANT: If you really want to know what I think, I don't like that kind of thing.

THE SA MAN: And what is it you don't like, may I ask?

THE MAIDSERVANT: The way you catch those poor down-and-outs by dressing up and playing tricks and all that. My father's unemployed too.

THE SA MAN: Ha, that's all I needed to hear. As if talking to that fellow Lincke hadn't already set me thinking.

THE MAIDSERVANT: Do you mean to say you're going to nail

him for what he did just to please you and with all of us
egging him on?

THE SA MAN: I'm not saying nothing. As I already told you.
And if you've anything against what I'm doing as part of
my duty then let me say just look in *Mein Kampf* and you'll
see how the Führer himself didn't think it beneath him to
test the people's attitude of mind, and it was actually his job
for a while when he was in the army and it was all for
Germany and the consequences were tremendously important.

THE MAIDSERVANT: If that's your line, Theo, then I'd just
like to know if I can have the twenty marks. That's all.

THE SA MAN: Then all I can say to you is I'm not in the mood
to have anything taken off me.

THE MAIDSERVANT: What do you mean, taken off you?
Whose money is it, yours or mine?

THE SA MAN: That's a nice way to be speaking about our joint
money all of a sudden. I suppose that's why we purged the
Jews from the life of our nation, so we could have our own
kith and kin suck our blood instead?

THE MAIDSERVANT: How can you say things like that on
account of twenty marks?

THE SA MAN: I've plenty of expenses. My boots alone set me
back twenty-seven marks.

THE MAIDSERVANT: But weren't they issued to you?

THE SA MAN: That's what we thought. And that's why I took
the better kind, the ones with gaiters. Then they demanded
payment and we were stung.

THE MAIDSERVANT: Twenty-seven marks for boots? So what
other expenses were there?

THE SA MAN: What d'you mean, other expenses?

THE MAIDSERVANT: Didn't you say you had lots of expenses?

THE SA MAN: Forgotten what they were. Anyway I'm not
here to be cross-examined. Keep your hair on, I'm not
going to swindle you. And as for the twenty marks I'll
think it over.

THE MAIDSERVANT *weeping*: Theo, I just can't believe you'd
tell me the money was all right and it wasn't true. Oh now I

don't know what to think. Surely there's twenty marks left in the savings bank out of all that money?

THE SA MAN *slapping her on the shoulder*: But nobody's suggesting for a minute that there's nothing left in our savings bank. Out of the question. You know you can rely on me. You trust something to me, it's like locking it in the safe. Well, decided to trust Theo again, have you?
*She weeps without replying.*

THE SA MAN: It's just nerves, you've been working too hard. Well, time I went off to that night exercise. I'll be coming for you on Friday, then. Heil Hitler! *Exit.*
*The maidservant tries to suppress her tears and walks distractedly up and down the kitchen. The cook comes back with a basket of linen.*

THE COOK: What's wrong? Had a quarrel? Theo's such a splendid boy. Pity there aren't more like him. Nothing serious, is it?

THE MAIDSERVANT *still weeping*: Minna, can't you go out to your brother's and tell him to watch out for himself?

THE COOK: What for?

THE MAIDSERVANT: Just watch out, I mean.

THE COOK: On account of tonight? You can't be serious. Theo would never do such a thing.

THE MAIDSERVANT: I don't know what to think any longer, Minna. He's changed so. They've completely ruined him. He's keeping bad company. Four years we've been going out together, and now it seems to me just as though . . . I even feel like asking you to look at my shoulder and see if there's a white cross on it.

# 4

## Peat-bog soldiers

With storm troopers parading
These men carry on debating
What Lenin and Kautsky meant
Till, clutching the tomes they've cited

They're forcibly united
By joint imprisonment.

*Esterwegen concentration camp, 1934. Some prisoners are mixing cement.*

BRÜHL *softly to Dievenbach*: I'd steer clear of Lohmann; he talks.

DIEVENBACH *aloud*: Oi, Lohmann, here's Brühl saying I should steer clear of you; you talk.

BRÜHL: Bastard.

LOHMANN: That's good coming from you, you bloody Judas. Why did Karl get given solitary?

BRÜHL: Nothing to do with me. Was it me got cigarettes from God knows where?

THE JEHOVAH'S WITNESS: Look out.
*The SS sentry up on the embankment goes by.*

THE SS MAN: Someone was talking here. Who was it? *Nobody answers.* If that happens just once more it'll be solitary confinement for the lot of you, get me? Now sing! *The prisoners sing verse 1 of the 'Song of the Peat-bog Soldiers'. The SS man moves on.*

PRISONERS:
See, whichever way one gazes
Naught but boggy heath lies there.
Not one bird his sweet voice raises
In those oak trees gaunt and bare.
  We are the peat-bog soldiers
  With shovels on our shoulders
  We march.

THE JEHOVAH'S WITNESS: Why do you people carry on quarrelling even now?

DIEVENBACH: Don't you worry, Jehovah, you wouldn't understand. *Indicating Brühl*: Yesterday his party voted for Hitler's foreign policy in the Reichstag. And he – *indicating Lohmann* – thinks Hitler's foreign policy means war.

BRÜHL: Not with us around.

LOHMANN: Last war we had you were around all right.

BRÜHL: Anyway the German armed forces are too weak.

LOHMANN: Still, your lot did at least bring Hitler a battle-cruiser as part of the wedding deal.

THE JEHOVAH'S WITNESS *to Dievenbach*: What were you? Communist or Social-democrat?

DIEVENBACH: I kept outside all that.

LOHMANN: But you're inside now all right, inside a camp I mean.

THE JEHOVAH'S WITNESS: Look out.

*The SS man appears again. He watches them. Slowly Brühl starts singing the third verse of the 'Song of the Peat-bog Soldiers'. The SS man moves on.*

BRÜHL:
Back and forth the guards keep pacing
Not a soul can get away.
Shots for those who try escaping
Thick barbed wire for those who stay.
   We are the peat-bog soldiers
   With shovels on our shoulders
   We march.

LOHMANN *hurls his shovel from him*: When I think I'm only in here because your lot sabotaged the united front I could bash your bloody brains out right now.

BRÜHL: Ha! 'Like your brother must I be/Or you'll turn and clobber me' – is that it? United front indeed. Softly softly catchee monkey: would have suited you nicely to sneak all our members away, wouldn't it?

LOHMANN: When you'd rather have Hitler sneak them away, like now. You traitors!

BRÜHL *furiously takes his shovel and brandishes it at Lohmann, who holds his own shovel at the ready*: I'll teach you something you won't forget!

THE JEHOVAH'S WITNESS: Look out.

*He hastily starts singing the last verse of the 'Song of the Peat-bog Soldiers'. The SS man reappears and the others join in as they resume mixing their cement.*

We've no use for caterwauling.
Sunshine follows after rain.
One day soon you'll hear us calling:

Homeland, you are ours again.
  And then we peat-bog soldiers
  Will rise, throw back our shoulders
  And march.

THE SS MAN: Which of you shouted 'Traitors'?
*Nobody answers.*
THE SS MAN: You people never learn, do you? *To Lohmann:*
Which?
*Lohmann stares at Brühl and says nothing.*
THE SS MAN *to Dievenbach:* Which?
*Dievenbach says nothing.*
THE SS MAN *to the Jehovah's Witness:* Which?
*The Jehovah's Witness says nothing.*
THE SS MAN *to Brühl:* Which?
*Brühl says nothing.*
THE SS MAN: I shall count up to five, then it'll be solitary
confinement for the whole lot of you till you turn blue.
*He waits for five seconds. They all stand in silence staring
straight ahead.*
THE SS MAN: So it's solitary.


## 5
## Servants of the people

  The camps are run by warders
  Narks, butchers and marauders –
  The people's servants they
  They'll crush you and assail you
  And flog you and impale you
  For negligible pay.

*Oranienburg concentration camp, 1934. A small yard
between the huts. In the darkness a sound of flogging. As it
gets light an SS man is seen flogging a detainee. An SS officer
stands in the background smoking; with his back to the scene.
Then he goes off.*

THE SS MAN *sits down on a barrel, exhausted*: Work on.

*The detainee rises from the ground and starts unsteadily cleaning the drains.*

Why can't you say no when they ask if you're a communist, you cunt? It means the lash for you and I have to stay in barracks. I'm so fucking tired. Why can't they give the job to Klapproth? He enjoys this sort of thing. Look, if that bastard comes round again – *he listens* – you're to take the whip and flog the ground hard as you can, right?

THE DETAINEE: Yes, sir.

THE SS MAN: But only because you buggers have flogged me out, right?

THE DETAINEE: Yes, sir.

THE SS MAN: Here he comes.

*Steps are heard outside, and the SS man points to the whip. The detainee picks it up and flogs the ground. This doesn't sound authentic, so the SS man idly points to a nearby basket which the detainee then flogs. The steps outside come to a stop. The SS man abruptly rises in some agitation, snatches the whip and begins beating the detainee.*

THE DETAINEE *softly*: Not my stomach.

*The SS man hits him on the bottom. The SS officer looks in.*

THE SS OFFICER: Flog his stomach.

*The SS man beats the detainee's stomach.*


6

## Judicial process

> The judges follow limply.
> They were told that justice is simply
> What serves our People best.
> They objected: how are we to know that?
> But they'll soon be interpreting it so that
> The whole people is under arrest.

*Augsburg 1934. Consultation room in a court building. A milky January morning can be seen through the window. A spherical gas lamp is still burning. The district judge is just putting on his robes. There is a knock.*

THE JUDGE: Come in.

*Enter the police inspector.*

THE INSPECTOR: Good morning, your honour.

THE JUDGE: Good morning, Mr Tallinger. It's about the case of Häberle, Schünt and Gaunitzer. I must admit the whole affair is a bit beyond me.

THE INSPECTOR: ?

THE JUDGE: I understand from the file that the shop where the incident occurred – Arndt's the jeweller's – is a Jewish one?

THE INSPECTOR: ?

THE JUDGE: And presumably Häberle, Schünt and Gaunitzer are still members of Storm Troop 7?

*The inspector nods.*

THE JUDGE: Which means that the Troop saw no reason to discipline them?

*The inspector shakes his head.*

THE JUDGE: All the same, I take it the Troop must have instituted some kind of inquiry in view of the disturbance which the incident caused in the neighbourhood?

*The inspector shrugs his shoulders.*

THE JUDGE: I would appreciate it, Tallinger, if you would give me a brief summary before we go into court. Would you?

THE INSPECTOR *mechanically*: On 2 December 1933 at 0815 hours SA men Häberle, Schünt and Gaunitzer forced their way into Arndt's jewellers in the Schlettowstrasse and after a brief exchange of words wounded Mr Arndt age 54 on the head. The material damage amounted to a total of eleven thousand two hundred and thirty-four marks. Inquiries were instituted by the criminal investigation department on 7 December 1933 and led to . . .

THE JUDGE: Come on, Tallinger, that's all in the files. *He points irritably at the charge sheet, which consists of a single page.* This is the flimsiest and sloppiest made-out indictment I've ever seen, not that the last few months have been much of a picnic, let me tell you. But it does say that much.

I was hoping you might be able to tell me a bit about the background.

THE INSPECTOR: Yes, your honour.

THE JUDGE: Well, then?

THE INSPECTOR: There isn't any background to this case, your honour, so to speak.

THE JUDGE: Tallinger, are you trying to tell me it's all clear as daylight?

THE INSPECTOR *grinning*: Clear as daylight: no.

THE JUDGE: Various items of jewellery are alleged to have vanished in the course of the incident. Have they been recovered?

THE INSPECTOR: Not to my knowledge: no.

THE JUDGE: ?

THE INSPECTOR: Your honour, I've got a family.

THE JUDGE: So have I, Tallinger.

THE INSPECTOR: Yes, sir.

*Pause.*

THE INSPECTOR: This Arndt fellow is a Jew, you know.

THE JUDGE: So one would infer from the name.

THE INSPECTOR: Yes, sir. There's been a rumour for some time in the neighbourhood that there was a case of racial profanation.

THE JUDGE *begins to get a glimmer*: Indeed. Involving whom?

THE INSPECTOR: Arndt's daughter. She's nineteen and supposed to be pretty.

THE JUDGE: Was there any official follow-up?

THE INSPECTOR *reluctantly*: Well, no. The rumour died a natural death.

THE JUDGE: Who set it going?

THE INSPECTOR: The landlord of the building. A certain Mr von Miehl.

THE JUDGE: I suppose he wanted the Jewish shop out of his building?

THE INSPECTOR: That's what we thought. But then he seems to have changed his line.

THE JUDGE: At least that would explain why there was a certain amount of resentment against Arndt round there.

Leading these young people to act from a kind of upsurge
of national feeling . . .

THE INSPECTOR *firmly*: I wouldn't say that, your honour.

THE JUDGE: What wouldn't you say?

THE INSPECTOR: That Häberle, Schünt and Gaunitzer will
try to get much mileage out of the racial profanation
business.

THE JUDGE: Why not?

THE INSPECTOR: As I told you, there hasn't been any official
mention of the name of the Aryan involved. It could be
anyone. Anywhere there's a bunch of Aryans you might
find him, you get me? And where d'you find those bunches
of Aryans? In other words the SA don't want this dragged
up.

THE JUDGE *impatiently*: Why tell me about it, then?

THE INSPECTOR: Because you said you'd got a family. To
stop you dragging it up. Any of the local witnesses might
mention it.

THE JUDGE: I see. But I can't see much else.

THE INSPECTOR: The less the better, if you want my personal
opinion.

THE JUDGE: It's easy for you to say that. I have to deliver a
judgement.

THE INSPECTOR *vaguely*: That's right . . .

THE JUDGE: So we're left with a direct provocation on
Arndt's part, or else there's no way of explaining what
happened.

THE INSPECTOR: Just what I'd say myself, your honour.

THE JUDGE: Then how were those SA people provoked?

THE INSPECTOR: According to their statements: partly by
Arndt himself and partly by some unemployed man he'd
got in to sweep the snow. Apparently they were on their
way to have a beer together and as they passed the shop
there were Wagner the unemployed man and Arndt himself
standing in the doorway and shouting vulgar terms of abuse
at them.

THE JUDGE: I don't suppose they have any witnesses, have
they?

THE INSPECTOR: Oh, they have. The landlord – you know,

von Miehl – said he was at the window and saw Wagner provoking the SA men. And Arndt's partner, a man called Stau, was round at Troop HQ the same afternoon and admitted in front of Häberle, Schünt and Gaunitzer that Arndt had always talked disparagingly about the SA, to him too.

THE JUDGE: Oh, so Arndt's got a partner? Aryan?

THE INSPECTOR: Aryan: what else? Can you really see him taking on a Jew as his front man?

THE JUDGE: But the partner wouldn't go and give evidence against him?

THE INSPECTOR *slyly*: Who's to say?

THE JUDGE *irritated*: What do you mean? There's no way the firm can claim damages if it can be proved that Arndt provoked Häberle, Schünt and Gaunitzer to assault him.

THE INSPECTOR: What makes you think Stau's interested in claiming damages?

THE JUDGE: I don't get you. Surely he's a partner?

THE INSPECTOR: That's it.

THE JUDGE: ?

THE INSPECTOR: We've found out – unofficially of course and off the record – that Stau's a regular visitor to Troop HQ. He used to be in the SA and may still be. Probably that's what made Arndt make him a partner. What's more, Stau's already been mixed up in a similar affair, where the SA dropped in on someone. They picked the wrong man that time and it took quite a bit of effort to get it all swept under the mat. Of course that's not to say that in our particular case Stau ... Well, anyhow he's someone to be careful of. I hope you'll treat this as completely confidential, given what you said about your family earlier.

THE JUDGE *shaking his head*: I don't quite see how it can be in Mr Stau's interest for his business to lose more than eleven thousand marks.

THE INSPECTOR: Yes, the jewellery has disappeared. Anyhow Häberle, Schünt and Gaunitzer haven't got it. And they haven't fenced it either.

THE JUDGE: Indeed.

THE INSPECTOR: Stau naturally can't be expected to keep

Arndt on as his partner if Arndt can be shown to have acted
in a provocative way. And any loss he has caused will have
to be made up to Stau, see?

THE JUDGE: Yes, I do indeed see. *For a moment he looks
thoughtfully at the inspector, who resumes his blank official
expression.* Yes, then I suppose the long and the short of it
will be that Arndt provoked the SA men. It seems that the
fellow had made himself generally disliked. Didn't you tell
me that the goings-on in his own family had already led the
landlord to complain? Ah well, I know this shouldn't really
be dragged up, but anyway we can take it that there will be
relief in those quarters if he moves out shortly. Thank you
very much, Tallinger, you've been a great help.

*The judge gives the inspector a cigar. The inspector leaves.
In the doorway he meets the official prosecutor, who is just
entering.*

THE PROSECUTOR *to the judge*: Can I have a word with you?

THE JUDGE *as he peels an apple for his breakfast*: You can
indeed.

THE PROSECUTOR: It's about the case of Häberle, Schünt and
Gaunitzer.

THE JUDGE *otherwise occupied*: Yes?

THE PROSECUTOR: It seems quite a straightforward case on
the face of it . . .

THE JUDGE: Right. I really don't see why your department
decided to prosecute, if you don't mind my saying so.

THE PROSECUTOR: What do you mean? The case has caused a
deplorable stir in the neighbourhood. Even members of the
party have thought it ought to be cleared up.

THE JUDGE: I simply see it as a plain case of Jewish
provocation, that's all.

THE PROSECUTOR: Oh, rubbish, Goll! Don't imagine our
indictments can be dismissed so lightly just because they
seem a bit tersely expressed these days. I could have guessed
you'd blithely settle for the most obvious interpretation.
Better not make a boob of this. It doesn't take long to get
transferred to the Silesian backwoods. And it's not all that
cosy there these days.

THE JUDGE *puzzled, stops eating his apple*: I don't understand

that one little bit. Are you seriously telling me you propose
to let the Jew Arndt go free?

THE PROSECUTOR *expansively*: You bet I am. The fellow had
no idea of provoking anyone. Are you suggesting that
because he's Jewish he can't expect justice in the courts of
the Third Reich? That's some pretty queer opinions you're
venting there, Goll.

THE JUDGE *irritably*: I was venting no opinions whatever. I
simply concluded that Häberle, Schünt and Gaunitzer were
provoked.

THE PROSECUTOR: But can't you see it wasn't Arndt who
provoked them but that unemployed fellow, what's his
damn name, the one clearing the snow, yes, Wagner?

THE JUDGE: There's not one single word about that in your
indictment, my dear Spitz.

THE PROSECUTOR: Of course not. It merely came to the
attention of the Prosecutor's office that those SA men had
made an assault on Arndt. Which meant that we were
officially bound to take action. But if witness von Miehl
should testify in court that Arndt wasn't in the street at all
during the dispute, whereas that unemployed fellow, what's
his damn name, yes, Wagner, was hurling insults at the SA,
then it will have to be taken into account.

THE JUDGE *tumbling to earth*: Is that what von Miehl is
supposed to be saying? But he's the landlord who wants to
get Arndt out of his building. He's not going to give
evidence for him.

THE PROSECUTOR: Come on, what have you got against von
Miehl? Why shouldn't he tell the truth under oath? Perhaps
you don't realise that, quite apart from the fact that he's in
the SS, von Miehl has pretty good contacts in the Ministry
of Justice? My advice to you, Goll old man, is to treat him
as a man of honour.

THE JUDGE: That's what I'm doing. After all, you can't call it
exactly dishonourable these days not to want a Jewish shop
in one's building.

THE PROSECUTOR *generously*: If the fellow pays his rent . . .

THE JUDGE *diplomatically*: I believe he's supposed to have
reported him already on another matter . . .

THE PROSECUTOR: So you're aware of that? But who told you it was in order to get the fellow out? Particularly as the complaint was withdrawn? That suggests something more like a particularly close understanding, wouldn't you say? My dear Goll, how can you be so naive?

THE JUDGE *now getting really annoyed*: My dear Spitz, it's not that simple. The partner I thought would want to cover him wants to report him, and the landlord who reported him wants to cover him. You have to know the ins and outs.

THE PROSECUTOR: What do we draw our pay for?

THE JUDGE: Shockingly mixed-up business. Have a Havana? *The prosecutor takes a Havana and they smoke in silence. Then the judge gloomily reflects.*

THE JUDGE: But suppose it's established in court that Arndt never provoked anybody, then he can go on and sue the SA for damages.

THE PROSECUTOR: To start with he can't sue the SA but only Häberle, Schünt and Gaunitzer, who haven't a penny – that's if he doesn't simply have to make do with that unemployed fellow, what's his damn name ... got it, Wagner. *With emphasis*: Secondly he may think twice before suing members of the SA.

THE JUDGE: Where is he at the moment?

THE PROSECUTOR: In hospital.

THE JUDGE: And Wagner?

THE PROSECUTOR: In a concentration camp.

THE JUDGE *with a certain relief*: Oh well, in those circumstances I don't suppose Arndt will be wanting to sue the SA. And Wagner won't be particularly keen to make a big thing of his innocence. But the SA aren't going to be all that pleased if the Jew gets off scot free.

THE PROSECUTOR: The SA will have proof in court that they were provoked. By the Jew or by the Marxist, it's all the same to them.

THE JUDGE *still dubious*: Not entirely. After all the dispute between the SA and the unemployed man did result in damage to the shop. Storm Troop 7 isn't altogether in the clear.

THE PROSECUTOR: Oh well, you can't have everything. You'll never be able to satisfy all parties. As for which you should aim to satisfy, that's a matter for your sense of patriotism, my dear Goll. All I can say is that patriotic circles – by which I mean the highest quarters of the SS – are looking to the German judiciary to show a bit more backbone.

THE JUDGE *with a deep sigh*: The process of law is getting a bit complicated these days, my dear Spitz, you must admit.

THE PROSECUTOR: Of course. But you have an excellent remark by our Minister of Justice to guide you. Justice is what serves the German people best.

THE JUDGE *apathetically*: Mm yes.

THE PROSECUTOR: Mustn't let it get you down, that's all. *He gets up.* So now you've got the background. Should be plain sailing. See you later, my dear Goll.

*He leaves. The judge is not at all happy. He stands by the window for a while. Then he leafs aimlessly through his papers. Finally he presses the bell. A court usher enters.*

THE JUDGE: Go and find Detective-Inspector Tallinger in the witnesses' room and bring him back here. Discreetly.

*Exit the usher. Then the inspector reappears.*

THE JUDGE: Tallinger, you nearly landed me in the cart with your idea of treating this as a case of provocation on Arndt's part. Apparently Mr von Miehl is all set to swear that it was Wagner the unemployed man who did the provoking and not Arndt.

THE INSPECTOR *giving nothing away*: So they say, your honour.

THE JUDGE: What's that mean: 'so they say'?

THE INSPECTOR: That Wagner shouted the offensive remarks.

THE JUDGE: Isn't it true?

THE INSPECTOR *offended*: Your honour, whether it's true or not it's not something we can...

THE JUDGE *firmly*: Listen to me, Detective-Inspector Tallinger. This is a German court you're in. Has Wagner admitted that or has he not?

THE INSPECTOR: Your honour, I didn't go to the concentration camp myself, if you want to know. The official report of his deposition – Wagner's supposed to have got something wrong with his kidneys – says that he admitted it. It's only that . . .

THE JUDGE: There you are, he did admit it. It's only that what?

THE INSPECTOR: He served in the war and was wounded in the neck, and according to Stau, you know, Arndt's partner, he can't talk above a whisper. So how von Miehl could have heard him from the first floor hurling insults isn't entirely . . .

THE JUDGE: I imagine it will be said that you don't need a voice in order to tell someone to 'get stuffed', as they put it. You can do it with a simple gesture. It's my impression the Prosecutor's department want to provide the SA with some way out of that sort. More precisely, of that sort and no other.

THE INSPECTOR: Yes, your honour.

THE JUDGE: What is Arndt's statement?

THE INSPECTOR: That he had no part in it and just hurt his head falling down the stairs. That's all we can get out of him.

THE JUDGE: The fellow's probably quite innocent and got into it accidentally, like Pontius Pilate and the Creed.

THE INSPECTOR *gives up*: Yes, your honour.

THE JUDGE: And it should be good enough for the SA if their men get off.

THE INSPECTOR: Yes, your honour.

THE JUDGE: Don't stand there saying 'yes, your honour' like a damn metronome.

THE INSPECTOR: Yes, your honour.

THE JUDGE: What are you trying to tell me? Don't get on your high horse now, Tallinger. You must make allowances for my being a bit on edge. I realise you're an honest man. And when you advised me you must have had something at the back of your mind?

THE INSPECTOR *being a kindly soul, plunges in*: Hasn't it struck you that our deputy prosecutor might simply be after your job and is putting the skids under you, sir? That's what they're saying. – Look at it this way, your honour: you find the Jew not guilty. He never provoked a soul. Wasn't around. Got his head bashed in by pure accident, some quarrel between a different lot of people. Then after a while, back he comes to the shop. No way Stau can prevent it. And the shop is about eleven thousand marks short. Stau will be just as hit by this loss, because now he can't claim the eleven thousand back from Arndt. So Stau, from what I know of his sort, is going to tackle the SA about his jewels. He can't approach them in person because being in partnership with a Jew counts as being sold out to Judah. But he'll have people who can. Then it will come out that the SA go pinching jewels in an upsurge of national feeling. You can guess for yourself how Storm Troop 7 is going to look at your verdict. And the man in the street won't understand anyway. Because how can it be possible for a Jew to win a case against the SA under the Third Reich?

*For some while there has been noise off. It now becomes quite loud.*

THE JUDGE: What's that shocking noise? Just a minute, Tallinger. *He rings. The usher comes in.* What's that din, man?

THE USHER: The courtroom's full. And now they're jammed so tight in the corridors that nobody can get through. And there are some people from the SA there who say they've got to get through because they've orders to attend.

*Exit the usher, while the judge just looks scared.*

THE INSPECTOR *continuing*: Those people are going to be a bit of a nuisance to you, you know. I'd advise you to concentrate on Arndt and not stir up the SA.

THE JUDGE *sits brokenly, holding his head in his hands. In a weary voice*: All right, Tallinger, I'll have to think it over.

THE INSPECTOR: That's the idea, your honour.

*He leaves. The judge gets up with difficulty and rings insistently. Enter the usher.*

THE JUDGE: Just go over and ask Judge Fey of the High Court if he'd mind looking in for a moment.

*The usher goes. Enter the judge's maidservant with his packed breakfast.*

THE MAIDSERVANT: You'll be forgetting your own head next, your honour. You're a terrible man. What did you forget this time? Try and think. The most important thing of all! *She hands him the packet.* Your breakfast! You'll be going off again and buying those rolls hot from the oven and next thing we'll have another stomach-ache like last week. Because you don't look after yourself properly.

THE JUDGE: That'll do, Marie.

THE MAIDSERVANT: Had a job getting through, I did. The whole building's full of brownshirts on account of the trial. But they'll get it hot and strong today, won't they, your honour? Like at the butcher's folk were saying 'good thing there's still some justice left'. Going and beating a business man up! Half the SA used to be criminals; it's common knowledge in the neighbourhood. If we didn't have justice they'd be making away with the cathedral. After the rings, they were; that Häberle's got a girl friend who was on the game till six months ago. And they attacked Wagner, him with the neck wound and no job, when he was shovelling snow with everyone looking on. They're quite open about it, just terrorising the neighbourhood, and if anybody says anything they lay for him and beat him senseless.

THE JUDGE: All right, Marie. Just run along now.

THE MAIDSERVANT: I told them in the butcher's: his honour will show them where they get off, right? All the decent folk are on your side, that's a fact, your honour. Only don't eat your breakfast too quickly, it might do you harm. It's so bad for the health, and now I'll be off and not hold you up, you'll have to be going into court, and don't get worked up in court or perhaps you'd better eat first, it'll only take a few minutes and they won't matter and you shouldn't eat when your stomach's all tensed up. Because you should take better care of yourself. Your health's your most precious possession, but now I'll be off, there's no need to tell you and I can see you're raring to get on with the case and I've got to go to the grocer's still.

*Exit the maidservant. Enter Judge Fey of the High Court, an elderly judge with whom the district judge is friends.*

THE SENIOR JUDGE: What's up?

THE JUDGE: I've got something I'd like to discuss with you if you've a moment. I'm sitting on a pretty ghastly case this morning.

THE SENIOR JUDGE *sitting down*: I know, the SA case.

THE JUDGE *stops pacing around*: How d'you know about that?

THE SENIOR JUDGE: It came up in discussion yesterday afternoon. A nasty business.

*The judge starts again nervously pacing up and down.*

THE JUDGE: What are they saying over your side?

THE SENIOR JUDGE: You aren't envied. *Intrigued*: What'll you do?

THE JUDGE: That's just what I'd like to know. I must say I didn't realise this case had become so famous.

THE SENIOR JUDGE *slightly amazed*: Indeed?

THE JUDGE: That partner is said to be a rather disagreeable customer.

THE SENIOR JUDGE: So I gather. Not that von Miehl is much of a humanitarian either.

THE JUDGE: Is anything known about him?

THE SENIOR JUDGE: Enough to go on with. He's got those sort of contacts.

*Pause.*

THE JUDGE: Very high ones?

THE SENIOR JUDGE: Very high.

*Pause.*

THE SENIOR JUDGE *cautiously*: Suppose you leave the Jew out of it and acquit Häberle, Schünt and Gaunitzer on the ground that the unemployed man provoked them before he dodged back into the shop, I imagine the SA might find that all right? Arndt won't sue the SA in any case.

THE JUDGE *anxiously*: There's Arndt's partner. He'll go to the SA and ask for his valuables back. And then, you know, Fey, I'll have the whole SA leadership gunning for me.

THE SENIOR JUDGE *after considering this argument, which apparently has taken him by surprise*: But suppose you don't leave the Jew out of it, then von Miehl will bring bigger guns to bear, to put it mildly. Perhaps you didn't realise he's being pressed by his bank? Arndt's his lifebelt.

THE JUDGE *appalled*: Pressed by his bank!

*There is a knock.*

THE SENIOR JUDGE: Come in!

*Enter the usher.*

THE USHER: Your honour, I really don't know what to do about keeping seats for the Chief State Prosecutor and President Schönling of the High Court. If only their honours would let one know in time.

THE SENIOR JUDGE *since the judge says nothing*: Clear two seats and don't interrupt us.

*Exit the usher.*

THE JUDGE: That's something I could have done without.

THE SENIOR JUDGE: Whatever happens, von Miehl can't afford to abandon Arndt and let him be ruined. He needs him.

THE JUDGE *crushed*: Someone he can milk.

THE SENIOR JUDGE: I said nothing of the sort, my dear Goll. And it seems to me quite extraordinary that you should imply I did. Let me make it crystal clear that I've not said one word against Mr von Miehl. I regret having to do so, Goll.

THE JUDGE *getting worked up*: But Fey, you can't take it that way. Not in view of our mutual relationship.

THE SENIOR JUDGE: What on earth do you mean, 'our mutual relationship'? I can't interfere in your cases. You have to choose for yourself whose toes you are going to tread on, the SA or the Ministry of Justice; either way it's your decision and nobody else's. These days everybody's his own best friend.

THE JUDGE: Of course I'm my own best friend. But what do I advise myself to do?

*He stands by the door, listening to the noise outside.*

THE SENIOR JUDGE: A bad business.

THE JUDGE *agitatedly*: I'll do anything, my God, can't you see my position? You've changed so. I'll give my judgement this way or that way, whatever way they want me to, but I've got to know first what they want me to do. If one doesn't know that, there's no justice left.

THE SENIOR JUDGE: I wouldn't go round shouting that there's no justice left if I were you, Goll.

THE JUDGE: Oh God, what have I said now? That's not what I meant. I just mean that with so many conflicting interests . . .

THE SENIOR JUDGE: There are no conflicting interests in the Third Reich.

THE JUDGE: Of course not. I wasn't saying there were. Don't keep weighing every single word of mine on your scales.

THE SENIOR JUDGE: Why shouldn't I? I am a judge.

THE JUDGE *who is breaking into a sweat*: But Fey, if every word uttered by every judge had to be weighed like that! I'm prepared to go over everything in the most careful and conscientious possible way, but I have to be told what kind of a decision will satisfy higher considerations. If I allow the Jew to have stayed inside the shop then I'll upset the landlord – I mean the partner; I'm getting muddled – and if the provocation came from the unemployed man then it'll be the landlord who – yes, but von Miehl would rather – Look, they can't pack me off to the backwoods in Silesia, I've got a hernia and I'm not getting embroiled with the SA, Fey, after all I've a family. It's easy for my wife to say I should just find out what actually happened. I'd wake up in hospital if nothing worse. Do I talk about assault? No, I'll talk about provocation. So what's wanted? I shan't condemn the SA of course but only the Jew or the unemployed man, only which of the two should I condemn? How do I decide between unemployed man and Jew or between partner and landlord. Whatever happens I'm not going to Silesia, Fey, I'd rather a concentration camp, the whole thing's impossible. Don't look at me like that. I'm not in the dock. I'm prepared to do absolutely anything.

THE SENIOR JUDGE *who has got to his feet*: Being prepared isn't enough, my dear fellow.

THE JUDGE: But how am I to make my decision?

THE SENIOR JUDGE: Usually a judge goes by what his conscience tells him, Judge Goll. Let that be your guide. It has been a pleasure.

THE JUDGE: Yes, of course: to the best of my heart and

conscience. But here and now; what's my choice to be, Fey? What?

*The senior judge has left. The judge looks wordlessly after him. The telephone rings.*

THE JUDGE *picks up the receiver*: Yes? – Emmy? – What have they put off? Our skittles session? – Who was it rang? – Priesnitz, the one who's just taken his finals? Where did he get the message? – What I'm talking about? I've got a judgement to deliver.

*He hangs up. The usher enters. The noise in the corridors becomes obtrusive.*

THE USHER: Häberle, Schünt, Gaunitzer, your honour.

THE JUDGE *collecting his papers*: One moment.

THE USHER: I've put the President of the High Court at the press table. He was quite happy about it. But the Chief State Prosecutor refused to take a seat among the witnesses. He wanted to be on the bench, I think. Then you'd have had to preside from the dock, your honour! *He laughs foolishly at his own joke.*

THE JUDGE: Whatever happens I'm not doing that.

THE USHER: This way out, your honour. But where's your folder got to with the indictment?

THE JUDGE *utterly confused*: Oh yes, I'll need that. Or I won't know who's being accused, will I? What the devil are we to do with the Chief State Prosecutor?

THE USHER: But your honour, that's your address book you've picked up. Here's the file.

*He pushes it under the judge's arm. Wiping the sweat off his face, the judge goes distractedly out.*


# 7

## Occupational disease

And as for the physicians
The State gives them positions
And pays them so much a piece.
Their job is to keep mending

The bits the police keep sending
Then send it all back to the police.

*Berlin 1934. A ward in the Charité Hospital. A new patient
has been brought in. Nurses are busy writing his name on the
slate at the head of his bed. Two patients in neighbouring beds
are talking.*

THE FIRST PATIENT: Know anything about him?

THE SECOND: I saw them bandaging him downstairs. He was
on a stretcher quite close to me. He was still conscious then,
but when I asked what he'd got he didn't answer. His
whole body's one big wound.

THE FIRST: No need to ask then, was there?

THE SECOND: I didn't see till they started bandaging him.

ONE OF THE NURSES: Quiet please, it's the professor.

*Followed by a train of assistants and nurses the surgeon
enters the ward. He stops by one of the beds and
pontificates.*

THE SURGEON: Gentlemen, we have here a quite beautiful
case showing how essential it is to ask questions and keep
on searching for the deeper causes of the disease if medicine
is not to degenerate into mere quackery. This patient has all
the symptoms of neuralgia and for a considerable time he
received the appropriate treatment. In fact however he
suffers from Raynaud's Disease, which he contracted in the
course of his job as a worker operating pneumatically
powered tools; that is to say, gentlemen, an occupational
disease. We have now begun treating him correctly. His
case will show you what a mistake it is to treat the patient
as a mere component of the clinic instead of asking where
he has come from, how did he contract his disease and what
he will be going back to once treatment is concluded. There
are three things a good doctor has to be able to do. What
are they? The first?

THE FIRST ASSISTANT: Ask questions.

THE SURGEON: The second?

THE SECOND ASSISTANT: Ask questions.

THE SURGEON: And the third?

THE THIRD ASSISTANT: Ask questions, sir.

THE SURGEON: Correct. Ask questions. Particularly concerning . . . ?

THE THIRD ASSISTANT: The social conditions, sir.

THE SURGEON: The great thing is never to be shy of looking
into the patient's private life – often a regrettably depressing
one. If someone is forced to follow some occupation that is
bound in the long run to destroy his body, so that he dies in
effect to avoid starving to death, one doesn't much like
hearing about it and consequently doesn't ask.

*He and his followers move on to the new patient.*

What has this man got?

*The sister whispers in his ear.*

Oh, I see.

*He gives him a cursory examination with evident reluc-
tance.*

*Dictates*: Contusions on the back and thighs. Open wounds
on the abdomen. Further symptoms?

THE SISTER *reads out*: Blood in his urine.

THE SURGEON: Diagnosis on admission?

THE SISTER: Lesion to left kidney.

THE SURGEON: Get him X-rayed. *Starts to turn away.*

THE THIRD ASSISTANT *who has been taking down his medical
history*: How was that incurred, sir?

THE SURGEON: What have they put?

THE SISTER: Falling downstairs, it says here.

THE SURGEON *dictating*: A fall down the stairs. Why are his
hands tied that way, Sister?

THE SISTER: The patient has twice torn his dressings off,
professor.

THE SURGEON: Why?

THE FIRST PATIENT *sotto voce*: Where has the patient come
from and where is he going back to?

*All heads turn in his direction.*

THE SURGEON *clearing his throat*: If this patient seems
disturbed give him morphine. *Moves on to the next bed*:
Feeling better now? It won't be long before you're fit as a
fiddle.

*He examines the patient's neck.*

ONE ASSISTANT *to another*: Worker. Brought in from Oranienburg.

THE OTHER ASSISTANT *grinning*: Another case of occupational disease, I suppose.

8

## The physicists

Enter the local Newtons
Dressed up like bearded Teutons –
Not one of them hook-nosed.
Their science will end up barbarian
For they'll get an impeccably Aryan
State-certified physics imposed.

*Göttingen 1935. Institute for Physics. Two scientists, X and Y.
Y has just entered. He has a conspiratorial look.*

Y: I've got it.

X: What?

Y: The answer to what we asked Mikovsky in Paris.

X: About gravity waves?

Y: Yes.

X: What about it?

Y: Guess who's written giving just what we wanted.

X: Go on.

*Y takes a scrap of paper, writes a name and passes it to X. As
soon as X has read it Y takes it back, tears it into small
pieces and throws it into the stove.*

Y: Mikovsky passed our questions on to him. This is his
answer.

X *grabs for it greedily*: Give me. *He suddenly holds himself
back.* Just suppose we were caught corresponding with him
like this . . .

Y: We absolutely mustn't be.

X: Well, without it we're stuck. Come on, give me.

Y: You won't be able to read it. I used my own shorthand, it's safer. I'll read it out to you.

X: For God's sake be careful.

Y: Is Rollkopf in the lab today? *He points to the right.*

X *pointing to the left*: No, but Reinhardt is. Sit over here.

Y *reads*: The problem concerns two arbitrary countervariant vectors *psi* and *nu* and a countervariant vector *t*. This is used to form the elements of a mixed tensor of the second degree whose structure can be expressed by $\Sigma^{-lr} = C_{hr}^{-l}$.

X *who has been writing this down, suddenly gives him a sign to shut up*: Just a minute.

*He gets up and tiptoes over to the wall, left. Having evidently heard nothing suspicious he returns. Y goes on reading aloud, with other similar interruptions. These lead them to inspect the telephone, suddenly open the door etc.*

Y: Where matter is passive, incoherent and not acting on itself by means of tensions $T = \mu$ will be the only component of the tensional energy depth that differs from o. Hence a static gravitational field is created whose equation, taking into account the constant proportionality factor $8\pi x$ will be $\Delta f = 4\pi x \mu$. Given a suitable choice of spatial coordinates the degree of variation from $c^2 dt^2$ will be very slight ...

*A door slams somewhere and they try to hide their notes. Then this seems to be unnecessary. From this point on they both become engrossed in the material and apparently oblivious of the danger of what they are doing.*

Y *reads on*: ... by comparison however with the passive mass from which the field originates the masses concerned are very small, and motion of the bodies implicated in the gravitational field is brought within this static field by means of a geodetic world line. As such this satisfies the variational principle $\delta \int ds = o$ where the ends of the relevant portion of the world line remain fixed.

X: But what's Einstein got to say about ...

*Y's look of horror makes X aware of his mistake so that he sits there paralysed with shock. Y snatches the notes which he has been taking down and hides away all the papers.*

Y *very loudly, in the direction of the left-hand wall*: What a typical piece of misplaced Jewish ingenuity. Nothing to do with physics.

*Relieved, they again bring out their notes and silently resume work, using the utmost caution.*

## 9

## The Jewish wife

Over there we can see men coming
Whom He's forced to relinquish their women
And coupled with blondes in their place.
It's no good their cursing and praying
For once He catches them racially straying
He'll whip them back into the Race.

*Frankfurt 1935. It is evening. A woman is packing suitcases. She is choosing what to take. Now and again she removes something from her suitcase and returns it to its original place in the room in order to pack another item instead. For a long while she hesitates whether to take a large photograph of her husband that stands on the chest of drawers. Finally she leaves the picture where it is. The packing tires her and for a time she sits on a suitcase leaning her head on her hand. Then she gets to her feet and telephones.*

THE WOMAN: This is Judith Keith. Hullo, is that you, doctor? Good evening. I just wanted to ring up and say you'll have to be looking for another bridge partner; I'm going away. – No, not long, but anyway a few weeks – I want to go to Amsterdam. – Yes, it's said to be lovely there in spring. – I've got friends there. – No, plural, believe it or not. – Who will you get for a fourth? – Come on, we haven't played for a fortnight. – That's right, Fritz had a cold too. It's absurd to go on playing bridge when it's as cold as this, I always say. – But no, doctor, how could I? – Anyway Thekla had her mother there. – I know. – What put that idea into my head? – No, it was nothing sudden, I kept putting it off, and

now I've really got to ... Right, we'll have to cancel our
cinema date, remember me to Thekla. – Ring him up on a
Sunday sometimes, could you perhaps? – Well, au revoir! –
Yes, of course I will. – Goodbye.
*She hangs up and calls another number.*
This is Judith Keith. Can I speak to Frau Schöck? – Lotte?
– I just wanted to say goodbye. I'm going away for a bit. –
No, nothing's wrong, it's just that I want to see some new
faces. – I really meant to say that Fritz has got the Professor
coming here on Tuesday evening, and I wondered if you
could both come too, I'm off tonight as I said. – Tuesday,
that's it. – No, I only wanted to tell you I'm off tonight,
there's no connection, I just thought you might be able to
come then. – Well, let's say even though I shan't be there,
right? – Yes, I know you're not that sort, but what about it,
these are unsettled times and everybody's being so careful,
so you'll come? – It depends on Max? He'll manage it, the
Professor will be there, tell him. – I must ring off now. –
Goodbye then.
*She hangs up and called another number.*
That you, Gertrud? It's Judith. I'm so sorry to disturb you.
– Thanks, I just wanted to ask if you could see that Fritz is
all right, I'm going away for a few months. – Being his
sister, I thought you ... Why not? – Nobody'd think that,
anyway not Fritz. – Well, of course he knows we don't ...
get on all that well, but ... Then he can simply call you if
you prefer it that way. – Yes, I'll tell him that. –
Everything's fairly straight, of course the flat's on the big
side. – You'd better leave his workroom to Ida to deal with,
she knows what's to be done. – I find her pretty intelligent,
and he's used to her. – And there's another thing, I hope
you don't mind my saying so, but he doesn't like talking
before meals, can you remember that? I always used to
watch myself. – I don't want to argue about that just now,
it's not long till my train goes and I haven't finished
packing, you know. – Keep an eye on his suits and remind
him to go to his tailor, he's ordered a new overcoat, and do
see that his bedroom's properly heated, he likes sleeping
with the window open and it's too cold. – No, I don't think

he needs to toughen himself up, but I must ring off now. –
I'm very grateful to you, Gertrud, and we'll write to each
other, won't we? – Goodbye.

*She hangs up and calls another number.*

Anna? It's Judith; look, I'm just off. – No, there's no way
out, things are getting too difficult. – Too difficult! – Well,
no, it isn't Fritz's idea, he doesn't know yet, I simply
packed my things. – I don't think so. – I don't think he'll
say all that much. It's all got too difficult for him, just in
everyday matters. – That's something we haven't arranged.
– We just never talked about it, absolutely never. – No, he
hasn't altered, on the contrary. – I'd be glad if you and Kurt
could look after him a bit, to start with. – Yes, specially
Sundays, and try to make him give up this flat. – It's too big
for him. – I'd like to have come and said goodbye to you,
but it's your porter, you know. – So, goodbye; no, don't
come to the station, it's a bad idea. – Goodbye, I'll write. –
That's a promise.

*She hangs up without calling again. She has been smoking.
Now she sets fire to the small book in which she has been
looking up the numbers. She walks up and down two or
three times. Then she starts speaking. She is rehearsing the
short speech which she proposes to make to her husband. It
is evident that he is sitting in a particular chair.*

Well, Fritz, I'm off. I suppose I've waited too long, I'm
awfully sorry, but . . .

*She stands there thinking, then starts in a different way.*

Fritz, you must let me go, you can't keep . . . I'll be your
downfall, it's quite clear; I know you aren't a coward,
you're not scared of the police, but there are worse things.
They won't put you in a camp, but they'll ban you from the
clinic any day now. You won't say anything at the time, but
it'll make you ill. I'm not going to watch you sitting around
the flat pretending to read magazines, it's pure selfishness
on my part, my leaving, that's all. Don't tell me anything . . .

*She again stops. She makes a fresh start.*

Don't tell me you haven't changed; you have! Only last
week you established quite objectively that the proportion

of Jewish scientists wasn't all that high. Objectivity is always the start of it, and why do you keep telling me I've never been such a Jewish chauvinist as now? Of course I'm one. Chauvinism is catching. Oh, Fritz, what has happened to us?

*She again stops. She makes a fresh start.*

I never told you I wanted to go away, have done for a long time, because I can't talk when I look at you, Fritz. Then it seems to me there's no point in talkng. It has all been settled already. What's got into them, d'you think? What do they really want? What am I doing to them? I've never had anything to do with politics. Did I vote Communist? But I'm just one of those bourgeois housewives with servants and so on, and now all of a sudden it seems only blondes can be that. I've often thought lately about something you told me years back, how some people were more valuable than others, so one lot were given insulin when they got diabetes and the others weren't. And this was something I understood, idiot that I was. Well, now they've drawn a new distinction of the same sort, and this time I'm one of the less valuable ones. Serves me right.

*She again stops. She makes a fresh start.*

Yes, I'm packing. Don't pretend you haven't noticed anything the last few days. Nothing really matters, Fritz, except just one thing: if we spend our last hour together without looking at each other's eyes. That's a triumph they can't be allowed, the liars who force everyone else to lie. Ten years ago when somebody said no one would think I was Jewish, you instantly said yes, they would. And that's fine. That was straightforward. Why take things in a roundabout way now? I'm packing so they shan't take away your job as senior physician. And because they've stopped saying good morning to you at the clinic, and because you're not sleeping nowadays. I don't want you to tell me I mustn't go. And I'm hurrying because I don't want to hear you telling me I must. It's a matter of time. Principles are a matter of time. They don't last for ever, any more than a glove does. There are good ones which last a long while. But even they only have a certain life. Don't get the idea that I'm angry. Yes, I am. Why should I always be understanding? What's wrong with the shape of my nose and the colour of my hair? I'm to leave the town where I was born just so they don't have to go short of butter. What sort of people are you, yourself included? You work out the quantum theory and the Trendelenburg test, then allow a lot of semi-barbarians to tell you you're to conquer the world but you can't have the woman you want. The artificial lung, and the dive-bomber! You are monsters or you pander to monsters. Yes, I know I'm being unreasonable, but what good is reason in a world like this? There you sit watching your wife pack and saying nothing. Walls have ears, is that it? But you people say nothing. One lot listens and the other keeps silent. To hell with that. I'm supposed to keep silent too. If I loved you I'd keep silent. I truly do love you. Give me those underclothes. They're suggestive. I'll need them. I'm thirty-six, that isn't too old, but I can't do much more experimenting. The next time I settle in a country things can't be like this. The next man I get must be allowed to keep me. And don't tell me you'll send me money; you know you won't be allowed to. And you aren't to pretend it's just a matter of four weeks either. This business is going to last rather more than four weeks. You know that, and so do I. So don't go telling me 'After all it's only for two or three weeks' as you hand me the fur coat I shan't need till next winter. And don't let's speak about disaster. Let's speak about disgrace. Oh, Fritz!

*She stops. A door opens. She hurriedly sees to her appearance. The husband comes in.*

THE HUSBAND: What are you doing? Tidying up?

THE WOMAN: No.

THE HUSBAND: Why are you packing?

THE WOMAN: I want to get away.

THE HUSBAND: What are you talking about?

THE WOMAN: We did mention the possibility of my going away for a bit. It's no longer very pleasant here.

THE HUSBAND: That's a lot of nonsense.

THE WOMAN: Do you want me to stay, then?

THE HUSBAND: Where are you thinking of going?

THE WOMAN: Amsterdam. Just away.

THE HUSBAND: But you've got nobody there.

THE WOMAN: No.

THE HUSBAND: Why don't you wish to stay here? There's absolutely no need for you to go so far as I'm concerned.

THE WOMAN: No.

THE HUSBAND: You know I haven't changed, you do, don't you, Judith?

THE WOMAN: Yes.

*He embraces her. They stand without speaking among the suitcases.*

THE HUSBAND: And there's nothing else makes you want to go?

THE WOMAN: You know that.

THE HUSBAND: It might not be such a bad idea, I suppose. You need a breather. It's stifling in this place. I'll come and collect you. As soon as I get across the frontier, even if it's only for two days, I'll start feeling better.

THE WOMAN: Yes, why don't you?

THE HUSBAND: Things can't go on like this all that much longer. Something's bound to change. The whole business will die down again like an inflammation – it's a disaster, it really is.

THE WOMAN: Definitely. Did you run into Schöck?

THE HUSBAND: Yes, just on the stairs, that's to say. I think he's begun to be sorry about the way they dropped us. He was quite embarrassed. In the long run they can't completely sit on filthy intellectuals like us. And they won't be able to run a war with a lot of spineless wrecks. People aren't all that standoffish if you face up to them squarely. What time are you off, then?

THE WOMAN: Nine-fifteen.

THE HUSBAND: And where am I to send money to?

THE WOMAN: Let's say poste restante, Amsterdam main Post-Office.

THE HUSBAND: I'll see they give me a special permit. Good God, I can't send my wife off with ten marks a month. It's all a lousy business.

THE WOMAN: If you can come and collect me it'll do you a bit
of good.
THE HUSBAND: To read a paper with something in it for once.
THE WOMAN: I rang Gertrud. She'll see you're all right.
THE HUSBAND: Quite unnecessary. For two or three weeks.
THE WOMAN *who has again begun packing*: Do you mind
handing me my fur coat?
THE HUSBAND *handing it to her*: After all it's only for two or
three weeks.


## 10

## The spy

    Here come the worthy schoolteachers
    The Youth Movement takes the poor creatures
    And makes them all thrust out their chest.
    Every schoolboy's a spy. So now marking
    Is based not on knowledge, but narking
    And on who knows whose weaknesses best.

    They educate traducers
    To set hatchet-men and bruisers
    On their own parents' tail.
    Denounced by their sons as traitors
    To Himmler's apparatus
    The fathers go handcuffed to gaol.

*Cologne 1935. A wet Sunday afternoon. The man, the wife
and the boy have finished lunch. The maidservant enters.*

THE MAIDSERVANT: Mr and Mrs Klimbtsch are asking if you
are at home.
THE MAN *snarls*: No.
*The maidservant goes out.*
THE WIFE: You should have gone to the phone yourself. They
must know we couldn't possibly have gone out yet.

THE MAN: Why couldn't we?

THE WIFE: Because it's raining.

THE MAN: That's no reason.

THE WIFE: Where could we have gone to? That's the first thing they'll ask.

THE MAN: Oh, masses of places.

THE WIFE: Let's go then.

THE MAN: Where to?

THE WIFE: If only it wasn't raining.

THE MAN: And where'd we go if it wasn't raining?

THE WIFE: At least in the old days you could go and meet someone.

*Pause.*

THE WIFE: It was a mistake you not going to the phone. Now they'll realise we don't want to have them.

THE MAN: Suppose they do?

THE WIFE: Then it wouldn't look very nice, our dropping them just when everyone else does.

THE MAN: We're not dropping them.

THE WIFE: Why shouldn't they come here in that case?

THE MAN: Because Klimbtsch bores me to tears.

THE WIFE: He never bored you in the old days.

THE MAN: In the old days . . . All this talk of the old days gets me down.

THE WIFE: Well anyhow you'd never have cut him just because the school inspectors are after him.

THE MAN: Are you telling me I'm a coward?

*Pause.*

THE MAN: All right, ring up and tell them we've just come back on account of the rain.

*The wife remains seated.*

THE WIFE: What about asking the Lemkes to come over?

THE MAN: And have them go on telling us we're slack about civil defence?

THE WIFE *to the boy*: Klaus-Heinrich, stop fiddling with the wireless.

*The boy turns his attention to the newspapers.*

THE MAN: It's a disaster, its raining like this. It's quite

intolerable, living in a country where it's a disaster when it rains.

THE WIFE: Do you really think it's sensible to go round making remarks like that?

THE MAN: I can make what remarks I like between my own four walls. This is my home, and I shall damn well say ... *He is interrupted. The maidservant enters with coffee things. So long as she is present they remain silent.*

THE MAN: Have we got to have a maid whose father is the block warden?

THE WIFE: We've been over that again and again. The last thing you said was that it had its advantages.

THE MAN: What aren't I supposed to have said? If you mentioned anything of the sort to your mother we could land in a proper mess.

THE WIFE: The things I talk about to my mother ...
*Enter the maidservant with the coffee.*

THE WIFE: That's all right, Erna. You can go now, I'll see to it.

THE MAIDSERVANT: Thank you very much, ma'am.

THE BOY *looking up from his paper*: Is that how vicars always behave, dad?

THE MAN: How do you mean?

THE BOY: Like it says here.

THE MAN: What's that you're reading?
*Snatches the paper from his hands.*

THE BOY: Hey, our group leader said it was all right for us to know about anything in that paper.

THE MAN: I don't have to go by what your group leader says. It's for me to decide what you can or can't read.

THE WIFE: There's ten pfennigs, Klaus-Heinrich, run over and get yourself something.

THE BOY: But it's raining.
*He hangs round the window, trying to make up his mind.*

THE MAN: If they go on reporting these cases against priests I shall cancel the paper altogether.

THE WIFE: Which are you going to take, then? They're all reporting them.

THE MAN: If all the papers are full of this kind of filth I'd sooner not read a paper at all. And I wouldn't be any worse informed about what's going on in the world.

THE WIFE: There's something to be said for a bit of a clean-up.

THE MAN: Clean-up, indeed. The whole thing's politics.

THE WIFE: Well, it's none of our business anyway. After all, we're protestants.

THE MAN: It matters to our people all right if it can't hear the word vestry without being reminded of dirt like this.

THE WIFE: But what do you want them to do when this kind of thing happens?

THE MAN: What do I want them to do? Suppose they looked into their own back yard. I'm told it isn't all so snowy white in that Brown House of theirs.

THE WIFE: But that only goes to show how far our people's recovery has gone, Karl.

THE MAN: Recovery! A nice kind of recovery. If that's what recovery looks like, I'd sooner have the disease any day.

THE WIFE: You're so on edge today. Did something happen at the school?

THE MAN: What on earth could have happened at school? And for God's sake don't keep saying I'm on edge, it makes me feel on edge.

THE WIFE: We oughtn't to keep on quarrelling so, Karl. In the old days . . .

THE MAN: Just what I was waiting for. In the old days. Neither in the old days nor now did I wish to have my son's imagination perverted for him.

THE WIFE: Where has he got to, anyway?

THE MAN: How am I to know?

THE WIFE: Did you see him go?

THE MAN: No.

THE WIFE: I can't think where he can have gone. *She calls*: Klaus-Heinrich!

*She hurries out of the room, and is heard calling. She returns.*

THE WIFE: He really has left.

THE MAN: Why shouldn't he?

THE WIFE: But it's raining buckets.

THE MAN: Why are you so on edge at the boy's having left?

THE WIFE: You remember what we were talking about?

THE MAN: What's that got to do with it?

THE WIFE: You've been so careless lately.

THE MAN: I have certainly not been careless, but even if I had what's that got to do with the boy's having left?

THE WIFE: You know how they listen to everything.

THE MAN: Well?

THE WIFE: Well. Suppose he goes round telling people? You know how they're always dinning it into them in the Hitler Youth. They deliberately encourage the kids to repeat everything. It's so odd his going off so quietly.

THE MAN: Rubbish.

THE WIFE: Didn't you see when he went?

THE MAN: He was hanging round the window for quite a time.

THE WIFE: I'd like to know how much he heard.

THE MAN: But he must know what happens to people who get reported.

THE WIFE: What about that boy the Schmulkes were telling us about? They say his father's still in a concentration camp. I wish we knew how long he was in the room.

THE MAN: The whole thing's a load of rubbish.

*He hastens to the other rooms and calls the boy.*

THE WIFE: I just can't see him going off somewhere without saying a word. It wouldn't be like him.

THE MAN: Mightn't he be with a school friend?

THE WIFE: Then he'd have to be at the Mummermanns'. I'll give them a ring. *She telephones.*

THE MAN: It's all a false alarm, if you ask me.

THE WIFE *telephoning*: Is that Mrs Mummermann? It's Mrs Furcke here. Good afternoon. Is Klaus-Heinrich with you? He isn't? – Then where on earth can the boy be? – Mrs Mummermann do you happen to know if the Hitler Youth place is open on Sunday afternoons? – It is? – Thanks a lot, I'll ask them.

*She hangs up. They sit in silence.*

THE MAN: What do you think he overheard?

THE WIFE: You were talking about the paper. You shouldn't have said what you did about the Brown House. He's so patriotic about that kind of thing.

THE MAN: What am I supposed to have said about the Brown House?

THE WIFE: You remember perfectly well. That things weren't all snowy white in there.

THE MAN: Well, nobody can take that as an attack, can they? Saying things aren't all white, or snowy white rather, as I qualified it – which makes a difference, quite a substantial one at that – well, it's more a kind of jocular remark like the man in the street makes in the vernacular, sort of, and all it really means is that probably not absolutely everything even there is always exactly as the Führer would like it to be. I quite deliberately emphasised that this was only 'probably' so by using the phrase, as I very well remember, 'I'm *told*' things aren't *all* – and that's another obvious qualification – so snowy white there. 'I'm told'; that doesn't mean it's necessarily so. How could I say things aren't snowy white? I haven't any proof. Wherever there are human beings there are imperfections. That's all I was suggesting, and in very qualified form. And in any case there was a certain occasion when the Führer himself expressed the same kind of criticisms a great deal more strongly.

THE WIFE: I don't understand you. You don't need to talk to me in that way.

THE MAN: I'd like to think I don't. I wish I knew to what extent you gossip about all that's liable to be said between these four walls in the heat of the moment. Of course I wouldn't dream of accusing you of casting ill-considered aspersions on your husband, any more than I'd think my boy capable for one moment of doing anything to harm his own father. But doing harm and doing it wittingly are unfortunately two very different matters.

THE WIFE: You can stop that right now! What about the kind of things you say yourself? Here am I worrying myself silly whether you make that remark about life in Nazi Germany being intolerable before or after the one about the Brown House.

THE MAN: I never said anything of the sort.

THE WIFE: You're acting absolutely as if I were the police. All I'm doing is racking my brains about what the boy may have overheard.

THE MAN: The term Nazi Germany just isn't in my vocabulary.

THE WIFE: And that stuff about the warden of our block and how the papers print nothing but lies, and what you were saying about civil defence the other day – when does the boy hear a single constructive remark? That just doesn't do any good to a child's attitude of mind, it's simply demoralising, and at a time when the Führer keeps stressing that Germany's future lies in Germany's youth. He really isn't the kind of boy to rush off and denounce one just like that. It makes me feel quite ill.

THE MAN: He's vindictive, though.

THE WIFE: What on earth has he got to be vindictive about?

THE MAN: God knows, but there's bound to be something. The time I confiscated his tree-frog perhaps.

THE WIFE: But that was a week ago.

THE MAN: It's that kind of thing that sticks in his mind, though.

THE WIFE: What did you confiscate it for, anyway?

THE MAN: Because he wouldn't catch any flies for it. He was letting the creature starve.

THE WIFE: He really is run off his feet, you know.

THE MAN: There's not much the frog can do about that.

THE WIFE: But he never came back to the subject, and I gave him ten pfennigs only a moment ago. He only has to want something and he gets it.

THE MAN: Exactly. I call that bribery.

THE WIFE: What do you mean by that?

THE MAN: They'll simply say we were trying to bribe him to keep his mouth shut.

THE WIFE: What do you imagine they could do to you?

THE MAN: Absolutely anything. There's no limit. My God!

And to think I'm supposed to be a teacher. An educator of
our youth. Our youth scares me stiff.

THE WIFE: But they've nothing against you.

THE MAN: They've something against everyone. Everyone's
suspect. Once the suspicion's there, one's suspect.

THE WIFE: But a child's not a reliable witness. A child hasn't
the faintest idea what it's talking about.

THE MAN: So you say. But when did they start having to have
witnesses for things?

THE WIFE: Couldn't we work out what you could have meant
by your remarks? Then he could just have misunderstood
you.

THE MAN: Well, what did I say? I can't even remember. It's all
the fault of that damned rain. It puts one in a bad mood.
Actually I'm the last person to say anything against the
moral resurgence the German people is going through these
days. I foresaw the whole thing as early as the winter of
1932.

THE WIFE: Karl, there just isn't time to discuss that now. We
must straighten everything out right away. There's not a
minute to spare.

THE MAN: I don't believe Karl-Heinrich's capable of it.

THE WIFE: Let's start with the Brown House and all the filth.

THE MAN: I never said a word about filth.

THE WIFE: You said the paper's full of filth and you want to
cancel it.

THE MAN: Right, the paper. But not the Brown House.

THE WIFE: Couldn't you have been saying that you won't
stand for such filth in the churches? And that you think the
people now being tried could quite well be the same as used
to spread malicious rumours about the Brown House
suggesting things weren't all that snowy white there? And
that they ought to have started looking into their own place
instead? And what you were telling the boy was that he
should stop fiddling with the wireless and read the paper
because you're firmly of the opinion that the youth of the
Third Reich should have a clear view of what's happening
round about them.

THE MAN: It wouldn't be any use.

THE WIFE: Karl, you're not to give up now. You should be strong, like the Führer keeps on...

THE MAN: I'm not going to be brought before the law and have my own flesh and blood standing in the witness box and giving evidence against me.

THE WIFE: There's no need to take it like that.

THE MAN: It was a great mistake our seeing so much of the Klimbtsches.

THE WIFE: But nothing whatever has happened to him.

THE MAN: Yes, but there's talk of an inquiry.

THE WIFE: What would it be like if everybody got in such a panic as soon as there was talk of an inquiry?

THE MAN: Do you think our block warden has anything against us?

THE WIFE: You mean, supposing they asked him? He got a box of cigars for his birthday the other day and his Christmas box was ample.

THE MAN: The Gauffs gave him fifteen marks.

THE WIFE: Yes, but they were still taking the socialist paper in 1932, and as late as May 1933 they were hanging out the old nationalist flag.

*The phone rings.*

THE MAN: That's the phone.

THE WIFE: Shall I answer it?

THE MAN: I don't know.

THE WIFE: Who could be ringing us?

THE MAN: Wait a moment. If it rings again, answer it.

*They wait. It doesn't ring again.*

THE MAN: We can't go on living like this!

THE WIFE: Karl!

THE MAN: A Judas, that's what you've borne me. Sitting at the table listening, gulping down the soup we've given him and noting down whatever his father says, the little spy.

THE WIFE: That's a dreadful thing to say.

*Pause.*

THE WIFE: Do you think we ought to make any kind of preparations?

THE MAN: Do you think he'll bring them straight back with him?

THE WIFE: Could he really?

THE MAN: Perhaps I'd better put on my Iron Cross.

THE WIFE: Of course you must, Karl.

*He gets it and puts it on with shaking hands.*

THE WIFE: But they've nothing against you at school, have they?

THE MAN: How's one to tell? I'm prepared to teach whatever they want taught; but what's that? If only I could tell . . . How am I to know what they want Bismarck to have been like? When they're taking so long to publish the new text books. Couldn't you give the maid another ten marks? She's another who's always listening.

THE WIFE *nodding*: And what about the picture of Hitler; shouldn't we hang it above your desk? It'd look better.

THE MAN: Yes, do that.

*The wife starts taking down the picture.*

THE MAN: Suppose the boy goes and says we deliberately rehung it, though, it might look as if we had a bad conscience.

*The wife puts the picture back on its old hook.*

THE MAN: Wasn't that the door?

THE WIFE: I didn't hear anything.

THE MAN: It was.

THE WIFE: Karl!

*She embraces him.*

THE MAN: Keep a grip on yourself. Pack some things for me.

*The door of the flat opens. Man and wife stand rigidly side by side in the corner of the room. The door opens and enter the boy, a paper bag in his hand. Pause.*

THE BOY: What's the matter with you people?

THE WIFE: Where have you been?

*The boy shows her the bag, which contains chocolate.*

THE WIFE: Did you simply go out to buy chocolate?

THE BOY: Whatever else? Obvious, isn't it?

*He crosses the room munching, and goes out. His parents look enquiringly after him.*

THE MAN: Do you suppose he's telling the truth?
*The wife shrugs her shoulders.*


11

# The black shoes

> These widows and orphans you're seeing
> Have heard Him guaranteeing
> A great time by and by.
> Meanwhile they must make sacrifices
> As the shops all put up their prices.
> That great time is pie in the sky.

*Bitterfeld, 1935. Kitchen in a working-class flat. The mother is peeling potatoes. Her thirteen-year-old daughter is doing homework.*

THE DAUGHTER: Mum, am I getting my two pfennigs?
THE MOTHER: For the Hitler Youth?
THE DAUGHTER: Yes.
THE MOTHER: I haven't any money left.
THE DAUGHTER: But if I don't bring my two pfennigs a week I won't be going to the country this summer. And our teacher said Hitler wants town and country to get to know each other. Town people are supposed to get closer to the farmers. But I'll have to bring along my two pfennigs.
THE MOTHER: I'll try to find some way of letting you have them.
THE DAUGHTER: Oh lovely, Mum. I'll give a hand with the 'taters. It's lovely in the country, isn't it? Proper meals there. Our gym teacher was saying I've got a potato belly.
THE MOTHER: You've nothing of the kind.
THE DAUGHTER: Not right now. Last year I had. A bit.
THE MOTHER: I might be able to get us some offal.
THE DAUGHTER: I get my roll at school; that's more than you do. Bertha was saying when she went to the country last

year they had bread and goose dripping. Meat too sometimes. Lovely, isn't it?

THE MOTHER: Of course.

THE DAUGHTER: And all that fresh air.

THE MOTHER: Didn't she have to do some work too?

THE DAUGHTER: Of course. But lots to eat. Only the farmer
was a nuisance, she said.

THE MOTHER: What'd he do?

THE DAUGHTER: Oh, nothing. Just kept pestering her.

THE MOTHER: Aha.

THE DAUGHTER: Bertha's bigger than me, though. A year
older.

THE MOTHER: Get on with your homework.

*Pause, then*:

THE DAUGHTER: But I won't have to wear those old black
shoes from the welfare, will I?

THE MOTHER: You won't be needing them. You've got your
other pair, haven't you?

THE DAUGHTER: Just that those have got a hole.

THE MOTHER: Oh dear, when it's so wet.

THE DAUGHTER: I'll put some paper in, that'll do it.

THE MOTHER: No, it won't. If they've gone they'll have to be
resoled.

THE DAUGHTER: That's so expensive.

THE MOTHER: What've you got against the welfare pair?

THE DAUGHTER: I can't stand them.

THE MOTHER: Because they look so clumsy?

THE DAUGHTER: So you think so too.

THE MOTHER: Of course they're older.

THE DAUGHTER: Have I *got* to wear them?

THE MOTHER: If you can't stand them you needn't wear
them.

THE DAUGHTER: I'm not being vain, am I?

THE MOTHER: No. Just growing up.

*Pause, then*:

THE DAUGHTER: Then can I have my two pfennigs, Mum?
I do so want to go.

THE MOTHER *slowly*: I haven't the money for that.

12

# Labour service

> By sweeping away class barriers
> The poor are made fetchers and carriers
> In Hitler's Labour Corps.
> The rich serve a year alongside them
> To show that no conflicts divide them.
> Some pay would please them more.

*The Lüneburger Heide, 1935. A Labour Service column at work. A young worker and a student are digging together.*

THE STUDENT: What did they put that stocky little fellow from Column 3 in clink for?

THE YOUNG WORKER *grinning*: The group leader was saying we'll learn what it's like to work and he said, under his breath like, he'd as soon learn what it's like to get a pay packet. They weren't pleased.

THE STUDENT: Why say something like that?

THE YOUNG WORKER: Because he already knows what it's like to work, I should think. He was down the pits at fourteen.

THE STUDENT: Look out, Tubby's coming.

THE YOUNG WORKER: If he looks our way I can't just dig out half a spit.

THE STUDENT: But I can't shovel away more than I'm doing.

THE YOUNG WORKER: If he cops me there'll be trouble.

THE STUDENT: No more cigarettes from me, then.

THE YOUNG WORKER: He'll cop me sure enough.

THE STUDENT: And you want to go on leave, don't you? Think I'm going to pay you if you can't take a little risk like that?

THE YOUNG WORKER: You've already had your money's worth and more.

THE STUDENT: But I'm not going to pay you.

THE GROUP LEADER *comes and watches them*: Well, Herr Doktor, now you can see what working is really like, can't you?

THE STUDENT: Yes, Herr Group Leader.
*The young worker digs half a spit of earth. The student
pretends to be shovelling like mad.*
THE GROUP LEADER: You owe it all to the Führer.
THE STUDENT: Yes, Herr Group Leader.
THE GROUP LEADER: Shoulder to shoulder and no class
  barriers; that's his way. The Führer wants no distinctions
  made in his labour camps. Never mind who your dad is.
  Carry on! *He goes.*
THE STUDENT: I don't call that half a spit.
THE YOUNG WORKER: Well, I do.
THE STUDENT: No cigarettes for today. Better remember
  there are an awful lot of people want cigarettes just as much
  as you.
THE YOUNG WORKER *slowly*: Yes, there are an awful lot of
  people like me. That's something we often forget.


# 13

# Workers' playtime

Then the media, a travelling circus
Come to interview the workers
With microphone in hand
But the workers can't be trusted
So the interview is adjusted
To fit what Goebbels has planned.

*Leipzig 1934. Foreman's office in a factory. A radio announcer
bearing a microphone is chatting to three workers; a middle-
aged worker, an old worker and a woman worker. In the
background are a gentleman from the office and a stocky
figure in SA uniform.*

THE ANNOUNCER: Here we are with flywheels and driving
  belts in full swing all around us, surrounded by our
  comrades working as busily as ants, joyously doing their bit
  to provide our beloved fatherland with everything it

requires. This morning we are visiting the Fuchs spinning mills. And in spite of the hard toil and the tensing of every muscle here we see nothing but joyous and contented faces on all sides. But let us get our comrades to speak for themselves. *To the old worker*: I understand you've been working here for twenty-one years, Mr ...

THE OLD WORKER: Sedelmaier.

THE ANNOUNCER: Mr Sedelmaier. Tell me, Mr Sedelmaier, how is it that we see nothing but these happy, joyous faces on every side?

THE OLD WORKER *after a moment's thought*: There's a lot of jokes told.

THE ANNOUNCER: Really? Right, so a cheerful jest or two makes work seem child's play, what? The deadly menace of pessimism is unknown under National Socialism, you mean. Different in the old days, wasn't it?

THE OLD WORKER: Aye.

THE ANNOUNCER: That rotten old Weimar republic didn't give the workers much to laugh about you mean. What are we working for, they used to ask.

THE OLD WORKER: Aye, that's what some of them say.

THE ANNOUNCER: I didn't quite get that. Oh, I see, you're referring to the inevitable grouses, but they're dying out now they see that kind of thing's a waste of time because everything's booming in the Third Reich now there's a strong hand on the helm once again. That's what you feel too – *to the woman worker* – isn't it, Miss ...

THE WOMAN WORKER: Schmidt.

THE ANNOUNCER: Miss Schmidt. And which of these steel mammoths enjoys your services?

THE WOMAN WORKER *reciting*: And then we also work at decorating our place of work which gives us great pleasure. Our portrait of the Führer was purchased thanks to voluntary contributions and we are very proud of him. Also of the geranium plants which provide a magical touch of colour in the greyness of our working environment, by suggestion of Miss Kinze.

THE ANNOUNCER: So you decorate your place of work with flowers, the sweet offspring of the fields. And I imagine

there've been a good few other changes in this factory since
Germany's destiny took its new turning?

GENTLEMAN FROM THE OFFICE *prompting*: Wash rooms.

THE WOMAN WORKER: The wash rooms were the personal
idea of Mr Bäuschle our managing director for which we
would like to express our heartfelt thanks. Anybody who
wants to wash can do so in these fine washrooms so long as
there isn't too much of a crowd fighting for the basins.

THE ANNOUNCER: Everybody wants to be first, what? So
there's always a jolly throng?

THE WOMAN WORKER: Only six taps for 552 of us. So there
are lots of quarrels. It's disgraceful how some of them
behave.

THE ANNOUNCER: But it's all sorted out perfectly happily.
And now we are going to hear a few words from Mr – if
you'd be so good as to tell me your name?

THE WORKER: Mahn.

THE ANNOUNCER: Mr Mahn. Right, Mr Mahn, would you
tell us what moral effect the great increase in the workforce
here has had on your fellow workers?

THE WORKER: How do you mean?

THE ANNOUNCER: Well, are all of you happy to see the
wheels turning and plenty of work for everybody?

THE WORKER: You bet.

THE ANNOUNCER: And everybody once more able to take his
wage packet home at the end of the week, that's not to be
sneezed at either.

THE WORKER: No.

THE ANNOUNCER: Things weren't always like that. Under
that rotten old republic many a comrade had to plod his
weary way to the public welfare and live on charity.

THE WORKER: 18 marks 50. No deductions.

THE ANNOUNCER *with a forced laugh*: Ha. Ha. A capital
joke! Not much to deduct, was there?

THE WORKER: No. Nowadays they deduct more.

*The gentleman from the office moves forward uneasily, as
does the stocky man in SA uniform.*

THE ANNOUNCER: So there we are, everybody's once again
got bread and work under National Socialism. You're

absolutely right, Mr – what did you say your name was? Not a single wheel is idle, not a single shaft needs to rust up in Adolf Hitler's Germany. *He roughly pushes the worker away from the microphone.* In joyful cooperation the intellectual worker and the manual worker are tackling the reconstruction of our beloved German Fatherland. Heil Hitler!

# 14

# The box

The coffins the SA carry
Are sealed up tight, to bury
Their victims' raw remains.
Here's one who wouldn't give in
He fought for better living
That we might lose our chains.

*Essen 1934. Working-class flat. A woman with two children. A young worker and his wife, who are calling on them. The woman is weeping. Steps can be heard on the staircase. The door is open.*

THE WOMAN: He simply said they were paying starvation wages, that's all. And it's true. What's more, our elder girl's got lung trouble and we can't afford milk. They couldn't possibly have harmed him, could they?
*The SA men bring in a big box and put it on the floor.*
SA MAN: Don't make a song and dance about it. Anybody can catch pneumonia. Here are the papers, all present and correct. And don't you go doing anything silly, now.
*The SA men leave.*
A CHILD: Mum, is Dad in there?
THE WORKER *who has gone over to the box*: That's zinc it's made of.
THE CHILD: Please can we open it?

THE WORKER *in a rage*: You bet we can. Where's your toolbox?

THE YOUNG WOMAN: Don't you open it, Hans. It'll only make them come for you.

THE WORKER: I want to see what they did to him. They're frightened of people seeing that. That's why they used zinc. Leave me alone!

THE YOUNG WOMAN: I'm not leaving you alone. Didn't you hear them?

THE WORKER: Don't you think we ought to just have a look at him?

THE WOMAN *taking her children by the hand and going up to the zinc box*: There's still my brother, they might come for him, Hans. And they might come for you too. The box can stay shut. We don't need to see him. He won't be forgotten.

## 15

## Release

Questioned in torture cellars
These men were no tale-tellers.
They held out all through the night.
Let's hope they didn't go under
But their wives and friends must wonder
What took place at first light.

*Berlin, 1936. Working-class kitchen. Sunday morning. Man and wife. Sound of military music in the distance.*

THE MAN: He'll be here any minute.

THE WIFE: None of you know anything against him, after all.

THE MAN: All we know is that they let him out of the concentration camp.

THE WIFE: So why don't you trust him?

THE MAN: There've been too many cases. They put so much pressure on them in there.

THE WIFE: How's he to convince you?

THE MAN: We'll find out where he stands all right.

THE WIFE: Might take time.

THE MAN: Yes.

THE WIFE: And he might be a first-rate comrade.

THE MAN: He might.

THE WIFE: It must be dreadful for him when he sees everybody mistrusting him.

THE MAN: He knows it's necessary.

THE WIFE: All the same.

THE MAN: I can hear something. Don't go away while we're talking.

*There is a ring. The man opens the door, the released man enters.*

THE MAN: Hullo, Max.

*The released man silently shakes hands with the man and his wife.*

THE WIFE: Would you like a cup of coffee with us? We're just going to have some.

THE RELEASED MAN: If it's not too much trouble.

*Pause.*

THE RELEASED MAN: You got a new cupboard.

THE WIFE: It's really an old one, cost eleven marks fifty. Ours was falling to pieces.

THE RELEASED MAN: Ha.

THE MAN: Anything doing in the street?

THE RELEASED MAN: They're collecting.

THE WIFE: We could do with a suit for Willi.

THE MAN: Hey, I'm not out of work.

THE WIFE: That's just why we could do with a suit for you.

THE MAN: Don't talk such nonsense.

THE RELEASED MAN: Work or no work, anybody can do with something.

THE MAN: You found work yet?

THE RELEASED MAN: They say so.

THE MAN: At Seimens?

THE RELEASED MAN: There or some other place.

THE MAN: It's not as hard as it was.

THE RELEASED MAN: No.

*Pause.*

THE MAN: How long you been inside?

THE RELEASED MAN: Six months.

THE MAN: Meet anyone in there?

THE RELEASED MAN: No one I knew. *Pause*. They're sending them to different camps these days. You could land up in Bavaria.

THE MAN: Ha.

THE RELEASED MAN: Things haven't changed much outside.

THE MAN: Not so as you'd notice.

THE WIFE: We live a very quiet life, you know. Willi hardly ever sees any of his old friends, do you, Willi?

THE MAN: Ay, we keep pretty much to ourselves.

THE RELEASED MAN: I don't suppose you ever got them to shift those rubbish bins from the hallway?

THE WIFE: Goodness, you remember that? Ay, he says he can't find anywhere else for them.

THE RELEASED MAN *as the wife is pouring him a cup of coffee*: Just give me a drop. I don't want to stay long.

THE MAN: Got any plans?

THE RELEASED MAN: Selma told me you looked after her when she was laid up. Thanks very much.

THE WIFE: It was nothing. We'd have told her to come over in the evening more, only we've not even got the wireless.

THE MAN: Anything they tell you is in the paper anyway.

THE RELEASED MAN: Not that there's much in the old rag.

THE WIFE: As much as there is in the *Völkischer Beobachter*, though.

THE RELEASED MAN: And in the *Völkischer Beobachter* there's just as much as there is in the old rag, eh?

THE MAN: I don't read that much in the evenings. Too tired.

THE WIFE: Here, what's wrong with your hand? All screwed up like that and two fingers missing?

THE RELEASED MAN: Oh, I had a fall.

THE MAN: Good thing it was your left one.

THE RELEASED MAN: Ay, that was a bit of luck. I'd like a word with you. No offence meant, Mrs Mahn.

THE WIFE: None taken. I've just got to clean the stove.

*She gets to work on the stove. The released man watches her, a thin smile on his lips.*

THE MAN: We've got to go out right after dinner. Has Selma quite recovered?

THE RELEASED MAN: All but for her hip. Doing washing is bad for her. Tell me ... *He stops short and looks at them. They look at him. He says nothing further.*

THE MAN *hoarsely*: What about a walk round the Alexanderplatz before dinner? See what's doing with their collection?

THE WIFE: We could do that, couldn't we?

THE RELEASED MAN: Sure.

*Pause.*

THE RELEASED MAN *quietly*: Hey, Willi, you know I've not changed.

THE MAN *lightly*: Course you haven't. They might have a band playing there. Get yourself ready, Anna. We've finished our coffee. I'll just run a comb through my hair. *They go into the next room. The released man remains seated. He has picked up his hat. He is aimlessly whistling. The couple return, dressed to go out.*

THE MAN: Come on then, Max.

THE RELEASED MAN: Very well. But let me just say: I find it entirely right.

THE MAN: Good, then let's go.

*They go out together.*

## 16

## Charity begins at home

With banners and loud drumming
The Winter Aid come slumming
Into the humblest door.
They've marched round and collected
The crumbs the rich have rejected
And brought them to the poor.

Their hands, more used to beatings
Now offer gifts and greetings.
They conjure up a smile.

Their charity soon crashes
Their food all turns to ashes
And chokes the uttered 'Heil!'

*Karlsruhe 1937. An old woman's flat. She is standing at a table
with her daughter while the two SA men deliver a parcel from
the Winter Aid Organisation.*

THE FIRST SA MAN: Here you are, Ma, a present from the
Führer.

THE SECOND SA MAN: So you can't say he's not looking after
you properly.

THE OLD WOMAN: Thanks very much, thanks very much.
Look, Erna, potatoes. And a woollen sweater. And apples.

THE FIRST SA MAN: And a letter from the Führer with
something in it. Go on, open it.

THE OLD WOMAN *opening the letter*: Five marks! What d'you
say to that, Erna?

THE SECOND SA MAN: Winter Aid.

THE OLD WOMAN: You must take an apple, young man, and
you too, for bringing these things to me, and up all those
stairs too. It's all I got to offer you. And I'll take one
myself.

*She takes a bite at an apple. All eat apples with the exception
of the young woman.*

THE OLD WOMAN: Go on, Erna, you take one too, don't just
stand there. That shows you things aren't like your husband
says.

THE FIRST SA MAN: What does he say, then?

THE YOUNG WOMAN: He doesn't say anything. The old
lady's wandering.

THE OLD WOMAN: Of course it's just his way of talking, you
know, it don't mean any harm, just the way they all talk.
How prices have gone up a bit much lately. *Pointing at her
daughter with the apple*: And she got her account book and
actually reckoned food had cost her 123 marks more this
year than last. Didn't you, Erna? *She notices that the SA
man seems to have taken this amiss.* But of course it's just
because we're rearming, isn't it? What's the matter, I said
something wrong?

THE FIRST SA MAN: Where do you keep your account book, young woman?

THE SECOND SA MAN: And who are you in the habit of showing it to?

THE YOUNG WOMAN: It's at home. I don't show it to no one.

THE OLD WOMAN: You can't object if she keeps accounts, how could you?

THE FIRST SA MAN: And if she goes about spreading alarm and despondency, are we allowed to object then?

THE SECOND SA MAN: What's more I don't remember her saying 'Heil Hitler' all that loudly when we came in. Do you?

THE OLD WOMAN: But she *did* say 'Heil Hitler' and I say the same. 'Heil Hitler'!

THE SECOND SA MAN: Nice nest of Marxists we've stumbled on here, Albert. We'd better have a good look at those accounts. Just you come along and show us where you live. *He seizes the young woman by the arm.*

THE OLD WOMAN: But she's in her third month. You can't ... that's no way for you to behave. After bringing the parcel and taking the apples. Erna! But she *did* say 'Heil Hitler', what am I do do, Heil Hitler! Heil Hitler!
*She vomits up the apple. The SA lead her daughter off.*

THE OLD WOMAN *continuing to vomit*: Heil Hitler!


## 17

## Two bakers

> Now come the master bakers
> Compelled to act as fakers
> And made to use their art
> On substitute ingredients –
> Spuds, bran and blind obedience.
> It lands them in the cart.

*Landsberg, 1936. Prison yard. Prisoners are walking in a*

*circle. Now and again two of them talk quietly to each other
downstage.*

THE ONE: So you're a baker too, new boy?
THE OTHER: Yes. Are you?
THE ONE: Yes. What did they get you for?
THE OTHER: Look out!
*They again walk round the circle.*
THE OTHER: Refusing to mix potatoes and bran in my bread.
    And you? How long've you been in?
THE ONE: Two years.
THE OTHER: And what did they get you for? Look out!
*They again walk round the circle.*
THE ONE: Mixing bran in my bread. Two years ago they still
    called that adulteration.
THE OTHER: Look out!

18

## The farmer feeds his sow

You'll notice in our procession
The farmer's sour expression:
They've underpriced his crop.
But what his pigs require
Is milk, whose price has gone higher.
It makes him blow his top.

*Aichach, 1937. A farmyard. It is night. The farmer is standing
by the pigsty giving instructions to his wife and two children.*

THE FARMER: I wasn't having you mixed up in this, but you
    found out and now you'll just have to shut your trap. Or
    else your dad'll go off to Landsberg gaol for the rest of his
    born days. There's nowt wrong in our feeding our cattle
    when they're hungry. God doesn't want any beast to starve.
    And soon as she's hungry she squeals and I'm not having a
    sow squealing with hunger on my farm. But they won't let
    me feed her. Cause the State says so. But I'm feeding her

just the same, I am. Cause if I don't feed her she'll die on me, and I shan't get any compensation for that.

THE FARMER'S WIFE: Too right. Our grain's our grain. And those buggers have no business telling us what to do. They got the Jews out but the State's the worst Jew of them all. And the Reverend Father saying 'Thou shalt not muzzle the ox that treadeth out the corn.' That's his way of telling us go ahead and feed our cattle. It weren't us as made their four-year plan, and we weren't asked.

THE FARMER: That's right. They don't favour the farmers and the farmers don't favour them. I'm supposed to deliver over my grain and pay through the nose for my cattle feed. So that that spiv can buy guns.

THE FARMER'S WIFE: You stand by the gate, Toni, and you, Marie, run into the pasture and soon as you see anyone coming give us a call.

*The children take up their positions. The farmer mixes his pig-swill and carries it to the sty, looking cautiously around him. His wife looks cautiously too.*

THE FARMER *pouring the swill into the sow's trough*: Go on, have a good feed, love. Heil Hitler! When a beast's hungry there ain't no State.


# 19

# The old militant

Behold several million electors.
One hundred per cent in all sectors
Have asked to be led by the nose.
They didn't get real bread and butter
They didn't get warm coats or fodder
They *did* get the leader they chose.

*Calw (Württemberg), 1938. A square with small shops. In the background a butcher's, in the foreground a dairy. It is a dark winter's morning. The butcher's is not open yet. But the dairy's lights are on and there are a few customers waiting.*

A PETIT-BOURGEOIS: No butter again today, what?

THE WOMAN: It'll be all I can afford on my old man's pay, anyway.

A YOUNG FELLOW: Stop grumbling, will you? Germany needs guns, not butter, no question about that. He spelled it out.

THE WOMAN *backing down*: Quite right too.

*Silence.*

THE YOUNG FELLOW: D'you think we could have reoccupied the Rhineland with butter? Everyone was for doing it the way we did, but catch them making any sacrifices.

A SECOND WOMAN: Keep your hair on. All of us are making some.

THE YOUNG FELLOW *mistrustfully*: What d'you mean?

THE SECOND WOMAN *to the first*: Don't you give something when they come round collecting?

*The first woman nods.*

THE SECOND WOMAN: There you are. She's giving. And so are we. Voluntary-like.

THE YOUNG FELLOW: That's an old story. Not a penny to spare when the Führer needs a bit of backing, as it were, for his mighty tasks. It's just rags, what they give the Winter Aid. They'd give 'em the moths if they could get away with it. We know the kind we got to deal with. That factory owner in number twelve went and gave us a pair of worn-out riding boots.

THE PETIT-BOURGEOIS: No foresight, that's the trouble.

*The dairywoman comes out of her shop in a white apron.*

THE DAIRYWOMAN: Won't be long now. *To the second woman*: Morning, Mrs Ruhl. Did you hear they came for young Lettner last night?

THE SECOND WOMAN: What, the butcher?

THE DAIRYWOMAN: Right, his son.

THE SECOND WOMAN: But he was in the SA.

THE DAIRYWOMAN: Used to be. The old fellow's been in the party since 1929. He was away at a livestock sale yesterday or they'd have taken him off too.

THE SECOND WOMAN: What're they supposed to have done?

THE DAIRYWOMAN: Been overcharging for meat. He was

hardly getting nothing on his quota and had to turn customers away. Then they say he started buying on the black market. From the Jews even.

THE YOUNG FELLOW: Bound to come for him, weren't they?

THE DAIRYWOMAN: Used to be one of the keenest of the lot, he did. He shopped old Zeisler at number seventeen for not taking the *Völkischer Beobachter*. An old militant, that's him.

THE SECOND WOMAN: He'll get a surprise when he comes back.

THE DAIRYWOMAN: *If* he comes back.

THE PETIT-BOURGEOIS: No foresight, that's the trouble.

THE SECOND WOMAN: Looks as if they won't open at all today.

THE DAIRYWOMAN: Best thing they can do. The police only have to look round a place like that and they're bound to find something, aren't they? With stock so hard to get. We get ours from the cooperative, no worries so far. *Calling out*: There'll be no cream today. *General murmur of disappointment*. They say Lettner's raised a mortgage on the house. They counted on its being cancelled or something.

THE PETIT-BOURGEOIS: They can't start cancelling mortgages. That'd be going a bit too far.

THE SECOND WOMAN: Young Lettner was quite a nice fellow.

THE DAIRYWOMAN: Old Lettner was always the crazy one. Went and shoved the boy in the SA, just like that. When he'd sooner have been going out with a girl, if you ask me.

THE YOUNG FELLOW: What d'you mean, crazy?

THE DAIRYWOMAN: Crazy, did I say? Oh, he always went crazy if anyone said anything against the Idea, in the old days. He was always speaking about the Idea, and down with the selfishness of the individual.

THE PETIT-BOURGEOIS: They're opening up, after all.

THE SECOND WOMAN: Got to live, haven't they?

*A stout woman comes out of the butcher's shop, which is now half-lit. She stops on the pavement and looks down the street for something. Then she turns to the dairywoman.*

THE BUTCHER'S WIFE: Good morning, Mrs Schlichter. Have

you seen our Richard? He should have been here with the meat well before now.

*The dairywoman doesn't reply. All of them just stare at her. She understands, and goes quickly back into the shop.*

THE DAIRYWOMAN: Act as though nothing's happened. It all blew up day before yesterday when the old man made such a stink you could hear him shouting right across the square. They counted that against him.

THE SECOND WOMAN: I never heard a word about that, Mrs Schlichter.

THE DAIRYWOMAN: Really? Didn't you know how he refused to hang that plaster ham they brought him in his shop window? He'd gone and ordered it cause they insisted, what with him hanging nothing in his window all week but the slate with the prices. He said: I've got nothing left for the window. When they brought that dummy ham, along with a side of veal, what's more, so natural you'd think it was real, he shouted he wasn't hanging any make-believe stuff in his window as well as a lot more I wouldn't care to repeat. Against the government, all of it, after which he threw the stuff into the road. They had to pick it up out of the dirt.

THE SECOND WOMAN: Ts, ts, ts, ts.

THE PETIT-BOURGEOIS: No foresight, that's the trouble.

THE SECOND WOMAN: How can people lose control like that?

THE DAIRYWOMAN: Particularly such a smooth operator.

*At this moment someone turns on a second light in the butcher's shop.*

THE DAIRYWOMAN: Look at that!

*She points excitedly at the half-lit shop window.*

THE SECOND WOMAN: There's something in the window.

THE DAIRYWOMAN: It's old Lettner. In his coat too. But what's he standing on? *Suddenly calls out*: Mrs Lettner!

THE BUTCHER'S WIFE: What is it?

*The dairywoman points speechlessly at the shop window. The butcher's wife glances at it, screams and falls down in a faint. The second woman and the dairywoman hurry over to her.*

THE SECOND WOMAN *back over her shoulder*: He's hung himself in his shop window.

THE PETIT-BOURGEOIS: There's a sign round his neck.

THE FIRST WOMAN: It's the slate. There's something written on it.

THE SECOND WOMAN: It says 'I voted for Hitler'.

20

# The Sermon on the Mount

> The Church's Ten Commandments
> Are subject to amendments
> By order of the police.
> Her broken head is bleeding
> For new gods are succeeding
> Her Jewish god of peace.

*Lübeck 1937. A fisherman's kitchen. The fisherman is dying. By his bed stand his wife and, in SA uniform, his son. The pastor is there.*

THE DYING MAN: Tell me: is there really anything afterwards?

THE PASTOR: Are you then troubled by doubts?

THE WIFE: He's kept on saying these last four days that there's so much talking and promising you don't know what to believe. You mustn't think badly of him, your Reverence.

THE PASTOR: Afterwards cometh eternal life.

THE DYING MAN: And that'll be better?

THE PASTOR: Yes.

THE DYING MAN: It's got to be.

THE WIFE: He's taken it out of himself, you know.

THE PASTOR: Believe me, God knows it.

THE DYING MAN: You think so? *After a pause*: Up there, I suppose a man'll be able to open his mouth for once now and again?

THE PASTOR *slightly confused*: It is written that faith moveth mountains. You must believe. You will find it easier then.

THE WIFE: Your Reverence, you mustn't think he doesn't believe. He always took Communion. *To her husband, urgently*: Here's his Reverence thinking you don't believe. But you do believe, don't you?

THE DYING MAN: Yes . . .

*Silence.*

THE DYING MAN: There's nothing else then.

THE PASTOR: What are you trying to say by that? There's nothing else then?

THE DYING MAN: Just: there's nothing else then. Eh? I mean, suppose there had been anything?

THE PASTOR: But what could there have been?

THE DYING MAN: Anything at all.

THE PASTOR: But you have had your dear wife and your son.

THE WIFE: You had us, didn't you?

THE DYING MAN: Yes . . .

*Silence.*

THE DYING MAN: I mean: if life had added up to anything . . .

THE PASTOR: I'm not quite sure I understand you. You surely don't mean that you only believe because your life has been all toil and hardship?

THE DYING MAN *looks round until he catches sight of his son*: And is it going to be better for them?

THE PASTOR: For youth, you mean? Let us hope so.

THE DYING MAN: If the boat had had a motor . . .

THE WIFE: You mustn't worry about that now.

THE PASTOR: It is not a moment to be thinking of such things.

THE DYING MAN: I've got to.

THE WIFE: We'll manage all right.

THE DYING MAN: But suppose there's a war?

THE WIFE: Don't speak about that now. *To the pastor*: These last times he was always talking to the boy about war. They didn't agree about it.

*The pastor looks at the son.*

THE SON: He doesn't believe in our future.

THE DYING MAN: Tell me: up there, does *he* want war?

THE PASTOR *hesitating*: It says: Blessed are the peacemakers.

THE DYING MAN: But if there's a war . . .

THE SON: The Führer doesn't want a war!

*The dying man makes a wide gesture of the hand, as if shoving that away.*

THE DYING MAN: So if there's a war . . .

*The son wants to say something.*

THE WIFE: Keep quiet now.

THE DYING MAN *to the pastor, pointing at his son*: You tell him that about the peacemakers.

THE PASTOR: We are all in the hand of God, you must not forget.

THE DYING MAN: You telling him?

THE WIFE: But his Reverence can't do anything to stop war, be reasonable. Better not talk about it nowadays, eh, your Reverence?

THE DYING MAN: You know: they're a swindling lot. I can't buy a motor for my boat. Their aeroplanes get motors all right. For war, for killing. And when it's stormy like this I can't bring her in because I haven't a motor. Those swindlers! War's what they're after! *He sinks back exhausted.*

THE WIFE *anxiously fetches a cloth and a bowl of water, and wipes away his sweat*: You mustn't listen. He doesn't know what he's saying.

THE PASTOR: You should calm yourself, Mr Claasen.

THE DYING MAN: You telling him about the peacemakers?

THE PASTOR *after a pause*: He can read for himself. It's in the Sermon on the Mount.

THE DYING MAN: He says it's all written by a Jew and it doesn't apply.

THE WIFE: Don't start on that again! He doesn't mean it like that. That's what he hears the others saying.

THE DYING MAN: Yes. *To the pastor*: Does it apply?

THE WIFE *with an anxious glance at her son*: Don't make trouble for his Reverence, Hannes. You shouldn't ask that.

THE SON: Why shouldn't he ask that?

THE DYING MAN: Does it apply or not?

THE PASTOR: It is also written: Render therefore unto Caesar
the things which are Caesar's; and unto God the things that
are God's.
*The dying man sinks back. His wife lays the damp cloth on
his forehead.*


**21**

# The motto

Their boys learn it's morally healthy
To lay down one's life for the wealthy:
It's a lesson that's made very clear.
It's far harder than spelling or figures
But their teachers are terrible floggers
So they're fearful of showing fear.

*Chemnitz, 1937. Meeting room of the Hitler Youth. A squad
of boys, mostly with gasmasks slung round their necks. A small
group are looking at a boy with no mask who is sitting by
himself on a bench and helplessly moving his lips as if learning
something.*

THE FIRST BOY: He still hasn't got one.
THE SECOND BOY: His old lady won't buy him one.
THE FIRST BOY: But she must know he'll get into trouble.
THE THIRD BOY: If she ain't got the cash . . .
THE FIRST BOY: And old Fatty's got a down on him in any
case.
THE SECOND BOY: He's back to learning it: 'The Motto'.
THE FOURTH BOY: That's four weeks he's been trying to
learn it, and it's just a couple of verses.
THE THIRD BOY: He's known it off for ages.
THE SECOND BOY: He only gets stuck cause he's frightened.
THE FOURTH BOY: That's terribly funny, don't you think?
THE FIRST BOY: Devastating. *He calls*: D'you know it,
Pschierer?

*The fifth boy looks up, distracted, gets the meaning and nods. Then he goes on learning.*

THE SECOND BOY: Old Fatty only keeps on at him cause he's got no gasmask.

THE THIRD BOY: The way he tells it, it's because he wouldn't go to the pictures with him.

THE FOURTH BOY: That's what I heard too. D'you think it's true?

THE SECOND BOY: Could be, why not? I wouldn't go to the pictures with Fatty either. But he wouldn't start anything with me. My old man wouldn't half kick up a stink.

THE FIRST BOY: Look out, here's Fatty.

*The boys come to attention in two ranks. Enter a somewhat corpulent Scharführer. The Hitler salute.*

THE SCHARFÜHRER: From the right, number!

*They number.*

THE SCHARFÜHRER: Gasmasks – on!

*The boys put on their gasmasks. Some of them have not got one. They simply go through the motions of the drill.*

THE SCHARFÜHRER: We'll start with 'The Motto'. Who's going to recite it for us? *He looks round as if unable to make up his mind, then suddenly*: Pschierer! You do it so nicely.

*The fifth boy steps forward and stands to attention in front of the others.*

THE SCHARFÜHRER: Can you do it, maestro?

THE FIFTH BOY: Yes, sir!

THE SCHARFÜHRER: Right, get cracking! Verse number one!

THE FIFTH BOY:

Thou shalt gaze on death unblinking –
Saith the motto for our age –
Sent into the fray unflinching
Heedless of the battle's rage.

THE SCHARFÜHRER: Don't wet your pants now. Carry on! Verse number two!

THE FIFTH BOY:

Victory is ours for gaining.
Beat, stab, shoot . . .

*He has got stuck, and repeats these words. One or two of the
boys find it difficult not to burst out laughing.*

THE SCHARFÜHRER: So once again you haven't learnt it?

THE FIFTH BOY: Yes, sir!

THE SCHARFÜHRER: I bet you learn something different at
home, don't you? *Shouts:* Carry on!

THE FIFTH BOY:

Beat, stab, shoot them so they fall.

Be a German ... uncomplaining, uncomplaining

Be a German uncomplaining

Die for this ... die for this, and give your all.

THE SCHARFÜHRER: Now what's so difficult about that?


## 22

## News of the bombardment of Almería gets to the barracks

The soldiers in His armed forces
Get full meat and pudding courses
And can also ask for more.
It helps them to face the firing
And not to think of enquiring
Who He is fighting for.

*Berlin, 1937. Corridor in a barracks. Looking around them
nervously, two working-class boys are carrying away something wrapped in brown paper.*

THE FIRST BOY: Aren't half worked up today, are they?

THE SECOND BOY: They say it's cause war could break out.
Over Spain.

THE FIRST BOY: White as a sheet, some of them.

THE SECOND BOY: Cause we bombarded Almería. Last night.

THE FIRST BOY: Where's that?

THE SECOND BOY: In Spain, silly. Hitler telegraphed for a
German warship to bombard Almería right away. As a
punishment. Cause they're reds down there, and reds have

got to be scared shitless of the Third Reich. Now it could lead to war.

THE FIRST BOY: And now they're scared shitless too.

THE SECOND BOY: Right. Scared shitless, that's them.

THE FIRST BOY: What do they want to go bombarding for if they're white as a sheet and scared shitless cause it could lead to war?

THE SECOND BOY: They just started bombarding cause Hitler wants it that way.

THE FIRST BOY: Whatever Hitler wants they want too. The whole lot are for Hitler. Cause he's built up our new armed forces.

THE SECOND BOY: You got it.

*Pause.*

THE FIRST BOY: Think we can sneak out now?

THE SECOND BOY: Better wait, or we'll run into one of those lieutenants. Then he'll confiscate everything and they'll be in trouble.

THE FIRST BOY: Decent of them to let us come every day.

THE SECOND BOY: Oh, they ain't millionaires any more than us, you know. They know how it is. My old lady only gets ten marks a week, and there are three of us. It's just enough for potatoes.

THE FIRST BOY: Smashing nosh they get here. Meatballs today.

THE SECOND BOY: How much d'they give you this time?

THE FIRST BOY: One dollop, as usual. Why?

THE SECOND BOY: They gave me two this time.

THE FIRST BOY: Let's see. They only gave one.

*The second boy shows him.*

THE FIRST BOY: Did you say anything to them?

THE SECOND BOY: No. Just 'good morning' as usual.

THE FIRST BOY: I don't get it. And me too, 'Heil Hitler' as usual.

THE SECOND BOY: Funny. They gave me two dollops.

THE FIRST BOY: Why d'they suddenly do that. I don't get it.

THE SECOND BOY: Nor me. Coast's clear now.

*They quickly run off.*

23
# Job creation

He sees that jobs are provided.
The poor go where they are guided:
He likes them to be keen.
They're allowed to serve the nation.
Their blood and perspiration
Can fuel His war machine.

*Spandau, 1937. A worker comes home and finds a neighbour there.*

THE NEIGHBOUR: Good evening, Mr Fenn. I just came to see if your wife could lend me some bread. She's popped out for a moment.

THE MAN: That's all right, Mrs Dietz. What d'you think of the job I got?

THE NEIGHBOUR: Ah, they're all getting work. At the new factory, aren't you? You'll be turning out bombers then?

THE MAN: And how.

THE NEIGHBOUR: They'll be needed in Spain these days.

THE MAN: Why specially Spain?

THE NEIGHBOUR: You hear such things about the stuff they're sending. A disgrace, I call it.

THE MAN: Best mind what you say.

THE NEIGHBOUR: You joined them now too?

THE MAN: I've not joined nothing. I get on with my work. Where's Martha gone?

THE NEIGHBOUR: I'd best warn you, I suppose. It could be something nasty. Just as I came in the postman was here, and there was some kind of letter got your wife all worked up. Made me wonder if I shouldn't ask the Schiermanns to lend me that bread.

THE MAN: Cor. *He calls*: Martha!
*Enter his wife. She is in mourning.*

THE MAN: What are you up to? Who's dead then?

THE WIFE: Franz. We got a letter.
*She hands him a letter.*

THE NEIGHBOUR: For God's sake! What happened to him?

THE MAN: It was an accident.

THE NEIGHBOUR *mistrustfully*: But wasn't he a pilot?

THE MAN: Yes.

THE NEIGHBOUR: And he had an accident?

THE MAN: At Stettin. In the course of a night exercise with troops, it says here.

THE NEIGHBOUR: He won't have had no accident. Tell me another.

THE MAN: I'm only telling you what it says here. The letter's from the commandant.

THE NEIGHBOUR: Did he write to you lately? From Stettin?

THE MAN: Don't get worked up, Martha. It won't help.

THE WIFE *sobbing*: No, I know.

THE NEIGHBOUR: He was such a nice fellow, that brother of yours. Like me to make you a pot of coffee?

THE MAN: Yes, if you would, Mrs Dietz.

THE NEIGHBOUR *looking for a pot*: That sort of thing's always a shock.

THE WIFE: Go on, have your wash, Herbert. Mrs Dietz won't mind.

THE MAN: There's no hurry.

THE NEIGHBOUR: So he wrote to you from Stettin?

THE MAN: That's where the letters always came from.

THE NEIGHBOUR *gives a look*: Really? I suppose he'd gone south with the others?

THE MAN: What do you mean, gone south?

THE NEIGHBOUR: Way south to sunny Spain.

THE MAN *as his wife again bursts into sobs*: Pull yourself together, Martha. You shouldn't say that sort of thing, Mrs Dietz.

THE NEIGHBOUR: I just wonder what they'd tell you in Stettin if you went and tried to collect your brother.

THE MAN: I'm not going to Stettin.

THE NEIGHBOUR: They always sweep things under the mat. They think it's heroic of them not to let anything come out. There was a fellow in the boozer bragging about how clever they are at covering up their war. When one of your bombers gets shot down and the blokes inside jump out with parachutes, the other bombers machine-gun them down in midair – their own blokes – so's they can't tell the Reds where they've come from.

THE WIFE *who is feeling sick*: Get us some water, will you, Herbert, I'm feeling sick.

THE NEIGHBOUR: I really didn't mean to upset you, it's just the way they cover it all up. They know it's criminal all right and that their war can't stand being exposed. Same in this case. Had an accident in the course of an exercise! What are they exercising at? A war, that's what!

THE MAN: Don't talk so loudly in here, d'you mind? *To his wife*: How are you feeling?

THE NEIGHBOUR: You're another of them keeps quiet about it all. There's your answer, in that letter.

THE MAN: Just shut up, would you?

THE WIFE: Herbert!

THE NEIGHBOUR: So now it's 'shut up, would you?'. Because you got a job. Your brother-in-law got one too, didn't he? Had an 'accident' with one of the same things you're making in that factory.

THE MAN: I don't like that, Mrs Dietz. Me working on 'one of the same things'! What are all the rest of them working on? What's your husband working on? Electric bulbs, isn't it? I suppose they're not for war. Just to give light. But what's the light for? To light tanks, eh? Or a battleship? Or one of those same things? He's only making light bulbs, though. My God, there's nothing left that's not for war. How am I supposed to find a job if I keep telling myself 'not for war!'? D'you want me to starve?

THE NEIGHBOUR *subduedly*: I'm not saying you got to starve. Of course you're right to take the job. I'm just talking about those criminals. A nice kind of job creation, I don't think.

THE MAN *seriously*: And better not go around in black like that, Martha. They don't like it.

THE NEIGHBOUR: The questions it makes people ask: that's what they don't like.

THE WIFE *calmly*: You'd rather I took it off?

THE MAN: Yes, if I'm not to lose my job any minute.

THE WIFE: I'm not taking it off.

THE MAN: What d'you mean?

THE WIFE: I'm not taking it off. My brother's dead. I'm going into mourning.

THE MAN: If you hadn't got it because Rosa bought it when Mother died, you wouldn't be able to go into mourning.

THE WIFE *shouting*: Don't anyone tell me I'm not going into mourning! If they can slaughter him I have a right to cry, don't I? I never heard of such a thing. It's the most inhuman thing ever happened! They're criminals of the lowest kind!

THE NEIGHBOUR *while the man sits speechless with horror*: But Mrs Fenn!

THE MAN *hoarsely*: If you're going to talk like that we could do more than lose our job.

THE WIFE: Let them come and get me, then! They've concentration camps for women too. Let them just put me in one of those because I dare to mind when they kill my brother! What was he in Spain for?

THE MAN: Shut up about Spain!

THE NEIGHBOUR: That kind of talk could get us into trouble, Mrs Fenn.

THE WIFE: Are we to keep quiet just because they might take your job away? Because we'll die of starvation if we don't make bombers for them? And die just the same if we do? Exactly like my Franz? They created a job for him too. Three foot under. He could as well have had that here.

THE MAN *holding a hand over her mouth*: Shut up, will you? It doesn't help.

THE WIFE: What does help then? Do something that does!

# 24

## Consulting the people

And as the column passes
We call with urgent voices:
Can none of you say No?

You've got to make them heed you.
This war to which they lead you
Will soon be your death-blow.

*Berlin. March 13th, 1938. A working-class flat, with two men
and a woman. The constricted space is blocked by a flagpole. A
great noise of jubilation from the radio, with church bells and
the sound of aircraft. A voice is saying 'And now the Führer is
about to enter Vienna.'*

THE WOMAN: It's like the sea.

THE OLDER WORKER: Aye, it's one victory after another for
that fellow.

THE YOUNGER WORKER: And us that gets defeated.

THE WOMAN: That's right.

THE YOUNGER WORKER: Listen to them shouting. Like
they're being given a present.

THE OLDER WORKER: They are. An invasion.

THE YOUNGER WORKER: And then it's what they call
'consulting the people'. 'Ein Volk, ein Reich, ein Führer!'
'A single people, a single empire, a single leader.' 'Willst du
das, Deutscher?' 'You're German, are you in favour?' And
us not able to put out the least little leaflet about this
referendum. Here, in a working-class district like Neukölln.

THE WOMAN: How d'you mean, not able?

THE YOUNGER WORKER: Too dangerous.

THE OLDER WORKER: And just when they've caught Karl.
How are we to get the addresses?

THE YOUNGER WORKER: We'd need someone to do the
writing too.

THE WOMAN *points at the radio*: He had a hundred thousand
men to launch his attack. We need one man. Fine. If he's the
only one who's got what's needed, then he'll score the
victories.

THE YOUNGER WORKER *in anger*: So we can do without Karl.

THE WOMAN: If that's the way you people feel then we may
as well split up.

THE OLDER WORKER: Comrades, there's no use kidding
ourselves. Producing a leaflet's getting harder and harder,
that's a fact. It's no good acting as if we just can't hear all

that victory din – *pointing at the radio. To the woman*: You've got to admit, anyone hearing that sort of thing might think they're getting stronger all the time. It really does sound like a single people, wouldn't you say?

THE WOMAN: It sounds like twenty thousand drunks being stood free beer.

THE YOUNGER WORKER: For all you know we might be the only people to say so.

THE WOMAN: Right. Us and others like us.

*The woman smoothes out a small crumpled piece of paper.*

THE OLDER WORKER: What have you got there?

THE WOMAN: It's a copy of a letter. There's such a din I can read it out. *She reads*: 'Dear son: Tomorrow I shall have ceased to be. Executions are usually at six a.m. I'm writing now because I want you to know I haven't changed my opinions, nor have I applied for a pardon because I didn't commit any crime. I just served my class. And if it looks as though I got nowhere like that it isn't so. Every man to his post, should be our motto. Our task is very difficult, but it's the greatest one there is – to free the human race from its oppressors. Till that's done life has no other value. Let that out of our sights and the whole human race will relapse into barbarism. You're still quite young but it won't hurt you to remember always which side you are on. Stick with your own class, then your father won't have suffered his unhappy fate in vain, because it isn't easy. Look after your mother, your brothers and sisters too, you're the eldest. Better be clever. Greetings to you all, Your loving Father.'

THE OLDER WORKER: There aren't really that few of us after all.

THE YOUNGER WORKER: What's to go in the referendum leaflet, then?

THE WOMAN *thinking*: Best thing would be just one word: NO!

# Señora Carrar's Rifles

*Partly based on an idea of J.M. Synge*

*Collaborator*: M. STEFFIN

*Translator*: WOLFGANG SAUERLÄNDER

*Characters*:

TERESA CARRAR, *a fisherwoman*
JOSÉ, *her younger son*
PEDRO JAQUERAS, *a worker, brother of Teresa Carrar*
THE WOUNDED MAN
MANUELA
THE PRIEST
OLD MRS PÉREZ
TWO FISHERMEN
WOMEN
CHILDREN

*A fisherman's cottage in Andalusia on a night in April, 1937.*
*In one corner of the whitewashed room a large black crucifix.*
*Teresa Carrar, a fisherwoman of forty, is baking bread. Her*
*son, José, fifteen, stands at the open window, whittling a float.*
*Roar of cannon in the distance.*

THE MOTHER: Can you still see Juan's boat?

JOSÉ: Yes.

THE MOTHER: Is his lantern still burning?

JOSÉ: Yes.

THE MOTHER: No other boat joined him?

JOSÉ: No.

   *Pause.*

THE MOTHER: That's strange. Why isn't anybody else out?

JOSÉ: You know why.

THE MOTHER *patiently*: If I knew, I wouldn't be asking.

JOSÉ: There's no one out but Juan; they've other things to do
than catch fish these days.

THE MOTHER: I see.

   *Pause.*

JOSÉ: If it was up to him Juan wouldn't be out either.

THE MOTHER: Right. It isn't up to him.

JOSÉ *whittling furiously*: No.

   *The mother puts the dough in the oven, wipes her hands and*
   *takes up a fish-net to mend it.*

JOSÉ: I'm hungry.

THE MOTHER: But you don't want your brother to go fishing.

JOSÉ: Because I can do that just as well and Juan ought to be
at the front.

THE MOTHER: I thought you wanted to go to the front too.

   *Pause.*

JOSÉ: Think the food ships will get through the British
blockade?

THE MOTHER: Anyhow there'll be no flour left when this bread is done.

*José shuts the window.*

THE MOTHER: Why are you shutting the window?

JOSÉ: It's nine o'clock.

THE MOTHER: Well?

JOSÉ: That swine is on the radio at nine and the Pérezes will tune in.

THE MOTHER *imploringly*: Please open the window! You can't see properly with the light on in here and the window reflecting it.

JOSÉ: Why should I sit here and watch? He won't run away. You're just afraid he'll go to the front.

THE MOTHER: Don't answer back! It's bad enough my having to keep an eye on the two of you.

JOSÉ: What do you mean, the two of us?

THE MOTHER: You're no better than your brother. Worse if anything.

JOSÉ: They only put on the radio for our benefit. This'll be the third time. They opened their window on purpose yesterday to make us listen; I saw them.

THE MOTHER: Those speeches are no different from the ones they made in Valencia.

JOSÉ: Why not just say they're better?

THE MOTHER: You know I don't think they're better. Why should I be for the generals? I'm against bloodshed.

JOSÉ: Who started it? Us, I suppose?

*The mother is silent. José has opened the window again. An announcement is heard from a near-by radio: 'Attention! Attention! His Excellency General Queipo de Llano will address you.' The radio general's voice comes through the night loud and clear as he delivers his nightly address to the Spanish people.*

THE GENERAL'S VOICE: Today or tomorrow, my friends, we propose to have a serious word with you. And we propose to have that word with you in Madrid, even if what's left of it doesn't look like Madrid any more. Then the Archbishop of Canterbury will really have something to shed crocodile tears for. Just wait till our splendid Moors are through.

JOSÉ: Bastard!

THE GENERAL'S VOICE: My friends, the so-called British Empire, that colossus on feet of clay, cannot stop us destroying the capital of a perverted people that has the effrontery to oppose the irresistible cause of nationalism. Rabble! We'll wipe them off the face of the earth!

JOSÉ: That's us, Mother.

THE MOTHER: We're not rebels and we're not opposing anybody. Perhaps you boys would if you had your way. You and that brother of yours, you're both reckless. You got that from your father and maybe I wouldn't like it if you were different. But this thing is no joke. Can't you hear their guns? We're poor; poor people can't make war.

*Knocking at the door. Pedro Jacqueras, a worker, Teresa Carrar's brother, enters. It is plain that he has walked a long way.*

THE WORKER: Good evening.

JOSÉ: Uncle Pedro!

THE MOTHER: What brings you here, Pedro? *She shakes hands with him.*

JOSÉ: Have you come from Motril, Uncle Pedro? How are things going?

THE WORKER: Ah, not too well. How are you getting along here?

THE MOTHER *hesitantly*: Not too bad.

JOSÉ: Did you leave today?

THE WORKER: Yes.

JOSÉ: Takes a good four hours, eh?

THE WORKER: More; the roads are clogged with refugees trying to get to Almería.

JOSÉ: But Motril's holding out?

THE WORKER: I don't know what has happened today. Last night we were still holding out.

JOSÉ: Then why did you leave?

THE WORKER: We need some stuff for the front. So I figured I'd look in on you.

THE MOTHER: Would you like a sip of wine? *She fetches wine.* The bread won't be done for another half hour.

THE WORKER: Where's Juan?

JOSÉ: Out fishing.

THE WORKER: Fishing?

JOSÉ: You can see his lantern from the window.

THE MOTHER: We've got to live.

THE WORKER: Of course. As I was coming down the street I heard the radio general. Who listens to him around here?

JOSÉ: The Pérezes across the street.

THE WORKER: Do they always tune in on that stuff?

JOSÉ: No. They're not Franco people, it isn't for their own benefit, if that's what you mean.

THE WORKER: Is that so?

THE MOTHER *to José*: Are you keeping an eye on your brother?

JOSÉ *reluctantly returns to the window*: Don't worry, he hasn't fallen overboard.

*The worker takes the wine jug, sits down by his sister and helps her mend the nets.*

THE WORKER: How old would Juan be now?

THE MOTHER: Twenty-one in September.

THE WORKER: And José?

THE MOTHER: Have you got something special to do around here?

THE WORKER: Nothing special.

THE MOTHER: You haven't shown your face in a long time.

THE WORKER: Two years.

THE MOTHER: How's Rosa?

THE WORKER: Rheumatism.

THE MOTHER: The two of you might have dropped in once in a while.

THE WORKER: I guess Rosa was a little put out about Carlos's funeral.

*The mother is silent.*

THE WORKER: She said you might have let us know. Of course we'd have come to your husband's funeral, Teresa.

THE MOTHER: It was all so sudden.

THE WORKER: What actually happened?

*The mother is silent.*

JOSÉ: Shot through the lung.

THE WORKER *amazed*: How come?

THE MOTHER: What do you mean 'How come'?

THE WORKER: Everything was quiet around here two years ago.

JOSÉ: There was the rising in Oviedo.

THE WORKER: How did Carlos get to Oviedo?

THE MOTHER: Took the train.

THE WORKER: From here?

JOSÉ: Yes, when he read about the rising in the papers.

THE MOTHER *with bitterness*: Same as other people go to America to stake everything on one card. Fools.

JOSÉ *rising*: Are you saying he was a fool?
*Silently, with trembling hands, she lays the net aside and goes out.*

THE WORKER: Must have been pretty bad for her.

JOSÉ: Yes.

THE WORKER: Did she take it very hard when he didn't come back?

JOSÉ: He did come back, she saw him again. That was the worst part of it. Up there in the Asturias, he seems to have managed to take a train with a field dressing under his blouse. He had to change twice, and then he died here at the station. One evening our door suddenly opened and the local women filed in, the way they do when someone gets drowned. They lined up along the walls without a word and reeled off an Ave Maria. Then he was brought in on a piece of sailcloth and laid down on the floor. She's been scurrying off to church ever since. And refusing to see the school teacher that everybody knew was a red.

THE WORKER: You mean she's got religion?

JOSÉ *nods*: Juan thinks it was mostly because people round here started talking about her.

THE WORKER: What did they say?

JOSÉ: That she put him up to it.

THE WORKER: Well, did she?
*José shrugs his shoulders. The mother returns, looks into the oven and sits down again with the net.*

THE MOTHER *to the worker who is again trying to help her*: Never mind that. Drink your wine and take it easy, you've been up and about since early morning.

*The worker takes the wine jug and returns to the table.*

THE MOTHER: Do you want to stay the night?

THE WORKER: No. I haven't that much time. I've got to go back tonight. But I'd like to wash. *He goes out.*

THE MOTHER *beckons José to come to her:* Did he tell you what he came for?

JOSÉ: No.

THE MOTHER: Are you sure?

*The worker returns with a wash basin; he washes himself.*

THE MOTHER: Are the old Lópezes still alive?

THE WORKER: Only him. *To José:* I suppose a good many of the villagers have gone to the front?

JOSÉ: Some are still here.

THE WORKER: In our town a lot of good Catholics have joined up.

JOSÉ: Some from here too.

THE WORKER: Have they all got rifles?

JOSÉ: No. Not all.

THE WORKER: That's bad. Guns are the main thing now. Aren't there any rifles left in this village?

THE MOTHER *quickly:* No!

JOSÉ: Some people hide them. They bury them like potatoes. *The mother looks at José.*

THE WORKER: I see.

*José ambles away from the window and withdraws into the background.*

THE MOTHER: Where are you going?

JOSÉ: Nowhere.

THE MOTHER: Get back to that window!

*José remains obstinately in the rear.*

THE WORKER: What's going on here?

THE MOTHER: Why have you left the window? Answer me!

THE WORKER: Is there someone outside?

JOSÉ *hoarsely:* No.

*Children's voices are heard howling outside.*

CHILDREN'S VOICES:
Juan's not a soldier
He'd rather stay in bed.
Juan's a lousy coward

Pulls the blanket over his head.

*The children's faces appear in the window.*

THE CHILDREN: Baah! *They run away.*

THE MOTHER *gets up, goes to the window*: Just let me catch you and I'll beat the stuffing out of you, stinking brats! *Talking back into the room.* It's those Pérezes again! *Pause.*

THE WORKER: You used to play cards, José. How about a little game?

*The mother sits down at the window. José gets the cards and they start playing.*

THE WORKER: Do you still cheat?

JOSÉ *laughing*: Did I?

THE WORKER: Used to think so. I'll just cut to be on the safe side. Right then, anything goes. All's fair in cards and war.

*The mother looks up suspiciously.*

JOSÉ: What lousy trumps.

THE WORKER: Thanks for letting me know. – Ha, look at him playing the ace of trumps. That was a bluff, but it didn't pay off, did it? Fired your big gun, and now here I come with my peashooter. *Slaps him down with a series of quick tricks.* You had it coming. Daring is all very well, my boy. You're daring all right, but you've a lot to learn about caution.

JOSÉ: Nothing venture, nothing gain.

THE MOTHER: They got those sayings from their father. 'A gentleman takes risks.' That it?

THE WORKER: Yes, he risks our skins. Don Miguel de Ferrante once lost seventy peasants to a colonel in a single card game. He was ruined, poor devil; had to make do with twelve servants for the rest of his life. – Look at that, he's playing his last ten.

JOSÉ: I had to. *He takes the trick.* It was my only chance.

THE MOTHER: That's the way they are. His father used to jump out of the boat when his net got caught.

THE WORKER: Maybe he didn't have all that many nets.

THE MOTHER: Didn't have all that many lives either.

*In the doorway stands a man in the uniform of the militia. His head is bandaged, one arm is in a sling.*

THE MOTHER: Come on in, Pablo.

THE WOUNDED MAN: You said I could come back to be bandaged, Mrs Carrar.

THE MOTHER: It's all soaked through again. *She runs out.*

THE WORKER: Where'd you get that?

THE WOUNDED MAN: Monte Solluve.

*The mother returns with a shirt which she tears into strips. She renews the dressing, constantly keeping an eye on those at the table.*

THE MOTHER: You've been working again, then.

THE WOUNDED MAN: Only with my right arm.

THE MOTHER: But they told you not to.

THE WOUNDED MAN: Yes, I know. – The rumour is, they'll break through tonight. We've no reserves left. Could they be through already?

THE WORKER *getting restless*: No, I don't think so. The gunfire would sound different.

THE WOUNDED MAN: That's right.

THE MOTHER: Am I hurting you? You must tell me. I'm not a trained nurse. I'm doing it as gently as I can.

JOSÉ: They'll never break through at Madrid.

THE WOUNDED MAN: There's no telling.

JOSÉ: Oh yes there is.

THE WOUNDED MAN: Fine. But you've gone and torn up another good shirt, Mrs Carrar. You shouldn't have done that.

THE MOTHER: Would you sooner have a dishrag around your arm?

THE WOUNDED MAN: You people aren't so well off either.

THE MOTHER: While it lasts it lasts. There now. But there wouldn't be enough for your other arm.

THE WOUNDED MAN *laughs*: I'll have to be more careful next time. *Gets up; to the worker*: If only they don't break through, the bastards! *He leaves.*

THE MOTHER: Oh God, those guns!

JOSÉ: And we go fishing.

THE MOTHER: You two can be glad you've still got sound limbs.

*The swelling and fading noise of trucks and singing is heard from outside. The worker and José step to the window and watch.*

THE WORKER: That's the International Brigade. They're being sent to the Motril front.

*The refrain of the 'Thälmann Column' is heard: 'Die Heimat ist weit . . .'.*

THE WORKER: Those are the Germans.

*A few measures of the 'Marseillaise'.*

THE WORKER: The French.

*The 'Warszawianka'.*

THE WORKER: Poles.

*'Bandiera rossa'.*

THE WORKER: The Italians.

*'Hold the Fort'.*

THE WORKER: Americans.

*'Los cuatro generales'.*

THE WORKER: And that's our men.

*The noise of trucks and singing fades away. The worker and José return to the table.*

THE WORKER: Everything depends on tonight! – I really ought to be going. That was the last hand, José.

THE MOTHER *approaching the table*: Who won?

JOSÉ *proudly*: He did.

THE MOTHER: Shouldn't I make up a bed for you?

THE WORKER: No, I've got to be going. *But he remains seated.*

THE MOTHER: Give Rosa my regards. And tell her to let bygones be bygones. None of us knows what's going to happen.

JOSÉ: I'll go a bit of the way with you.

THE WORKER: No need.

*The mother, standing up, looks out of the window.*

THE MOTHER: I suppose you'd have liked to see Juan?

THE WORKER: Yes, I'd have liked to. But he won't be back all that soon, will he?

THE MOTHER: He's gone pretty far out. Must be close to the Cape. *Talking back into the room.* We could go and get him. *A young girl appears in the doorway.*

JOSÉ: Hello, Manuela. *Under his breath to the worker*: It's Juan's girl, Manuela. *To the young girl*: This is Uncle Pedro.

THE YOUNG GIRL: Where's Juan?

THE MOTHER: Juan's at work.

THE YOUNG GIRL: We thought you'd bundled him off to kindergarten to play ball.

THE MOTHER: No, he went fishing. Juan's a fisherman.

THE YOUNG GIRL: Why didn't he come to the meeting at the schoolhouse? Some of the fishermen were there.

THE MOTHER: He had no business there.

JOSÉ: What was the meeting about?

THE YOUNG GIRL: They decided whoever can be spared must go to the front this very night. You people knew what the meeting was about. We sent Juan a message.

JOSÉ: That's not possible. Juan wouldn't have gone fishing in that case. Or did they tell you, Mother?

*The mother is silent. She has crawled all the way into the oven.*

JOSÉ: She didn't give him the message! *To the mother*: So that's why you sent him out fishing!

THE WORKER: You shouldn't have done that, Teresa!

THE MOTHER *straightening up*: God gave people trades. My son is a fisherman.

THE YOUNG GIRL: Do you want to make us the laughing stock of the whole village? Wherever I go people point at me. Just hearing Juan's name makes me sick. What kind of people are you anyway?

THE MOTHER: We're poor people.

THE YOUNG GIRL: The government has called on all able-bodied men to take up arms. Don't tell me you didn't read that.

THE MOTHER: I've read it. Government this, government that. I know they want us to end up in the boneyard. But I'm not volunteering to wheel my children there.

THE YOUNG GIRL: No. Sooner wait till they're lined up against the wall, wouldn't you? I've never seen anything so stupid. It's because of your sort that things are how they are and a swine like Queipo dares talk to us the way he does.

THE MOTHER *weakly*: I'm not having such things said in my house.

THE YOUNG GIRL *beside herself*: She's all for the generals now, I suppose.

JOSÉ *somewhat impatiently*: No! But she doesn't want us to fight.

THE WORKER: Neutrality: that it?

THE MOTHER: I know you people want to turn my house into a den of conspirators. And *you* won't lay off till you see Juan stood up against a wall.

THE YOUNG GIRL: And they said *you* helped your husband when he went off to Oviedo.

THE MOTHER *softly*: Hold your tongue! I did not help my husband. Not for a thing like that. I know I'm being blamed for it, but it's a lie. All dirty lies! Anybody'll tell you.

THE YOUNG GIRL: Nobody's blaming you, Mrs Carrar. They said that with the deepest respect. All of us in the village knew that Carlos Carrar was a hero. But now we know that he probably had to sneak out of the house in the dead of night.

JOSÉ: My father did not sneak out of the house in the dead of night, Manuela.

THE MOTHER: Shut up, José!

THE YOUNG GIRL: Tell your son I'm through with him. And there'll be no more need for him to keep out of sight for fear I'll ask why he isn't where he should be. *She leaves.*

THE WORKER: You oughtn't to have let the girl go like that, Teresa. In the old days you wouldn't have.

THE MOTHER: I'm the same as I've always been. They probably made bets to see who could get Juan off to the front. – Anyway, I'll go and get him. Or you go, José. No, wait, better go myself. I'll be right back. *Goes out.*

THE WORKER: Look, José, you're not stupid, there's no need to tell you a story you know already. All right, where are they?

JOSÉ: What?

THE WORKER: The rifles.

JOSÉ: Father's?

THE WORKER: They must be around somewhere. He couldn't have taken them on the train when he went off.

JOSÉ: That what you came for?

THE WORKER: What else?

JOSÉ: She'll never let them go. She's hidden them.

THE WORKER: Where?

*José indicates a corner. The worker gets up and is starting in that direction when they hear footsteps.*

THE WORKER *sits down quickly*: Quiet now!

*The mother comes in with the local priest. He is a tall, strong man in a worn-out cassock.*

THE PRIEST: Good evening, José. *To the worker*: Good evening.

THE MOTHER: Father, this is my brother from Motril.

THE PRIEST: I'm glad to make your acquaintance. *To the mother*: I really must apologise for coming with yet another request. Could you stop in at the Turillos' at noon tomorrow? Mrs Turillo has joined her husband at the front and now the children are alone.

THE MOTHER: I'll be glad to.

THE PRIEST *to the worker*: What brings you to our village? I'm told it's not so easy to get here from Motril.

THE WORKER: Still pretty quiet around here, ain't it?

THE PRIEST: Beg your pardon? – Yes.

THE MOTHER: Pedro, I believe the Father asked you something. What brings you here?

THE WORKER: I figured it was time to see how my sister was getting along.

THE PRIEST *with an encouraging glance at the mother*: It's very kind of you to take an interest in your sister. As you probably know, she's been having a hard time of it.

THE WORKER: I hope you find her a good parishioner.

THE MOTHER: You must take a sip of wine. – The Father keeps an eye on children whose parents have gone to the front. You've been running around all day again, haven't you? *She puts down a jug of wine for the priest.*

THE PRIEST *sits down, takes the jug*: If only I knew who was going to get me a new pair of shoes.

*At this moment the Pérezes' radio starts up again. The mother is about to close the window.*

THE PRIEST: You can have the window open, Mrs Carrar. They saw me come in. They resent my not mounting the barricades, so they treat me to one of those speeches now and then.

THE WORKER: Does it bother you much?

THE PRIEST: As a matter of fact, it does. But never mind, leave the window open.

THE GENERAL'S VOICE: ... but we know the dastardly lies with which they try to besmirch the national cause. We may not pay the Archbishop of Canterbury as much as the Reds do, but to make up for that we could give him the names of ten thousand dead priests, whose throats have been cut by his honourable friends. Even if there's no cheque with the message, there is one thing his Grace ought to know: in the course of its victorious advance, the Nationalist army has found plenty of hidden bombs and arms, but not one surviving priest.

*The worker offers the priest his pack of cigarettes. The priest takes one with a smile, though he is no smoker.*

THE GENERAL'S VOICE: Fortunately, the right cause can win without depending on Archbishops so long as it has decent planes. And men like General Franco, General Mola ...

*The broadcast is abruptly cut off.*

THE PRIEST *good-humouredly*: Thank God, even the Pérezes can't stand more than three sentences of that stuff! I can't believe speeches like that make a good impression.

THE WORKER: They say even the Vatican is putting out the same kind of lies.

THE PRIEST: I don't know. *Miserably.* In my opinion it's not the Church's job to turn black into white and vice versa.

THE WORKER *looking at José*: Certainly not.

THE MOTHER *hastily*: My brother's with the militia, Father.

THE PRIEST: In which sector?

THE WORKER: Málaga.

THE PRIEST: It must be horrible.

*The worker smokes in silence.*

THE MOTHER: My brother thinks I'm not a good Spaniard.
He says I ought to let Juan go to the front.

JOSÉ: And me too. That's where we belong.

THE PRIEST: You know, of course, Señora Carrar, that in my
heart and conscience I consider your attitude justified. In
many places the lower clergy are supporting the legal
government. Out of eighteen parishes in Bilbao seventeen
have declared for the government. Quite a few of my fellow
priests are doing service at the front. Some have been killed.
But I myself am not a fighter. God has not given me the gift
of marshalling my parishioners in a loud clear voice to fight
for – *groping for a word* – anything. I stand by the Lord's
commandment: 'Thou shalt not kill.' I am not a rich man. I
don't own a monastery and what little I have I share with
my flock. Maybe that is what gives my words a certain
weight in times like these.

THE WORKER: True. But maybe you're more of a fighter than
you think. Please don't misunderstand me. But suppose a
man is about to be killed and wants to defend himself; then
you tie his hands with your 'Thou shalt not kill', so he lets
himself be slaughtered like an ox; in that case, perhaps,
you'd be participating in the fight – in your own way of
course? If you'll forgive me for saying so.

THE PRIEST: For the time being I'm participating in hunger.

THE WORKER: And how do you think we'll get back the daily
bread you ask for in the Lord's Prayer?

THE PRIEST: I don't know. I can only pray.

THE WORKER: Then you might be interested to know that
God made the supply ships turn back last night.

JOSÉ: Is that true? – Mother, the ships have turned back.

THE WORKER: Yes, that's neutrality. *Suddenly*: You're neutral
too, aren't you?

THE PRIEST: What do you mean by that?

THE WORKER: Let's say, in favour of non-intervention. And
by being for non-intervention you objectively approve
every bloodbath the generals inflict on the Spanish people.

THE PRIEST *raising his hands level with his head in protest*: I
don't approve at all.

THE WORKER *looks at him with half-closed eyes*: Keep your

hands like that for a moment. With that gesture, I've heard, five thousand of our people stepped out of their besieged houses in Badajoz. With that gesture they were gunned down.

THE MOTHER: Pedro, how can you say such a thing!

THE WORKER: It only struck me, Teresa, that the gesture of disapproval is horribly like the gesture of capitulation. I've often read that people who wash their hands in innocence do so in blood-stained basins. And their hands bear the traces.

THE MOTHER: Pedro!

THE PRIEST: Never mind, Mrs Carrar. Tempers are heated at a time like this. We shall take a calmer attitude when it's all over.

THE WORKER: I thought we were to be wiped off the face of the earth because we are a perverted people.

THE PRIEST: Who says such things?

THE WORKER: The radio general. Didn't you hear him just now? You don't listen to the radio enough.

THE PRIEST *disgustedly*: Oh, that general ...

THE WORKER: Don't say 'Oh, that general'! That general has hired all the scum of Spain to wipe us off the face of the earth, not to mention the Moors, Italians and Germans.

THE MOTHER: Yes, they shouldn't have brought in all those people who just do it for money.

THE PRIEST: Don't you think there might be some sincere people on the other side too?

THE WORKER: I don't see what they could be sincere about. *Pause.*

THE PRIEST *takes out his watch*: I've still got to call on the Turillos.

THE WORKER: The government had a clear majority in the Chamber of Deputies. Don't you believe the election was honest and above-board?

THE PRIEST: Yes, I do.

THE WORKER: When I spoke about tying the hands of a man who wants to defend himself, I meant it literally, because we haven't got all that much apart from our bare hands and ...

THE MOTHER *interrupting him*: Please, don't start in again, it's no use.

THE PRIEST: Man is born with bare hands, as we all know. The Creator does not bring him forth from the womb with a weapon in his hand. I know the theory that all the misery in the world comes from the fact that the fisherman and the worker – you are a worker, I believe – have only their bare hands to fight for their livelihood with. But nowhere does Scripture say that this is a perfect world. On the contrary, it is full of misery, sin and oppression. Blessed the man who perchance may suffer from being sent into this world unarmed, but can at least leave it without a weapon in his hand.

THE WORKER: You said that beautifully. I won't contradict anything that sounds so beautiful. I only wish it impressed General Franco. The trouble is that General Franco is armed to the teeth and hasn't shown the slightest inclination to depart from this world. We'd gladly throw all the weapons in Spain after him if only he'd leave this world. Here's a leaflet his pilots have thrown down to us. I picked it up on the street in Motril. *He takes a leaflet from his pocket. The padre, the mother and José look at it.*

JOSÉ *to the mother*: You see? It's always the same, they're going to destroy everything.

THE MOTHER *while reading*: They can't do that.

THE WORKER: Oh yes, they can. What do you think, Father?

JOSÉ: Yes!

THE PRIEST *not sure*: Well, technically, I think, they might be able to. But if I understand Mrs Carrar correctly, she means that it's not just a question of aeroplanes. They may be making these threats in their leaflets in order to convince the population of the seriousness of the situation; but to carry out such threats for military reasons would be a very different matter.

THE WORKER: I don't quite follow you.

JOSÉ: Neither do I.

THE PRIEST *even less sure*: I thought I was being very clear.

THE WORKER: Your sentences are clear, but your opinion is

not clear to me or José. You mean they're not going to drop bombs?

*A short pause.*

THE PRIEST: I believe it's a threat.

THE WORKER: Which won't be carried out?

THE PRIEST: No.

THE MOTHER: The way I see it, they're trying to avoid bloodshed by warning us not to resist them.

JOSÉ: Generals avoiding bloodshed?

THE MOTHER *showing him the leaflet*: Here it says: All who lay down their arms will be spared.

THE WORKER: In that case, I have another question for you, Father: Do you believe the people who lay down their arms will be spared?

THE PRIEST *looking around helplessly*: They say General Franco himself always makes it very clear that he is a Christian.

THE WORKER: Meaning he'll keep his promise?

THE PRIEST *vehemently*: He must keep it, Mr Jaqueras!

THE MOTHER: They can't do anything to the people who don't bear arms.

THE WORKER: Look, Father – *apologetic* – I don't know your name . . .

THE PRIEST: Francisco.

THE WORKER *continuing*: . . . Francisco, I didn't mean to ask you what in your opinion General Franco *must* do but what in your opinion he *will* do. You understand my question?

THE PRIEST: Yes.

THE WORKER: You understand that I'm asking you as a Christian, or maybe we should say, as a man who doesn't own a monastery, to use your own words, and who will tell the truth when it's a matter of life and death. Because it is, don't you agree?

THE PRIEST *very upset*: I understand.

THE WORKER: It might make it easier for you to answer if I remind you of what happened in Málaga.

THE PRIEST: I know what you mean. But are you sure there was no resistance in Málaga?

THE WORKER: You know that fifty thousand men, women and children were mowed down by shelling from Franco's ships and by bombs and machine-gun fire from his planes, while trying to escape to Almería on a highway that's a hundred and forty miles long.

THE PRIEST: That might be an atrocity story.

THE WORKER: Like the one about the executed priests?

THE PRIEST: Like the one about the executed priests.

THE WORKER: In other words they weren't mowed down?
*The priest is silent.*

THE WORKER: Mrs Carrar and her sons are not taking up arms against General Franco. Does that mean Mrs Carrar and her sons are safe?

THE PRIEST: To the best of my knowledge...

THE WORKER: Really? To the best of your knowledge?

THE PRIEST *in agitation*: Surely you don't want me to give you a guarantee?

THE WORKER: No. I only want you to give me your true opinion. Are Mrs Carrar and her sons safe?
*The priest is silent.*

THE WORKER: I think we understand your answer. You're an honest man.

THE PRIEST *getting up, confused*: Well, Mrs Carrar, then I can count on you to look after the Turillo children?

THE MOTHER *also quite disconcerted*: I'll take them something to eat. And thank you for your visit.
*The priest nods to the worker and José as he leaves. The mother accompanies him.*

JOSÉ: Now you've heard the kind of stuff they're drumming into her. But don't leave without the rifles.

THE WORKER: Where are they? Quick!
*They go to the rear, remove a chest and rip the floor open.*

JOSÉ: She'll be back in a second.

THE WORKER: We'll put the rifles outside the window. I can pick them up later.
*Hurriedly they take the rifles from a wooden box. A small tattered flag in which they were wrapped falls to the floor.*

JOSÉ: And there's the little flag from the old days. How could you sit still so long when it's so urgent?

THE WORKER: I had to have them.

*Both are testing the rifles. José suddenly pulls a cap – the cap of the militia – from his pocket and puts it on triumphantly.*

THE WORKER: Where the hell did you get that?

JOSÉ: Swapped it. *With a furtive glance at the door he puts it back in his pocket.*

THE MOTHER *has come in again*: Put those rifles back! Is that what you came for?

THE WORKER: Yes, we need them, Teresa. We can't stop the generals with our bare hands.

JOSÉ: Now you've heard from Father Francisco himself how things really are.

THE MOTHER: If you came just to get the rifles you needn't wait any longer. And if you people don't leave us in peace, I'll take my children and clear out.

THE WORKER: Teresa, have you ever looked at our country on a map? We're living on a broken platter. Where the break is there's water, around the edge there are guns. And above us are the bombers. Where will you go? Straight into the guns?

*She goes up to him, takes the rifles from his hands and carries them off in her arms.*

THE MOTHER: Your lot can't have the rifles, Pedro.

JOSÉ: You've got to let him have them, Mother. Here they'll only rot away.

THE MOTHER: You shut up, José! What do you know about these things?

THE WORKER *has calmly sat down on his chair again and lights a cigarette*: Teresa, you have no right to hold back Carlos's rifles.

THE MOTHER *packing the rifles in the box*: Right or no right: you can't have them. You can't just rip up my floor and take things out of my house against my will.

THE WORKER: These things aren't exactly part of the house. I won't tell you what I think of you in front of your boy and we won't argue about what your husband would think of you. He fought. I suppose it's worry about your boys that's affected your mind. But of course we can't let that influence us.

THE MOTHER: What do you mean?

THE WORKER: I mean that I'm not leaving without the rifles. That's definite.

THE MOTHER: You'll have to knock me down first.

THE WORKER: That I won't do. I'm not General Franco. But I'll talk to Juan. That way I'll get them.

THE MOTHER *quickly*: Juan won't be back.

JOSÉ: But you called him yourself!

THE MOTHER: I did not call him. I don't want him to see you, Pedro.

THE WORKER: I thought as much. But I have a voice too. I can go down to the shore and call him. Two, three words will do it, Teresa, I know Juan. He's no coward. You can't hold him back.

JOSÉ: I'll go with you.

THE MOTHER *very calmly*: Leave my children alone, Pedro. I told them I'd hang myself if they went. I know it's a great sin before God and gets you eternal damnation. But there's nothing else for me to do. When Carlos died – died the way he did – I went to see Father Francisco or I'd have hanged myself then. I know perfectly well that I was partly to blame, though he was the worst of the lot with his hot temper and his violent ways. We aren't all that well off, and it isn't an easy life to bear. But guns won't help. I realised that when they brought him in and laid him out on the floor. I'm not for the generals and it's disgraceful to say I am. But if I keep quiet and watch my temper, maybe they'll leave us in peace. It's a very simple calculation. I'm not asking much. I don't want to see this flag any more. We're unhappy enough as it is.

*She calmly walks over to the little flag, picks it up and rips it apart. At once she stoops down, collects the tatters and puts them in her pocket.*

THE WORKER: It would be better if you hanged yourself, Teresa.

*Knocking at the door. Mrs Pérez, an old woman in black, comes in.*

JOSÉ *to the worker*: That's old Mrs Pérez.

THE WORKER *under his breath*: What kind of people are they?

JOSÉ: Good people. The ones with the radio. Her daughter was killed at the front last week.

OLD MRS PÉREZ: I waited until I saw the Father leave. I thought I ought to drop in, on account of my family. I wanted to tell you I don't think it's right of them to make trouble for you because of your opinions.

*The mother is silent.*

OLD MRS PÉREZ *who has sat down*: You're worried about your children, Mrs Carrar. People always forget how hard it is to bring up children in times like these. I had seven. *She half turns to the worker to whom she has not been introduced.* There aren't many left now that Inez has been killed. I lost two before they were six. Those were the lean years of ninety-eight and ninety-nine. I don't even know where Andrés is. He last wrote from Rio. That's in South America. Mariana, as you know, is in Madrid. She has had a hard time too. She never was very strong. It always seems to us old people as if the younger folk had turned out kind of sickly.

THE MOTHER: But you still have Fernando.

OLD MRS PÉREZ: Yes.

THE MOTHER *confused*: I'm sorry, I didn't mean to offend you.

OLD MRS PÉREZ *calmly*: No need to apologise. I know you didn't.

JOSÉ *softly to the worker*: He's with Franco.

OLD MRS PÉREZ *quietly*: We don't talk about Fernando any more. *After a short pause*: You know, you can't really understand my family unless you keep in mind that we're all in great sorrow over Inez's death.

THE MOTHER: We were always very fond of Inez. *To the worker*: She taught Juan to read.

JOSÉ: Me too.

OLD MRS PÉREZ: Some people think you're for the other side. But I always contradict them. Our kind knows the difference between rich and poor.

THE MOTHER: I don't want my boys to be soldiers. They're not cattle to be slaughtered.

OLD MRS PÉREZ: You know, Mrs Carrar, I always say there's

no life insurance for the poor. I mean they get it either way. The ones who get it all the time are the ones we call the poor people. No amount of foresight can save the poor, Mrs Carrar. Our Inez was always the most timid of the children. You can't imagine how my husband had to coax her before she got up the courage to swim.

THE MOTHER: What I mean is that she could still be living.

OLD MRS PÉREZ: But how would she be living?

THE MOTHER: Why did your daughter, a teacher, have to take up a gun and fight the generals?

THE WORKER: Who are being financed by the Holy Father, no less.

OLD MRS PÉREZ: She said she wanted to go on being a teacher.

THE MOTHER: Couldn't she have done just that at her school in Málaga, generals or no generals?

OLD MRS PÉREZ: We discussed that with her. Her father gave up smoking for seven years and her brothers and sisters never got a drop of milk in all that time so she could become a schoolteacher. But then Inez said she couldn't teach children that twice two is five and that General Franco was sent by God.

THE MOTHER: If Juan were to come and tell me he wouldn't be able to fish any more I'd let him have a piece of my mind. Do you think the speculators would give up trying to skin us if we got rid of the generals?

THE WORKER: I think it will be slightly harder for them when we have the guns.

THE MOTHER: Guns again, always guns! The shooting will never stop.

THE WORKER: That's not the point. If sharks attack you, are you the one that's using force? Did we march on Madrid or did General Mola come down over the mountains? For two years there was a little light, a very feeble light, not really a dawn, but now it's to be night again. And that's not the whole of it. It's not just that teachers won't be allowed to tell children that twice two is four, they're to be extermi- nated if they ever said so in the past. Didn't you hear him spell out tonight that we're to be wiped off the face of the earth?

THE MOTHER: Only those who have taken up arms. Don't hammer at me like this all the time. I can't argue with all of you. My sons look at me as if I were a policeman. When the flour chest is empty, I can see in their faces that I'm to blame. When the planes appear, they look away as if I had sent them. Why does Father Francisco keep silent when he ought to speak out? You all think I'm out of my mind because I believe the generals are human beings too, very wicked, yes, but not an earthquake you can't argue with. Why do you sit down in my room, Mrs Pérez, and keep telling me these things? Do you really think I don't know everything you're saying? Your daughter's been killed; now it's to be the turn of my boys. Is that what you want? You haunt my house like bloody tax collectors, but I've already paid.

OLD MRS PÉREZ *getting up*: Mrs Carrar, I didn't mean to make you angry. I don't agree with my husband that you should be forced to do anything. We thought a lot of your husband, and I only wanted to apologise if my family is bothering you. *She leaves, nodding to the worker and José. Pause.*

THE MOTHER: The worst of it is, the way they keep on at me they goad me into saying things I don't mean at all. I'm not against Inez.

THE WORKER *furious*: Yes, you are against Inez. By not helping her you were against her. You keep on saying you're not for the generals. And that's not true either, whether you know it or not. If you don't help us against them, you're for them. You can't stay neutral, Teresa.

JOSÉ *suddenly walking up to her*: Come on, Mother, you haven't got a chance. *To the worker*: She's gone and sat on the box to keep us from getting them. Come on, Mother, let's have them.

THE MOTHER: Best wipe the snot off your nose, José.

JOSÉ: Mother, I want to go with Uncle Pedro. I'm not waiting here till they slaughter us like pigs. You can't stop me fighting like you stopped me smoking. There's Felipe who can't sling a stone half as straight as me, and he's at the front already, and Andrés is a year younger than me and he's been killed. I won't have the whole village laughing at me.

THE MOTHER: Yes, I know. Little Pablo promised a truck driver his dead mole if he'd take him to the front. That's ridiculous.

THE WORKER: It's not ridiculous.

JOSÉ: Tell Ernesto Turillo he can have my little boat. – Let's go, Uncle Pedro. *He intends to leave.*

THE MOTHER: You stay right here!

JOSÉ: No, I'm going. You can say you need Juan, but if he's here you don't need me too.

THE MOTHER: I'm not keeping Juan just to fish for me. And I won't let you go either. *She rushes to him and embraces him.* You can smoke if you like, and if you want to go fishing by yourself, I won't say a word, even in Father's boat once in a while.

JOSÉ: Let go of me!

THE MOTHER: No, you're staying here.

JOSÉ *trying to free himself*: No, I'm going. – Quick, take the rifles, Uncle!

THE MOTHER: Oh!
*She releases José and limps away, putting one foot down gingerly.*

JOSÉ: What's wrong?

THE MOTHER: A fat lot you mind. Just go. You've got the better of your mother.

JOSÉ *suspiciously*: I wasn't rough. You can't be hurt.

THE MOTHER *massaging her foot*: Of course not. Run along.

THE WORKER: Want me to set it for you?

THE MOTHER: No, I want you to go. Out of my house! How dare you incite my children to assault me.

JOSÉ *furiously*: Me assault her! *White with rage he goes to the rear.*

THE MOTHER: You'll finish up a criminal. Why not take the last loaf of bread from the oven too? Yes, you could tie me to the chair with a rope. After all there are two of you.

THE WORKER: Stop playing games.

THE MOTHER: Juan is another madman, but he'd never use force against his mother. He'll give you what for when he gets back. Juan. *She suddenly gets up, struck by an idea, and rushes to the window. She forgets to limp and José indignantly points at her feet.*

JOSÉ: All of a sudden her foot's all right.

THE MOTHER *looks out; suddenly*: I don't know, I can't see Juan's lantern any longer.

JOSÉ *sulkily*: Don't tell me it just vanished.

THE MOTHER: No, it's really gone.

*José goes to the window, looks out.*

JOSÉ *with a strange voice to the worker*: Yes, it's gone! Last time he was way out at the Cape. I'm running down. *He runs out quickly.*

THE WORKER: He may be on his way back.

THE MOTHER: We'd still see his light.

THE WORKER: What could have happened?

THE MOTHER: I know what's happened. She's rowed out to meet him.

THE WORKER: Who? The girl? Not her!

THE MOTHER: I'm sure they went out to get him. *With mounting agitation*: It was a plot. They planned it beforehand. They went on sending one visitor after another all evening so I wouldn't be able to keep watch. They're murderers! The whole lot of them!

THE WORKER *half joking, half angry*: Don't tell me they sent the priest.

THE MOTHER: They won't stop till they've dragged everyone in.

THE WORKER: You mean he's made off for the front?

THE MOTHER: They're his murderers, but he's no better than they are. Sneaking off at night. I never want to see him again.

THE WORKER: I just don't understand you any more, Teresa. Can't you see there's nothing worse you can do to him now than hold him back from fighting? He won't thank you for it.

THE MOTHER *absently*: It wasn't for my sake I told him not to fight.

THE WORKER: You can't call it not fighting, Teresa; when he's not fighting on our side, he's fighting for the generals.

THE MOTHER: If he has done this to me and joined the militia I'm going to curse him. Let them hit him with their bombs! Let them crush him with their tanks! To show him that you can't make a mockery of God. And that a poor man can't beat the generals. I didn't bring him into the world to ambush his fellow men behind a machine gun. Maybe there has to be injustice in this world, but I didn't teach him to take part in it. When he comes back telling me he's defeated the generals, it's not going to make me open the door to him. I'll tell him from behind the door that I won't have a man in my house who has stained himself with blood. I'll cut him off like a bad leg. I will. I've already had one brought back to me. He too thought luck would be on his side. But there's no luck for us. Maybe that will dawn on you all before the generals are through with us. They that take the sword shall perish with the sword.

*Murmuring is heard outside the door, then the door opens and three women come in, hands folded over their breasts, murmuring an Ave Maria. They line up along the wall. Through the open door two fishermen carry the dead body of Juan Carrar on a blood-soaked sailcloth. José, deadly pale, walks behind. He is holding his brother's cap in his hand. The fishermen set the body on the floor. One of them holds Juan's lantern. While the mother sits there petrified and the women pray louder, the fishermen explain to the worker with subdued voices what happened.*

FIRST FISHERMAN: It was one of their fishing cutters with machine-guns. They gunned him down as they passed him.

THE MOTHER: It can't be! There must be a mistake! He only went fishing!

*The fishermen are silent. The mother sinks to the floor, the worker picks her up.*

THE WORKER: He won't have felt anything.

*The mother kneels down beside the dead body.*

THE MOTHER: Juan.

*For a while only the murmur of the praying women and the muffled roar of the cannon in the distance are heard.*

THE MOTHER: Could you life him up on the chest?

*The worker and the fishermen lift the body, carry it to the rear and place it on the chest. The sailcloth remains on the floor. The prayers of the women grow louder and rise in pitch. The mother takes José by the hand and leads him to the body.*

THE WORKER *in front again, to the fishermen*: Was he on his own? No other boats out with him?

FIRST FISHERMAN: No. But he was close to the shore. *He points at the second fisherman.*

SECOND FISHERMAN: They didn't even question him. They just flicked their searchlight over him, and then his lantern fell into the boat.

THE WORKER: They must have seen he was only fishing.

SECOND FISHERMAN: Yes, they must have seen that.

THE WORKER: He didn't call out to them?

SECOND FISHERMAN: I'd have heard.

*The mother comes forward, holding Juan's cap which José had brought in.*

THE MOTHER *simply*: Blame it on his cap.

FIRST FISHERMAN: What do you mean?

THE MOTHER: It's shabby. Not like a gentleman's.

FIRST FISHERMAN: But they can't just loose off at everybody with a shabby cap.

THE MOTHER: Yes they can. They're not human. They're a canker and they've got to be burned out like a canker. *To the praying women, politely*: I'd like you to leave now. I have a few things to do and, as you see, my brother is with me.

*The people leave.*

FIRST FISHERMAN: We've made his boat fast down below.

*When they are alone the mother picks up the sailcloth and gazes at it.*

THE MOTHER: A minute ago I tore up a flag. Now they've brought me a new one.

*She drags the sailcloth to the rear and covers the body with it. At this moment the distant thunder of the guns changes. Suddenly it is coming closer.*

JOSÉ *listlessly*: What's that?

THE WORKER *suddenly looking harassed*: They've broken through! I've got to go!

THE MOTHER *going to the oven in front, loudly*: Take the guns! Get ready, José! The bread's done too.

*While the worker takes the rifles from the box she looks after the bread. She takes it out of the oven, wraps it in a cloth and goes over to the men. She reaches for one of the rifles.*

JOSÉ: What, you coming too?

THE MOTHER: Yes, for Juan.

*They go to the door.*

Dansen

*Translators*: ROSE *and* MARTIN KASTNER

*Characters*:

DANSEN
THE STRANGER

*On the stage are three house fronts. One is a tobacco shop with the sign: 'Austrian – Tobacconist'. The second is a shoe shop with the sign: 'Czech – Boots and Shoes'. The third is not a shop, but a sign in the window reads: 'Fresh ham'. Next to this house front there is a large iron door with a sign saying: 'Svendson. Iron'.*

I

*Beside the door sits Dansen. He is a small man. In front of him is a tub. He is holding a pig under his arm.*

DANSEN *to the audience*: I'm a little man, respected, well-off and independent. I get along perfectly with my neighbours. We settle all disagreements between us peacefully through an organisation to which almost all of us belong. We have contracts that cover everything. So far we've been doing fine. I have my freedom and my business connections, I have my friends and my customers, I have my principles and I raise pigs. *He starts scrubbing the pig in the tub.* There. And now, my boy, hold still and let me wash your rosy ears. We've got to look nice when the customers turn up: healthy, happy, and succulent. If we're good and eat properly, we'll go far in life. The customer will say: That's a good little pig. After all, what do you want in this world? What does your little heart desire? You desire to be sold. Oh, you're clever. Whenever you suspect that I'm neglecting you, that I've forgotten your heart's desire for one moment, you let out a loud squeal and remind me. If anyone passes by who looks the least bit as if he hadn't eaten yet, you squeal. That way I myself have nothing to worry ab . . .
*The pig squeals.*

DANSEN *looks up, pleased*: What is it? What is it? Is somebody coming? A customer?

*Stealthily, looking anxiously around, an armed man approaches the tobacco shop; his hat is drawn down over his eyes. He stops outside the closed door and takes a bunch of passkeys out of his trouser pocket. He tries them one after another, meanwhile smiling at Dansen, whose hair is beginning to stand on end. Finally the burglar loses patience and climbs in through the window, holding a large pistol. Immediately a terrible din is heard from inside: a falling chair, loud cries for help. Dansen jumps up in horror. With the pig under his arm, he runs around wildly. Then he rushes to the telephone.*

DANSEN: Svendson, Svendson! What should I do? They're shouting for help in the tobacco shop across the street. A stranger has broken in before my very eyes. – What, you can hear the screams from where you are? – No, of course I can't go in, I have no right to barge into someone else's house. But what should I do when he comes out? I'm trembling with indignation. – Don't worry, I'll give him a good piece of my mind. You know my policy, no, not insurance policy, policy ... *After warily looking around, he sings into the telephone in a muffled voice*:

A Dansen does his duty
In every town and land
For his sincere opinions
He bravely takes his stand.

In short, I'll fling my loathing in his face. As I said, I'm trembling with indignation.

*The calls for help have stopped. A scream, a pistol shot, and a loud thud are heard.*

DANSEN: I've got to hang up. I have to sit down. I think my hair has turned grey.

*Deep in gloom, he sits down again outside the house, his pig under his arm. The stranger comes out of the tobacco shop, quickly crosses out the word 'Austrian' with chalk and writes 'Ostmarker & Co.' over it. Then he steps up to Dansen.*

THE STRANGER: Why are you looking so pale?

DANSEN: My dear fellow, I'll tell you. I'm pale with pent-up agitation.

THE STRANGER: You could learn from your charming little pig. He's pink and he stays pink.

DANSEN: But a pig isn't human. I'm pale with human emotion, and you know why.

THE STRANGER: What a *good* little pig!

DANSEN *points accusingly at the tobacco shop*: What . . . what . . . happened in there?

THE STRANGER: Do you really want to know?

DANSEN: Of course I want to know! Anything that happens to my fellow man . . .

*The pig squeals a second time.*

DANSEN: What is it? What is it?

THE STRANGER: You mean you don't want to know!

DANSEN *to the pig*: But that man . . . *He points at the tobacco shop.*

THE STRANGER: Did you know him?

DANSEN: Did I know him? No, yes, I'm sorry, I'm all mixed up. *Reproachfully*: We belonged to the same club.

THE STRANGER: What did you do in your club? Sell pigs?

DANSEN *morosely*: We played cards. We played non-intervention.

THE STRANGER: I can't afford that game. Too expensive.

DANSEN: We only play once a week. On Saturdays. *Points at the tobacco shop.* He comes too.

THE STRANGER: I don't think he'll be coming any more.

DANSEN: Are you going to tell him not to? That would be an outrage. I mean it. Austrian is a free man.

THE STRANGER *hesitantly*: Nobody'll be telling him anything now. *He laughs mirthlessly.*

DANSEN *indignantly*: What do you mean by that?

THE STRANGER: Do you really want to know?

DANSEN: Do I want to know? Yes, no. I don't know, my head is swimming. You stand here talking as if . . . and just a minute ago, with my own eyes, I saw . . . Of course I want to know! Abso . . .

*The pig under his arm squeals a third time in terror, as though cruelly maltreated.*

DANSEN *tonelessly, completes the word*: . . . lutely. *His confidence is gone; he is afraid to meet the eyes of the stranger, who is now stroking the pig.*

DANSEN: I don't understand the world any more. I'm a peace-loving man. I loathe violence and respect contracts. I have business connections and I have my freedom, a few customers and a few friends, I have my pig farm and my . . . *Almost without thinking*: Would you care to buy a pig?

THE STRANGER *flabbergasted*: I beg your pardon?

DANSEN: A pig? Three or four pigs? I could let you have them cheap. I've got so many. Too many. I've got pigs to burn.

THE STRANGER: Let's have one.

DANSEN *intently*: Sure you don't want two?

THE STRANGER: One.

DANSEN: But what will I do with the rest? They breed like rabbits. Every night I drown half a dozen in the cesspit, and every morning another dozen are born. *Gestures to the stranger to look into the pigsty.* You see, there are fourteen of them again.

THE STRANGER: *One.*

DANSEN: Take a good look at them. Aren't they healthy, amiable, and succulent? Don't they make your mouth water?

THE STRANGER *whose mouth is watering, with an effort*: They're a luxury.

DANSEN: How can you say such a thing when they're a hundred per cent edible? Even the ears. Even the toes. Fried pig's toes.

THE STRANGER: A luxury.

DANSEN *grieved, to the pig*: You a luxury! *Disappointed, to the stranger*: In that case, we'll make it just two.

THE STRANGER *loudly*: One. I don't waste money on luxuries.

DANSEN: You buy iron, though. You buy all the iron my friend Svendson can deliver.

THE STRANGER: Iron isn't a luxury. Iron is a necessity.

DANSEN *gives him the pig; his hands are trembling*: My nerves are shot. That terrible experience just now ... *He wipes the sweat off his neck with a red handkerchief.*

THE STRANGER: What's that red rag you've got there?

DANSEN: This?

THE STRANGER *roughly*: Yes, that. *He puts the pig back in the tub.*

DANSEN *eager to please*: It's not red. Look, it's got a white cross on it. *He points at it.*

THE STRANGER: Okay. *He throws money down.*

DANSEN: I'll wrap it up for you.

THE STRANGER: Take this paper. Otherwise you'll charge me for the wrapping. *He hands him a large sheet of paper he has taken out of his pocket.*

DANSEN *smoothing out the paper*: But this is a contract!

THE STRANGER: What kind of a contract?

DANSEN: With Mr Austrian, I think. Friendship pact, it says. Don't you need it any more?

THE STRANGER: No. What's the use of a friendship pact with a stiff? *He takes the paper away from him and tears it up.*

DANSEN *almost fainting*: Quick, take the pig. I'm feeling sick. *The stranger takes the pig out of his hands. Dansen puts his handkerchief on his head.*

THE STRANGER *looking at the cross with irritation*: Put that cross away!

*Dansen puts the handkerchief back in his pocket.*

THE STRANGER: I'll take the pig as it is. Maybe I'll cut off a chunk on the way. *He takes it under his arm. But before he goes, he looks at the shoe shop.* Nice place, that shoe shop.

DANSEN: Yes, very nice.

THE STRANGER: Plenty of room. Your house isn't bad either.

DANSEN *without thinking*: I like it.

THE STRANGER *looking at it dreamily*: Well, I'll be seeing you. *Goes out.*

DANSEN *wiping his forehead, unnerved*: I'll be seeing you – I was so indignant I went and sold him a pig. Look what he's done to that nice peace-loving Mr Austrian. Just simply ... The damn brute! *Looking anxiously around, he goes into the corner between his house and the warehouse door and grumbles*: Barbarian! Inhuman monster! What a way to treat a contract!

2

*Dansen is sitting in front of his house with a pig on his lap.*

DANSEN: I'm a respected man, but a little one. I have a feeling things aren't right any more. The dreadful incidents lately have really got me down. Contracts are wonderful things, but if they're not held sacred . . . My two friends next door and I have been toying with the idea of arming ourselves. We're not entirely helpless. There aren't many supplies of iron beside my friend Svendson. Right here in the warehouse – *he points to Svendson's warehouse* – we've got quite a supply of iron. If we used it to forge weapons . . . It would be sheer madness to bury our heads in the sand. On the other hand, we can't afford a repetition of those dreadful events. Whatsisname can't do such a thing twice.

*Stealthily, looking anxiously around, the stranger approaches the shoe shop; his cap is drawn down over his eyes. He stops outside the closed door and takes a bunch of passkeys out of his trouser pocket. He tries them one after another, shaking his head now and then and smiling at Dansen, whose hair is beginning to stand on end. Finally the stranger loses patience and climbs in through the window, holding a large pistol. Immediately a terrible din is heard from inside: a falling chair, loud cries for help.*

DANSEN: He's done it again. This is terrible. And to think that the poor old woman had an agreement with him. There's something sick about that man's greed. Whatever he sees he wants. What about my own house? Not bad, he said. I'll have to take very firm steps immediately. And whatever I do, I mustn't attract his attention. I'll have to disappear. But how can I prevent him from seeing me? Ah, the tub! *With the pig under his arm, he pulls the tub, which he ordinarily uses to wash his pigs in, over his head.*

*The stranger steps out of the shoe shop. He hurriedly crosses out the name 'Czech' with chalk and writes 'Böhm & Mohr,*

*Inc.' At this moment Dansen's pig is heard squealing inside the tub.*

DANSEN: What is it? What is it? Is somebody coming? A customer? *He looks out cautiously, sees the stranger writing, and ducks back in again.*

*The stranger steps forward, takes a sheet of paper from his pocket and tears it up. The scraps fall to the ground.*

THE STRANGER: Hey, what's become of that pig farmer? Probably stepped out for a drink. Good chance to take a look at Svendson's iron warehouse. *Looking around, he saunters over to the warehouse door and, turning his back to it, tries the handle. But the door is locked.*

*Suddenly Dansen's phone rings. At first Dansen sits motionless. When it goes on ringing, he is obliged to answer it. With extreme caution he gets up and with the tub still over him goes to the phone. The stranger looks with amazement at the walking tub.*

THE STRANGER *instantly*: *Mighty* suspicious!

*Since Dansen, under the tub, cannot see the stranger, he almost bumps into him, but the stranger, grinning, steps out of his way. Reaching the telephone, which rests on a low lard crate in front of the house, Dansen settles down, bent over the crate.*

DANSEN *under his breath into the telephone, but the receiver reverberates slightly under the tub*: That you, Svendson? – Oh, you've heard the latest terrible news? – No, good God, not my place. Why do you keep thinking it happened at my place? It gives me the creeps. – Of course we've got to do something together. We'll have to consider taking very firm action. No, not take, consider. – Arm ourselves? Out of the question! – Stand united, yes, but arm, no. – United in what? In not arming! That would only attract his attention, and I've done everything in my power to avoid that. – Yes, I said we've got to be united. Our unity must be iron-clad and directed against no one. *Very emphatically*: Against no one. Then it can't attract attention. – Yes, Svendson, you can rely on me. – I understand perfectly that your mind wouldn't be at ease about your warehouse, no, not for a minute, if I were to give up one grain of my independence.

I'll keep my nose strictly out of the whole business. And stick to selling my pigs, period. – Where I keep the key to your warehouse? Where I always keep it, of course, on a string around my neck, under my shirt. – Naturally I keep my eyes open. – That burglary the other day, when your letter to me was stolen? Yes, but that was a burglary, there's nothing we can do about that. – Of course I won't give anybody the key, never! – Let somebody take it? What do you think I am? – Under pressure? Nobody has ever put pressure on me, I've never given anyone reason to. – I'm being watched? Ridiculous! Nobody's watching me, I'd notice it, wouldn't I? – You insist on strong action? I'm all for it. I suggest we sign a contract. Before the day's over we must absolutely sign a contract. – That's it, against everybody who doesn't keep their contracts. Listen. I have a brilliant idea, we'll agree not to sell any more iron to a certain notorious troublemaker and disturber of the peace, we'll offer it to decent people instead. – Not so brilliant? Why? – You say the big shots are already discussing effective measures?

*The stranger, who has sat down and has been quietly listening, knocks on the tub.*

DANSEN *in his tub, alarmed*: Hold on! I'll have to break off for a second. – No, I've got to wait on a customer. We'll go on with our discussion right away.

*The stranger pulls him out of the tub by the seat of his pants.*

THE STRANGER: Looks like I got here in the nick of time. How did you get stuck in that tub? If I hadn't come along, you'd have suffocated.

*Dansen sits on the ground in sullen silence.*

THE STRANGER: Why are you so quiet? Is something worrying you? You know, Dansen, I've been thinking the two of us ought to get better acquainted. It's really nice sitting here with you. The house is small but not at all bad. What would you say to a mutual friendship pact?

DANSEN *his hair standing on end*: Friendship pact . . .

THE STRANGER: Friendship pact. *He strokes Dansen's pig.* You're a good little pig! Are you a good little pig? I suggest we sign a pact. Saying we're friends. *He takes a pencil stub from his waistcoat pocket, stands up and picks up one of the paper scraps from the ground. On the back of the scrap he scribbles a few words.* You simply agree not to attack me under any circumstances, if for instance I take one of your pigs or something. And I agree in return that you can call on me for protection at any time. Well, what do you say?

DANSEN: No offence, but I wouldn't want to make that kind of decision on the spur of the moment.

THE STRANGER: You wouldn't?

*Dansen's pig squeals for the second time.*

DANSEN *aside to his pig*: You keep quiet! *To the stranger*: I'd have to phone my friend Svendson first.

THE STRANGER: Oh, so you won't sign? *Dansen is silent.* That's funny. Didn't I hear you say you wanted a contract before the day's over? *To Dansen's pig, stroking it*: You're a smart little pig. We understand each other. There'd never be any disagreement between us. But I guess it's no go. I don't force myself on anyone. If my offers of friendship are trampled underfoot, there's nothing for me to do but leave. *Looking offended, he stands up.*

*The pig squeals a third time.*

DANSEN *wipes the sweat from his neck with his red handkerchief*: Wait! *The stranger turns around.* Maybe I was a little hasty. I've been so confused by the recent events. You wanted to buy a pig?

THE STRANGER: Why not?

DANSEN *hoarsely*: Then give me the contract. *He signs.* But don't you need a duplicate?

THE STRANGER: Not necessary. *He takes the pig under his arm.* Send me the bill in the New Year. *On his way out*: And kindly don't forget that you're friends with *me* now and you're to choose your company accordingly. I'll be seeing you.

DANSEN *in amazement*: Now I've made a friendship pact with him. *Holding the contract, he returns hesitantly to the phone.* Hello, Svendson. It's Dansen. I've got something to tell you. No sooner said than done, I've made a contract. – With whom? With Whatsisname. – He doesn't keep to contracts? But I've got his personal signature. Hold on, let's see what it says ... I haven't read it through yet ... oh yes, *he* agrees not to attack me, and *I* agree not to help anyone he attacks. – If he attacks you? Out of the question. He can't keep on doing these things. Your warehouse is as safe as the Bank of England. – Who you can rely on? On me! You can rely on me. And I can rely on him.

3

*Dansen is standing in front of his house, still on the phone.*

DANSEN: I don't see how you can say our unity is in danger when I've been telling you now for three days and three nights that it's not in danger. – All right, let me tell you this: if he doesn't keep to this contract, I won't hesitate for one moment to invest every penny I've saved out of my pig business in the last five years on arming ourselves to the teeth with your iron. What do you think of that? – Right now it would be madness. There's no reason for it. – What *about* the sky? *He looks around.* Yes, my goodness, it really is red.
*During the conversation the sky has turned slightly red. Muffled thunder in the distance.*
DANSEN: Say, that's funny thunder. I think we'll have to break off. Got to take a look at my pigs. – Yes, of course, your warehouse too. I'm really glad about that contract now, especially for your sake. – Now you'll see what a shrewd move I made. Want to bet that Whatsisname is beginning to feel sorry he made me that promise? In any case we'll keep in tou ... Hello! Are you there, Svendson? *He shakes the telephone, but the line has gone dead.* Damn it, this is a fine time for the phone to go dead! *He goes to the tub and fishes out his contract. Then he unties the rope attaching the pig to the tub.* Indeed, where would I be now without this paper? I'm dog-tired. The pigs were so restless I had to tie them up, and all this phoning has been a strain. And to make matters worse I'll have to stand guard outside the warehouse tonight, I owe that to my friend Svendson. *Shouldering the rolled-up contract like a rifle, he marches up*

*and down in front of the warehouse, occasionally shading his eyes with one hand and peering into the distance. He soon begins to drag his feet.* If I let my vigilance flag for so much as one second, the consequences for myself and my friends up the street will be incalculable. *He sits down with his back to the warehouse wall; the pig is now on his lap. He yawns.* It's unbelievable. Now he's even picking a fight with Pollack, the horse trader. *Dozes off, wakes with a start, reaches for the big warehouse key that he is wearing around his neck, under his shirt, and pulls it out.* Anyway I've got the key. *He puts it back.* I don't see why Pollack doesn't just sign ... a contract ... with him ... *He falls asleep.*

*It gets dark. Only the reddish horizon remains visible. Slowly a sign with the words 'Dansen's Dream' on it comes down from the flies.*

*A rosy light fills the stage. Dansen and the stranger stand facing each other. Dansen is leading his pig on a rope and shouldering his contract. The stranger, still in civilian clothes, is armed to the teeth. He is wearing a steel helmet; he has hand-grenades in his belt, and a tommy-gun under his arm.*

THE STRANGER: I've been attacked. I was paying an innocent little visit to a certain Pollack, I'd arranged to meet a friend of mine at his place. While I was in the house, the neighbours surrounded me and attacked me. You've got to help me.

DANSEN: But ...

THE STRANGER: Don't talk so much. I haven't a moment to lose. There's not enough iron in my house. I need the key to my friend Svendson's warehouse right away.

DANSEN: But I can't let it out of my hands.

THE STRANGER: You can give it to me. The warehouse definitely needs protection, it's full of iron and you're in no position to defend it. Give me the key! Quick!

DANSEN: But the key was given to me for safekeeping. I'll at least have to phone my friend Svendson first ...

THE STRANGER: Your safekeeping is my safekeeping. This is no time to quibble. Hands up! *He threatens him with his tommy-gun.*

*Dansen suddenly aims his contract at the stranger and stands motionless in this menacing position.*

THE STRANGER *not believing his eyes*: Are you out of your mind? What's that you've got there?

DANSEN: My contract!

THE STRANGER *contemptuously*: Contracts! Who says I have to respect contracts?

DANSEN: Maybe you don't have to respect the others. But you've got to respect this one with me!

THE STRANGER *letting his gun drop*: This is terrible! I *need* that iron. Everybody's against me.

DANSEN: I'm sorry.

THE STRANGER: But I'm lost without it. I'll be trampled to a pulp, do you hear me, a pulp!

DANSEN: You should have thought of that before, my friend.

THE STRANGER: My whole livelihood is at stake! I've got to get in there! I've got to, I've got to!

DANSEN *holds up the paper*: I'm sorry, it can't be done.

THE STRANGER: I'll buy all your pigs, Dansen, if you'll co-operate!

DANSEN: I can't do it, friend.

*Dansen's pig squeals. A gong sounds in the distance.*

DANSEN: Shut up! When freedom is at stake. *To the stranger*: We're sorry.

THE STRANGER *going down on his knees, sobbing*: Please, I beg you, the key! Don't be heartless! My family, my wife, my children, my mother, my grandmother! My aunts!

DANSEN: It can't be done. I deeply sympathise, but it can't be done. A contract's a contract.

THE STRANGER *broken, stands up with difficulty*: There's only one thing left for me to do: hang myself. This contract is costing me, one of your best customers, my life. *Crushed, he turns to go.*

*The pig squeals a second time. Again the distant gong.*

DANSEN: Shut up. You make me sick. You haven't got a pennyworth of morality. *To the stranger*: And you, don't come to me any more with your immoral demands, understand! They won't wash with me, the next time I might lost my patience! *As the stranger staggers away,*

*Dansen, clutching the contract in his fist, sings the third stanza of 'King Christian Stood by the Tall Mast'.*

Niels Juel he shouted to the gale
'The time has come!'
Hoisted the red flag like a sail
And bade the enemy turn tail.
Aloud he shouted in the gale
'The time has come!'
'Vile knaves,' he shouted, 'leave the stage!
For who will not to Dansen's rage
Succumb!'

*But when he comes to the last line, he is horrified to hear the pig squeal a third time. The stranger suddenly turns around looking triumphant. Darkness. Another sign is lowered. On it is written 'And Dansen's Awakening'.*
*The light goes on. The pig has gone on squealing. Beside Dansen, who is still leaning against the warehouse door asleep, stands the stranger, armed to the teeth. He gives Dansen a kick. Dansen wakes up with a start.*

THE STRANGER: Give me that key!

DANSEN: I can't let anyone have it!

THE STRANGER: Then you're breaking the contract, you swine. You think you can make a friendship pact with me and then refuse me your friendship? *Kicks him.* You think you can cheat me out of the key I need to get at the iron? Now you've proved you're my enemy, one of the worst. *He grabs the contract out of his hands and tears it up.* And now for the last time: give me that key!
*Dansen reaches for the key and, staring at the stranger, takes it out. The stranger grabs it and opens the door.*

DANSEN *amazed*: Goodness, I've honoured the contract by giving him Svendson's key!

THE STRANGER *in the doorway, turns around to Dansen, takes the pig's rope out of his hands and says menacingly*: I expect you to hand over the rest of the pigs without being asked, and I don't expect to see any bills! *He goes into Svendson's warehouse with Dansen's pig.*

# How Much Is Your Iron?

*Translators*: ROSE *and* MARTIN KASTNER

*Characters*:

SVENDSON
THE CUSTOMER
MR AUSTRIAN, *a tobacconist*
MRS CZECH, *owner of a shoe shop*
THE GENTLEMAN
THE LADY

An Englishman, dear friends, not long ago
Spun a story which we'd like to show.
With two young Swedes he'd met near the Old Vic
He downed a few, and talked of politics;
But though they quaffed much brandy, ale, and rye
He and the Swedes could not see eye to eye.
Next day, the Englishman took pen in hand
And wrote a parable that all could understand.
This fable made his point both sharp and clear –
For your diversion, now, we'll show it here.
The scene: a shop with iron bars for sale.
You'll recognise the merchant without fail.
The shoe-shop lady and tobacconist
Are figures that can't easily be missed.
And by our playlet's end – if not before –
You'll know which fellow's grabbing all the ore.
Even a simpleton, we dare to say
Will get the point: so now let's start the play!

*An iron dealer's shop. A wooden door and a wooden table.*

I

*On the table lie iron bars. The shopkeeper is polishing them
with a cloth. On an easel an enormous calendar showing the
date: 1938. A tobacconist comes in with cigar boxes under his
arm.*

MR AUSTRIAN: Good morning, Mr Svendson. How are you
for smokes? I've got some fine cigars here, thirty cents
apiece, genuine Austrillos.

SVENDSON: Good morning, Mr Austrian. Let's have a look! What an aroma. You know how crazy I am about your cigars. Unfortunately my business hasn't been doing very well. I'll have to cut down on my smoking. No, I can't take any today. I can't see my way clear. No hard feelings, Mr Austrian. Maybe next time.

MR AUSTRIAN: This is a bit of a disappointment. But of course I understand. *He packs up his wares.*

SVENDSON: Been having a pleasant round, Mr Austrian?

MR AUSTRIAN: Not very pleasant, Mr Svendson. I'm afraid your store is rather out of the way.

SVENDSON: Out of the way? Nobody ever told me that before.

MR AUSTRIAN: I'd never thought of it before myself. The fact is, we all live pretty far from each other. But today I met a man on the way here and I've had a funny feeling ever since.

SVENDSON: How come? Was he rude to you?

MR AUSTRIAN: Far from it. He spoke to me like an old friend. He called me by my first name and said we were related. News to me, I told him. What, he says, you didn't know? And he glares at me like I was a bad penny. And then he starts explaining exactly how we're related and the longer he talks the more related we are.

SVENDSON: Is that so bad?

MR AUSTRIAN: No, but he said he'd be coming to see me soon.

SVENDSON: You make it sound like a threat.

MR AUSTRIAN: There was nothing unusual about his words. He said that maybe he had one weakness, an over-developed family sense. When he discovers he's even remotely related to someone he just can't live without them.

SVENDSON: That's not such a bad thing to say.

MR AUSTRIAN: No, but he shouted so when he said it.

SVENDSON: And that frightened you?

MR AUSTRIAN: To tell you the truth, it did.

SVENDSON: Good Lord, you're shaking. Like a leaf.

MR AUSTRIAN: Because I can't get him out of my head.

SVENDSON: Nerves. You ought to live up here, in this pure air.

MR AUSTRIAN: Maybe. The one good thing is that he didn't seem to be armed. If he were, I might be really worried. Oh, well, we all have our headaches, and no one can have them for us.

SVENDSON: No.

MR AUSTRIAN: Another thing that struck me as odd was that before he let me go he suggested we sign an agreement never to say anything detrimental about each other.

SVENDSON: That sounds fair enough. A mutual agreement.

MR AUSTRIAN: Think so?

*Pause.*

MR AUSTRIAN: Maybe I ought to have some kind of weapon.

SVENDSON: Yes. It might come in handy.

MR AUSTRIAN: Unfortunately weapons are expensive.

SVENDSON: That's a fact.

MR AUSTRIAN: Well, goodbye, Mr Svendson.

SVENDSON: Goodbye, Mr Austrian.

*Mr Austrian goes out. Svendson stands up and does Swedish exercises with his iron bars, in time to monotonous music. A customer in an ill-fitting suit enters.*

THE CUSTOMER *in a hoarse voice*: How much is your iron?

SVENDSON: A crown a bar.

THE CUSTOMER: Expensive.

SVENDSON: I've got to earn my living.

THE CUSTOMER: I see.

SVENDSON: Your face looks familiar.

THE CUSTOMER: You knew my brother. He often came here.

SVENDSON: How's he getting along?

THE CUSTOMER: Dead. He left me the business.

SVENDSON: I'm sorry to hear it.

THE CUSTOMER *menacingly*: Really?

SVENDSON: I didn't mean about your having the business, I meant about his being dead.

THE CUSTOMER: You seem to have been very close friends with him.

SVENDSON: Not really. But he was a good customer.

THE CUSTOMER: And now I'm your customer.

SVENDSON: At your service. I suppose you want two bars, same as your brother?

THE CUSTOMER: Four.

SVENDSON: That will be four crowns.

THE CUSTOMER *pulls some notes out of his pocket. Hesitantly*: They've got a few spots on them. Coffee stains. Do you mind?

SVENDSON *examining the notes*: This isn't coffee.

THE CUSTOMER: What is it then?

SVENDSON: It's reddish.

THE CUSTOMER: Then it must be blood. *Pause.* I cut my finger. *Pause.* Do you want the money or not?

SVENDSON: I don't think I'll have any trouble getting rid of it.

THE CUSTOMER: No. I'm sure you won't.

SVENDSON: Very well. *He puts the notes in the cash drawer while the customer takes his bars under his arm. Casually*: Oh, by the way. My old friend the tobacconist dropped in a little while ago. He complained of being stopped and molested by a stranger on the way here. Has anybody molested you?

THE CUSTOMER: No. No one has molested me. No one even spoke to me, which rather surprised me, I must say. Your friend seems to be a liar of the worst kind.

SVENDSON *taking offence*: You have no right to say that.

THE CUSTOMER: The world is full of liars, thieves, and murderers.

SVENDSON: I don't subscribe to that. My friend seemed really worried. I was even thinking of giving him one of my iron bars to defend himself with if necessary.

THE CUSTOMER: I wouldn't advise you to do that. It would make for bad blood in the neighbourhood if you started arming everybody free of charge. Take it from me, they're all a lot of thieves and murderers. And liars. Your best bet is to keep your nose clean and peacefully attend to your iron business. I'm speaking as a peace-loving individual. Just don't put any weapons into those people's hands! They don't know where the next meal is coming from. You put weapons into the hands of a hungry man and . . .

SVENDSON: I see what you mean.

THE CUSTOMER: Say, aren't we related?

SVENDSON *surprised*: What makes you think that?

THE CUSTOMER: I'm pretty sure. Through our great-grandfathers or something.

SVENDSON: I believe you're mistaken.

THE CUSTOMER: Really? Well, I'll be going now. Good iron you've got here. It's expensive, but I need it. What can I do if I need it? You think the price will come down?

SVENDSON: I doubt it.

*The customer turns towards the door. A rumbling sound is heard.*

SVENDSON: Did you say something?

THE CUSTOMER: Me? No, that's my stomach. I'd been eating too much fatty food for a while. Now I'm fasting.

SVENDSON *laughs*: Oh! Well, good day.

*The customer goes out.*

SVENDSON *picks up the phone*: Is that you, Dansen? Listen, that new man has just been here. – Oh, he's been at your place too? He bought some of my merchandise. – Oh, he's bought from you too? Well, as long as he pays he's good enough for me. – Of course he's good enough for you too as long as he pays.

*The stage grows dark.*


2


*The calendar in the iron shop reads 1939. Mrs Czech comes in with some shoe-boxes under her arm.*

MRS CZECH: Good morning, Mr Svendson. Can I interest you in some shoes? *She takes out a pair of large yellow shoes.* Good sturdy shoes, eleven crowns a pair, genuine Czech workmanship.

SVENDSON: Good morning, Mrs Czech. I'm always glad to see you. My business hasn't been doing very well lately, so I'm afraid I can't afford new shoes at the moment, but rest assured, I won't buy from anyone else. But you look rather upset, Mrs Czech.

MRS CZECH *looking around fearfully from time to time*: Does that surprise you? Haven't you heard the terrible news about the tobacconist?

SVENDSON: What about him?

MRS CZECH: This tobacconist, a Mr Austrian, was attacked on the street. Robbed and murdered.

SVENDSON: You don't say so! Why, that's terrible.

MRS CZECH: The whole neighbourhood's talking about it. They want to organise a police force. We must all join up. You too, Mr Svendson.

SVENDSON *dismayed*: Me? No, that's impossible. I'm not cut out for police work, Mrs Czech, not in the least. I'm a peace-loving man. Besides, my iron business takes up all my time. I want to sell my iron in peace, that's enough for me.

MRS CZECH: The man who attacked the tobacconist must have been well armed. I want a weapon too, I'm frightened. Send me one of your iron bars, Mr Svendson.

SVENDSON: Glad to. With the greatest pleasure, Mrs Czech. One iron bar, that will be one crown.

MRS CZECH *fumbling in her purse*: There must be a crown in here somewhere.

SVENDSON: Why, your hands are trembling, Mrs Czech.

MRS CZECH: Here it is. *She has brought out the crown.* On my way here a man spoke to me. He offered me his protection. It scared me out of my wits.

SVENDSON: Why?

MRS CZECH: Well, you see, I haven't any enemies among the people I know. But this was somebody I didn't know. He wanted to come home with me to protect me, so he said. Isn't that creepy? Tell me: don't you feel threatened?

SVENDSON: Me? No. They all have to keep on good terms with me, because they all need my iron in these uncertain times. Even when they're at each other's throats, they've got to treat me with respect. Because they need my iron.

MRS CZECH: Yes, you're a lucky man. Good day, Mr Svendson. *She goes out.*

SVENDSON *calls after her*: Good day, Mrs Czech. I'll have your bar delivered. *He stands up and does Swedish gymnastics in time to the monotonous music. The customer comes in. He has something hidden under his coat.*

THE CUSTOMER: How much is your iron?

SVENDSON: A crown a bar.

THE CUSTOMER: Price hasn't come down yet? Let's have it.

SVENDSON: Four bars again?

THE CUSTOMER: No, eight.

SVENDSON: That will be eight crowns.

THE CUSTOMER *slowly*: I'd like to make you a proposition, in view of the fact that after all we're slightly related.

SVENDSON: Not that I know of, Mr . . .

THE CUSTOMER: You may not know it yet, but never mind. I'd like to suggest a new way of doing business: barter. I bet you smoke cigars. Well, I've got cigars. *He takes a box full of big cigars from under his coat.* I can let you have them cheap, because I got them for nothing. I inherited them from a relative. And I don't smoke.

SVENDSON: You don't smoke. You don't eat. You don't smoke. And these are Austrillos.

THE CUSTOMER: Ten cents apiece. That makes ten crowns for a box of a hundred. But between cousins I'll let you have it for eight, the price of your iron. Is it a deal?

SVENDSON: The tobacconist was a good friend of mine. How did he die?

THE CUSTOMER: Peacefully, my friend, very peacefully. Quietly and peacefully. A peace-loving man. He suddenly sent for me. And then a Higher Power sent for him. It all happened very quickly. He barely had time to say: Brother, don't let the tobacco dry out, and then he was gone. He'd hung a wreath on the door to welcome me. I laid it on his coffin. *He wipes a tear from his eye. As he does so, a revolver falls out of his sleeve. He puts it back hastily.* He has departed this cruel world. A world where everyone distrusts everyone else. A world of violence, where the streets aren't safe any more. I always carry a weapon nowadays. Unloaded, just as a deterrent. How about the cigars?

SVENDSON: I can't afford cigars. If I could buy anything, I'd buy myself a pair of shoes.

THE CUSTOMER: I haven't got any shoes. I have cigars. And I need the iron.

SVENDSON: What do you need so much iron for?

THE CUSTOMER: Oh, iron always comes in handy. *Again his stomach rumbles loudly.*

SVENDSON: Maybe you'd better buy some food instead?

THE CUSTOMER: All in good time. All in good time. I've got to go now, it looks like rain, and my suit is made out of synthetic wool, my own invention, it won't stand up under rain. Would you be interested in a bolt of this excellent material?

SVENDSON: All right, I'll take the Austrillos. My business isn't doing very well. *He takes the box.*

THE CUSTOMER *laughs scornfully and picks up his eight iron bars*: Good day, Mr Svendson.

SVENDSON *picks up the phone, voluptuously puffing on an Austrillo*: Is that you, Dansen? What do you say about the recent events? – Yes, that's what I say. I don't say anything. – Oh, you're not sticking your neck out? Right, I'm not sticking my neck out either. – Oh, you're still doing business with him? Right, I'm still doing business with him too. – So you're not worried? Fine, I'm not worried either. *The stage grows dark.*

3

*The calendar in the iron store reads February 1939. Svendson sits smoking an Austrillo. A lady and a gentleman come in.*

THE GENTLEMAN: My dear Mr Svendson, Mrs Gall and I would like a word with you if you can spare the time.

SVENDSON: Rest assured, Mr Britt, that I always have time for my best customer.
*The lady and the gentleman sit down.*

THE GENTLEMAN: We wished to speak to you about the dreadful assault on Mrs Czech.

SVENDSON: An assault on Mrs Czech?

THE GENTLEMAN: Last night our neighbour Mrs Czech was assaulted, robbed, and murdered by Whatsisname. He was armed to the teeth.

SVENDSON: What, Mrs Czech murdered? How can that be?

THE GENTLEMAN: How indeed? We're quite beside ourselves, we just don't understand. Mrs Gall was a special friend of hers. Last night Mrs Gall heard loud cries for help coming from her house. She rushed straight over to my place and we sat there for hours discussing what we could do. Then we went to the poor woman's house and found her engaged in a violent argument with that Whatsisname. He was asking for something that supposedly belonged to a relative of his, and we advised her to let him have it if he promised to leave her in peace. She consented and he promised. But later in the night it seems he came back and murdered the poor woman.

THE LADY: Of course we'd never have left if we hadn't trusted him to keep his promise.

THE GENTLEMAN: Now we've decided to form an organisation of all our neighbours to make sure such a thing never happens again. We've come to ask if you wish to join our law-enforcement organisation and add your name to our membership list. *He hands him the list.*

SVENDSON *takes it hesitantly. Uneasily*: But you see, I've only got a small iron business. I can't get mixed up in the quarrels of the big corporations. Some of my customers might take it amiss if I were to join this kind of organisation.

THE LADY: I see. You wish to sell your iron no matter what happens, to no matter whom?

SVENDSON: Not at all. How can you say such a thing? My conscience, it seems to me, is as sensitive as yours. But I'm just not the warlike type, don't you see. My business has nothing to do with it. Let's be a little more relaxed about all this. *To the gentleman*: Do you smoke?

THE GENTLEMAN *looks at the cigars*: Austrillos!

THE LADY: I'd appreciate it if the gentlemen didn't smoke.

SVENDSON *annoyed, puts away the box and his own cigar*: I beg your pardon.

THE GENTLEMAN: You were speaking of your conscience, Mr Svendson.

SVENDSON: Was I? Yes, of course. I can assure you that I abhor all violence. I haven't had a good night's sleep since these dreadful things started happening. To tell you the truth, madame, it's only on account of my nerves that I've been smoking so much.

THE LADY: Then you have no basic objection to the idea of an organisation to combat violence?

SVENDSON: Basic or not, my motives are of the purest.

THE GENTLEMAN: We wouldn't think of questioning the purity of your motives. It's obvious that if you sell your iron to Whatsisname it's not because you approve of his conduct.

SVENDSON: Of course not. I abominate it.

THE GENTLEMAN: And you don't consider yourself related to him, as he is said to claim?

SVENDSON: Certainly not.

THE GENTLEMAN: You only sell because he pays and you'll only sell as long as he pays.

SVENDSON: That's right.

THE GENTLEMAN: And you think Whatsisname wouldn't need your iron any more if you were to join our peace league that would guarantee your security and everyone else's?

SVENDSON: Of course he needs my iron. I honestly don't know what he does with it . . .

THE LADY *amiably*: He makes machine-guns!

SVENDSON *ignoring her information*: As I've said, I don't know, but he'd probably have to buy it even then. Only, as I said before, it might make him angry, and, you see, I just happen to be the peaceful kind. To be perfectly frank, I'm expecting him now, and I'd rather he didn't find you in my shop. He's uncommonly sensitive and quick to take offence. So you'd be doing me a big favour if . . .

*The customer comes in with a package under his arm.*

THE CUSTOMER: How much is your iron?

SVENDSON: A crown a bar.

THE CUSTOMER: Ah, I see we have company. Friends of yours, Svendson?

SVENDSON: Hm. Yes. No. In a way. A business call.

THE GENTLEMAN: We've been talking about Mrs Czech, the lady you murdered, sir.

THE CUSTOMER: Me?

THE LADY: Yes.

THE CUSTOMER: Lies! Calumny! Slander!

THE GENTLEMAN: What, you deny that you murdered Mrs Czech?

THE CUSTOMER: Of course I deny it. Mrs Czech was recommended to me by some close relatives of mine who were lodgers in her house. She asked me for protection. When my relatives got down on their knees and begged me, I gave in, and yesterday I started protecting her. It was her last great joy on earth. A few minutes later she died peacefully of old age in my arms. That's the truth, and that's what you and certain other people choose to represent as murder! What's more, it was because of you that Mrs Czech came to me! You let her down and you'll let all your friends down. That ought to give you pause, Mr Svendson.

THE LADY: So you just took care of Mrs Czech?

THE CUSTOMER: Why would I have wanted to hurt her? *His stomach rumbles.*

THE GENTLEMAN: And you really mean to deny that you threaten everyone who lives anywhere near you?

THE CUSTOMER: Of course I deny it! I've come here to buy sixteen bars of iron, Mr Svendson. But I find an atmosphere of hostility. Obviously you can't be expected to sell iron to anyone who threatens you. So let me ask you a question; think carefully before you answer: Do you feel threatened by me?

SVENDSON: Me? How can you ask? How many bars did you say? Oh yes, sixteen. Do I feel threatened by you? Whatever put that into your head? Do you really want an answer?

THE GENTLEMAN, THE LADY *and* THE CUSTOMER: Yes.

SVENDSON *counting out the bars*: In that case I'll tell you: No. I don't feel threatened.

*The lady and the gentleman leave in indignation.*

THE CUSTOMER *while Svendson wipes off the bars with the membership list*: Splendid. There's a man who still has the courage of his convictions. We must be related in some way, Svendson. Even if you deny it. People deny a lot of things. By the way, since we're both so passionately devoted to peace, couldn't we make a little pact entitling you to attack anyone you please with iron bars except me, and me to attack anyone but you?

SVENDSON *in a choked voice*: I wouldn't like to do that. My biggest customer . . .

THE CUSTOMER: But I need more iron, Svendson. People are plotting against me. They're planning to attack me. They all want to attack me. Because they can't bear to see how well I'm getting along. *His stomach rumbles again.* They accuse me of killing that woman! Lies! Lies! Lies! And do you know what I found in her house afterwards? An iron bar! She was going to attack me! You're right to keep out of these disgusting quarrels. You're an iron dealer, not a politician, Svendson. You sell your iron to anyone who can pay. And I buy from you because I like you and because I see that you have to make a living. Because you're not against me and don't let my enemies incite you against me – that's why I buy your iron. Why else would I buy it? You've no reason to make an enemy of me! Weren't you saying something about shoes? Here, I've brought you some shoes. *He takes out a pair of large yellow shoes.* Just what you need, Svendson. I can let you have them cheap. Do you know how much they cost me?

SVENDSON *feebly*: How much?

THE CUSTOMER: Nothing. See. And you get the benefit, Svendson. Oh yes, you and I are going to be great friends, especially when we've come to a perfect agreement about the price of iron. And we will, Svendson, we will. Give me a hand with these bars, Svendson.

*Svendson helps him to pick up the bars. He takes six under each arm, loads the rest on his back, and thus heavily laden hobbles out.*

SVENDSON: Good day.

THE CUSTOMER *turning with difficulty in the doorway. Smiling*: See you soon.

4

*The calendar in the iron store now reads 19??. Svendson is strolling around, smoking an Austrillo and wearing Mrs Czech's shoes. Suddenly the sound of guns is heard. Very much upset, Svendson tries in vain to telephone. The telephone is dead. He turns on the radio. The radio is dead. He looks out the window and sees the glow of flames.*

SVENDSON: War!

*He hurries to the blackboard showing the price of iron, rubs out the figure 3 with a sponge and in feverish haste writes in a 4. The customer comes in with all sorts of things under his coat. His face is chalky-white.*

SVENDSON *listening*: Do you know where that gunfire is coming from?

THE CUSTOMER: It's coming from my rumbling stomach. I'm on my way to get some food. But for that I need more iron. *He throws open his coat, uncovering two machine-guns at the ready.*

SVENDSON: Help! Help!

THE CUSTOMER: *How much is your iron?*

SVENDSON *stammers*: Nothing.

# The Trial of Lucullus

*A radio play*

*1940 version*

*Collaborator*: MARGARETE STEFFIN

*Translator*: H.R. HAYS

*Characters*:

LUCULLUS, *a Roman general*
THE COURT CRIER
THE JUDGE OF THE DEAD
*Jury of the Dead*: THE TEACHER, THE COURTESAN, THE
    BAKER, THE FISHWIFE, THE FARMER
*Figures on the Frieze*: THE KING, THE QUEEN, TWO GIRLS
    WITH A TABLET, TWO SLAVES WITH A GOLDEN GOD, TWO
    LEGIONARIES, LUCULLUS'S COOK, THE CHERRY-TREE
    BEARER
THE HOLLOW VOICE
AN OLD WOMAN
THE THREEFOLD VOICE
TWO SHADOWS
THE HERALD
THE CROWD: TWO GIRLS, TWO MERCHANTS, TWO WOMEN,
    TWO PLEBEIANS, A DRIVER
CHORUS OF SOLDIERS
CHORUS OF SLAVES
CHILDREN'S CHORUS

Bracketed numbers show where passages were subsequently added in *Versuche 11*, 1951 (English translation in *Bertolt Brecht: Plays* Volume 1, Methuen, 1960) or else included in the 'Notes to the Opera' in those publications. Such passages and changed scenes are separately listed as 'New passages included in the 1951 radio play' (pp. 383–90).

THE FUNERAL PROCESSION

*Noise of a great crowd.*

THE HERALD:
Hark, the great Lucullus is dead!
The general who conquered the East
Who overthrew seven kings
Who filled our city of Rome with riches.
Behind his catafalque
Borne by soldiers
Walk the most distinguished men of mighty Rome
With covered faces, beside it
Walks his philosopher, his advocate, and before it
Slaves drag a tremendous frieze
Setting forth his deeds and destined to be his tombstone.
Once more
The entire people pays its respects to an amazing lifetime
Of victory and conquest
And they remember his former triumphal processions.
SONG OF THE SOLDIERS CARRYING THE CATAFALQUE:
Hold it steady, hold it shoulder-high.
See that it does not waver in front of thousands of eyes
For now the Lord of the Eastern Earth
Betakes himself to the shadows. Take care, do not stumble.
That flesh and metal you bear
Has ruled the world. (1)
SLAVES DRAGGING THE FRIEZE:
Careful, do not stumble!
You who haul the frieze with the scene of triumph
Ay, though the sweat runs down to your eyelids
Still keep your hands to the stone! Think, if you drop it
It might crumble to dust.

THE CROWD

A GIRL:
See the red plume! No, the big one.

ANOTHER GIRL:
He squints.

FIRST MERCHANT:
All the senators.

SECOND MERCHANT:
All the tailors too.

FIRST MERCHANT:
Why no, this man has pushed on even to India.

SECOND MERCHANT:
But he was finished long ago
I'm sorry to say.

FIRST MERCHANT:
Greater than Pompey
Rome would have been lost without him.
Enormous victories.

SECOND MERCHANT:
Mostly luck.

FIRST WOMAN:
My Reus
Perished in Asia.
All this fuss won't bring him back to me.

FIRST MERCHANT:
Thanks to this man
Many a man made a fortune.

SECOND WOMAN:
My brother's boy too never came home again.

FIRST MERCHANT:
Everyone knows what Rome reaped, thanks to him
In fame alone.

FIRST WOMAN:
Without their lies
Nobody would walk into the trap.

FIRST MERCHANT:
Heroism, alas
Is dying out.

FIRST PLEBEIAN:
When
Will they spare us this twaddle about fame?
SECOND PLEBEIAN:
Three legions in Cappadocia
Not one left to tell the tale.
A DRIVER:
Can
I get through here?
SECOND WOMAN:
No, it's closed off.
FIRST PLEBEIAN:
When we bury our generals
Oxcarts must have patience.
SECOND WOMAN:
They dragged my Pulcher before the judge:
Taxes due.
FIRST MERCHANT:
We can say
Except for him Asia would not be ours today.
FIRST WOMAN:
Has tunnyfish jumped in price again?
SECOND WOMAN:
Cheese too.
*The noise of the crowd increases.*
THE HERALD:
Now
They pass through the arch of triumph
Which the city has built for her great son.
The women hold their children high. The mounted men
Press back the ranks of the spectators.
The street behind the procession lies deserted.
For the last time
The great Lucullus has passed through it.
*The noise of the crowd and the sound of marching fade.*

2

SUDDEN SILENCE AND RETURN TO NORMALITY

THE HERALD:
   The procession has disappeared. Now
   The street is full again. From the obstructed side-alleys
   The carters drive out with their oxcarts. The crowd
   Returns to its business, chattering. Busy Rome
   Goes back to work.

3

IN THE SCHOOLBOOKS

CHILDREN'S CHORUS:
   In the schoolbooks
   Are written the names of great generals.
   Whoever wants to emulate them
   Learns their battles by heart
   Studies their wonderful lives.
   To emulate them
   To rise above the crowd
   Is our task. Our city
   Is eager to write our names some day
   On the tablets of immortality. (2)

4

THE BURIAL

THE HERALD:
   Outside, on the Appian Way
   Stands a little structure, built ten years before
   Meant to shelter the great man
   In death.
   Before it, the crowd of slaves that drags the triumphal frieze
   Turns in.
   Then the little rotunda with the boxtree hedge receives it.

A HOLLOW VOICE:
Halt, soldiers!
THE HERALD:
Comes a voice
From the other side of the wall
Giving orders from now on.
THE HOLLOW VOICE:
Tilt the bier! No one is carried
Behind this wall. Behind this wall
Each man goes alone.
THE HERALD:
The soldiers tilt the bier, the General
Stands up now, a little uncertain.
His philosopher makes as if to accompany him
A wise saw on his lips. But...
THE HOLLOW VOICE:
Stand back, Philosopher. Behind this wall
No one heeds your sophistry.
THE HERALD:
Says the voice that gives orders here
And thereupon the advocate steps forward
To raise an objection.
THE HOLLOW VOICE:
Overruled.
THE HERALD:
Says the voice that gives orders here. And it says to the
    General:
THE HOLLOW VOICE:
Now step through the gateway.
THE HERALD:
And the General goes to the little gateway
Stands there a moment, looking about him
And stares with grave eyes at the soldiers
Stares at the slaves who haul the sculpture
Stares at the boxtree, the last green thing. He lingers.
As the portico stands open, a breath of wind
Blows in from the street.
*A gust of wind.*

THE HOLLOW VOICE:
Take your helmet off. Our gateway is low.
THE HERALD:
And the General takes off his splendid helmet
And steps in with bowed head. With a sigh of relief
The soldiers crowd out of the burial place, chattering gaily.


5

DEPARTURE OF THE LIVING

CHORUS OF THE SOLDIERS:
So long, Lakalles.
Now we're quits, old goat.
Out of the boneyard
Up with the glass!
Fame isn't everything
You've got to live too.
Who'll come along?
Down by the dock
There's wine and song. You weren't in step.
I'll come along.
Be sure of that.
Who'll pay the bill?
They'll chalk it up.
Look at his grin!
I'm off to the cattle market.
To the little brunette? Hey, we'll come along.
No, three's a crowd.
You'll put her off.
Then
We're for the dog races.
Man
That costs money. Not if they know you.
I'll come along.
Attention! Break ranks!
March.

6

THE RECEPTION

*The Hollow Voice is the voice of the gatekeeper of the Realm of Shadows. It continues the narration.*

THE HOLLOW VOICE:
Ever since the newcomer has entered
He has stood near the door, motionless, his helmet under
    his arm
Like his own statue.
The other dead who are newly arrived
Crouch on the bench and wait as they have often waited
For good fortune and for death
Waited in the tavern until they got their wine
Waited at the well until the lover came
Waited in the wood, in battle, for the word of command.
But the newcomer
Does not seem to have learned how to wait.
LUCULLUS *suddenly*:
By Jupiter
What does this mean? I stand and wait here.
The greatest city on the globe still rings
With lamentations for me, and here
There is no one to receive me. Outside my war tent
Seven kings once waited for me.
Is there no order here? (3)
*Pause.*
I demand to be conducted from this place.
*Pause.*
Must I stand here among these people?
*Pause.*
I object. Two hundred armoured ships, five legions
Used to advance at the crook of my little finger.
I object.
*Pause.*
THE HOLLOW VOICE:
No answer but from the bench of those who wait
An old woman says:

THE VOICE OF AN OLD WOMAN WAITING:
  Sit down, newcomer.
  All that metal you haul, the heavy helmet
  And the breastplate must be tiring.
  So sit down.
  *Lucullus is silent.*
  Don't be arrogant. You can't stand the whole time
  You must wait here. My turn comes before yours.
  No one can say how long the hearing inside will last.
  There's no doubt that each one will be strictly examined
  To determine whether he shall be sentenced to go
  Down into dark Hades
  Or into the Elysian Fields. Sometimes
  The trial is quite short. One glance is enough for the judges.
  This one here, they say
  Has led a blameless life and he was able
  To be of use to his fellow men.
  With them a person's usefulness counts the most.
  They say to him, go take your rest.
  Of course with others
  The hearing may last for whole days, especially
  With those who have sent someone down here to the Realm
    of the Shadows
  Before the appointed span of his life was over.
  It won't take long with the one who went in just now.
  He's a harmless little baker. As for my affair
  I'm a little anxious, but put my faith in this –
  Among the jury within, they tell me
  There are little people who know well enough
  How hard life is for those of us in times of war.
  My advice to you, newcomer...
THE THREEFOLD VOICE *interrupting*:
  Tertullia! (4)
THE HOLLOW VOICE:
  The newcomer stands stubbornly on the sill
  But the burden of his decorations
  His own roaring
  And the friendly words of the old woman have changed
    him.
  He looks around to see if he is really alone.

Now he goes to the bench after all, but before he can sit
   down
He'll be called. A glance at the old woman
Was enough for the judge.

THE THREEFOLD VOICE:
   Lakalles!

LUCULLUS:
   My name is Lucullus! Isn't my name known here?
   I come from a distinguished family
   Of statesmen and generals. Only in the slums
   In the docks and soldiers' taverns, in the unwashed
   Jaws of the vulgar, the scum
   Is my name Lakalles.

THE THREEFOLD VOICE:
   Lakalles!

THE HOLLOW VOICE:
   And so yet again called
   In the despised language of the slums
   Lucullus, the general
   Who conquered the East
   Who overthrew seven kings
   And filled the city of Rome with riches.
   At nightfall, when Rome sits down to the funeral feast
   Lucullus presents himself before the highest tribunal of the
      Realm of the Shadows.


7

CHOICE OF SPONSOR

THE COURT CRIER:
   Before the highest tribunal of the Realm of the Shadows
      appears
   General Lakalles, who calls himself Lucullus.
   Presided over by the Judge of the Dead
   Five jurors pursue the examination:
   One, formerly a farmer
   One, formerly a slave who was a teacher
   One, formerly a fishwife
   One, formerly a baker

And one, formerly a courtesan.
They sit upon a high bench
Without hands to take and without mouths to eat
Insensible to magnificence, these long-extinguished eyes
Incorruptible, these ancestors of the world-to-come.
The Judge of the Dead begins the hearing.

THE JUDGE OF THE DEAD:

Shadow, you shall be heard.
You must account for your life among men.
Whether you have served them or harmed them
Whether we wish to see your face
In the Elysian Fields.
You need a sponsor.
Have you a sponsor in the Elysian Fields?

LUCULLUS:

I propose the great Alexander of Macedon be called.
Let him speak to you as an expert
On deeds like mine.

THE THREEFOLD VOICE *calls out in the Elysian Fields*:

Alexander of Macedon!
*Silence.*

THE COURT CRIER:

The person called does not answer.

THE THREEFOLD VOICE:

In the Elysian Fields
There is no Alexander of Macedon.

THE JUDGE OF THE DEAD:

Shadow, your expert is unknown
In the Fields of the Blessed.

LUCULLUS:

What? He who conquered from Asia to India
The never-to-be-forgotten one
Who so indelibly pressed his footprint in the globe of the
    earth
The mighty Alexander . . .

THE JUDGE OF THE DEAD:

Is unknown here. (5)

LUCULLUS:

Then I propose

That the frieze from my memorial
On which my triumphal procession is set forth, be fetched.
But how can it be fetched? Slaves haul it. Surely
Entrance is forbidden here
To the living.

THE JUDGE OF THE DEAD:
  Not to slaves. So little divides them
  From the dead that one can say
  They scarcely live. The step from the world above
  Down to the Realm of the Shadows
  Is to them a short one.
  The frieze shall be brought.


8

THE FRIEZE IS PRODUCED


THE HOLLOW VOICE:
  His slaves still huddle
  By the wall, uncertain
  Where the frieze should go. Until a voice
  Suddenly speaks through the wall.

THE COURT CRIER:
  Come.

THE HOLLOW VOICE:
  And changed to shadows
  By this single word
  They drag their burden
  Through the wall with the box hedge.

CHORUS OF SLAVES:
  Out of life into death
  Without protest, we haul the burden.
  Long ago our time ceased to be ours
  And the goal of our journey unknown.
  And so we follow the new voice
  Like the old. Why question it?

We leave nothing behind; we expect nothing. (6)

THE COURT CRIER:

And so they go through the wall
For nothing holds them back, neither can this wall keep
   them back.
And they set their burden down
Before the highest tribunal of the Realm of the Shadows –
This frieze with the triumphal procession.
The jurymen of the dead, look upon it:
A captured king, sad of countenance
A strange-eyed queen with provocative thighs
A man with a cherry tree, eating a cherry
A golden god, borne by two slaves, very fat
Two girls with a tablet, upon it the names of fifty-three
   cities
A dying legionary, greeting his general
A cook with a fish.

THE JUDGE OF THE DEAD:

Are these your witnesses, Lakalles?

LUCULLUS:

They are. But how shall they speak?
They are stone, they are dumb.

THE JUDGE OF THE DEAD:

Not to us. They shall speak.
Are you ready, you stony shadows
You shapes, to give testimony here?

CHORUS OF FIGURES IN THE FRIEZE:

We figures, stony shadows of vain sacrifice
Once destined to remain above in the daylight
Either to speak or to keep silent
We figures once destined by the conqueror's order to
   portray
Those conquered, robbed of breath
Silenced, forgotten
Are willing to keep silent and willing to speak.

THE JUDGE OF THE DEAD:

Shadow, the witnesses of your greatness
Are ready to testify.

9

THE HEARING

THE COURT CRIER:
  And the General steps forward and
  Points to the king.
LUCULLUS:
  Here you see one whom I vanquished.
  In these few days
  His empire crumbled like a hut struck by lightning.
  He began to fly when I appeared on his frontier
  And the first few days of the war
  Were scarcely enough for us both
  To reach the other frontier of his realm.
  So short was the campaign that a ham
  My cook had hung up to smoke
  Was not yet thoroughly cured when I returned.
  And of seven I struck down he was but one.
THE JUDGE OF THE DEAD:
  Is that true, O King?
THE KING:
  It is true.
THE JUDGE OF THE DEAD:
  Your questions, jurors.
THE COURT CRIER:
  And the shadowy slave who was once a teacher
  Bends darkly forward and asks:
THE TEACHER:
  How did it happen?
THE KING:
  As he says. We were attacked
  As the farmer loading hay
  Stood with raised fork
  His half-filled waggon was taken from him
  And strange hands seized the baker's breadloaf
  Before it was fully baked. All that he says
  Concerning the lightning that strikes a hut is true.
  The hut is destroyed. Here
  Is the lightning.

THE TEACHER:
And of seven you were ...
THE KING:
But one.
THE COURT CRIER:
The jurymen of the dead
Consider the testimony of the king.
*Silence.*
And the shadow who was once a courtesan
Puts a question.
THE COURTESAN:
You there, O Queen
How did you get here?
THE QUEEN:
One day by the Taurion I
Went to bathe there early
From among the olive trees
Down came fifty strangers.
Those men were my conquerors.

Had no weapon but a sponge
In the limpid water.
And their armour shielded me
Only for a moment.
Quickly I was conquered. (7)
THE COURTESAN:
And why do you walk here in the procession?
THE QUEEN:
Oh, as a proof of the victory.
THE COURTESAN:
What victory, the one over you?
THE QUEEN:
And the lovely Taurion.
THE COURTESAN:
And what does he call a triumph?
THE QUEEN:
That the king, my husband
Could not with his whole army
Protect his property
From prodigious Rome.

THE COURTESAN:
 Sister, then our fates are the same.
 For I too
 Found prodigious Rome
 No shield against prodigious Rome.
THE COURT CRIER:
 And there was silence. The jurymen
 Of the dead consider the testimony of the queen.
 *Silence.*
 And the Judge of the Dead
 Turns to the General.
THE JUDGE OF THE DEAD:
 Shadow, do you wish to proceed?
LUCULLUS:
 Yes, I mark well how the conquered
 Have a sweet voice. However
 Once it was rougher. This king here
 Who captures your sympathy, when he was in power
 Was especially ruthless. (8)
 In taxes and tribute
 He took no less than I. The cities
 I snatched from him
 Lost nothing in him, but Rome won
 Fifty-three cities, thanks to me.
TWO YOUNG GIRLS WITH A TABLET:
 With streets and people and houses
 Temples ·and waterworks
 We sprang out of the landscape.
 Today only our names remain on this tablet.
THE COURT CRIER:
 And the shadowy juror who was once a baker
 Bends darkly forward and asks:
THE BAKER:
 Why so?
GIRL WITH A TABLET:
 One day at noon an uproar broke loose.
 Into the streets swept a flood
 Whose waves were men, and carried
 Our goods away. In the evening

Only a foul smoke marked the spot
That was once a city.

THE BAKER:

And what then
Did he carry away, he who sent the flood and says
He gave fifty-three cities to Rome?

THE COURT CRIER:

And the slaves who haul the golden god
Began to tremble and cry:

THE SLAVES:

Us.
Once happy, now cheaper than oxen
To haul away booty, ourselves booty.

GIRL WITH A TABLET:

Formerly the builders of fifty-three cities, of which
Only name and smoke remain.

LUCULLUS:

Yes, I carried them off.
There were two hundred and fifty thousand
Formerly foes but now no longer foes.

THE SLAVES:

Formerly men, but now no longer men.

LUCULLUS:

And with them I carried away their god
So that the whole earth might see our gods
Were greater than all other gods.

THE SLAVES:

And the god was very welcome
Because he was of gold and weighed two hundredweight
And we too are each worth a piece of gold
The size of a fingerbone.

THE COURT CRIER:

And the shadowy juryman
Who was once a baker
In Marsilia, the city by the sea
Bends forward and says quietly:

THE BAKER:

Then we write to your credit, shadow
Simply this: Brought gold to Rome.

THE COURT CRIER:
>  And there is silence.
>  The jurymen of the dead
>  Consider the testimony of the cities.

THE JUDGE OF THE DEAD:
>  The accused seems tired.
>  I allow a recess.

10

ROME

THE COURT CRIER:
>  And the judge goes away.
>  The accused sits down.
>  He crouches by the railing
>  And leans back his head. He is exhausted, but he overhears
>  Talk behind the door
>  Where new shadows have appeared.

A SHADOW:
>  I came to grief through an oxcart.

LUCULLUS *softly*:
>  Oxcart.

THE SHADOW:
>  It brought a load of sand to a building site.

LUCULLUS *softly*:
>  Building site. Sand.

ANOTHER SHADOW:
>  Isn't it meal time now?

LUCULLUS *softly*:
>  Meal time?

FIRST SHADOW:
>  I had my bread and onions
>  With me. I haven't a room any more.
>  The horde of slaves
>  They herd in from every spot under heaven
>  Has ruined the shoemaking business.

SECOND SHADOW:
>  I too was a slave.

Say rather, the lucky
Catch the unlucky's bad luck.
LUCULLUS *somewhat louder*:
You there, is there wind up above?
SECOND SHADOW:
Hark, someone's asking a question.
FIRST SHADOW *loudly*:
Whether there's wind up above? Perhaps.
There may be in the gardens.
In the suffocating alleys
You don't notice it.


11

THE HEARING IS CONTINUED

THE COURT CRIER:
The jurymen return.
The hearing begins again.
And the shadow that was once a fishwife
Speaks.
THE FISHWIFE:
There was talk of gold.
I too lived in Rome.
Yet I never noticed any gold where I lived.
I'd like to know where it went.
LUCULLUS:
What a question!
Should I and my legions set out
To capture a new stool for a fishwife?
THE FISHWIFE:
Though you brought nothing to us in the fish market
Still you took something from us in the fish market:
Our sons.
THE COURT CRIER:
And the jurywoman
Speaks to the warriors in the frieze.
THE FISHWIFE:
Tell me, what happened to you in the two Asias?

FIRST WARRIOR:
  I ran away.
SECOND WARRIOR:
  And I was wounded.
FIRST WARRIOR:
  I dragged him along.
SECOND WARRIOR:
  So then he fell too.
THE FISHWIFE:
  Why did you leave Rome?
FIRST WARRIOR:
  I was hungry.
THE FISHWIFE:
  And what did you get there?
SECOND WARRIOR:
  I got nothing.
THE FISHWIFE:
  You stretch out your hands.
  Is that to greet your general?
SECOND WARRIOR:
  It was to show him
  They were still empty.
LUCULLUS:
  I protest.
  I rewarded the legionaries
  After each campaign.
THE FISHWIFE:
  But not the dead.
LUCULLUS:
  I protest.
  How can war be judged
  By those who do not understand it?
THE FISHWIFE:
  I understand it. My son
  Fell in the war.
  I was a fishwife in the market at the Forum.
  One day it was reported that the ships
  Returning from the Asian war
  Had docked. I ran from the market place

And I stood by the Tiber for many hours
Where they were being unloaded and in the evening
All the ships were empty and my son
Came down none of the gangplanks.
Since it was chilly by the harbour at night
I fell into a fever, and in the fever sought my son
And ever seeking him more deeply
I grew more chilled, died, came here
Into the Realm of Shadows, and still sought him.
Faber, I cried, for that was his name.
And I ran and ran through shadows
And from shadow to shadow
Crying Faber, until a gatekeeper over there
In the camp of fallen warriors
Caught me by the sleeve and said:
Old woman, there are many Fabers here, many
Mothers' sons, many, deeply mourned
But they have forgotten their names
Which only served to line them up in the army
And are no longer needed here. And their mothers
They do not wish to meet again
Because they let them go to the bloody war.
And I stood, held by my sleeve
And my cries died out in my mouth.
Silently I turned away, for I desired no longer
To look upon my son's face.

THE COURT CRIER:
And the Judge of the Dead
Seeks the eyes of the jurymen and announces:

THE JUDGE OF THE DEAD:
The court recognises that the mother of the fallen
Understands war.

THE COURT CRIER:
The jurymen of the dead
Consider the testimony of the warriors.
*Silence.*

THE JUDGE OF THE DEAD:
But the jurywoman is moved
And in her trembling hands

The scales may tip. She needs
A recess.


12

ROME, ONCE AGAIN

THE COURT CRIER:
And again
The accused sits down and listens
To the talk of the shadows behind the door.
Once again a breath is wafted in
From the world above.
SECOND SHADOW:
And why did you run so?
FIRST SHADOW:
To make an enquiry. It got about that they were recruiting
Legionaries in the taverns by the Tiber for the war in the
West
Which is now to be conquered. The land is called Gaul.
SECOND SHADOW:
Never heard of it.
FIRST SHADOW:
Only the big folks know these countries.


13

THE HEARING IS CONTINUED

THE COURT CRIER:
And the Judge smiles at the jurywoman
Calls the accused and regards him sadly.
THE JUDGE OF THE DEAD:
Our time runs out. You do not make use of it.
Anger us no more with your triumphs!
Have you no witnesses
To any of your weaknesses, mortal?
Your business goes badly. Your virtues

Seem to be of little use.
Perhaps your weaknesses will leave some loopholes
In the chain of violent deeds.
I counsel you, shadow
Recollect your weaknesses.

THE COURT CRIER:
And the juryman who was once a baker
Puts a question.

THE BAKER:
Yonder I see a cook with a fish.
He seems cheerful. Cook
Tell us how you came to be in the triumphal procession.

THE COOK:
Only to show
That even while waging war
He found time to discover a recipe for cooking fish.
I was his cook. Often
I think of the beautiful meat
The gamefowl and the black venison
Which he made me roast.
And he not only sat at table
But gave me a word of praise
Stood over the pots with me
And himself mixed a dish.
Lamb *à la* Lucullus
Made our kitchen famous.
From Syria to Pontus
They spoke of Lucullus's cook.

THE COURT CRIER:
And the juror who was once a teacher says:

THE TEACHER:
What is it to us that he liked to eat?

THE COOK:
But he let me cook
To my heart's content. I thank him for it.

THE BAKER:
I understand him, I who was a baker.
How often I had to mix bran with the dough
Because my customers were poor. This fellow here

Could be an artist.

THE COOK:

Thanks to him!

In the triumph

He ranked me next to the kings

And gave my art recognition. That is why I call him
  human. (9)

And I know

That in Amisus, the daughter city of splendid Athens

Brimming with art treasures and books

His rapacious troops promised not to burn it.

Wet with tears he returned to his supper.

That too was human, mark you.

THE COURT CRIER:

There was silence. The jurymen consider

The testimony of the cook.

*Silence.*

And the juryman who was once a farmer

Puts a question.

THE FARMER:

Over there is someone too who carries a fruit tree.

THE TREE BEARER:

This is a cherry tree.

We brought it from Asia. In the triumphal procession

We carried it along. And we planted it

On the slopes of the Apennines.

THE FARMER:

Oh, so it was you, Lakalles, who brought it?

I once planted it too, but I did not know

That you introduced it.

THE COURT CRIER:

And with a friendly smile

The juryman who was once a farmer

Discusses with the shadow

Who was once a general

The cherry tree.

THE FARMER:

It needs little soil.

LUCULLUS:
 But it doesn't like the wind.
THE FARMER:
 The red cherries have more meat.
LUCULLUS:
 And the black are sweeter.
THE FARMER:
 My friends, this of all the detestable souvenirs
 Conquered in bloody battle
 I call the best. For this sapling lives.
 It is a new and friendly companion
 To the vine and the abundant berrybush
 And growing with the growing generations
 Bears fruit for them. And I congratulate you
 Who brought it to us. When all the booty of conquest
 From both Asias has long mouldered away
 This finest of all your trophies
 Renewed each year for the living
 Shall in spring flutter its white-flowered branches
 In the wind from the hills.


14

THE WHEAT AND THE CHAFF (10)

THE JUDGE OF THE DEAD:
 And so I close the hearing.
 Among your witnesses, shadow
 The most brilliant did not serve you best. In the end
    however
 Some small ones came forward. Not wholly empty
 Were your bloody hands. Of course your
 Best contribution was a very costly one; the cherry tree:
 You could have paid for that conquest with just one more
    man.
 But eighty thousand were what you sent below. Against
    that
 We must set a few happy moments for your cook, tears
 For damaged books and suchlike trivialities.

Alas, all that violence and victory serves to extend just one
    realm
The realm of shadows!

THE JURORS OF THE DEAD:

But we who are chosen to judge the dead
Observe, on their departure from the earth, what they gave
    it.

THE COURT CRIER:

And from the high bench they rise up
The spokesmen of the world-to-be
Of those with many hands, to take
Of those with many mouths, to eat
Of the rarely gullible, eagerly gathering
Joyful world-to-be.
The court
Withdraws for consultation.

Notes and Variants

# ROUND HEADS AND POINTED HEADS

**Texts by Brecht**

'MEASURE FOR MEASURE, OR THE SALT TAX' (1931)

Act One, scene 1

*Duke. Eskaler. Sitting over the books.*

DUKE:
Now it's enough, Eskaler.
The day is dawning: all our endless sums,
Creative twists, accounting sleights of hand
Have demonstrated, each and every time,
Precisely what we can't afford to know,
And what, if we sat here till doomsday counting,
Would always be the outcome: the economic
Meltdown of the state. In short: we're bankrupt.

ESKALER:
My lord!

DUKE:
A stronger hand than mine is needed now,
I'd fain withdraw a while from public view
To think things over. There is our commission.
For now a stronger man must take my place,
Undaunted by the task in hand and eager.
Call hither, no, bid Angeler approach.
*Exit servant.*
How well d'you think he'll represent my office?
For you must know, I have a special purpose
Electing him our absence to supply;
I've lent him all our power of justice and
Of mercy, furnished him with all the organs
Of our power! But speak – what think you of it?

ESKALER:
If any in Vienna be of worth
To take on such a matter
It is Graf Angeler.

SERVANT:
Graf Angeler.

DUKE:
  Bid him come in.
  *Enter Angeler.*
ANGELER:
  Always obedient to Your Grace's will,
  I come to know your pleasure.
DUKE:
  Angeler!
  You oughtn't so to hide yourself!
  Yourself and your wise words are not your own!
  God does with us as we with torches do,
  Not light them for themselves. So too our power.
  If it should not go forth from us – it were
  As well we had it not. But to the point.
  The finances of state – you know – lie ruined.
  And what tomorrow holds is anybody's guess.
  And so it's up to us to hold the fort
  Until new money streams from sources new.
  The two of us have reckoned all the night
  And think we've found a way . . .

[. . . and so on. This abrupt first scene then ends, a page later:]

DUKE:
  So fare you well.
ESKALER:
  May God be with you.
ANGELER:
  Come back well rested, sire.
DUKE:
  I thank you both. *Exit.*
ESKALER:
  As I, dear Angeler, am now your subject,
  I'd know what role you have in mind for me?
ANGELER:
  For now I'll take the government to myself
  Since I bear all responsibility.
  In detail, well, I'd rather not commit.
  Yet straight away I'll give you one word, Eskaler:
  Reform. And now I beg you to excuse me.
ESKALER:
  Of course.
  *Exit Angeler.*
ESKALER:
  Reform.

Reform. (In the beginning was the word.)
*Exit.*

[BBA 266 (9/10), 264 (50) and 262 (01/02). These are the most important folders of material for this play (see also Editorial Note, below); and these sheets represent the very first stage of the Shakespeare adaptation, such as it has survived. Brecht's text is typed beneath stuck-on pages cut out from the standard German translation, from which Brecht has borrowed only a few lines and phrases. In most cases he has subjected even these to a process of simplification and colloquialisation, which we have attempted to represent by similarly abusing Shakespeare's original.]


CHEATED HOPES

On our travels through Peru we met a tenant farmer and his family living in indescribable misery. A conversation with the farmer revealed that these unfortunate people had sunk to such unimaginable depths of poverty not because of despair, as we had thought, but rather because of hope, a commodity of which they had rather more than of other things. The farmer told us how, towards the end of the previous year after a poor harvest, he could see no way, after he had paid the rents and dues which were too high in any case, that he could buy in winter provisions for his family and above all for his cows. Unable to help himself by other means, with a hardhearted landlord and an uninterested government, he had been on the point of joining the Association of the Black Flag, which was then rallying the discontented farmers in preparation for an uprising. Given the feebleness of the government and the parlous state of the economy, the farmers' movement had been not without prospects. Like most Czuchish* farmers he had, however, been dissuaded when the anti-Czich Thomaso Angelas, a schoolteacher from Lima, took the reins of government. Angelas had the reputation of being a friend of the people and, coming himself from the lower classes, he seemed originally to have genuinely populist intentions. And indeed, there was a proper lawsuit against the landlord, a Czich, in which the landlord was even condemned to death, albeit not for rack-renting but for seducing the farmer's daughter. At the time this affair had in fact brought the family some relief, and had enabled the girl to get

---

* In spite of all the other changes, the 'races' in Brecht's texts and notes towards the play are consistently the 'Tschuchen' and 'Tschichen', Round Heads and Pointed Heads. Here in the notes we have translated them as Czuchs and Czichs, in the text of the play as Zaks and Ziks.

into a public brothel in Lima. And in this explication of a judgement
apparently so favourable lay the seeds of all the farmer's further
misfortunes.

[BFA 19, p. 337. This sketch from 1932 may have originally been
intended as an independent short story.]

NOTES FOR DRAWINGS

1

Two Round Heads reading the newspaper. The Viceroy of Yahoo
and his advisor learn from the press that the country is bankrupt.
(Champagne bottles, cigars.)
The Viceroy receives the racial theorist Iberin. The Privy Councillor
introduces him.
'I hear that you've discovered what has caused
These small misfortunes in the fiscal realm. Is that correct?'
The Viceroy discovers the symbol of the rebel Sickle in his own
study. (Eskahler hides the chalk behind his back.)

2

The wealthy Czichish landowner de Guzman is denounced as a
Czich by the daughter of one of his tenant farmers.
(The three Hatsos, the girl, a Czich, de Guzman, three other wealthy
gentlemen.)
'A Czich!'

3

The Czuchish tenant farmer Callas leaves his Czichish comrade
Lopez to the mercy of the Iberin thugs.
(Run-down hut, open door, the two families, the Pointed Head
Lopez with his rifle, Callas has no gun – it's on the ground, or his
wife is putting it away.)
'We used to be united by our woes
But now our different head shapes make us bitter foes.'

4

Angelo Iberin condemns the Czich de Guzman to death for abusing
his power.
(Bench for the accused. Judge's throne – very high –)
'Look at the wretch there with his pointed head!
Discovered in the vile abuse of power!'
Czuchish landowners leave their Czichish fellow to the mercy of the
Iberin forces.

(as portrayed in the letter)
'... You my lords
You must stand by me in my hour of need!'

5
The attorney and Mother Superior haggle over the admission of the young Isabella de Guzman to the convent.

6
The Czuchish tenant farmer Callas parades his looted horses.
'And why shouldn't they, say I, and untie the horses.'

7
Encouraged by the propitious course of the civil war, Angelo Iberin enjoins Farmer Callas to return the horses.
'Sir, does that mean I don't get to keep the horses?'
'No!'

8
Isabella de Guzman flees from the terrible demands of her imprisoned brother.
'Such talk is just a token of despair!'
'This close to death and everything is fair!'
The victory bells are still tolling when Farmer Callas brings his daughter back to the establishment of Madame Cornamontis.
'Ah, Madame Cornamontis, the ways of the world are strange.'

9
The landowner's daughter instructs the farmer's daughter in the three primary virtues.

10
Just as the attorneys are seeking a man who might go to the gallows in the landowner's stead, Farmer Callas turns up and requests a deferment of the rents.
'Señor de Guzman! Señor de Guzman, it's Farmer Callas!'
On death row, de Guzman barters with Farmer Callas over the terms on which the latter would take his place.
'Landlord and peasant: always picking fights.
One's in the right, the other one has rights.'

11
The Viceroy shows Señor Iberin that he nearly hanged the poor Czuch instead of the rich Czich.
'Dear Iberin, permit me to reveal
The fish that have so hopelessly enmeshed

Themselves within your closely knotted net.'

Final tableau:

> [BFA 24, pp. 201–3. Early 1935. Brecht and his publisher Wieland
> Herzfelde wanted George Grosz to do drawings for Brecht's plays
> in the *Gesammelte Werke* edition. These are Brecht's (incomplete)
> notes for his guidance. The numbers refer to the scenes of the play.
> In 1937 Grosz, regrettably, turned his back on the commission.
> The reference in §4 is to a letter to Grosz of January 1935.]

PROPS FOR 'THE ROUND HEADS'

The judge's table in the Viceroy's palace must clearly be the same
table as that from which the victors dine at the end.

In the convent the only piece of furniture is a small cupboard with an
altar tableau on the door. When the Mother Superior locks away the
deeds to the de Guzman estates it turns out in fact to be a safe.

> [BFA 24, p. 203. 1936, for the Copenhagen production.]

'ROUND HEADS AND POINTED HEADS'

The play *Round Heads and Pointed Heads* is a new creative
adaptation of the old Italian tale which Shakespeare used in his play
*Measure for Measure*. Many people think that *Measure for Measure*
is the most philosophical of all Shakespeare's works, and it is
certainly his most progressive. It demands from those in positions of
authority that they shouldn't measure others by standards different
from those by which they themselves would be judged. It demonstrates that they ought not to demand of their subjects a moral stance
which they cannot adopt themselves. The play *Round Heads and
Pointed Heads* seeks to propose for our own age a progressive stance
similar to that which the great poet of humanism proposed for his.

> [BFA 24, p. 203. October 1936. Published in Danish: *'Rundhoder
> og Spidshoder'* in *Riddersalen* (3, 1936), the journal of the
> Copenhagen theatre of that name where the play was first
> performed (4 November 1936).]

THE COPENHAGEN PRODUCTION

In the wake of a crisis on the grain market the country of Yahoo, with its tenant farmers and landowning classes, faces the prospect of rebellion by the peasant farmers, who have joined forces in an association called 'The Sickle'. A certain Iberin suggests to the Viceroy, who is himself a landowner, that the farmers' opposition could be disrupted by a new division of the populace into Round Heads and Pointed Heads, and by the persecution of the Pointed Heads, who are to be designated the enemies of Yahoo. The Viceroy delegates power to Señor Iberin. The parable develops as follows. The round-headed farmer Callas discovers that, in a show-trial staged by Iberin, his pointed-headed landlord has been sentenced to death for seducing the round-headed daughter of one of his tenants. Encouraged by this news Callas leaves the Sickle and expropriates for himself two of his landlord's horses, which he needs for ploughing. Ownership of the landlord's estate has however, in the meantime, passed *pro forma* to the San Barabas convent, and in another trial, initiated by the convent and again used by Señor Iberin as a show-trial, the farmer is compelled to return the horses. Iberin finds himself able to make this judgement because the Sickle has been dispersed and is defeated. The tenant farmer, hoping at least to secure himself a rent reduction, declares himself prepared to go to the gallows in the place of his landlord, for whose release things are already well under way. Equally, his daughter agrees, for money, to submit to the attentions of one of Iberin's high officials in the place of the landlord's sister. Now the Viceroy returns at the head of his victorious troops. Since the farmers would refuse to pay the rents if a landlord was hanged, the Viceroy releases the landlord. He sends the disillusioned tenant farmer back to his field, but with the prospect that he'll shortly send for him again: for a great war that he's planning with a neighbouring race of Square Heads.

The play was performed with the means of Brecht's epic theatre. Set design by S. Johansen. Masks by H. Horter. Remarkable actorly contributions by Anderson as Iberin and Langberg as Farmer Callas, and a charming performance in the role of the farmer's daughter by Lulu Ziegler.

The parable form made it possible, despite the censorship in Denmark, to perform an anti-Nazi play in a small country which abuts Germany and absolutely depends on trade with Germany. None the less, the bourgeois critics attacked the play fiercely and threatened to remove it from the programme within a week. The local fascists handed out leaflets in front of the theatre, and there were attempts to mobilise the Ministry of Justice against the play. These attempts, together with the growing public interest, had as their result that, despite the hostile press, the play can go on being performed.

> [BFA 24, pp. 204–5. November 1936. On 12 November 1936 the Copenhagen daily newspaper *Berlingske Tidende* reported that the writer Olga Eggers had personally asked the Minister of Justice to protest against the production of Brecht's play in the Riddersalen Theatre.]

NOTES ON 'POINTED HEADS AND ROUND HEADS'
*Description of the Copenhagen première*

*General*
The première was given in Copenhagen on 4 November 1936 in the Riddersalen Theatre under Per Knutzon's direction. One can smoke and eat in this theatre; it holds 220. The stage is 7 metres wide, 8 metres deep and 10 metres high.

*Special characteristics of the parable form*
This play, the parable type of non-aristotelian drama, demanded a considerable sacrifice of effects of illusion on the part of actors and stage set. The preparations made so as to give point to the parable had themselves to be transparent. The playing had to enable and encourage the audience to draw abstract conclusions. During Missena's final speech the barrel of an enormous gun was lowered on wires so that it dangled above the banquet. The tenant farmer Callas on his way to gaol (scene 10) went right through the auditorium, telling his story over again to the spectators. Small adjustments were made to the parable, so that the trial (scene 7) was conducted by Missena himself rather than by the judge, and so that (in scene 3) it was Iberin's speech that brought about the split between the farmers' families. (The voice from off continued after the words, 'has taken over the government', 'and for us the most important thing is that our landlord has already been arrested'. After the sentence, 'The years of misery, my children, are at an end', came the speech during which the families move apart, and then Mrs Callas's words, 'I'm afraid the news isn't quite so good for you, you're Czichs. Señor de Guzman himself was arrested because he's a Czich'. The arrival of the other farmers was cut.)

*Building up a part (inductive method)*
The parts were built up from a social point of view. The modes of behaviour shown by the actors had transparent motives of a social-historical sort. It was not the 'eternally human' that was supposed to

emerge, not what any man is alleged to do at any period, but what men of specific social strata (as against other strata) do in our period (as against any other). Since actors are accustomed to rely primarily on the spectator's empathy, which means exploiting his most easily-accessible emotions, they nearly always run a whole sequence of sentences together and give a common expression to them. But with the kind of drama under consideration it is essential that each separate sentence should be treated for its underlying social gesture [*Gestus*]. The characters' unity is in no way upset by exactly reproducing their contradictory behaviour; it is only in their development that they really come to life. Nanna Callas, for example, demonstrates (in scene 6) quite clearly that she believes her father's case to be hopeless; all the same, in front of the judge (in 7) she uses all her charm and fights like a tigress for the horses. She does not conceal from Madame Cornamontis (in 8) that she thinks her father is an ass, but immediately afterwards she is none the less moved and grateful when she bids him farewell. The figure of the leading Hatso became, by a process of a precise consideration of each individual sentence, an inductive process from sentence to sentence, one of the principal figures. A single cry of 'Hail Iberin!', in the scene (4) where Iberin walks amongst the crowds ('But you, you see how hard it is . . .'), was enough to express his conviction. And in just a few sentences (in 6) he could make palpable the fact that his hatred for the landlord and his sympathy for the farmer come from one and the same source. Even with this great wealth of important social content, a bourgeois spectator would probably declare the characterisation to be primitive, simply because the figures do not provoke the conventional emotions; unless the actor works very carefully this may be a justified response. The work of the actors is made all the more difficult because they have more than one task. The role of Nanna Callas does not only require that the actress portray a sensible and unpretentious soul when she's alone or amongst her own kind, and the rest of the time take on the professional airs of a prostitute; she must also speak some of the explanatory passages (in 11), as it were as the mouthpiece of the playwright, directly to the spectators. Her attitude to the whole situation casts light on the role. And that attitude must in turn be derived from the role.

*Farmer Callas* was portrayed as a man worn out by work, who abandons the cause (in 3) with considerable embarrassment. He listens reluctantly to the stupid words of his wife, who is both more stupid and more of a traitor than he. It is only when Farmer Lopez refuses to understand his (Callas's) special circumstances that he becomes a little more impatient. His incomprehension of the idealistic clichés of Iberin (in 6) makes him sympathetic; his reluctance to concern himself with the honour of his daughter has good reasons; later (in 6), when he thinks he's got the horses, he is quite prepared to defend his daughter's honour. In this first court scene, however, he clearly manifests that distinctive incapacity to think realistically which leads him to value a legal judgement more highly than the armed struggle. Yet he knows how much he owes to the struggle by the Sickle; that is clear from his drunken toast to Lopez (in 6). However much the actor seemed to be setting up the farmer for our disapproval, even contempt, because of his treacherous opportunism, he was still able to retain that degree of sympathy appropriate to the cheated peasant; those who had ruined him would always be more contemptible than him; and at the moment when he is beaten (in 7) he shares once more the fate of all his class (even though they are ruined more by him than by their enemies) and so gains our sympathy for the rage and despair that their defeat must inspire.

*The Viceroy*, characterised as a landlord by his dress and manner of speech, is just a shade the coquette when he allows (in 1) his advisor to treat him as if he were inexperienced in business matters and uninterested in economic affairs; he prefers to adopt an unbiased stance as observer. After he has reached his decision about Iberin over the billiard table (after the words, 'Just spit it out then: Iberin', he brushes the remaining newspapers from the table and starts to play billiards), he exits through the stalls and returns (in 11) the same way; he could watch the whole presentation of the Iberin experiment from the stalls. In this case he could (after scene 8) hold a little speech from the stalls:

> It seems my town has put me out of mind,
> So now it's time to contemplate return,
> With luck I may accomplish it unnoticed.
> These bells confirm that victory is mine.
> I'll wait a while, but soon I shall be bold
> And join my friends at table, 'ere the food grows cold.
> The dark times cede, I'm sure, to a new light;
> The new moon rocks the old to sleep for one last night.

In any case it would be good if the actor could sit in the auditorium during the rehearsals and, as Viceroy, take a stance on things. In order to deprive the Viceroy, in the last scene where he is the master of political fudge, of the utter superiority of the *deus ex machina*, he was portrayed as an alcoholic.

*Angelo Iberin* was given no outward similarity to Hitler. The very fact that he is a sort of idealised image of a racist prophet (that is enough for the parable) prohibited that, even had the police allowed it. However, a few gestures were borrowed, partly from photographic sources. The two bows in front of the Viceroy (in 1 and 11) can only really be envisaged with the help of such material. Many people thought the tears of Iberin, who got out a large handkerchief when he heard about the return of the Viceroy (in 11), were too naive, but it is a characteristic and established ploy of such figures, like the demagogic exploitation of exhaustion after big speeches. Iberin's use of the microphone (in 7) achieved a certain notoriety, the actor demonstrated Iberin's almost erotic relationship with the instrument.

*The waitress Nanna Callas* was portrayed as a type who as a consequence of twofold exploitation (as waitress and prostitute) has an even less developed political attitude than the farmer. Her attitude only seems to be more realistic, in fact it is bereft of all hope. The actress expressed this particularly clearly in the 'Song of the Waterwheel', but on many other occasions too.

*Influence the audience (by the inductive method)*
A considerable sacrifice of the spectator's empathy does not mean sacrificing all right to influence him. The representation of human behaviour from a social point of view is meant indeed to have a decisive influence on the spectator's own social behaviour. This sort of intervention necessarily is bound to release emotional effects; they are deliberate and have to be controlled. A creation that more or less renounces empathy need not by any means be an 'unfeeling' creation, or one which leaves the spectator's feelings out of account. But it has to adopt a critical approach to his emotions, just as it does to his ideas. Emotions, instincts, drives are generally presented as being deeper, more eternal, less easily influenced by society than ideas, but this is in no way true. The emotions are neither common to all humanity nor incapable of alteration; the instincts neither infallible nor independent of reason; the drives neither uncontrollable nor only spontaneously engendered, and so on. But above all the actor must bear in mind that no worthwhile feeling can be compromised by being brought clearly and critically to the conscious level. The character's piecemeal development, as he initiates more and more relationships with other characters, consolidating or expanding himself in continually new situations, produces a rich and sometimes complicated emotional curve in the spectator, a fusion of feelings and even a conflict between them.

*Verfremdung* [Alienation]
Certain incidents in the play should be treated as self-contained scenes and raised – by means of inscriptions, musical or sound effects and the actors' way of playing – above the level of the everyday, the obvious, the expected (i.e. they are *verfremdet*).

*In scene 1:*
the Viceroy of Yahoo reads in the newspapers that his country is bankrupt;
the Viceroy learns, over a game of billiards, that according to the racist prophet Iberin it is not he and the other landlords who are responsible for the misery of the tenant farmers, but people with pointed heads;
the Viceroy receives and takes a good look at the racist prophet Iberin.

*In scene 2:*
the petty bourgeois learn from the newspaper that they have a new ruler;
the brothel madam Cornamontis, who is the first to fly the Iberin flag, announces that she won't be employing Czich girls in her establishment any more;
the economic rivalries between shopkeepers develop into pogroms; a pointed-headed grocer is threatened for not flying the Iberin flag; but when he does so he's arrested;
Nanna Callas recognises a way out for her landlord's sister which does not involve the oath of chastity and the convent;
Nanna Callas denounces her landlord and onetime lover to the Hatsos as a Pointed Head;

*In scene 3:*
Iberin's exhortation to the Round Heads to wage war on the Pointed Heads divides two farmers who had been going to join forces to resist their landlords;
Farmer Lopez's wife takes up the rifle that Farmer Callas has laid aside;
Farmer Callas refuses shelter to Farmer Lopez's family of Pointed Heads.

*In scene 4:*
the Hatsos throw dice for the rings of the captured landowners;
the people and the judge disagree whether the landlord or the waitress should be in the dock;
Iberin instructs the judge to pass judgement, not according to the case files, but according to the progress of the civil war;
Farmer Callas accuses his landlord, not of seducing his daughter, but of rack-renting;

Iberin condemns Señor de Guzman, not as a landowner, but as a Pointed Head, and not for rack-renting, but for racial violation; round-headed landowners sacrifice their pointed-headed class comrade;

*In scene 5:*

the attorney doubts that the rents are sufficiently high to enable the landlord's sister to fulfil her wish and enter the convent;

the Convent of San Barabas is content to take the estates of the Pointed Head de Guzman under their protection, but refuses shelter to his sister.

*In scene 6:*

Farmer Callas interprets a comment by Iberin about the unimportance of property as permitting him to take the horses he needs for his plough;

Callas, thinking the horses are his, rejects the de Guzman family's proposal that he should sacrifice the honour of his daughter;

Nanna complains that the way Iberin has honoured her has driven away her customers;

landlords, who have been beaten up by Iberin soldiers, are lectured by a high official about the need to pay his bodyguards.

*In scene 7:*

Iberin waits for the outcome of the civil war to decide whether or not to grant the farmer the Czich's horses;

the Mother Superior of the Convent, which is suing for the restitution of the Pointed Head's horses, shows Callas that her head is round;

Farmer Parr gives the reason why he took the horses, that he needs them for ploughing; Farmer Callas denounces him for it;

Farmer Callas, having lost the horses, wants to join the Sickle again; he learns that it has been defeated.

*In scene 8:*

Farmer Callas, unable to feed his daughter, takes her back to the brothel;

Farmer Callas recognises that by defeating the Sickle Iberin has defeated him too;

the landlord de Guzman demands of his sister that she submits to his gaoler; his attorneys don't understand his faint-heartedness;

Nanna Callas declares that she isn't interested in the death sentence hanging over her father's landlord;

*In scene 9:*

the landed lady discovers that she too is well-suited to be a prostitute; the only thing that speaks against her submitting to this fate is that she is so well-heeled;

for a suitable payment, Nanna Callas is prepared to prostitute herself, in order to save the landlord who has himself been condemned to death for prostituting her.

*In scene 10:*
in the face of death the landlord and the tenant are still arguing about the rent;
the round-headed Farmer Callas, in exchange for a rent reduction, accepts the risk that he'll be hanged in the place of his pointed-headed landlord.

*In scene 11:*
Iberin, to keep a hold on power, declares he is prepared to cash in his doctrine of Round and Pointed Heads;
the Viceroy shows Señor Iberin the fish that got tangled in his net;
the Viceroy declares that he needs the tenant farmers because there's to be a war with a neighbouring people of square heads;
seeing the execution of the people of the Sickle, Farmer Callas rejects the Viceroy's soup;
under the Viceroy's gallows and at his table Round and Pointed Heads hang and sit side by side.

*Examples of 'Verfremdung' in the Copenhagen production*
When Nanna Callas sang her introductory song (scene 2), she stood beneath the signboards of the small traders (see 'stage set and masks'), a commodity amongst other commodities, beckoning to the audience before the third verse with a mechanical prostitute's smile which she promptly switched off.

Before the fifth scene a young nun entered through the Neher-curtain carrying a gramophone and sat down on some steps. A record of organ music accompanied the first, pious section of the scene (up to the sentence 'What does the young lady bring with her?'). The nun then got up and went out with the gramophone.

The meeting of the two de Guzmans in the eighth scene (a street in the old town) was based on Claudio's conversation with Isabella in Shakespeare's *Measure for Measure*. The scene has to be played with complete seriousness in the heightened and impassioned style of the Elizabethan theatre. The Copenhagen production 'estranged' this style by having it rain during the scene and giving umbrellas to all appearing in it. In this way the heightened style of playing was given a certain artistic *Verfremdung*. The spectator, however, having had his attention drawn to the outmoded nature of such conduct, was not as yet brought to notice that heightened means of expression are bound up with individual problems of the upper class. This could be achieved e.g. by having the inspector and the Hatso who escorted the prisoner adopt a particularly offhand or even amused, but at the same time slightly surprised attitude to the event.

This demonstration of historic theatrical forms continued with the ninth scene in Madame Cornamontis's coffeehouse, which contained elements of the late eighteenth-century French conversation piece. Isabella had a completely white make-up in this scene.

*Stage set and masks*
The basic set consisted of four ivory-coloured screens, slightly curved horizontally, which could be arranged in various ways. The lights were shown, in so far as they were movable. The two pianos were illuminated while working; their mechanism was laid open. Scene changes took place behind a small Neher curtain, which did not completely interrupt vision but allowed bridge scenes to be played.

The set was constructed and elaborated during the rehearsals.

The following were used:

*Scene 1:* a low chair for the Viceroy; a billiard table covered with newspapers; a map on a wooden stand; a broken lamp with just one functioning bulb; a hatstand for the Viceroy's hat and cane; a door-frame with a door with a small emblem, a hyena with a sceptre; a wooden chair for Iberin waiting outside the door.

*Scene 2:* two rough wooden window-frames for Callamassi and Nanna; a sign 'Palmosa Tobacconist'; a red lantern with the legend 'Café Paradiso'; a wicker chair for Madame Cornamontis; a door-frame leading to the café; two painted two-metre-high four-storey houses with little food-shops; 6 shop-signs to suggest small shops, hanging from wires (Gorelik's idea): a baker's golden pretzel, a silver top-hat, a black cigar, a golden barber's bowl, a red child's boot, a red glove (these emblems of small-scale commerce were lowered as Nanna appeared for her song); flags with Iberin's portrait.

*Scene 3:* a big well with rough wooden benches; hanging up, a straw mat.

*Scene 4:* the Viceroy's chair for the judge, on a little wooden balcony to one side outside the stage proper; illuminated text scrolling on the back wall of the stage above the screens; a rough wooden staircase; an old bench for the accused; a damaged statue of Justice.

*Scene 5:* a pew for the Superior; a painted church window on metal legs, which could be opened at the bottom; two wooden chairs; a safe with a portrait of a saint.

*Scene 6:* a door-frame with a little wooden step; a table; 6 chairs;

the red lantern; sawn wooden letters 'Café Paradiso'; a candle; on one of the screens the silhouette of two horses.

*Scene 7:* a wooden staircase with a blue carpet; a chandelier; the Justice statue repaired, lowered on pulleys at the end of the 'Song of the stimulating effect of cash' in the place of the damaged statue, which was removed; a small board 'Convent of San Barabas versus Farmer Callas. At issue 2 horses'; the chair for the judge; a new carved dock for the accused; hanging at mid height two horses made of wood offcuts which could be drawn up at the judgement.

*Scene 8:* dirty flags, otherwise as in the second scene.

*Scene 9:* door-frame with a red fringed curtain; a tray with a glass of water; a wooden chair; an old Récamier sofa; a green artificial house palm, used by Nanna as a screen; a red bulb above the sofa; a visitor leaving the bar that Isabella is about to enter.

*Scene 10:* a large wooden frame with ropes painted black as prison bars, front stage; 2 wooden stools for de Guzman and Callas right behind the bars; a small stage with stools for the bound farmers; a lighting rig so that Callas can come into the auditorium when he speaks his monologue; 3 gallows behind one of the screens.

*Scene 11:* 3 sets of gallows behind the screen; blackboard outside the stage area 'Execution of 1 landlord and 200 farmers'; a set table with golden chairs; silhouettes of soldiers made of offcuts, visible when the Viceroy enters; a huge gun barrel lowered on a wire above the table and aimed into the auditorium when Missena talks of peace.

Heads were about 20 centimetres high. The masks showed drastic distortions of nose, ears, hair and chin. The Hatsos had unnaturally large hands and feet.

The women's costumes were coloured and not restricted to any particular fashion; the farmers wore black trousers, linen shirts and clogs; the rich landowners were dressed to go to the races; Missena in uniform; the small bourgeoisie in ordinary suits.

## Sound effects

Recently the gramophone industry has started supplying the stage with records of real noises. These add substantially to the spectator's illusion of *not* being in a theatre. Theatres have fallen on them avidly; so that Shakespeare's *Romeo and Juliet* is now accompanied by the real noise of the mob. So far as we know the first person to make use of records was Piscator. He applied the new technique entirely correctly. In his production of the play *Rasputin* a record of Lenin's voice was played. It interrupted the performance. In another production a new technical achievement was demonstrated: the transmission by wireless of the sound of a sick man's heart. A film simultaneously showed the heart contracting. The fact that one can now get a specialist's opinion for a case of illness on board ship or in some remote place played no part in the play. The point was simply to show how greatly human communications have been simplified by science, and that social conditions at present act as an obstacle to the full exploitation of the fact.

In a parable-type play sound effects should only be used if they too have a parable function, and not in order to evoke atmosphere and illusion. The marching feet of Iberin's troops as they go to war (scene 11) can come from a record. So can the victory bells (scenes 7 and 8) and the execution bell (in scene 11). A noise that should not come from a record is that, for example, of the well at which the tenants are working (scene 3). Synthetic popular noises can accompany Iberin's entry (scene 4); while the reaction of the crowd outside the courtroom (scene 4) to the tenants' demands and the decisions of the governor, and the crowd noises at the news of victory (scene 7), can likewise be artificial.

It is best to place the record player, like the orchestra, so that it can be seen. But if such an arrangement would shock the audience unduly, or give too much cause for amusement it should preferably be dropped.

[BFA 24, pp. 207–19. Brecht's notes probably written shortly after the Copenhagen production at the end of 1936, and in any case before 1938 when the text was published in London, in volume two of the Malik edition of the works. The text, which refers in part to a different order of scenes from the published play, is a practical record, comparable to the later and much more detailed models. It is the first instance of Brecht applying the theory of *Verfremdung* practically to his own work.

Some photographs and caricatures of Hitler, as well as other visual material, are preserved amongst the material for this play.

The Neher-curtain (mentioned under 'Examples of *Verfremdung*') is the characteristic half-height curtain devised by Caspar Neher, which Brecht and Neher subsequently used for nearly all the productions in which they were involved.

Brecht got to know Mordecai Gorelik, the American stage designer mentioned under 'Stage set: scene 2', in New York in 1935 during rehearsals there for *The Mother*. He visited some of the rehearsals for *Round Heads and Pointed Heads* in Copenhagen in autumn 1936.

Erwin Piscator produced *Rasputin* (mentioned under 'Sound

effects') in the Theater am Nollendorfplatz, Berlin, on 12 November 1927. Brecht helped with the adaptation, derived from Alexei Tolstoy.

A photograph of the Copenhagen production of *Round Heads and Pointed Heads* is in *Brecht on Theatre*, facing p. 97; further photographs are preserved in the Brecht-Archive.]

## Editorial Notes

This is one of Brecht's plays, like *Galileo*, for which a vast number of sketches, drafts, fragments and variants are preserved. They bear witness to a long struggle with the material over a period of political upheaval, a period in which Brecht reflected on the relationship between an experimental progressive theatre and direct political engagement (see also Introduction). The texts discussed below also bear the hands of a great many collaborators: Ludwig Berger and Elisabeth Hauptmann were involved in the original work of adaptation; Emil Hesse-Burri (who had stayed in Germany and was credited under the pseudonym H. Emmel), Margarete Steffin and Hermann Borchardt all had a hand in the later development of the play, as of course had Hanns Eisler.

We have only fragmentary evidence of Brecht's efforts, late in 1931, to adapt Shakespeare's *Measure for Measure* for a production planned by Ludwig Berger for the Berlin Volksbühne. As well as mapping out the essentials of the plot as he wished to realise it, he also began detailed textual work, sticking pages out of an old Reclam edition of the play (in the translation by Wolf Graf von Baudissin for the Schlegel/Tieck edition) onto large sheets, and typing his own text underneath. An extract from the first scene of this text is translated (with reference to the Shakespeare original) above. It shows a drastic tendency to abbreviate and simplify, as well as to modernise and colloquialise the language of the original.

As work proceeded several far-reaching changes were introduced and Brecht quickly drifted away from the idea of a straightforward Shakespeare adaptation. He moved the setting to the late nineteenth century, and then from Vienna (as in Shakespeare) to Bohemia (hence perhaps the later racial division into 'Tschuchen' and 'Tschichen', in German reminiscent of 'Tschechen' – Czechs). Later the action shifted to Peru (whence all the South American and Hispanic names and references) and eventually to Yahoo (a name borrowed from Swift's *Gulliver's Travels*). Brecht's Yahoo has the features of a twentieth-century country with a hesitantly developing economy: for the most part it seems agrarian and feudal, but there is a power station and a relatively developed financial set-up. Brecht uses a similar 'mixed' economic setting in *The Good Person of Szechwan*. It permits a stark and simplified presentation of class differences and of the relations of power and ownership. In the course of adaptation, the names also changed: the Duke became a Viceroy; Angelo became Graf von Angeler, Tomaso Angelas, and then Angelo Iberin; Escalus became Eskaler, Fernando Eskahler, and finally Missena; and so on.

Above all, however, other elements were introduced to the plot. The plot of a change of government was initially exploited as a parable about how little is to be hoped from a populist reformism which contents itself with the superficial problems of a capitalist society and moral order. Angelo is merely a deputy of the old order. Not only in the Shakespeare adaptation, but also in the first complete drafts of an independent play, Angeler/Angelas's motto is 'reform'. From the outset Brecht was concerned also to create a clear economic motivation for the transfer of power. He introduced a crisis of overproduction with clear echoes of the world economic crash of 1929. The deputy takes power with the backing of the big capitalists. And as this theme was gradually fleshed out, the motif of a salt tax was introduced (ultimately removed again), an inequitable measure to be forced on the populace in order to restock the state's coffers. A salt tax was a historical reality in Germany: it had been dropped in 1926 only to be reintroduced as one of the first emergency decrees of the von Papen government in January 1932. Brecht was responding closely to a real political and economic situation, despite the elements of distant parable and caricature which are so important to his play.

Lower-class resistance to such a tax had of course to be overcome, and Brecht developed scenes illustrating the popular reaction to the change in government and creating a clear social stratification. He organised the labouring class under the sign of the 'Black Flag', later the Sickle. At a relatively late stage (it is impossible to date it precisely from the evidence) the motif of racial politics was introduced. This racism was understood as a political ploy: to divide and overcome the resistance of the lower classes, at this stage still for the purpose of imposing the salt tax and rescuing the economy. A peasant family (Meixner or Meixenego) plays a part in even the earliest drafts, but their role and the relationship between the families of peasant farmers, Callas and Lopez, only emerged later, alongside the theme of race (see 'Cheated hopes', above). It has been suggested that the emphasis on a rural labouring class and on landownership may derive from Brecht's observation of the conditions of developing Fascism in Italy.

The story of Callas's horses is derived from another literary source, Kleist's *Michael Kohlhaas* (1810). However, whereas Kohlhaas fights for his horses out of a sense of justice, Brecht's Callas is driven only by economic necessity. His hope that the law will provide social justice for the lower classes is one of several hopes that are cheated. At the other end of this strand of the plot: whereas Kohlhaas gets his horses back but is condemned to death for his treasonable uprising, Callas abandons the uprising, escapes death on the scaffold, but then loses the horses – and is effectively condemned by the powers-that-be to a just somewhat more gradual death (or to death in war).

Brecht's other significant literary source is Pietro Aretino's *Ragionamenti* (1534/36), which provided the basis for the scene in which Madame Cornamontis instructs Nanna (originally Judith) how to conduct herself in her role as the false Isabella. More or less from the beginning Brecht had determined that, when she goes to plead for her brother with Angelo, Claudio's sister Isabella (as they are in the Shakespeare original; in Brecht: Isabella von Klausner, Calausa, and eventually de Guzman) should have her place taken, not by Angelo's betrothed, but by a prostitute. Thus he introduced one of his favourite motifs: the sex industry as an extreme case of commodification and self-alienation in a capitalist society (versions of which appear also in *The Threepenny Opera*, *Mahagonny*, and *The Good Person of Szechwan*). The theme is entirely congruent with the understanding of sexual relations and prostitution propagated by many early socialists: 'Prostitution is only a *particular* expression of the *general* prostitution of the labourer, and since prostitution is a relationship which includes not only the prostituted but also the prostitutor – whose vileness is even greater – so also the capitalist etc. fall in this category' (Karl Marx, 1844).

In later versions of the first scene, Angelas's nature and the nature of his task were sketched out in far more detail than in the quoted extract. And of course the conclusion of Shakespeare's parable was altered also. The Viceroy is very far from Shakespeare's image of the ideal ruler, indeed he too represents little more than class interest. Any fragmentary hope of a political, social, moral 'measure for measure' is satirised as a foolish illusion. In the 'rosy dawn' of the final scene, war is revealed as another, still more terrible political distraction by which to govern the oppressed. And yet the old regime is not restored undamaged. The landowners' verse at the end insistently repeats 'perhaps'; and Brecht gives the last word to the peasants' song: since death awaits us all beyond this world of illusion and betrayal, let us take whatever little opportunity we have on earth, and assert ourselves.

All of these alterations, adaptations and versions had already been undertaken by the end of 1932, at which point the play was published as a stage manuscript by the theatre publisher Felix Bloch Erben,

Berlin-Wilmersdorf. At the beginning of 1933 an almost identical text, under the title *Pointed Heads and Round Heads or Money Calls to Money* was prepared for volume 8 of Brecht's *Versuche* ('Experiments') series, as the seventeenth 'Versuch'. The subtitle, 'Reich und reich gesellt sich gern', which survived all subsequent changes, is a play on the saying 'Gleich und gleich gesellt sich gern', a loose equivalent of the English 'Birds of a feather flock together'. Although publication of this volume of the *Versuche* was prevented by the Nazis, type was set and page-proofs printed. Brecht took the proofs with him into exile, and the surviving text is reproduced in full in BFA 4, pp. 7–145.

By this time only a couple of isolated lines of text and the slogan 'measure for measure' still survived as direct quotations from the Shakespeare translation, although of course many elements of the plot and several important motifs remained.

In the original work on *Measure for Measure* neither fascist demagogy nor racial politics played a part. Indeed, the text may have been as much directed against the reformist Social Democratic Party as against right-wing politics. The rise of Fascism, first in Italy and then in Germany, directed Brecht to the possibility of adapting his parable into a satire against 'völkisch' idealist politics. In the work on the 1933 version the new governor appears as an honest fanatic who takes his own anti-capitalist slogans seriously and is exploited cynically by the ruling class. However, the working notes for the play, preserved in the Archive, also contain a lengthy article by Adolf Hitler (from the *Völkische Beobachter*, 21 October 1932), quotations from which begin to appear in Angelas's speeches. And so the attack on reformism and unjust taxation and the elements of a deluded populist idealism begin to make way for ever more explicit references to National Socialism and to the person of Hitler, albeit still in a clearly agrarian context.

In 1934, by now in exile in Denmark, Brecht undertook what he called 'a complete reformulation' of the play. He removed the motif of the salt tax, and tightened the plot (removing four scenes and making the social and political relationships clearer). He introduced the 'Hutabschlägerstaffel', or Hatsos, a clear parody of the SA, and their leader Zazarante; and the other names arrived at their final versions. The Governor was given a programme with distinct echoes of the social and economic measures of the Nazi government of 1933 and '34. The Viceroy was confined to the first and last scenes. The title now became *Round Heads and Pointed Heads*.

This version benefited also from the participation of Brecht's second major musical collaborator, Hanns Eisler. Most of the songs and musical elements were introduced in 1934 (although some of the settings go back to 1932 and a few were only completed later in the 1930s, and the instrumentation was only completed in 1954 and 1962). The Dagmar Theatre production in Copenhagen, towards which all this effort had been expended, collapsed however, amidst fears of censorship.

After 1934 Brecht came back to his material several more times. At first his inclination was to develop the references to National Socialism, and above all to introduce the whole sorry political tale as a preparation for war. A version of this text was published in Russian, both as a pamphlet volume and in the journal *International Literature* (1936, no. 8). In the course of 1936, however, in rehearsal for a new Copenhagen production (the eventual première in the Riddersalen) Brecht started to remove the specific references to German Fascism. The play became a more generalised parable about the role of racism and war in right-wing capitalist politics. This general direction was underlined by the prologue, written for the Riddersalen production.

After the eventual Copenhagen première the play was further altered, partly, it seems, in response to the experience of the text in production. A version appeared in English in *International Literature* (1937, no. 5) in a translation by N. Goold-Verschoyle, entitled *Round Heads, Peak Heads or Rich and Rich Make Good Company (A Thriller)*. The version on which our translation for this volume is based was first published in Brecht's *Collected Works* vol. 2, London: Malik-Verlag, 1938, where it appeared alongside the 'Notes on *Pointed Heads and Round Heads*' (see above). This is the text that has formed the basis for all further publications.

# FEAR AND MISERY OF THE THIRD REICH

## Texts by Brecht

FEAR AND MISERY OF THE THIRD REICH

Undoubtedly the sight of Germany, our home country, has today become terrifying to the rest of the world: that is, in so far as the world is bourgeois, to the bourgeois world. Even among the Third Reich's friends there can hardly be one that has never been terrified by Germany as it now is.

Anyone who talks about Germany becomes a diviner of mysteries. One favourite interpretation of the mystery which we have read on various occasions and in various languages, not excluding our own, goes like this: here is a country at the heart of Europe, a long-established nursery of culture, which was plunged overnight into barbarism, a sudden horrible senseless outbreak of savagery. The forces of good were defeated and the forces of evil got the upper hand.

Such is the interpretation, and it argues that barbarism springs from barbarism. The impetus comes from impulse. The impulse comes from nowhere but was always there. In this interpretation the Third Reich is a natural event, comparable with a volcanic eruption which lays waste fertile land.

The most powerful living English statesman has spoken of the German overestimation of the State. To him, naturally, the State is something natural; once you overestimate it, however, it becomes something unnatural. Think of Schiller's lines:

Fire is to our benefit
Only if one watches it

– and the object lesson that follows them.

According to this interpretation a particular unnatural state derives from overestimation of the State. How this overestimation comes about in the first place is left open.

Some interpretations are more realistic: for instance the following. Germany is a great state and industrially very strong. It has to make sure that it gets provided with markets and sources of raw materials. Twenty years ago it fought for markets and raw materials and was defeated. The victors hamstrung the State as such while promoting still further expansion of its industry by means of loan aid. Its industry's former markets and raw material reserves were never enough and now they had been partly taken away. No wonder that industry got the State functioning again. The State will have another shot at the old objectives.

People who talk that way at least have some explanation for the German 'overestimation' of the State, but even they have no explanation for the barbarism prevalent in Germany short of saying yet again that it springs from barbarism. Perhaps they see that state as an ordinary state which has got into an exceptional situation and therefore must have recourse to exceptional means; all the same the means inevitably terrify them.

For these exceptional means clearly have something of the character of malignant growths. They can't just be explained away by the exceptional situation.

This is why such people find the persecution of the Jews, for instance, so exasperating, because it seems such an 'unnecessary' excess. They regard it as something extraneous, irrelevant to the business in hand. In their view pogroms are not essential to the conquest of markets and raw materials, and accordingly can be dispensed with.

They fail to understand that barbarism in Germany is a consequence of class conflicts, and so they cannot grasp the Fascist principle which demands that class conflicts be converted into race conflicts. They can keep their parliaments, because they have parliamentary majorities.

But the bourgeois world is profoundly reluctant to look and see what exceptional means a state can employ to master exceptional situations; what's more, virtually all rules were at one time exceptions. Is it really possible that culture might become the ballast that has to be jettisoned so that this particular balloon may rise?

The same powerful English statesman who regretted the German tendency to overestimate the State was voicing this reluctance when he spoke of conditions under which life would no longer be worth while. Does it ever strike him that there are also 'natural' states to whose inhabitants the same thing applies?

Germany, our home, has transformed itself into a people of two million spies and eighty million people being spied on. Life for these people consists in the case being made against them. They are composed exclusively of the guilty.

When the father says something to his son it is to avoid being arrested. The priest thumbs through his Bible to find sentences he can quote without being arrested. The teacher puzzles over some action of Charlemagne's, looking for motives that he can teach without somebody arresting him. The doctor who signs a death certificate chooses a cause of death that is not going to lead to his arrest. The poet racks his brains for a rhyme he won't be arrested for. And it is to escape arrest that the farmer decides not to feed his sow.

As you can see, the measures which the State is driven to take are exceptional.

The bourgeois world desperately seeks to prove that the State is making a mistake, that it is not forced to take them; that force may be necessary (what with the exceptional circumstances), but not all that much force, just so much force and no more; that moderate punishment is enough; that occasional spying will suffice; that military preparations within rational limits are to be preferred.

And the bourgeois world has a vague feeling that it is wrong. This question of the degree of compulsion necessary in Germany is preoccupying the bourgeoisie of many nations, including the German. The way the German upper bourgeoisie saw it was this: large-scale property-owning had to be maintained, and the deal was 'by whatever means'. The State was massively built up. There are now supposed to be odd pockets of incomprehension among the upper bourgeoisie, restrictions placed on the means. All of a sudden it's no longer supposed to be by whatever means, just by some. Grumbling can be heard.

Now and then a head rolls, and now and then the odd grumble is heard. 'That signifies discontent,' say those who have fled. Does it? Does a 27-year-old student mother have to be beheaded for the same reason that the Rhineland industrialists' memorandum had to be torn up? If this really is discontent, just tell me how much.

Has the regime outstayed its welcome, does it really 'represent nobody but itself'?

The expression 'discontent rules' is not a happy one. Discontent does anything but rule. The regime is a foreign body? But the knife in a bandit's hand is a foreign body too. The industrialists are having to be kept down now? Down on top of what? Of the workers? The loss of freedom affects all alike? Does this mean that all wish all to be free?

The regime forces the workers to submit to exploitation and accordingly strips them of their trade unions, parties, newspapers. The regime forces the employers to exploit the workers, lays down specific forms of exploitation, makes it conform to plan and foists General Goering on the employers, hence the unfreedom felt 'on all sides'.

The regime's great strength, it is said, lies in the absence of any sign of opposition. This can't apply to the workers; now and then a head rolls. It can apply to the bourgeoisie, even though now and then the odd grumble is heard. Such grumbles are not an opposition.

Admittedly that leaves the great middle class, the mass of petty bourgeoisie and peasantry. Of every ten of these people two can be seen as holding down the other eight. For them the great question, what degree of culturally destructive means should be tolerated so that the regime can maintain large-scale ownership, boils down to this: is small-scale ownership dependent on large? Certain groups get some marginal droppings from the loot, or hope to do so. Others have been unable to see the difference between their own possessions and possession of the means of production. Anyhow they aren't asked.

Whoever clings to cultural concepts will get arrested. In the great war which will shortly have to be authorised for the maintenance of large-scale ownership, those who cling to life (which is also a cultural value) will be punished by death. This fear is beginning to overshadow all others.

The regime and the middle orders confront one another in a frenzied bargaining process. The regime is brandishing a list of luxuries due to be sacrificed for the maintenance of ownership. The middle orders are haggling. 'All right, scrap Goethe. But can't we keep religion?' – 'No.' – 'Surely a little freedom of opinion can't do any harm?' – 'Yes it can.' – 'But our children, can't we . . . ?' – 'What are you thinking of?' – 'Our bare life?' – 'Will have to be committed.'

The thought that barbarism springs from barbarism won't help solve the dreadful problem of Germany. The degree of violence employed implies the degree of opposition: to that extent the acts of violence are due not to spontaneous impulses but to deliberate reckoning, and have a touch of rationality however much stupidity, ambiguity and miscalculation may also be involved. But just as the oppression is of varying kinds, so also is the opposition. Those sections of the people who are now nervously asking '*how many* culturally destructive means are really needed to maintain large-scale ownership of capital, land and machinery?' probably get a truthful answer from the regime when it bellows back 'Just as many as we are using.' Might the sections in question have to be forced into the same condition of extreme dehumanisation that the proletariat, according to the Socialist classics, is resisting by its fight for the dignity of mankind? Will it be the misery that eventually defeats the fear?

[BFA 22, pp. 472–7. Unpublished in Brecht's lifetime. The 'British statesman' referred to appears to be Neville Chamberlain, who became PM in May 1937. See the short note 'Mr Chamberlain's

Dream' which precedes this in BFA and duplicates certain of its
arguments.]


NOTE TO 'FEAR AND MISERY OF THE THIRD REICH'

The play 'Fear and Misery of the Third Reich' offers the actor more
temptation to use an acting method appropriate to a dramaturgically
Aristotelian play than do other plays in this collection. To allow it to
be performed immediately, under the unfavourable circumstances of
exile, it is written in such a way that it can be performed by tiny
theatre groups (the existing workers' groups) and in a partial
selection (based on a given choice of individual scenes). The workers'
groups are neither capable nor desirous of conjuring up the
spectators' empathetic feeling: the few professionals at their disposal
are versed in the epic method of acting which they learnt from the
theatrical experiments of the decade prior to the fascist regime. The
acting methods of these professionals accord admirably with those of
the workers' groups. Those theorists who have recently taken to
treating the *montage* technique as a purely formal principle are
hereby confronted with montage as a practical matter, and this may
make them shift their speculations back to solid ground.

[BFA 24, p. 225. Possibly intended for the Malik-Verlag edition.
The last sentence is aimed at Georg Lukács.]


FURTHER NOTE

The cycle 'Fear and Misery of the Third Reich' is a documentary
play. Censorship problems and material difficulties have hitherto
prevented the available small workers' theatre groups from performing more than a few isolated scenes. Using simple indications of
scenery (for instance, playing against dimly lit swastika flags),
however, almost any theatre with a revolving or a multiple set could
resolve the play's technical problems. It should be feasible to stage at
least a selection of 17 scenes (1, 2, 5, 6, 8, 9, 12, 13, 16, 18, 19, 20, 22,
23, 25, 27). The play shows behaviour patterns typical of people of
different classes under Fascist dictatorship, and not only the gests of
caution, self-protection, alarm and so forth but also that of resistance
need to be brought out. In the series of *Versuche* whose publication
began in 1930 this play constitutes no. 20.

[BFA 24, pp. 226–7. May also have been intended for the Malik
publication, which was interrupted in 1938/39.]

NOTES TO 'FEAR AND MISERY OF THE THIRD REICH'

'Fear and Misery of the Third Reich' derives from eyewitness accounts and press reports. Collaborator: *Margarete Steffin.*

The Malik-Verlag had these scenes printed in Prague in 1938, but distribution was prevented by Hitler's invasion.

A stage version for America was performed in New York and San Francisco under the title 'The Private Life of the Master Race'. This comprises:

in Part I, scenes 1, 3, 4, 13 and 14
in Part II, scenes 8, 9, 6 and 10
in Part III, scenes 15, 19, 17, 11, 18, 16, 20 and 24.

The basic constituent of the set is the classic armoured troop-carrier of the Nazi army. This appears four times, at the beginning, between the parts and at the end. The individual scenes are separated by a voice and by the rumbling of the troop-carrier. This rumbling also becomes audible during the scenes, at the onset of the terror which the carrier's crew bring with them.

For instance:

Part I. To the sound of a barbaric military march a large signpost looms out of the darkness bearing the inscription 'TO POLAND' and with the troop-carrier beside it. This is manned by 12–16 soldiers with rifles between their knees, steel helmets and chalk-white faces. Thereupon:

CHORUS: Now that the Führer...
　　　　...by his steely hand.

The scene grows dark again. The dull rumble of the waggon continues for a few seconds. Then the lights go up and a landing is seen. Over the stage are suspended big black letters: 'BRESLAU, SCHUSTERGASSE 2'. This is followed by scene 1. Thereupon:

VOICE: That's how neighbour...
　　　　...taken on to our waggon.

CHORUS IN THE ARMOURED TROOP-CARRIER

*Before Part I:*
Now that the Führer has created order
In his own country with his steely hand
He's made us take up arms and drive across the border
To do the same in every neighbouring land.
So we set out as told by our superiors

With all our might – it was a summer day
And launched a blitzkrieg on those German-peopled areas
Whose ancient towns were under Polish sway.
Scarlet with blood, our tanks rolled ever faster
Right from the Seine to Volga's ice strand.
Thanks to the Führer the world must acknowledge us a Master
Race, forged for ever by his steely hand.

*Before Part II:*
Treason and discord split the world we live in
And all the time our tank accelerates:
Their discord hoists white flags to show they give in
Their treason now will help us force the gates.
They saw our tank roll on its sacred mission
To Denmark's shores through fields of blue-green flax.
Those peoples who deny the Führer's vision
Will soon be crushed beneath our rumbling tracks.
For what he's done for our own German nation
He's going to do for Europe as a whole
Iceland to Italy will be one vast plantation
Of our New Order's swastika symbol.

*Before Part III:*
You see, our tank was made by Krupp von Bohlen
And three old bankers played a useful part
And then von Thyssen made it tracks to roll on
Twelve landed Junkers gave it a good start.

*After Part III:*
But after two more winters making war
We found our tanks began to show the strain
Until we got cold feet because we'd come too far
And felt we'd never see our home again.
We pressed on east across each conquered land till
Fresh snow clogged up the crown our Führer wore
And then at last our tanks came to a total standstill
Once we had reached the country of the poor.
Thus we went forth to impose the chains that bind us
And, violated, turned to violence.
Now we see death in front and death behind us.
Our homes are far away, the cold intense.

THE VOICE

*After scene 1:*
That's how neighbour betrayed his neighbour
How the little people ripped one another apart
And enmity grew in tenements and city districts
And we strode in confidently
And took on to our battle waggon
All who had not been beaten to death:
This whole people of betrayers and betrayed
Was taken on to our waggon.

*After scene 3:*
From factories and kitchens and labour exchanges
We collected a crew for our waggon.
Pauper dragged pauper to our waggon.
With the kiss of Judas we took him on our waggon
With a friendly pat on the shoulder
We took them on our battle waggon.

*After scene 4:*
The people's disunity gave us our greatness.
Our prisoners still fought each other in the concentration camps
Then they all ended up on our waggon.
The prisoners came on our waggon
Tormentors and tormented
The whole lot came on our battle waggon.

*After scene 13:*
We covered the good worker with approval
And heaped him high with menaces.
We put flower boxes round the sweatshop he worked in
And SS men at the exit.
With salvoes of applause and salvoes of rifle fire
We loaded him on our battle waggon.

*Before scene 8:*
Pressing their children closer
Mothers in Brittany stand and humbly search
The skies for the inventions of our learned men.
For there are learned men too on our waggon
Pupils of the notorious Einstein
First given an iron schooling by the Führer
And taught what Aryan science is.

*Before scene 9:*
A doctor too is on our waggon
He decides which Polish miners' wives
Shall be sent off to the brothel in Krakow
And he does this well and without any fuss
In memory of the loss of *his* wife
Who was Jewish and got sent away
Because a member of the Master Race has to be carefully coupled
And the Führer decides who he is to lie with.

*Before scene 6:*
And there are also judges on our waggon
Adept at taking hostages, picked from a hundred victims
Accused of being Frenchmen
And found guilty of loving their country
For our judges are well versed in German law
And know what is demanded of them.

*Before scene 10:*
And there is a teacher too on our waggon
A captain now, with a hat of steel
Who delivers his lessons
To Norway's fishermen and the wine-growers of Champagne
For there was a day seven years ago
Now faded but never forgotten
When in the bosom of his own family he learned
Hatred of spies.
And whenever we arrived we incited father against son
And friend against friend.
And the mischief we made in foreign countries was no different
    from
The mischief we made in our own.

*Before scene 19:*
And there is no other business but ours
And nobody knows how long we shall keep it.

*Before scene 17:*
Here we come as hungry as locusts
And eat out entire countries in a single week
For we were given guns instead of butter
And we have long mixed bran with our daily bread.

*Before scene 11:*
And whenever we arrive no mother is safe, and no child
For we did not spare
Our own children.

*Before scene 18:*
And the corn in the barn is not safe from us
Nor the cattle in the byre
For our cattle were taken away from us.

*Before scene 16:*
And we take away their sons and their daughters
And toss them potatoes in the goodness of our hearts
And tell them to shout 'Heil Hitler' like our own mothers
As if they were skewered.

*Before scene 20:*
And there is no god
But Adolf Hitler.

*Before scene 24:*
And we subjugated foreign peoples
As we have subjugated our own.

[BFA 24, pp. 227–32. These notes document the stage version, *The Private Life of the Master Race* (first published by New Directions: New York, 1944), performed in June 1945 in Berkeley (directed by Henry Schnitzler) and New York (directed by Berthold Viertel). A version of the chorus appeared in English (a different translation by Eric Bentley) in the New York (1944) edition. This German text was published the following year (Aurora: New York, 1945). Scene 1 in this version was 'A case of betrayal'.]


SIX ADDITIONAL SCENES

## Ersatz feelings

*Family of Gnauer the bookbinder. Gnauer is sitting in his SA uniform. It is eight in the evening. The doctor is examining the bookbinder's sick sister in the next room.*

THE SON *standing indecisively by the radio*: I wonder if we ought to have the radio just now. Aunt Frieda's so feeble. It might just get her worked up.

THE FATHER: She's always been keen on our national resurgence. She lives for that. Which is more than can be said of you. Put it on.

THE SON: I was thinking, what with the doctor being in there. It'll give him the wrong idea.

THE FATHER: That's a phony excuse. In other words, un-German.

Frieda would never let us miss anything on her account. I'd say Germany's food position was an important enough matter.

THE MOTHER: You're to put it on.

VOICE ON THE RADIO: Professor Dr Seifner of the Health Advisory Council will now give a talk on 'The Scientist's view of the Four-Year Plan with particular regard to the availability of edible fats'.

ANOTHER VOICE: It is a regrettable if all too familiar fact that mankind is not always aware what is in its own best interest and what not. Certain of our national comrades have been known to judge the comprehensive measures which the government takes in the interests of the whole people, according to the degree of sacrifice demanded of the individual judging. This is of course a very human characteristic. Looked at closely, however, this presumed sacrifice often turns out to be no sacrifice but an act of kindness. Thus suppose we take nutrition in the context of the Four-Year Plan: a certain amount of petty grumbling might be heard to the effect that there are slight shortages of milk here and of fat there. Those concerned will be surprised to learn from science that such a shortage of fat for instance may constitute a positive act of kindness to their body. Recently a committee of scientific experts conducted a thorough investigation of the way in which the human body reacts to a low-fat diet. Let us consider the conclusions that this committee of top academics came to.

*Drying his hands, the doctor enters from the next room. The father makes a sign to his son, who turns off the radio.*

THE FATHER: What's the verdict, doctor?

THE DOCTOR: Not good. She'll have to have an operation.

THE MOTHER: That's dreadful.

THE DOCTOR: Yes, it's a serious business at her age.

THE MOTHER: We thought it would be all right if she was properly looked after. That's why we got a nurse in. She isn't cheap.

THE DOCTOR: But now an operation's unavoidable. The tumour's practically blocked the entrance to her stomach. She'll die if she's not operated.

THE FATHER: That's a major operation, I suppose.

THE DOCTOR: It is.

THE FATHER: Expensive?

THE DOCTOR: You'd have to reckon somewhere between two and three thousand marks.

THE FATHER: That's rather more than we could manage, you know.

THE MOTHER: Poor Frieda.

THE FATHER: So I must ask you for an absolutely straight answer, doctor. Will this operation cure my sister?

THE DOCTOR: There's a good chance.

THE FATHER: What do you mean, a good chance? In other words it's not even certain she'll be cured?

THE DOCTOR: I mean that we shall remove the tumour and hope it doesn't return. In other words there's a good chance of a cure and at least she'll gain time.

THE MOTHER: I wonder if that kind of time is much gain. When she's suffering.

THE DOCTOR: Starving to death isn't pleasant either, Mrs Gnauer. If we leave her as she is she'll starve.

THE FATHER: But the tumour might return?

THE DOCTOR: It might.

THE FATHER: So it isn't even certain the operation will cure her.

THE DOCTOR: No, but it's certain she'd die without it.

THE FATHER: Of course.

THE DOCTOR: Yes, of course. Think it over, but don't take too long. Good night.

THE FATHER: Good night, doctor.

*The doctor leaves.*

THE FATHER: Well, there we are.

THE SON: Poor Aunt Frieda.

*The daughter stands up, goes to the mirror and prepares to go out.*

THE FATHER: Where are you off to?

THE DAUGHTER: We've a lecture. 'Race and Home'.

THE FATHER: You'll have to stay here a moment. I'm due over at the SA myself. But first of all there's a decision to be taken, and I want you all to be present.

THE DAUGHTER *pouting*: What am I supposed to decide?

*The nurse enters from the next room.*

THE NURSE: Miss Gnauer is asking if Mrs Gnauer would come in for a minute.

THE MOTHER: Yes, I'll come.

*The nurse goes back; the mother remains seated.*

THE SON: What is there to decide? She's got to be operated.

THE FATHER: Don't be so smart. An operation is no joke.

THE MOTHER: At her age.

THE FATHER: Didn't you hear what the doctor said? About that?

THE SON: He also said she'd die without it.

THE FATHER: And that she might die if she has it.

THE MOTHER: I never realised she was in such a bad way.

THE SON: A very bad way, if you ask me.

THE FATHER *suspiciously*: What d'you mean by that?

THE DAUGHTER: Just another of his mean remarks.

THE MOTHER: Stop quarrelling, you two.

THE FATHER: Any sauce from you and you needn't bother to ask for your next pocket-money.

THE SON: Then I won't be able to cycle to school. My inner tubes are past mending now. And I can't get new ones of real rubber. Just ersatz rubber. Same way school nowadays is ersatz school. And this family's an ersatz family.

THE MOTHER: Hans!

THE FATHER: Right. No more pocket-money. And as for the other thing, I wonder if that quack really knows his business. He isn't exactly brilliant. Or he'd charge more than three marks for a visit.

THE MOTHER: His coat is all coming away at the seams and his shoes are patched.

THE FATHER: Anyway there are better doctors than him. I don't go by what he says.

THE SON: Consult a more expensive one, then.

THE MOTHER: Don't talk to your father like that. A more expensive one wouldn't necessarily be better. Not that the nurse isn't dear enough.

THE FATHER: Even the best of them will never give an unbiased verdict, because he gets part of the surgeon's fee. It's the usual practice with surgeons.

THE SON: The doctor seemed straight, I thought.

THE FATHER: You thought. I didn't think so at all. And however straight they are, people act in their own interests. I've yet to come across a man who doesn't put his own interests first. What he says may sound all very humanitarian and idealistic, but what he actually thinks is another kettle of fish.

THE MOTHER: So you think the operation mayn't be at all necessary?

THE FATHER: Who can tell?

*The nurse again appears at the door.*

THE NURSE: Couldn't you come, Mrs Gnauer? My patient's worried on account of the doctor being there.

THE MOTHER: Right, I'm just coming. We've a small matter to discuss. Tell her I'll come at once.

*The nurse goes back.*

THE FATHER: Take the paper in to her. *The son takes a paper and is about to leave.*

THE FATHER: When'll you learn not to give her today's paper before I've read it?

THE MOTHER: But that's yesterday's. Why do you think I put it on the music stand?

THE SON: But cancer's not infectious.

THE FATHER: It is for me, given that the possibility's not ruled out.

THE MOTHER: The news will be the same anyway. Give her last month's and it'll hardly be any different.

THE SON: Ersatz newspapers. All the same the nurse might notice.

THE FATHER: I'm not paying her to read papers.

*The son takes the previous day's newspaper into the next room.*

THE FATHER: All I want to say is that it's a great deal of money.

THE MOTHER: What with there being no certainty of a cure.

THE FATHER: Exactly. *Pause.* What she's got in the bank would cover it, but there'd be very little over. Three thousand.

THE MOTHER: It'd be a crime to waste all that money on an uncertain operation. Poor Frieda earned every bit of it penny by penny working as a maidservant.

*The son returns.*

THE SON: She's pretty scared.

THE FATHER: Did the doctor tell her there was question of an operation?

THE SON: No.

THE FATHER: I wouldn't have put it beyond him to upset her like that.

THE SON: I think she's more scared of what you people are talking about here.

THE FATHER: Well, of course she's upset. She can't help knowing she's ill. What with not being able to eat now.

THE MOTHER: It's a bad business. For us too. There are you, having to work all day and you come back to such misery.

THE SON: Have you made your minds up yet?

THE FATHER: It is a great responsibility.

THE SON: It certainly is.

THE MOTHER: If only it was definite and not just a possibility.

THE FATHER: Definite my foot. It's a pure experiment.

THE MOTHER: When he shrugged his shoulders like that I could tell at once he wasn't sure.

THE FATHER: In fact he made no bones about it. All they want is to make experiments. Won't even let you die in peace. Just cut you open once more and talk about good chances. After which they say 'we tried everything'. You bet, with us paying!

THE MOTHER: Shoving a poor old woman in hospital. Away from her own home surroundings. I don't like that one little bit.

THE FATHER: That's not at all what I'm talking about. If the operation was a sure way of getting her back to health I'd be for it right away. This very night. Nobody would have any right to turn down an operation like that.

THE SON: I wouldn't say we had the right in any case. Because there *is* a good chance and it'd be her own money.

THE FATHER: Who's talking about money? Did I mention money? I'm saying it'd be sheer cruelty to inflict another major operation on my sister after all she's had to go through already. Haven't you got any feelings? How can you speak of money? You should be thoroughly ashamed of yourself.

THE SON: I wouldn't say I had any cause to be ashamed of myself.

THE MOTHER: Hans!

THE FATHER: You haven't got two pence worth of feelings in your makeup. All you think about's that bike of yours. And the fact that you'll have to put up with ersatz rubber. Here's our people fighting for its existence, and you've got your mind on your bike. The Führer's raising an army from nothing while we're ringed round by enemies watching us for the least sign of weakness. The whole people is tightening its belts. Look at me collecting all my old toothpaste tubes for the common good. And you've got your mind on your bike and start grumbling about ersatz. With our people confronting its hour of decision. It's for us to decide now. Are we to come up, or are we to sink irretrievably? I'd like to know who is doing as much for our people as the present government. And who takes his responsibilities as seriously. And then we've got this mob, this band of subhumans, who aren't prepared to sacrifice their miserable selfish selves because they can't see that it's all for their own good. But why am I wasting my time talking to you about it? You're not even prepared to sacrifice one of your inner tubes.

THE SON: I simply said I'd need extra pocket-money because ersatz rubber costs more than the real thing.

THE FATHER: That's enough of that. I'm fed up with all your unpatriotic talk. Here's the nation undergoing its biggest moral upsurge since the wars of independence and he talks about pocket-money. It's just that kind of materialism that we have to extirpate root and branch. Go off to your room. I don't want to see you. *The son walks to the door in silence.*

THE SON *pausing in the doorway*: It isn't her illness she's scared of, it's you two. *He goes out.*

THE MOTHER *calls after him*: That was horrid of you, Hans.

THE DAUGHTER: I've got to be off to the League of German Maidens, Mother. *By the window*: It doesn't look as if it's going to rain. So I'll be able to wear my new jacket. Or do you think it might? Our uniforms are made of synthetic wool, and every drop of rain leaves a mark.

THE MOTHER: Don't you budge.

*The nurse appears in the doorway.*

THE NURSE: I don't want to disturb you, but my patient is getting into a state. She'd like to talk to one of her family.

THE FATHER: Tell her we'll all come in as soon as we've finished discussing a domestic matter.

*The nurse goes back in.*

THE FATHER: Not a pleasant character. She's a luxury. What does Frieda need a nurse for? You couldn't ask for anyone less demanding.

THE MOTHER: You wanted to save hospital expenses. And after she was sick that last time who could say it'd be more than a matter of days?

THE FATHER: If I were prepared to take the responsibility for it I'd much sooner hand the whole business over to the doctors. This way I'm just worrying myself to death.

THE MOTHER: In that case they'd surely operate.

THE FATHER: Definitely.

THE MOTHER: Poor Frieda. Getting lugged out of her quiet cosy room yet again.

THE FATHER: Who says I've got anything against operations? Let her have herself cut open as often as she wants: it's up to her.

THE MOTHER: You shouldn't say that. After all, she's your sister. We have to do what's best for her.

THE FATHER: How am I to tell that? Maybe they should operate. I'm not having people say I let my sister starve to death. All I can do is point out that anyone after a major operation like that isn't going to find eating much fun. When nothing's healed up yet.

THE MOTHER: For heaven's sake. Pain with every mouthful. This way at least she won't notice and will just gently flicker out into the beyond.

THE FATHER: You people do as you like. But if they operate and tell you 'it's been cut out but nothing's changed from before', just don't turn on me. It's my considered opinion that when one's ill one has every right to a bit of peace and quiet.

THE MOTHER: Fancy Frieda in hospital. When she's used to having all of us around.

THE FATHER: Here she's with her family. Everything in its accustomed place. She gets looked after. But put her in hospital if you like. Why should I mind?

THE MOTHER: Whoever's suggesting that? Nobody wants her put away. After all she eats like a bird.

THE FATHER: You may find it too much work.

THE MOTHER: No question of that. Frieda's so sensible.

THE FATHER: If you're to be tied because of her . . .

THE MOTHER: We really would miss her. She gave Lotte her new jacket. And then there's her pension too.

THE FATHER: If you ask *me* it'd be in her own best interest to have no more excitements, not: yet another doctor, yet another move, yet more new faces. And if money really has to come into it, then let me point out that the monstrous sum such an operation would cost would be just enough for us to buy that shop in the Möschstrasse for a knockdown price, what with Kott and Sons having gone bankrupt as a Jewish-owned business. That's a bargain that won't occur twice.

THE MOTHER: Did you see their lawyers?

THE FATHER: Without committing us to anything. But of course that shouldn't enter into it. It's Frieda's money.

THE MOTHER: Of course.

THE FATHER: I don't want to be told afterwards that there was anything we failed to do for Frieda.

THE MOTHER: How could they say that? We're doing absolutely everything.

THE FATHER: People are mean enough. You heard how your own son talked.

THE MOTHER: It's really only for Frieda's sake that we're against an operation.

THE FATHER: We can't keep her waiting indefinitely. Of course she's worked up, what with the doctor having been. She'll imagine we're talking about her.

THE MOTHER: In that case I'll tell her . . .

*She gets up.*

THE FATHER: That the doctor decided there need be no question of an operation.

THE MOTHER: And she needn't worry.

THE FATHER: And that we have gone into it all most conscientiously and decided that it's in her own best interest to stay resting here peacefully rather than go into a nursing home.

THE MOTHER: Where she'd be surrounded by a lot of strangers who wouldn't bother about her.

*She goes into the next room. The father turns the radio on once more.*

VOICE ON THE RADIO: Accordingly the committee established that too much fat was commonly being eaten. There is no need to consider special measures to counter the fat shortage. In the words of the report, we have examined the problem more carefully and conscientiously and come to the conclusion that there is no call for the population to worry since its present diet is not merely adequate but actually much healthier than in the past. Statistics teach us that the effects of a low-fat diet are far from harmful. On the contrary, the human organism is incapable of tolerating as much fat as is generally supposed. We would merely cite the example of China and Japan, where the greater part of the people keeps in excellent health on the plainest diet of rice. Too fatty a diet is more likely to cause disease. A low-fat diet guarantees greater energy and longer life. It is not for nothing that the worker is better fitted for physical effort than the so-called intellectual. His supposedly inferior diet is in reality the better of the two. Thus even if our economic situation and lack of colonies did not force our people to save on fat and apply its resources in other ways we are honestly convinced that it would be in its own best interest to do with less fat.

## The Internationale

Enter the hangman and floggers
The sadists and the sloggers
From their war on the 'inner front'.
Their arms are tired of flaying
And one of them keeps saying
'What's the point of this bloody stunt?'

*Yard in a concentration camp. Prisoners and SS. A prisoner is being flogged.*

THE SS MAN: My arm's hurting. Are you or aren't you going to sing us another verse of that Internationale of yours, you pig?
*The prisoner groans under the lash.*
THE SS MAN: What about you sods showing how angry you feel when you hear a pig like this singing the Internationale? *To a prisoner*: Hey, you, comrade, take this whip and beat him, but good and hard or it'll be your turn next.
*The prisoner in question hesitates.*
THE SS MAN: Stubborn, eh?
*He hits him. The second prisoner takes the whip and flogs the first.*
THE SS MAN: I said good and hard. Ten strokes for you for disobeying orders.
*The second prisoner beats harder.*
THE SS MAN: Another ten strokes for you, that's twenty in all.

*The second prisoner beats harder still. The first prisoner starts singing the Internationale in a hoarse voice. The second stops beating and joins in the song. The SS men fall on the prisoners.*

## The vote

> With well-armed thugs to lead them
> And nothing much to feed them
> Their groans rose to the sky.
> We asked them, all unknowing:
> Poor things, where are you going?
> They said 'to victory'.

*29th March 1936. Polling booth. One wall with a big banner:* THE GERMAN PEOPLE NEEDS LIVING SPACE (ADOLF HITLER). *SA men standing around. Likewise the official in charge is in SA uniform. Enter an old woman and a blind man of about forty, escorted by two SA men. They are very poorly clothed.*

GUARD *announces*: WAR VICTIM!
   *All rise and give the Nazi salute.*
SA MAN *who has been to collect the pair*: Jakob Kehrer, 34 Rummelsburger Allee, and his mother Mrs Anna Kehrer.
   *The pair are given slips and envelopes.*
THE OLD WOMAN *to the civilians present*: Do you think there'll be another war now?
   *Nobody answers. An SA man coughs.*
THE OFFICIAL IN CHARGE *to the old woman*: Just show your son where to put the cross. *To the SA men, but also addressed to the waiting electors*: This man was blinded in the war. But he knows where to put his cross. There are plenty of comrades can learn from him. This man gladly and joyfully gave his eyesight for the nation. But now on hearing his Führer's call he has no hesitation about giving his vote once again for Germany's honour. His loyalty to our nation has brought him neither possessions nor money. You need only look at his coat to see that. Many a habitual grumbler among our comrades would do well to think what has led such a man to the poll. *He points the old woman to the booth*: Step in. *The old woman hesitantly guides her blind son to the booth. At one moment she stops mistrustfully and looks around. All the SA men are staring at her. She is clearly frightened. And shyly, looking back over her shoulder, she draws the blind man into the booth.*

## The new dress

Look: clothes whose classy label
Won't say how they're unable
To stand the slightest rain.
For they're made of wood and paper
The wool has been saved for later
For German troops in Spain.

*Hall of a building. It is raining. Two SA men are standing there.*
*Enter a couple who are taking shelter from the rain.*

THE MAN: Just a few specks. It'll stop in a moment.
THE GIRL: Look at my dress. A few drops, and just look at my dress.
And it cost 28 marks. Now it's a bit of old rag. Made in Germany.
Two drops of rain and just one rag. Who do they think they are,
treating a wage-earner that way? 22 marks a week I get.
THE MAN: Pipe down.
THE GIRL: But you bet the wool goes for uniforms. And we'll soon
be left naked. It's a bloody fraud, I saved up for three months.
Gave up coffee. Nobody can make that up to me. They're a load
of . . .
ONE OF THE SA MEN: Well, miss?
*The girl notices the SA men and gives a scream.*
THE MAN: She's just a bit worked up about her dress.
THE GIRL *stammers*: I only meant it shouldn't rain, should it?


## Any good against gas?

They come with rubber nozzles
And masks with perspex goggles
Forceps and sterile gauze.
They know that gas is fatal
It's a part of modern battle
And of aggressive wars.

*Working-class flat. A worn-out woman and her brother, a worker. It*
*is evening.*

THE WOMAN: Potatoes have gone up again.
THE BROTHER: They'll go higher.
THE WOMAN: If they've got nothing for folk to eat they can't make
war.

THE BROTHER: Wrong. They can't make war if they've got nothing for folk to eat, but then they'll have to make war.

THE WOMAN: I'm having trouble with the boy 'cause he won't stop talking about war, don't you do the same.

THE BROTHER: How's the girl?

THE WOMAN: She's coughing.

THE BROTHER: Seen the doctor, has she?

THE WOMAN: Yes.

THE BROTHER: What d'he say?

THE WOMAN: She needs proper food. *The brother laughs.*

THE WOMAN: That's nothing to laugh about.

THE BROTHER: What's your husband say about it?

THE WOMAN: Nothing.

THE BROTHER: See anything of the Minzers these days?

THE WOMAN: No. What's there to talk about?

THE BROTHER: Plenty, I'd have thought.

THE WOMAN: But you can't talk about that. As you know.

THE BROTHER: There are people beginning to talk again. And the fewer potatoes there are the more talking they'll do.

THE WOMAN: But you were saying there'd be a war.

THE BROTHER: Someone at the door.

*The woman leaves the cooker, and goes and opens the door. She recoils. In the doorway stand three Hitler Youth members wearing gas-masks.*

THE BROTHER: What sort of a bad joke is this?

THE THREE: Heil Hitler!

THE WOMAN: What d'you want?

THE THREE: Heil Hitler!

THE WOMAN: Paul's not here.

THE THREE: Heil Hitler! *One of them takes off his gas-mask.*

THE WOMAN: Paul!

THE BOY: Cos you're always going on about when gas comes. We only wanted to show you we're prepared.

THE WOMAN *has to sit down*: I didn't recognise you.

*One boy throws his gas-mask on the table as the three say 'Heil Hitler' and go off laughing.*

THE WOMAN: They're already at war.

THE BROTHER *picking up the gas-mask*: A thing like that's no better than papier maché. That filter'll let anything through. It's rubbish.

THE WOMAN: What'd be the good of telling him? I've still got weak knees. I just didn't recognise him.

THE BROTHER: Right, once they get their hooks on anyone he's not a son any longer.

THE WOMAN: But what am I to tell him?

THE BROTHER: That gas-masks are no good against gas.

THE WOMAN: What is then?

THE BROTHER *in an undertone*: I was on the Eastern front in 1917. The fellows in the trenches opposite did something that was. They threw out their government. That was the only thing that was any good, and it was the first time in the history of the world that anyone did it.

THE WOMAN: You know how thin these walls are.

THE BROTHER: Bloody muzzle! *He throws the gas-mask into the corner.* We'll stay muzzled till we're forced to open our mouths: once the gas is there.
*There is a ring. The woman quickly and anxiously rises and picks up the gas-mask from the floor.*


## A possible last scene for Basel

*Hamburg. 1938. In an impoverished flat three young men in SA uniform are getting themselves ready. The pregnant young wife of the oldest of them stands and watches. The radio blares the final sentences of a militant Hitler speech.*

HITLER'S VOICE *over a storm of applause*: I have only one thing to say to the world: Nothing, but nothing will halt our progress. Whosoever is against us, lone voices or certain whole nations, they will be ruthlessly overthrown and trampled underfoot.
*Renewed applause.*

FIRST SA MAN: The Führer's telling them straight, eh? I just don't get it, how some people still want to swim against the tide. They're mad.

SECOND: Off with their heads, that's the only answer to these international animals. Lechner calls it 'topping' them, good eh? *Laughs uproariously.* Topping! Yesterday they topped another couple. One of 'em passed a note for his wife to Lechner, I've got it here. I'll read it for you.

OLDEST: Later. Handkerchief, Anna. *The wife gives him a handkerchief.* Now you've gone and washed my blues. And I told you you should get Müller to do the washing, in your condition. I should smack you one.

SECOND: You're right, you just won't let yourself be mollycoddled, Mrs Hall. Great things lie in store for this boy. – Just listen to what the swine wrote before they topped him.

OLDEST: I'd rather hear what they're saying on the radio.

SECOND *turns it off and reads from a crumpled letter*: 'My dear son! . . .'

[See letter from the scene 'Consulting the people'.]

FIRST: What's up, Anna?

*The woman has sat down.*

OLDEST: She's just not feeling so well. *He brings her a glass of water.* Don't let it bother you.

FIRST: The letter wasn't right for her.

SECOND: Rubbish. Why not? All I can say is: if you say A, you've got to be prepared to say B. *He turns the radio back on. The cheers have given way to the Horst Wessel Song.* As the Führer says: In the end, it's the strongest who triumph.

## Editorial Notes

There is no trace of any structural scheme for this work, whose scenes were individually conceived, arranged in different orders at different times, and eventually published in what seems to have been conceived as chronological order, following the dates given in the initial stage directions. The nucleus evidently consisted of five scenes – 1 The spy. 2 The Jewish wife. 3 A matter of justice. 4 Occupational disease. 5 The chalk cross – under the overall title *Die Angst (Fear)*: and subtitled *Spiritual Upsurge of the German People under Nazi Domination.* This was dated 20th–24th August 1937 by Brecht's collaborator Margarete Steffin. Three months later Brecht told Karl Korsch that he had written seven. By the spring of 1938 the number had grown to seventeen, at which point Brecht added the introductory 'March-past' poem and had copies made which he sent to Piscator, Dudow and no doubt others. He described this to Piscator as a 'cycle of very short plays which might for performance purposes be called *German Marchpast*' but had the overall title *Fear and Misery of the Third Reich.* Scenes in our text which were not included in this first full script were 2, 4, 11, 12, 13, 14, 20 and 22.

This was the script used for 99%, the version performed that May in Paris under Dudow's direction, though only eight of its scenes were played.

But Brecht had evidently got the bit between his teeth, and he sent Dudow a number of additional scenes till by late May the total had risen to 27. This was the number included in the new duplicated script which served as a basis for the unrealised third volume of the Malik-Verlag edition of Brecht's works, where the play was to be entitled *Germany – an Atrocity Story*; this went for type-setting in August 1938. A copy also went to Ferdinand Reyher who spent the first half of 1939 making a first American adaptation.

Several scenes were also published individually and in small groups in 1938 and 1939: in German in *Das Wort, Internationale Literatur, Die neue Weltbühne* and *Mass und Wert*, in French in *La Nouvelle Revue Française, L'Europe* and *La Commune,* and in English in *New Writing.* At some point too Brecht sent (or took) the play to Mezhdunarodnaya Kniga in Moscow, who, following the German invasion in 1941, published a selection of thirteen scenes: 1, 2, 5, 7, 10,

13, 14, 16, 18, 19, 22, 23 and 'The vote' – oddly enough omitting 'The Jewish wife' and 'The chalk cross'.

By this time, however, the scenes had also provided the material for an even odder event. In December 1940 the BBC Home Service broadcast selections of four and five scenes in two programmes which were late repeated on the Overseas Service, thus providing Brecht, who knew nothing of the broadcasts, with perhaps his biggest wartime audience. The translation, with the title *Under the Crooked Cross*, was by Albert Lloyd and music was composed by Walter Goehr.

The wartime *The Private Life of the Master Race* version was originally made in May 1942 in German for Max Reinhardt, and now only survives in its translation by Eric Bentley, subtitled *A Documentary Play*. It is composed of 17 scenes divided into three parts, as detailed in the note on p. 328, with new introductory verses for the different parts and scenes. When in 1945 the Aurora-Verlag (successor to the Malik-Verlag) at last published a full German text – the 24-scene basis for the subsequent Gesammelte Werke and for our own translation – it restored the pre-war verses and loose chronological form, relegating the wartime version to Brecht's note (as above). For the first time it included 'Peat-bog soldiers', while five scenes from one or other of the earlier versions were omitted. The more recent Berliner und Frankfurter Ausgabe gives the run of 27 scenes from the unrealised Malik edition, and puts 'Ersatz feelings' and 'Peat-bog soldiers' into an appendix. Since that volume appeared, a further scene has been discovered, 'A possible last scene for Basel', which we reproduce above (now in BFA Registerband, pp. 736–7).

The extremely adaptable and accessible nature of the scene cycle enabled *Fear and Misery*, in its various arrangements, to become Brecht's most widely distributed and performed text in anti-Nazi exile.

In the notes on all 30 scenes which follow, the 17-scene script of spring 1938 is referred to as '17-sc.', the duplicated 27-scene script as '27-sc.', and *The Private Life of the Master Race* (1942) as '*PLMR*'. The complete set of Brecht's working scripts, including scenes later omitted, is referred to by its archive number, BBA 420. The main early productions are referred to as '*99%*' (Dudow, 1938), 'BBC' (Laurence Gilliam for the BBC, 1940), '1942 production' (Viertel, New York, 1942, in German) and '1945 production' (*The Private Life of the Master Race*, New York, 1945, initiated by Piscator and finally directed by Viertel).

Prologue. The German march-past. *Der deutsche Heerschau.*
   Was included, along with the introductory verses to the individual scenes, in 99%. In the 1945 production and in *PLMR* it was replaced by the chorus's verses on pp. 328–9.

1 One big family. *Volksgemeinschaft.*
   First in 17-sc. Much shorter in BBA 420, which starts approximately with the same stage direction, but goes on:

> THE FIRST: What I say is once we're one big family we can go on and make war. They'll scatter like crap off a boot when we come along, one solid People of brothers. Our mission is to ... *He stops, freezes and listens. Somewhere a window has been opened.*
>
> THE SECOND: Wozzat?

   Continuing roughly as on page 120 except for the omission of the Second's last exclamation.

2 A case of betrayal. *Der Verrat.*
   First in 27-sc. Included in 1945 production and *PLMR*. Derived primarily from the poem 'The Neighbour' of 1934:

> I am the neighbour. I reported him.
> None of us want
> Agitators in our building.
>
> When we put out the swastika flag
> He put out nothing.
> Then when we tackled him about it
> He asked if our living room –
> Lived in by us and our four children –
> Had enough space for a flagpole
> When we told him we'd believe in the future once more
> He laughed.
>
> When they beat him up on the staircase
> We didn't like that. They ripped his shirt.
> That wasn't necessary. Our kind aren't
> All that well off for shirts.
>
> Still, at least we're rid of him now, and the house is quiet.
> We've plenty to worry about, so
> Quiet at least is essential.
> We've begun to notice one or two people

Looking away when we run into them. But
Those who came for him tell us
We did the right thing.

3 The chalk cross. *Das Kreidekreuz.*
   In *Die Angst.* Dated 18–20 viii 37 by Margarete Steffin in BBA
   420. Based on poem of 1934 with the same title (*Poems
   1913–1956*, p. 226). Brecht has later added the passages (a) from
   'THE SA MAN: That's what women want' to 'We're glad to help'
   on p. 123; (b) the SA man's three lines as '*he puts his hand on hers
   in a friendly way*' on p. 124; and (c) the worker's 'Give me the
   Marxists and the Jews' on p. 127. Included in *99%*, 1942 and 1945
   productions and *PLMR* but not in Moscow edition of 1941.

4 Peat-bog soldiers. *Moorsoldaten.*
   Presumably written during Brecht's stay in the US. According to
   Eric Bentley, Elisabeth Hauptmann wrote the closing third, from
   the SS man's final entrance. The scene was included in 1945
   production and *PLMR*. The 'Song of the Peat-bog Soldiers' is an
   actual concentration camp song.

5 Servants of the people. *Dienst am Volke.*
   In 17-sc. Not played in the early productions.

6 A matter of justice. *Rechtsfindung.*
   In *Die Angst.* Included in *99%*, BBC (as last scene), 1942 and
   1944 productions and *PLMR* but not in Moscow edition 1942.
   Passages added on or after BBA 420 are (a) on p. 150 from '*For
   some while*' to '*The judge just looks scared*'; (b) the whole episode
   with the maidservant from her entrance on p. 150 to her exit on p.
   151; (c) the usher's second appearance on p. 153 from 'THE
   SENIOR JUDGE: Come in!' to the judge's 'That's something I
   could have done without' eight lines later; and (d) the concluding
   seventeen lines following the judge's 'One moment', apart from
   his final exit.

7 Occupational disease. *Die Berufskrankheit.*
   In *Die Angst.* Included in Moscow edition 1942 but not in *PLMR*
   or US productions. In BBA 420 the surgeon originally began with
   one long speech up to his query 'What has this man got?'; this
   was subsequently broken up by the exchange with the three
   assistants, amplified with medical details (e.g. the naming of
   Raynaud's Disease) and extensively reworded. His exchanges
   with the sister were also added later, as was his 'Why?' and the
   first patient's sotto voce question.

8 The physicists. *Die Physiker.*
In 17-sc. Included in *PLMR*. BBA 420 omits the five lines from '*grabs for it greedily*' on p. 158 to 'Without it we're stuck' and the whole passage read out by Y from 'The problem concerns' (p.159) to 'remain fixed'. Instead it has Y reading '*the whole incomprehensible text with its plethora of formulas in a hushed voice*', broken by interruptions as in the final stage directions. It seems likely that the 'Mikovsky' referred to is an error for (Rudolph) Minkovsky, the name of an eminent astronomer who emigrated to the US in the 1930s and his uncle (Hermann) who contributed to the general theory of relativity and died in 1909.

9 The Jewish wife. *Die jüdische Frau.*
In *Die Angst.* Was included in 99%, BBC, 1942 and 1945 productions and *PLMR*. Not in the Moscow edition, though a script destined for it is in the Lenin Library. There is a script worked on by Brecht (BBA 415/25–35) which shows that at one point the order of the woman's four telephone calls was different: first to Anna, second to Gertrude, third to the bridge-playing doctor and fourth to Mrs Schöck. After that she made a fifth (promptly deleted) call to an asylum to ask whether equivalent institutions in Holland would take in a Jewish woman without means, and another (likewise deleted) to order a photograph for her husband. Two of her imaginary conversations with the husband were added on the same script: those beginning 'Don't tell me you haven't changed' (p. 162) and 'I never told you' (p. 163).

10 The spy. *Der Spitzel.*
In *Die Angst.* Dated 18 viii 1937 by Steffin. Published in the Moscow *Internationale Literatur* (Deutsche Blätter) no. 3, March 1938 and (as 'The Informer') in Charles Ashleigh's translation in *New Writing*, London. Included in 99%, BBC, 1942 and 1945 productions and *PLMR*. Relates to poem of *c.* 1934 'Ich bin der Lehrer' (BFA 94, p. 247).

11 The black shoes. *Die schwarzen Schuhe.*
In 27-sc. Also called 'Children's shoes' (*Die Kinderschuhe*) and *Fleisch für Fleisch* (untranslatable pun on the exchanging of flesh for meat). Included in *PLMR* but not played in main early productions.

12 Labour service. *Arbeitsdienst.*
In 27-sc. Written by April 1938. Not included in early productions or *PLMR*. The student's final line ended with 'for today', to

which the young worker replied simply: 'Wait till we're out of here and I'll give you something to remember'.

13 Workers' playtime. *Die Stunde des Arbeiters.*
In 27-sc. Was among the six newly written scenes sent to Dudow on 24 April 1938. Included in BBC and *PLMR*.

14 The box. *Die Kiste.*
In 27-sc. Included in 1945 production and *PLMR*. Due to be played in Viertel's 1942 production but omitted at the last moment.

15 Released. *Der Entlassene.*
In 27-sc. Included in *PLMR* but not played in early productions except BBC.

16 Charity begins at home. *Winterhilfe.*
In 17-sc. Included in 99% and BBC. 'Winter Aid' was the organised Nazi charity for the poor, for which the SA and others went out collecting.

17 Two bakers. *Zwei Bäcker.*
In 17-sc. Included in 99% and *PLMR*.

18 The farmer feeds his sow. *Der Bauer füttert die Sau.*
In 17-sc. Included in 99% and *PLMR*.

19 The old campaigner. *Der alte Kämpfer.*
In 17-sc. In *PLMR* but not staged in any early productions.

20 The Sermon on the Mount. *Die Bergpredigt.*
In 27-sc. Also called 'The question' or 'The pastor's question' (*Die Frage* or *Die Frage des Pfarrers*). Included in BBC, 1945 and *PLMR*.

21 The motto. *Das Mahnwort.*
In 27-sc. In the working script BBA 420, the initial stage direction specifies that it is Hitler's birthday but gives no indication of year and city. Not staged in early productions.

22 The barracks learn that Almería has been bombarded. *In den Kasernen wird die Beschiessung von Almeria bekannt.*
In 27-sc. Included in BBC and in 1942 Moscow edition.

23 Job creation. *Arbeitsbeschaffung.*
In 17-sc. Also called *Arbeitsbeschaffung 1937*. In 99% and 1942 Moscow edition, both times as closing scene. Also in BBC.

24 Consulting the people. *Volksbefragung.*
In 17-sc. Also called 'The Missing Man' (*Der Fehlende* or *Der fehlende Mann*). In 1945 production and *PLMR*. 13 March 1938 was the official date of the Anschluss with Austria, two days after German troops moved into that country. According to Eric Bentley, Elisabeth Hauptmann added the references to class at the end.

Epilogue

An unfinished epilogue goes (in loose translation):

> We'll watch them follow the band till
> The whole lot comes to a standstill –
> A beaten, bogged-down élite.
> We'd laugh till we were crying
> If it weren't for our brothers dying
> To bring about his defeat.

> And yet historians tell us
> Of other mighty fellows
> Who came to a sticky end.
> The people had revolted
> Thrown off their chains [...]

BBA 429/06

Additional scenes

25 Ersatz feelings. *Der Gefühlsersatz.*
This scene is in one of the complete scripts, but is at the end of the working script BBA 420. It has no introductory verse, though the following epigraph may be meant as the theme for one:

> Meanness was always shrouded in a little cloak. But nowadays the cloak is made of synthetic material.

Evidently the scene was discarded at an early stage.

26 The Internationale. *Die Internationale.*
In 17- and 27-sc. and unpublished Malik-Verlag proof. Omitted from the Aurora edition of 1945, possibly because of similarities with scene 5, 'Servants of the people'.

27 The vote. *Die Wahl.*
In 27-sc. and unpublished Malik-Verlag proof. Omitted from Aurora edition of 1945, and thereafter. 29 March 1936 was the date of the German elections in which 99 per cent of the voters

voted Nazi. The Rummelsburger Allee was in a working-class area of Berlin.

28 The new dress. *Das neue Kleid.*
In 27-sc. and unpublished Malik-Verlag proof. Omitted from Aurora edition of 1945, and thereafter.

29 Any good against gas? *Was hilft gegen Gas?*
In 17-sc. and unpublished Malik-Verlag proof. Proposed by Brecht for inclusion in 99%, but not staged. Omitted from Aurora edition of 1945, and thereafter.

30 A possible last scene for Basel. Untitled.
Only preserved as a single sheet in Caspar Neher's papers, now in the archive (BBA E61/15), with Brecht's handwritten note, 'a possible last scene of Fear + Misery for Basel'. It was written in October 1946 in Santa Monica. The reference is to the Swiss première of the play in January 1947, directed by Ernst Ginsberg, designed by Neher. Brecht had been asked to produce a scene which gave a 'post-war', future perspective, but his response was not used.

Sketches and fragments (including some in verse) provide the following hints that Brecht at one time or another planned further scenes:

(a) The prospect of war frightens her less than the warden for her block. (A neighbouring tenant gets mistaken for the warden.)
(b) A posh youth loses 10 pfennigs. (Reproaches.)
(c) A lady gets insulted because of her rings. Her husband: 'Next time besides bringing your gas-mask don't forget to wear your gloves.'
(d) When can paterfamilias still sit there in his SA uniform after supper?

(a–d, BBA 464/30)

(e) A verse introducing General Goering. (BBA 9/10)
(f) A voice introduces the builder of the Atlantic Wall – i.e. probably Albert Speer. (98/34)
(g) A verse introduces the hygiene experts. (353/6)
(h) Corner of a cellar during an air-raid precautions exercise. Seufert, a business manager, is crouching against the wall with his wife and child. They are trying on gas-masks. (464/11, with twelve lines of dialogue in which a working-class family enter and are asked to sit on the other side of the cellar; they take no notice.)

(i)   A fragment of dialogue in which two concentration camp prisoners, named Rullmann and Lüttge, discuss whether the local Group Leader should be termed a neo-pagan or a freethinker. (464/10)

# SEÑORA CARRAR'S RIFLES

## Texts by Brecht

NOTE TO 'SEÑORA CARRAR'S RIFLES'

The little play was written during the first year of the Spanish Civil War for a German group in Paris. It is Aristotelian (empathy-) drama. The drawbacks of this technique can to some extent be made up for by performing the play together with a documentary film showing the events in Spain, or with a propaganda manifestation of any sort.

[BFA 24, p. 225. The text dates from 1938.]

## ART OR POLITICS?

I understand your question. You see me sitting here and looking out across the Sound, which has nothing warlike about it. So what leads me to concern myself with the struggle of the Spanish people against its generals? But you shouldn't forget why I am sitting here. How can I clear my writing of everything that has so affected my life? And my writing too? For I am sitting here as an exile, and one who has been deprived above all else of his listeners and readers – the people whose language I write in and who moreover are not just the customers for my writings but the objects of my most profound interest. I can only write for people I am interested in. Then imaginative writing becomes just like writing letters. And at present the people in question are being subjected to unspeakable sufferings. How am I to keep that out of my writing? And wherever I look, the moment I see a little way beyond this Sound I see people subjected to sufferings of the same kind. However, if mankind is destroyed there will not be any more art. Stringing beautiful words together is not art. How is art to move people if it is not itself moved by what happens to them? If I harden my heart to people's sufferings how can their hearts be uplifted by what I write? And if I make no effort to find them some way out of their suffering, how are they to find their way into my works? The little play we are talking about deals with an Andalusian fisherman's wife and her fight against the generals. I've tried to show how difficult it is for her to decide to fight them: how only the most extreme necessity makes her take up a rifle. It is an appeal to the oppressed to revolt against their oppressors in the name of humanity. For humanity has to become warlike in times like these if it is not to be wiped out. At the same time it is a letter to the fisherman's wife to assure her that not everybody who speaks the German language is in favour of the generals and is despatching bombs and tanks to her country. This letter I write in the name of many Germans both inside and outside Germany's frontiers. They are the majority of Germans, I am sure.

BFA 22.1, pp. 356–7, dated February 1938. On the 13th of that month the play was performed in German under the direction of Brecht and Ruth Berlau in Copenhagen at Borups Højskole, with Helene Weigel as Carrar.]

DIFFERENT WAYS OF ACTING
(Weigel and Andreasen as Mrs Carrar)

A comparison of Weigel's and Andreasen's performances in the German and Danish productions of *Señor Carrar's Rifles* leads to some useful conclusions about the principles of the epic theatre. Weigel is a highly qualified professional actress and a communist, Andreasen an amateur and a communist. The two productions involved exactly the same movements and used the same set.

The question of talent is irrelevant, since the acting differences that concern us would also be observable if the degree of talent was more or less equal.

The greater 'impressiveness' which everyone saw in Weigel's performance was attributable to factors other than superior talent.

Both actresses respected epic principles in so far as they largely dispensed with empathy in portraying the character, and by so doing allowed the audience to dispense with it too. The difference lay in the fact that Andreasen made this less interesting than did Weigel.

Unlike Andreasen, Weigel managed by every attitude and every sentence to permit, if not force the audience to take a line – to such an extent that those sitting near me several times expressed their displeasure at the attitude of the fisherman's wife as she argued in favour of neutrality – by continually taking a line herself. Andreasen's way of acting had the audience passively following the story. Carrar's opinions ('you have to be neutral') seemed entirely natural and understandable given her environment and what we had been told of her previous history; she could in effect be no different from what she was. Her change of opinion due to a specific experience (the death of the son she had kept out of the battle, in a battle which neutrality had not eliminated) was understood in the same way. It was like following a piece of natural history wherein one repeatedly acknowledges the laws of nature. Even the detailed contradictions in the character's attitude never emerged: Carrar's neutrality as acted by Weigel was never one hundred per cent complete; she hadn't always favoured neutrality and even now had her reservations about it, her appreciation of her sons' attitude, her traits of bellicosity, her disapproval of the priest's attitude, her traits of compromise and so on. The character Andreasen portrayed was far more passive than Weigel's; things happened *to* her rather than by her agency. Nor did Andreasen show the fighter she eventually becomes as a fighter of a specific, contradictory kind (a fighter for the renunciation of force). Weigel showed a fighter for neutrality being transformed into a fighter for the abolition of fighting.

In other words Andreasen's performance didn't make the story sufficiently interesting, and as a result one missed – as one did not with Weigel – any chance to empathise with the character and participate strongly and effectively in her emotions. One actually missed any use of those hypnotic powers which one is normally able to feel in the theatre. Her noble renunciation of such methods, springing from a natural sense of modesty and a high conception of dignity, became something close to a disadvantage. This way of playing the incidents, as naturally involving no contradictions, seemed to call for another type of acting if interest was to be maintained: the suggestive acting of the old-style theatre.

The lesson for Andreasen, in view of her lack of experience and technique – in old- and new-style methods alike – is that there are two ways in which she can develop: she can master the one technique or the other. She has to learn either to make her acting suggestive, to practise empathy and induce it, to mobilise more powerful emotions, or else to define her own attitude to the character portrayed and induce the same attitude in the audience. If she wishes to do the latter, then she must develop to the point of recognition what she now more or less obscurely feels, and find ways of turning this recognition into a recognition by the audience. She must know what she is doing, and show that she knows it. She must not just *be* a proletarian when she acts one, but show how a proletarian woman differs from a member of the middle or lower middle class. She must be conscious of everything that is special about a proletarian and portray this in a special way.

[BFA 24, pp. 223–5. This refers to two productions in Copenhagen, both directed by Ruth Berlau. Dagmar Andreasen played the title role in a Danish amateur production which opened on 20 December 1937, and Helene Weigel in the German production at the Borups Højskole on 13 February 1938 (as well as at the première in Paris, 16 October 1937).]

DIALOGUE ABOUT AN ACTRESS OF THE EPIC THEATRE

THE ACTOR: I've read what you've written about the epic theatre. And now having seen your little Spanish Civil War play, with the outstanding actress of this new method in the title part, I'm quite frankly astounded. Astounded to find it was proper theatre.

ME: Really?

THE ACTOR: Does it surprise you to hear that what you've written about this new method of acting made me expect something utterly dry, abstract, not to say schoolmasterly?

ME: Not specially. No one likes learning these days.

THE ACTOR: It's not considered entertaining certainly; but it wasn't only your demand for instruction that led me to expect something very remote from theatre, but also the fact that you seemed to be denying the theatre everything that makes it theatrical.

ME: What, for instance?

THE ACTOR: Illusion. Suspense. An opportunity to empathise.

ME: And did you feel suspense?

THE ACTOR: Yes.

ME: Did you empathise?

THE ACTOR: Not entirely. No.

ME: Wasn't there any illusion?

THE ACTOR: Not really. No.

ME: But you still thought it was theatre?

THE ACTOR: Yes, I did. That was what astounded me. Don't start crowing, though. It was theatre, but all the same it wasn't anything like as new as I'd expect from what you wrote.

ME: To be as new as that it would have to stop being theatre, I suppose?

THE ACTOR: All I'm saying is that it's not all that difficult to do what you're asking for. Apart from Weigel in the lead part, it was performed by amateurs, simple workers who'd never been on a stage before; and Weigel is a great technician who quite clearly got her training in that ordinary old-style theatre which you keep running down.

ME: You're quite right. The new method results in proper theatre. It allows amateurs to make theatre under certain conditions, so long as they haven't quite mastered the old methods, and it allows professionals to make theatre so long as they have partly forgotten them.

THE ACTOR: Ha. I'd have said Weigel displayed too much technique rather than too little or just enough.

ME: I thought she displayed not just technique but the attitude of a fisherman's wife to the generals too?

THE ACTOR: Certainly she displayed that. But technique as well. I mean, she *wasn't* the fisherman's wife, just acting her.

ME: But she really isn't a fisherman's wife. She really was just acting her. And that's just a fact.

THE ACTOR: Of course; she's an actress. But when she plays a fisherman's wife she has to make you forget that. She showed everything that was remarkable about the fisherman's wife's, but she also showed she was showing it.

ME: I get you. She didn't create any illusion that she *was* the fisherman's wife.

THE ACTOR: She was far too conscious of what was remarkable. You could see she was conscious of it. She actually showed you that she was. But of course a real fisherman's wife isn't conscious of that; she's unconscious, of course, of what's remarkable about her. So if you see a character on stage who is conscious of that, then it plainly won't be a fisherman's wife that you're seeing.

ME: – But an actress. I get you.

THE ACTOR: The only thing lacking was for her to look at the audience at certain points as if to ask 'Well, do you see the sort of person I am?'. I'm sure she had developed a complete technique for sustaining this feeling in the audience, the feeling that she is not what she portrays.

ME: Do you think you could describe such a technique?

THE ACTOR: Suppose she had tacitly thought 'And then the fisherman's wife said' before every sentence, then that sentence would have emerged very much as it did. What I mean is, she was plainly speaking another woman's words.

ME: Perfectly right. And why do you make her say 'said'? Why put it in the past tense?

THE ACTOR: Because it's equally plain that she was re-enacting something that had happened in the past; in other words, the spectator is under no illusion that it's happening now or that he himself is witnessing the original incident.

ME: But the fact is that the spectator is not witnessing an original incident. The fact is that he's not in Spain but in the theatre.

THE ACTOR: But after all, one goes to the theatre to get the illusion of

having been in Spain, if that is the play's location. Why else go to
the theatre?

ME: Is that an exclamation or a question? I think one can find reasons
for going to the theatre without wanting to be under any illusion
of being in Spain.

THE ACTOR: If you want to be here in Copenhagen you don't have to
go to the theatre and see a play which is set in Spain, do you?

ME: You might as well say that if no one wants to be in Copenhagen
one doesn't have to go to the theatre and see a play set in
Copenhagen, mightn't you?

THE ACTOR: If you don't experience anything in the theatre that you
could not equally well experience at home, then you don't have to
go there, that's a fact.

ME:

[BFA 22, pp. 353–5. Incomplete. Possibly based on conversation
with Per Knutzon, who had directed *Round Heads and Pointed
Heads*.]

PROLOGUE TO 'SEÑORA CARRAR'S RIFLES'

*Internment camp for Spanish refugees in Perpignan. Barbed wire
separates a couple of French soldiers, one of whom is on guard while
the other reads a paper, from three Spaniards: a worker in the
uniform of the Republican militia, a youth wearing a soldier's cap and
a woman sitting motionless on the bare ground leaning against a post.*

THE NEWSPAPER READER: It's all come out now about why the
Czechoslovakian Republic didn't fight when the Germans invaded.
That ex-president of theirs fled to Chicago in the United States,
and at last he's talking.

THE SENTRY: And what's he said?

*The worker is intrigued and steps up to the wire to listen.*

THE NEWSPAPER READER: Here, just listen: that makes the second
republic they've polished off this year. Well, the ex-president, he's
called Beneš...

*The worker nods impatiently.*

THE NEWSPAPER READER: What, you've heard of him, have you?
How come?

THE WORKER: We read all that in our papers last September. We had
hopes. If Czechoslovakia had fought...

THE NEWSPAPER READER: She didn't, and you know why? She had
an alliance with the Soviet Union and when the Germans started

making noises this fellow Beneš asked Moscow if the Soviets would come to her aid. They said yes they would. But what happened? The big landowners formed up to Beneš and told him he mustn't accept that aid, and they threatened to revolt if he did. They'd sooner see their country under Prussian jackboots than let the people fight alongside the Soviet Union.

THE SENTRY: Think that's true?

THE NEWSPAPER READER: Of course we can't tell. It's in the paper, so probably it isn't.

THE WORKER: I'd say it was true even though it's in the paper. Our big landowners used foreigners against their own people too.

THE SENTRY: What did they do that for?

THE WORKER: Don't you know? Not even now? That's bad, mate. How they sent the bombers in to make us keep our wooden ploughs? The forces of oppression have their own International.

THE NEWSPAPER READER: So what you're saying is that one people gets attacked from inside, then the big shots throw open the door to let the foreign aggressors in so they can help them, while the other is attacked from outside by foreign aggressors, then the big shots throw open the door and help them attack.

THE WORKER: That's how you have to see it if you've been through what we have.

THE SENTRY: Perhaps it's just no use fighting. The Czechs didn't fight, so of course they were beaten. But you lot fought. Well, you've been beaten too, so what's the point of fighting?

THE NEWSPAPER READER: What you got to say to that?

THE WORKER: Plenty. Your best answer would come from that woman, only she doesn't know your language. She's my sister. She used to live in a small fishing village in Catalonia with her two sons. That boy's the only one she's got left. She asked the same question: What's the point of fighting? She didn't keep on asking it right up to the last moment, but for a very long time she did, almost up to the last moment, and a lot of her sort went on like her asking that question 'What's the point of fighting?' for a very long time, almost up to the last moment. And the fact that they went on asking it for so long was one of the reasons why we got beaten, see, and if one day you find yourself asking the same question as them you'll get beaten too.

THE NEWSPAPER READER: Tell us how it all happened, will you?

THE WORKER: Right, I will. As I said, she was living in a village in Catalonia when the generals and the big landowners began their revolt. She had two sons and kept them out of the fighting for a long time. But one evening...

EPILOGUE TO 'SEÑORA CARRAR'S RIFLES'

*The internment camp at Perpignan. The worker on the other side of the barbed wire has finished telling his story. The newspaper reader passes him a cigarette.*

THE WORKER: Yes, that's how Maria Carrar went into the fight – even her – against our own generals and against a whole world, of which one part helped to crush us while the other part looked on; and that's how she was defeated. And her rifles once again disappeared beneath some floorboards, somewhere.

THE NEWSPAPER READER: Do you suppose they'll be brought out again ever?

THE WORKER: I know they will, because she knows what the fight is about now.

[BFA 4, pp. 335-7. The Prologue and Epilogue were written in 1939, after the fall of the Spanish Republic, for Curt Trepte's Swedish amateur production (Västerås, autumn 1938), which went to a youth festival in Eskilstuna in August 1939.]

ANOTHER CASE OF APPLIED DIALECTICS

The little play *Señora Carrar's Rifles*, which B. had based on a one-acter by Synge, was being rehearsed for the Ensemble by a young director, with Carrar being played by Weigel who had played her years before in exile under B.'s direction. We had to tell B. that the ending, where the fisherman's wife gives her young son and her brother the buried rifles, then goes off to the front with them, did not carry conviction. Weigel herself was unable to say what was wrong. As B. came in she was giving a masterly performance showing how the woman, having grown pious and embittered over the use of force, became increasingly worn down in spirit by the repeated visits and continually renewed arguments of the villagers; likewise how she collapsed when they brought in the body of her son who had been out peacefully fishing. Nonetheless B. too saw that her change of mind was not really credible. We gathered round and swapped views. 'You could understand it if it was just the effect of all that agitation by her brother and the neighbours,' said one of us, 'but the death of the son is too much.' 'You lay too much store by agitation,' said B., shaking his head. 'Better if it was only the son's death,' said another. 'She'd just collapse,' said B. 'I don't get it,' said Weigel eventually. 'She suffers one blow after another, yet nobody believes they have an effect.' 'Just say that again,' said B. Weigel repeated the sentence. 'It's that one-thing-after-another that weakens it,' said B. We had located the flaw. Weigel had allowed Carrar to flinch under each successive blow and collapse under the heaviest one. Instead she ought to have played the way Carrar steeled herself after each blow had devastated her, then all of a sudden collapsed after the last. 'Yes, that's how I played it in Copenhagen,' said Weigel, surprised, 'and it worked there.' 'Curious,' remarked B. after the rehearsal had confirmed our supposition, 'how a fresh effort is needed every time if the laws of the dialectic are to be respected.'

[BFA 23, pp. 404–5. This outwardly impersonal account of Egon Monk's rehearsals for the November 1952 production appears to have been written by Brecht himself. It forms part of his 'Dialectics in the Theatre', for which see *Brecht on Theatre*, pp. 281–2.]

## Editorial Notes

It was in September 1936 that Slatan Dudow wrote to Brecht suggesting that he should write a play about the Spanish Civil War which had just broken out. The work seems to have overlapped with the writing of the first five scenes of *Fear and Misery of the Third Reich*, and it too was typed out and dated 24 August 1937, nearly a year after Dudow's letter. By then Franco's troops had taken Bilbao and Santander and were on their way to conquering the whole north-west corner of the country. Originally the play had been titled *Generals over Bilbao*, which suggests that most of the writing must have been done between 19 April – the date given for the action in one version of the script – and 18 June, when Bilbao itself fell. The title however was not changed to the present one till the scripts were ready, when the location too was altered from the Basque coast to that of Andalucia in the far south.

The play is based on motifs from J.M. Synge's *Riders to the Sea* (1904).

There are two of Brecht's characteristic outline schemes. One, seemingly the earlier, lists eleven episodes:

  1 the brother visiting, the food ships are on the way
  2 the conversation over cards
              hunger
  3 manuela. theresa goes to tell juan
  4 search for rifles
  5 the tearing of the flag
  6 the priest
  7 old mrs perez. the women in the window
  9 where is juan?
 10 here is juan
 11 three rifles for bilbao

The other, seven-episode scheme slightly changes the order, thus:

  1 the brother's visit
  2 mistrustful, she catches her brother and her son bent over her dead husband's case of rifles, she tears up the flag in which the rifles are packed
  3 the card game

4 where is juan?
5 he that taketh the sword shall perish by the sword
6 here is juan
7 the departure

In the text as typed the names of the mother and her son were
Theresa Pasqual and Fernando. Brecht changed them first to Mrs
Pasqual and José, then to the Mother and the Boy, as now. On what
looks like a final script the present title has been written on the cover,
while in the opening stage direction 'Basque' has been amended to
'Andalusian' for the fisherman's house and 'Pasqual' changed to
'Carrar'. The prologue and epilogue (pp. 360–2) suggest that Brecht
later thought of Theresa as Maria and shifted the setting up to
Catalonia, but these changes were never carried out.

The play was premièred in October 1937 in Paris, directed by
Slatan Dudow and with Helene Weigel in the title role. After this
there were fourteen further productions before 1945, notably in
Denmark, Sweden and Prague. It remained one of the plays most
often performed in Brecht's lifetime and was especially popular with
amateur and student groups. It was first published as a 'Sonderdruck'
or advance offprint from the second volume of the collected Malik
edition of Brecht's works, which was printed in Prague a bare year
before the Nazis moved in. The offprint was dated 1937, the
complete volume March 1938. The former was prefaced by Brecht's
poem 'The actress in exile' (BFA 14, p. 355), which is dedicated to
Helene Weigel:

Now she is making up. In the white cubicle
She sits hunched on the wretched stool.
With easy gestures
She puts on her greasepaint before the mirror.
Carefully she wipes from her face
All individuality: the slightest sensation
Will change it. Now and again
She lets the noble and delicate shoulders
Fall forward, as with those who do
Hard work. She is already wearing the coarse blouse
With the patched elbow. Her canvas shoes
Are still on the dressing table.
When she has finished she
Asks eagerly if the drum has arrived
Which is to create the noise of gunfire
And if the big net is
Already hanging. Then she stands up, small figure

Great fighter
Ready to don the canvas shoes and show
How an Andalusian fisherman's wife
Fights the generals.

**Glossary/Historical Notes** (for *Fear and Misery* and *Señora Carrar*)

Almería: Spanish coastal town, shelled by German fleet on 31 May 1937.

Aryan: Of Indo-European origin. Term properly used of languages, but serving in Nazi race theory to denote a superior Nordic Germanic breed of human.

BDM: League of German Maidens. Nazi girls' organisation.

Brown: Nazi colour. Brown House: party HQ in Munich, cradle of the movement. Brownshirts: the SA.

Ersatz: Substitute. A term much used of synthetic materials, whose use was forced on the Nazis by economic problems.

Goebbels, Josef: Nazi Propaganda Minister (suicide 1945).

Goering, Hermann: Nazi Economics Minister (suicide 1946).

Kautzky, Karl: Austrian Socialist leader/theorist of Social-Democracy and opponent of Lenin.

Labour Service: Conscripted labour force run on quasi-military lines.

Ley, Dr: Nazi Labour Minister.

Oranienburg: Early concentration camp near Berlin, better known as Sachsenhausen.

Queipo de Llano: Spanish Nationalist general. Principal Franco propagandist.

Racial profanation (*Rassenschande*): Sexual relations between Aryans and Jews (or Blacks), prohibited in 1934.

Radio General: Queipo de Llano, q.v.

Scharführer: Nazi paramilitary officer's rank.

Silesia: South-eastern province of Germany, now partly incorporated into Poland.

Strength through Joy (*Kraft durch Freude*): Nazi travel and leisure organisation, directed to the workers.

Subhumans (*Untermenschen*): Term used of Slavs, Jews, Blacks and other 'non-Aryans'.

Thälmann, Ernst: German Communist Party secretary, imprisoned and executed by the Nazis. Gave his name to German anti-Fascist forces in the Spanish Civil War.

Thyssen: Dynasty of Rhineland heavy industrialists, who flourished before, during and after Fascism.

United Front: Short-lived Communist policy of alliance with Socialist rank and file, *c.* 1934.

*Völkischer Beobachter*: Nazi Party daily paper.

Winter Aid. Nazi relief organisation, distributing clothing and food parcels to the poor.

# DANSEN and
# HOW MUCH IS YOUR IRON?

**Text by Brecht**

NOTE [FOR 'HOW MUCH IS YOUR IRON?']

This little play must be performed in slapstick style. The iron dealer must have a wig with hair that can be made to stand on end; the shoes and cigar are enormous. The backdrop should if possible be plastered with quotations from Scandinavian statesmen.

['Note' to *Was kostet das Eisen*, BFA 24, p. 257, for the première, August 1939, in the polytechnic at Tollare, near Stockholm.]

## Editorial Notes

These two agitprop one-acters, with extremely close references to the contemporary political situation, were written in spring and early summer 1939. *Dansen* may have been started before Brecht left Denmark (April 1939), with a view to performance by a Danish workers' theatre group with whom he had contact through Ruth Berlau. The plays were completed together in June, when the Brechts were living on Lidingö near Stockholm, in response to the opportunity – mediated by Henry Peter Matthis and Ruth Berlau – to work with a Swedish amateur theatre group. Only *How Much Is Your Iron?* was actually performed, with Ruth Berlau as director and in a mixed Danish/Swedish translation. Since Brecht himself was not supposed to take any part in political activities while living in Sweden, he gave the author's name as John Ken, an echo of his early 'Ballad of Hannah Cash'. The first script, entitled *Little Deals in Iron* (*Kleine Geschäfte mit Eisen*), was dated by Margarete Steffin 'Lidingö 2 vi 1939'. About this time Brecht wrote a number of essays on amateur political theatre.

A fragmentary scene suggests that there was to have been a third playlet, set in the house of Norsen the Norwegian. Dansen and Svendson call to see him, to the sound of thunder and the glow of a distant fire. He reproaches them with giving in so easily and failing to make a threefold alliance against the stranger/customer which would certainly have kept him out. The stranger/customer then appears wearing a steel helmet, takes over the meeting and forces them to make an alliance, but under his protection and in order to carry out his wishes. The three thereupon shake hands.

Presumably history intervened. The Norsen piece was not finished, *Dansen* (so far as we know) not performed. None the less he rounded off the latter with three brief dialogues that seem to have been designed as a framework for it, introducing each of the three successive scenes. They go thus:

*Two Scandinavians sitting over breakfast.*

1

THE OPTIMIST: You are an incorrigible pessimist.

THE PESSIMIST: And you are an incorrigible optimist.

THE OPTIMIST: If only you wouldn't always turn up here with your prophecies just as I am sitting having a meal!

THE PESSIMIST: When else am I to turn up? You're always sitting having a meal.

THE OPTIMIST: But every time I listen to you I lose my appetite.

THE PESSIMIST: Mine goes every time I see you.

THE OPTIMIST *gives an irritated grunt.*

THE PESSIMIST: It's bound to end badly. Look at what has happened.

THE OPTIMIST: What has happened?

THE PESSIMIST: Shall I tell you a little story to remind you? Eh?

THE OPTIMIST: All right.

2

THE PESSIMIST: Was that, or was that not how it was?

THE OPTIMIST: An extremely pessimistic view. And a very uncharitable picture of Dansen. Not a word about his undisputed love of freedom, etc., etc.

THE PESSIMIST: My dear fellow! I was positively flattering Dansen. Now comes his big moment.

THE OPTIMIST: Really? That sounds promising.

THE PESSIMIST: Let me just go on with the story.

3

THE OPTIMIST: Well?

THE PESSIMIST: Well what?

THE OPTIMIST: Well, what's wrong with that contract? Suppose I go on with the story this time? I'll show you how the contract is going to work out. You'll be amazed.

THE PESSIMIST: I certainly will. Just watch out!

# THE TRIAL OF LUCULLUS

## Texts by Brecht

At the beginning of the year 63 AD Rome was full of unrest. In a series of protracted campaigns Pompey had conquered Asia for the Romans, and now they were filled with fear as they waited for the victor to return. Following his victory of course not only Asia but Rome too was his to do what he liked with.

On one of those days of tension, a short, thin man issued from a palace situated in the vast gardens along the Tiber and walked as far as the marble steps to meet a visitor. He was the former general Lucullus, and his visitor (who had come on foot) was the poet Lucretius.

In his time the old general had launched the Asiatic campaign, but thanks to a variety of intrigues Pompey had managed to ease him out of his command. Pompey knew that in many people's eyes Lucullus was the real conqueror of Asia, and so the latter had every reason to view the victor's arrival with alarm. He was not receiving all that many visits in those days.

The general greeted the poet warmly and led him into a small room where he could take some refreshment. The poet however ate nothing but a few figs. His health was poor. His chest troubled him, he could not stand the spring mists.

At first the conversation contained no reference to political matters, not one word. There was some airing of philosophical questions.

Lucullus expressed reservations about the treatment of the gods in Lucretius's didactic poem *On the Nature of Things*. He considered it was dangerous simply to write off religious feeling as superstition. Religious feeling and morality were the same. Renouncing the one meant renouncing the other. Such superstitious notions as are refutable are bound up with other notions whose value cannot be proved but which are none the less needed etc., etc.

Lucretius naturally differed and the old general tried to support his views by describing a dream which he had had during one of his Asiatic campaigns – in point of fact the last. 'It was after the battle of Gasiura. Our position was pretty desperate. We had been counting on some quick victories. Triarus, my deputy at that time, had led his reserves into an ambush. I was forced to extricate him at once or all would have been lost. This at the very moment when the army was becoming dangerously infected with insubordination due to prolonged holdups over pay.

'I was shockingly overworked, and one afternoon I nodded off over the map and had a dream which I will now recount to you.

'We had established our camp by a big river, the Halys, which was in full spate, and I dreamed that I was sitting in my tent at night working on a plan which would definitely destroy my enemy Mithridates. The river was then impassable, and in my dream it split Mithridates' army in two. If I went ahead and attacked the part on our side of the river it would get no help from the part on the other side.

'Morning came. I paraded the army and saw that the proper sacrifices were carried out before my legions. Since I had had a word with the priest the omens proved exceptionally favourable. I made a great speech in which I referred to our unusually good opportunity to destroy the enemy, to the backing given us by the gods who had filled the river, to the splendidly propitious omens which proved that the gods were looking forward to the battle etc., etc. As I spoke a strange thing happened.

'I was standing fairly high up and had a good view of the plain behind our ranks. Not all that far away I could see the smoke going up from Mithridates' camp fires. In between the two armies lay fields; the corn in them was already quite tall. To one side, close by the river, was a farm that was about to get flooded. A peasant family was engaged in rescuing its household possessions from the low house.

'Suddenly I saw the peasants waving in our direction. Some of my legionaries apparently heard them shouting and turned round. Four or five men began moving towards them, at first slowly and uncertainly, then breaking into a run.

'But the peasants pointed in the opposite direction. I could see what they meant. A wall of earth had been banked up to our right. The water had undermined it and it was threatening to collapse.

'All this I saw as I went on speaking. It gave me an idea.

'I thrust out my arm and pointed at the wall so that all eyes were turned towards it, raised my voice and said: "Soldiers, this is the hand of the gods! They have ordered the river to break down the enemy's dyke. In the gods' name, charge!"

'My dream of course was not entirely clear, but I distinctly remember that moment as I stood in the middle of the whole army and paused for effect while they watched the crumbling dyke.

'It was very brief. Suddenly, with no transition, hundreds of soldiers began running towards the dyke.

'Likewise four or five who had already hastened to the peasants' assistance started shouting back to us as they helped the family drag the cattle from their stalls. All I could hear was "The dyke! the dyke!".

'And now there were thousands running that way.

'Those standing behind me ran past me till finally I was swept along too. It was a stream of men, rolling forward against a stream of water.

'I called to the nearest bystanders – by-runners, more like – "On to glory!" "Right, on to the dyke!", they enthusiastically yelled back as if they had not understood me. "How about the battle?" I yelled. "Later!" they assured me.

'I stood in the way of one disorganised cohort.

'"I command you to halt", I shouted peremptorily.

'Two or three of them actually halted. One was a tall fellow with a twisted chin, and to this day I have not forgotten him even though I only saw him in a dream. Turning to his comrades he said "Who's this?". And it was not mere insolence; he honestly meant it. And equally honestly, as I could see, the others replied "No idea". Then they all ran on towards the dyke.

'For a short while I stood there alone. Beside me the sacrifices still smouldered on the field altars. But even the priests were following the soldiers down to the river, I saw. A bit more slowly of course, on account of their being fatter.

'Yielding to a preternaturally strong impulse I decided that I too would examine the dyke. Vaguely I felt the thing would have to be organised. I walked along, a prey to conflicting feelings. But soon I broke into a run because I was worried that the operation might be badly directed and the dyke still collapse. This, I suddenly realised, would mean the loss not only of the farm buildings but also of the fields with the half-grown corn. I had, you see, already been infected by everyone else's feelings.

'When I got there however everything was under control. The fact that our legionaries were equipped with spades for revetting the camp perimeter was a great help. No one thought twice about sticking his sword into the fascines to reinforce them. Shields were used for bringing up earth.

'Seeing me standing there with nothing to do, a soldier grabbed me by the sleeve and handed me a spade. I started digging as directed by a centurion. A man beside me said, "Back home in Picenum there was a dyke burst in '82. The harvest was a total loss." Of course, I realised, most of them were peasants' sons.

'Just once, so I remember, the idea of the enemy again crossed my mind. "Let's hope the enemy doesn't take advantage of this," I told the man beside me. "Nonsense," he said mopping his forehead, "it's not the moment." And true enough when I looked up I could see some of Mithridates' soldiers further downstream working on the dyke. They were working alongside our men, making themselves understood by nods and gestures since of course they spoke a different language – which shows how exact the details of my dream were.'

The old general broke off his story. His little yellow shrivelled-up face bore an expression somewhere between cheerfulness and concern.

'A fine dream,' said the poet placidly.

'Yes. Eh? No.' The general's look was dubious. Then he laughed. 'I wasn't too happy about it,' he said quickly. 'When I woke up I felt disagreeably disturbed. It seemed to me evidence of great weakness.'

'Really?' asked the poet, taken aback. There was a silence. Then Lucretius went on, 'What did you conclude from your dream, at the time?'

'That authority is an extremely shaky business, of course.'

'In the dream.'

'Yes, but all the same . . .'

Lucullus clapped his hands and the servants hastened to clear the dishes. These were still full. Nor had Lucullus eaten anything. In those days he had no appetite.

He proposed to his guest that they should visit the blue room, where some newly acquired *objets d'art* were on display. They walked through open colonnades to a lateral wing of the great palace.

Striking the marble paving hard with his stick, the little general continued:

'What robbed me of victory was not the indiscipline of the common man but the indiscipline of the great. Their love of their country is just love of their palaces and their fishponds. In Asia the Roman tax-farmers banded together with the big local landowners to oppose me. They swore they would paralyse me and my army. In return the landowners handed the peasantry of Asia Minor over to them. They found my successor a better proposition. "At least he's a real general," they said. "He takes." And they weren't only referring to strongpoints. There was one king in Asia Minor on whom he imposed a tribute of fifty millions. As the money had to be paid into the state treasury he "lent" him that sum, with the result that he now draws forty per cent interest each year. That's what I call conquests!'

Lucretius was scarcely listening to the old man, who had not done all that badly out of Asia himself – witness this palace. His thoughts were still focused on the dream, which struck him as an interesting counterpart to a true incident that had occurred during the capture of Amisus by Lucullus's troops.

Amisus, a daughter city of glorious Athens and full of irreplaceable works of art, had been looted and set on fire by Lucullus's soldiers even though the general – reputedly in tears – had besought the looters to spare the art works. There too his authority had not been respected.

The one event had been dream, the other reality. Should it be said that authority, having forbidden the troops the one, could not deny them the other? That was what Lucullus seemed to have felt, though hardly to have acknowledged.

The best of the new *objets d'art* was a little earthenware figure of Nike. Lucretius held it delicately in his skinny hand and looked at it, smiling.

'A good artist,' he said. 'That carefree stance and that delicious smile! His idea was to portray the goddess of victory as a goddess of peace. This figure must date from before those peoples were first defeated.'

Lucullus looked mistrustfully at him and took it in his hand too.

'The human race,' he said abruptly, 'tends to remember the abuses to which it has been subjected rather than the endearments. What's left of kisses? Wounds however leave scars.'

The poet said nothing, but in turn gave him a peculiar look.

'What's the matter?' asked the general. 'Did I surprise you?'

'Slightly, to be honest. Do you really fear you'll get a bad name in the history books?'

'No name at all, perhaps. I don't know what I fear. Altogether this is a month of fear, isn't it? Fear has become rampant. As always after a victory.'

'Though if my information is correct you should be fearing fame these days more than oblivion.'

'True enough. Fame is dangerous for me. More than anything. And between you and me, that's a strange business. I'm a soldier and I must say death has never scared me. But there has been a change. The lovely sight of the garden, the well-cooked food, the delicious works of art bring about an extraordinary weakness in me and even if I still don't fear death I fear the fear of death. Can you explain that?'

The poet said nothing.

'I know,' said the general a little hurriedly. 'That passage from your poem is very familiar to me; in fact I think I even know it by heart, which is another bad sign.'

And he began in a rather dry voice to recite Lucretius' famous lines about fear of death:

'Death, then, is nothing to us, it is not of the slightest importance.
So when you see some man resenting his own destination
Either, when dead, to rot where his mortal body is buried
Or be destroyed by flames or by the jaws of predators
Then you can tell he's a fraud whose heart is surely affected
By some latent sting, however he may keep denying
Any belief that death does not deprive one of feeling.
That which he claims to admit, he does not admit, nor its basis
Nor does he tear out his roots and hurl himself from this existence
But he makes something survive of himself, though he doesn't
    know it.
For if someone who lives can see himself enter a future
Where when he's dead wild beasts and birds will mangle his body
Then he pities himself, for he can't see the thing with detachment
Nor can he stand back enough from the body that he has rejected;
Rather he stands beside it, infecting it with his own feelings.
So he fills with resentment at having been born a mere mortal
Failing to see true death can allow no new self to be, which
Living, could tell itself how much it regrets the deceased and
Standing, lament that, prone, either wounding or fire will consume
    it.'

The poet had listened carefully while his verses were recited, though he had to struggle slightly not to cough. This night air . . . However he could not resist the temptation to acquaint his host with a few lines which he had cut from the work so as not to depress his readers unduly. In them he had set out the reasons for this same effort to cling to what is disappearing. In a hoarse voice, very clearly, slowed down by the need to remember, he spoke these verses:

'When they complain their life has been stolen from them, they're
    complaining
Of an offence both practised on them and by themselves practised
For the same life that they've lost was stolen by them in the first
    place.
Yes, when the fisherman snatches his fish from the sea, then the
    traders
Snatch it in turn from him. And the woman who's hoping to fry it

Ruefully eyes the bottle and pours the oil with reluctance
Into the waiting pan. O fear of a shortage! The risk of
Never replacing what's gone! The awful prospect of robbery!
Violence suited our fathers. And once their inheritance passes
See how their heirs will stoop to criminal acts to preserve it.
Trembling, the dyer will keep his lucrative recipe secret
Fearful of leaks. While in that circle of roistering writers
One will bite off his tongue on betraying some new inspiration.
Flattery serves the seducer to wheedle his girl into bed with
Just as the priest knows tricks to get alms from penurious tenants
While the doctor finds industrial disease is a goldmine.
Who in a world like this can confront the concept of dying?
"Got it" and "drop it" alone determine how life will develop.
Whether you snatch or you hold, your hands begin curving like
    talons.'

'You know the answer, you versifiers,' said the little general
pensively. 'But can you explain to me why it is only now, in these
particular days, that I again start hoping that not everything I've done
will be forgotten – even though fame is hazardous for me and I am
not indifferent towards death?'

'Perhaps your wish for fame is at the same time fear of death?' The
general seemed not to have heard. He looked nervously round and
motioned the torchbearer to withdraw. When he was a few paces
away he asked half-ashamedly, in something like a whisper:

'Where do you think my fame might lie?'

They started walking back. A gentle puff of wind broke the
evening stillness that lay over the garden. The poet coughed and said,
'The conquest of Asia perhaps?' He realised that the general was
holding him by the sleeve and gazing round in alarm, and hastily
added, 'I don't know. Perhaps also the delicious cooking of the
victory banquet.'

After saying this casually he came to a sudden stop. Extending his
finger he pointed at a cherry tree which stood on a small rise, its
white blossom-covered branches waving in the wind.

'That's something else you brought back from Asia, isn't it?'

The general nodded.

'That could be it,' said the poet intensely. 'The cherry tree. I don't
suppose it will recall your name to anyone. But what of that? Asia
will be lost once more. And it won't be long before the general
poverty forces us to give up cooking your favourite dishes. But the
cherry tree ... There might all the same be one or two people who
would know it was you that brought it. And even if there aren't, even

if every trophy of every conqueror has crumbled to dust, this loveliest trophy of yours, Lucullus, will still be waving each spring in the wind of the hillsides; it will be the trophy of an unknown conqueror.'

[It was in autumn 1937 that Brecht began reading Roman history with a view to writing a play about Julius Caesar. A fairly detailed description of its scope will be found in his letter to the Paris lawyer Martin Domke on 13 November. Within a few months however he was changing it into a novel, only to lose interest around the time of the Munich Agreement.

Lucullus, another product of his historical researches, came to the surface of his concerns in Sweden at the beginning of 1939 when he wrote this story, which was first published in his *Geschichten*, 1962, *GW* 11 (our version comes from *Collected Short Stories*, Methuen, 1983). There is nothing in his subsequent radio and opera versions to echo the story's picture of the great general as a little man, with a 'skinny hand' and a 'little yellow shrivelled-up face'. Lucretius would occupy him further during his exile in the US, where he would base his verse rendering of the Communist Manifesto on the hexameters of Lucretius's great poem *De Rerum Natura*. The second passage quoted in this story is taken from Brecht's adaptation.]

DISCUSSION OF 'THE CONDEMNATION OF LUCULLUS'

The opera had already been accepted when the anti-formalist campaign was launched. Misgivings were being expressed in the Ministry of Education. The authors were urged to withdraw it. But they were only prepared to cancel the contract, not to withdraw the opera, since they did not consider it formalist. The arguments adduced failed to convince them; those put forward by musicians being indeed formalist themselves. They stressed the importance of the content, to wit the condemnation of predatory war. As to the work on the opera, which had already begun, they suggested that it should be carried on up to the point where a closed performance could be staged for the enlightenment of the artists and a responsible audience. This was accepted, and massive resources were devoted for that enlightenment to be promoted. At the performances the content had a very strong effect on the audience, if only because it stood for the peaceful policy of the GDR, with its condemnation of wars of conquest. At the same time many reservations were felt, and from a three-hour discussion between the authors and leading government members, with the President in the chair, it appeared that the work in its present form could cause a certain amount of confusion in the recently launched campaign whose importance lies in healing the undeniable breach now separating the arts from their audience. The element of parable in the text was an obstacle to understanding, and the music did not make allowance for the current state of musical education among the wider public; it spurned the classical tradition. What is more, a disproportionate importance was given to describing the aggressor, and the results were depressing and hard on the ear. Brecht and Dessau agreed to make additions in the spirit of the discussion, and to resubmit the results. A further discussion under similar conditions led to the submission of fresh texts, along with an undertaking by the composer to make certain changes. It was then decided that the work should be prepared for performance and offered for criticism by the public.

[BFA, vol. 24, pp. 276–7, May 1951.]

## Editorial Notes

In the case of *Lucullus* Brecht was writing two distinctly different works. The first was the radio play, initially without music, which he wrote in Scandinavia in November 1939, immediately after his great war play *Mother Courage*; it took him six days while Germany and Russia were partitioning Poland, and was first broadcast from Switzerland in the following May. The second was an opera, conceived before he left America, but mainly worked on with the composer Paul Dessau, starting in 1949 when both men were back in Berlin. The additions and revisions which followed were of various kinds. Partly they were changes made before the 1951 publication of the radio play; partly they reflected the demands of the opera medium and the change of title that followed. But the most radical and the most controversial were caused by the changed times – notably by the impact of Nazi war crimes, the revival of Socialist Realism and the pressures of the Cold War. And, far more than the first version, the alterations became news.

In 1951 there were two new publications of Brecht's still changeable text, both of them differing radically from that of 1940. In the *Versuche* series of his works, the radio play version was introduced thus:

> *The Trial of Lucullus* is a radio play. It forms the basis of the opera *The Condemnation of Lucullus*, whose music was written by Paul Dessau.

– while the separate opera libretto appeared in the same year from Aufbau in East Berlin, giving the work its third version as:

THE CONDEMNATION OF LUCULLUS

OPERA BY

PAUL DESSAU AND BERTOLT BRECHT

There are thus three main versions of Brecht's text, and it is their differences that have been the centre of critical and political interest ever since the Dessau–Brecht project was first accepted by Ernst Legal at the East Berlin State Opera in February 1950. We include on p. 391ff the *Condemnation* text as approved for the definitive public première on 12 October 1951, following the much publicised discussions and closed performances. As our primary text, however, we have reproduced Brecht's original *Trial* text as broadcast in 1940 (and subsequently known by that date), which was long unpublished except in the Moscow *Internationale Literatur* of that time and is now given its first publication in English. Frank Jones, who translated the 'Play for Radio' for our Vintage Books edition in 1972, called this 1940 text 'on paper at least, much the most effective of the three versions', and we agree. But prior to the current Berlin and Frankfurt edition of Brecht's *Werke* it was shoved away in favour of the ambiguous 1951 radio play ('Hörspiel') version which finished with the *Condemnation* closing scene. All we give here of that second version is the passages which differ from the original rapidly and unhesitantly written *Trial*. The Brecht/Dessau 'Notes to the Opera' were written subsequently and appended to the 1951 radio play text in the *Versuche* series after the opera's trial performances that spring. Along with the new passages, these make up a slightly flawed midway stage of the work, linking the two main texts.

NOTES TO THE OPERA 'THE CONDEMNATION OF LUCULLUS' (1951, signed Brecht, Dessau)

The 'Hörspiel' *The Trial of Lucullus* was the basis for the opera *The Condemnation of Lucullus*. The former work ended with the verses

> The court
> Withdraws for consultation.

'The Judgement' (scene 14) was borrowed from the latter. It kept its title, however, the better to distinguish it from this. [NB: This is both confusing and inaccurate. See the added scene as reproduced below, pp. 388–90. The Brecht/Dessau notes only give the new chorus of warriors (or legionaries).]

The opera does not include the testimony of the stone figures from the frieze. Instead, the shadows represented there are summoned to give evidence.

NEW PASSAGES INCLUDED IN THE 1951 RADIO PLAY

Additions made in the *Versuche* edition of the radio play (no. 14, Suhrkamp, 1951), followed by later alterations from its endnotes on the further development of the opera version. Their positions in the original text of 1940 are marked there by corresponding numbers.

(1)   Add to 'The Funeral Procession':

VOICES:
  Remember the mightly, the undefeated hero!
  Remember the terror of both Asias
  And the darling of Rome and of the gods
  As he drove through Rome
  In a golden chariot, bringing you
  Alien kings and curious animals
  Elephants, camels, panthers!
  And the carts full of captive women
  The baggage waggons rattling with furniture
  Ships, pictures and beautiful vessels
  Of ivory, a whole Corinth
  Of brazen statues dragged through
  A roaring sea of people! Remember the spectacle!
  Think of the coins for the children
  And the wine and sausages
  As he drove through the city
  In the golden chariot.
  He, the mighty, the undefeated
  The terror of both Asias
  Darling of Rome and of the gods.

(2)   Add to 'In the Schoolbooks':

  Sextus conquers Pontus.
  And you, Flaccus, conquer the three regions of Gaul.
  But you, Quintilian
  Cross over the Alps.

(3)   Add to 'The Reception':

  Where, at least, can Lasus my cook be?
  A man always able to whip up a little titbit
  Out of nothing at all!
  If, for example, they had sent him to meet me –
  For he is down here too –
  I should feel more at home. Oh, Lasus!
  Your lamb with the bayleaves and dill!
  Cappadocian roast game! Your lobsters from Pontus!
  And your Phrygian cakes with bitter berries!

(4)   Add to 'The Reception':

THE WOMAN:
They're calling me.
You'll have to get through as best you can
Newcomer.

(5)   Add to 'Choice of Sponsor':

*Silence.*
THE JUDGE OF THE DEAD:
Unhappy man! Great names
No longer arouse terror down here.
Here
They can threaten no more. Their utterances
Are counted as lies. Their deeds
Are not recorded. And their fame
To us is like smoke showing
That a fire has once raged.
Shadow, your attitude reveals
That mighty enterprises
Are connected with your name.
The enterprises
Are unknown here.

(6)   In scene 8, 'The Frieze is Produced', substitute after 'we expect
nothing':

LUCULLUS:
You jurymen of the dead, observe my frieze.
A captured king, Tigranes of Pontus.
His strange-eyed queen. Look at her lovely thighs.
A man with a cherry tree, eating a cherry.
Two girls with a tablet, on it the names of fifty-three cities.
A dying legionary, greeting his general.
My cook with a fish!
CHORUS:
O see, this is how they build themselves monuments
With stony figures of vain sacrifice
To speak or keep silence above.
Lifeless witnesses, those who have been conquered
Robbed of breath, silenced, forgotten
Must face the daylight for their conqueror's sake
Willing to keep silent and willing to speak.
THE COURT CRIER:
Shadow, the jury take

Note of your triumphal frieze.
They wish to know more about your
Triumphs than your frieze can tell.
They suggest that all those should
Be called who have been portrayed by you
On your frieze.

THE JUDGE OF THE DEAD:

Let them be called.
Always
The victor writes the history of the vanquished.
He who beats
Distorts the faces of the beaten. The weaker
Depart from this world and
The lies remain. Down here we
Have no need of your stones. So many
Of those who crossed your path, General, are with us
Down here – instead of the portrayal
We call those portrayed. We reject the stones
For the shadows themselves.

LUCULLUS:

I object.
I wish not to see them.

VOICES OF THE THREE CITIES:

The victims of General Lucullus
And his Asiatic campaigns!
*The shadows of those portrayed on the triumphal frieze emerge
from the background and stand opposite the frieze.*

[This concludes 'The Frieze is Produced'. The remainder of p. 282 is
cut.]

(7)   Add third verse in scene 9, 'The Hearing':

Fearfully I looked around
Shrieking for my maidens
While the maidens fearfully
Shrieked from out the bushes.
We were all assaulted.

After the trial performance which the Ministry of Education
organised in the Berlin State Opera two interpolations were made as
a result of thoroughgoing discussions. The first shows why the king
(who in this version appears as a shadow, not merely as a figure on
the frieze) has survived a trial similar to that which Lucullus will not.

(8)   In 'The Hearing', after Lucullus's 'Was especially ruthless', cut
the next five lines and substitute:

The silver whose production he favoured
Did not pass through him to the people.
THE TEACHER *to the king*:
Why then
Are you here amongst us, King?
THE KING:
Because I built cities
Because I defended them when you
Romans demanded them from us.
THE TEACHER:
Not we, him!
THE KING:
Because, to defend my country, I summoned
Man, wife and child
In hedgerow and waterhole
With axe, billhook and ploughshare
By day, by night
By their speech, by their silence
Free or captive
In face of the enemy
In face of death.
THE TEACHER:
I propose that we all
Rise to our feet before this witness
And in honour of those
Who defended their cities.
*The jurors rise.*
LUCULLUS:
What sort of Romans are you?
Your enemy gets your plaudits!
I did not act for myself
I acted on orders
I was sent by
Rome.
THE TEACHER:
Rome! Rome! Rome!
Who is Rome?
Were you sent by the masons who built her?
Were you sent by the bakers and fishermen
And the peasants and the carters

And the gardeners who feed her?
Was it the tailors and the furriers
And the weavers and the sheepshearers who clothe her?
Were you sent by the marble-polishers
And the wool-dyers who beautify her?
Or were you sent by the tax-farmers
And the silver merchants and the slave dealers
And the bankers of the Forum who plunder her?
*Silence.*

LUCULLUS:
Whoever sent me:
Rome won
Fifty-three cities, thanks to me.

THE TEACHER:
And where are they?
Jurors, let us question the cities.

TWO YOUNG GIRLS WITH A TABLET:
With streets and people and houses . . .

[Then continue as on p. 285.]

(9)   In 'The Hearing is Continued' the next six lines are cut, p. 293.

(10)   The *Versuche* edition of 1951 tacitly substituted a new last scene (14, 'The Judgement') for that in our (1940) text entitled 'The Wheat and the Chaff'. Here it is. The warriors' chorus was subsequently interpolated in this at (11).

Scene 14

THE JUDGEMENT

THE COURT CRIER:
And up jumps the jurywoman, formerly a fishwife in the market.

THE FISHWIFE:
And have you still got
A penny left in those bloody hands?
Does the murderer
Bribe the court with the booty?

THE TEACHER:
A cherry tree! That conquest
Could have been made
With just one man!
But he sent eighty thousand down here.

THE BAKER:
How much
Must they pay up there
For a glass of wine and a bun?

THE COURTESAN:
Must they always put their skins
On sale in order to sleep with a woman?

THE FISHWIFE:
Yes, into oblivion with him!

THE TEACHER:
Yes, into oblivion with him!

THE BAKER:
Yes, into oblivion with him!

THE COURT CRIER:
And they look at the farmer
Who praised the cherry tree:
Farmer, what do you say?
*Silence.*

THE FARMER:
Yes, into oblivion with him!

THE JUDGE OF THE DEAD:
Yes, into oblivion with him! For
With all this violence and conquest
Only one realm is extended:
The Realm of Shadows.

THE JURORS:
And already
Our grey underworld
Is full of half-lived lives. Yet here
We have no ploughs for strong arms, nor
Hungry mouths, when above
You have so many of both. What except dust
Can we heap over the
Slaughtered eighty thousand? And you up there
Need homes! How often still
Shall we meet them on our paths which lead nowhere
And hear their terrible eager questions – what
Is the summer like this year, and the autumn
And the winter?

THE COURT CRIER:
And the legionaries on the frieze
Move and cry out:

[(11)   Insert chorus of the legionaries (the warriors), see below.]

THE COURT CRIER:
   And the slaves who drag the frieze
   Move and cry out:
THE SLAVES:
   Yes, into oblivion with him! How long
   Shall he and his kind sit
   Inhumanly above other humans and raise
   Lazy hands and fling peoples
   Against each other in bloody warfare?
   How long shall we
   And our kind endure them?
ALL:
   Yes, into oblivion with him and into oblivion
   With all like him!
THE COURT CRIER:
   And from the high bench they rise up
   The spokesmen of the world-to-be
   The world with many hands, to take
   The world with many mouths, to eat –
   The eagerly gathering
   Gladly living world-to-be.

(11)   The subsequent interpolation comes near the end of the new
final scene, where the warriors who fell in his Asiatic campaigns join
in Lucullus's condemnation.

THE WARRIORS:
   In the murderer's tunic
   In the ravager's plunder gang
   We fell
   The sons of the people.
   Yes, into oblivion with him!
   Like the wolf
   Who breaks into the herd
   And has to be destroyed
   We were destroyed
   In his service.
   Yes, into oblivion with him!
   Had we but
   Left the aggressor's service!
   Had we but
   Joined with the defenders!
   Into oblivion with him!

# The Condemnation of Lucullus

OPERA BY
PAUL DESSAU AND BERTOLT BRECHT

*Translator:* H.R. HAYS

*Characters:*

LUCULLUS, *a Roman general (tenor)*
*Figures on the Frieze:*
  THE KING *(bass)*
  THE QUEEN *(soprano)*
  TWO CHILDREN *(soprano and mezzo)*
  TWO LEGIONARIES *(basses)*
  LASUS, *cook to Lucullus (tenor)*
  THE CHERRY-TREE BEARER *(baritone)*
*Jury of the Dead:*
  THE FISHWIFE *(contralto)*
  THE COURTESAN *(mezzo)*
  THE TEACHER *(tenor)*
  THE BAKER *(bass)*
  THE FARMER *(bass)*
TERTULLIA, *an old woman (mezzo)*
THREE ROMAN WOMEN *(sopranos)*
VOICES OF THE THREE WOMEN HERALDS
THE JUDGE OF THE DEAD *(high bass)*
VOICE OF A WOMAN COMMENTATOR
THE COURT CRIER
THREE HERALDS
TWO GIRLS
TWO MERCHANTS
TWO WOMEN
TWO PLEBEIANS
A DRIVER
Chorus of the crowd; soldiers, slaves, shadows, children

I

THE FUNERAL PROCESSION

*Noise of a great crowd.*

FIRST HERALD:
   Hark, the great Lucullus is dead!
   The general who conquered the East
   Who overthrew seven kings
   Who filled our city of Rome with riches.
SECOND HERALD:
   Before his catafalque
   Borne by soldiers
   Walk the most distinguished men of mighty Rome
   With covered faces, beside him
   Walk his philosopher, his advocate
   And his charger.
SONG OF THE SOLDIERS CARRYING THE CATAFALQUE:
   Hold it steady, hold it shoulder-high.
   See that it does not waver in front of thousands of eyes
   For now the Lord of the Eastern Earth
   Betakes himself to the shadows. Take care, do not stumble.
   That flesh and metal you bear
   Has ruled the world.
THIRD HERALD:
   Before him
   They drag a tremendous frieze
   Setting forth his deeds and destined to be his tombstone.
   Once more
   The entire people pays its respects to an amazing lifetime
   Of victory and conquest
   And they remember his former triumphal processions.
SONG OF THE THREE ROMAN WOMEN:
   Think of the powerful, think of the unbeatable
   Think of the terror of the two Asias
   And favourite of Rome and the gods
   As he rode through the city on the golden waggon
   Bringing you foreign kings and foreign animals!
   Think of the coins for the children
   And the wine and the sausages!
   As he rode through the city

On the golden waggon
He the unbeatable, he the powerful
He the terror of the two Asias
Favourite of Rome and the gods!

SLAVES DRAGGING THE FRIEZE:
Careful, do not stumble!
You who haul the frieze with the scene of triumph
Ay, though the sweat runs down to your eyelids
Still keep your hands to the stone! Think, if you drop it
It might crumble to dust.

A GIRL:
See the red plume! No, the big one.

ANOTHER GIRL:
He squints.

FIRST MERCHANT:
All the senators.

SECOND MERCHANT:
All the tailors too.

FIRST MERCHANT:
Why no, this man has pushed on even to India.

SECOND MERCHANT:
But he was finished long ago
I'm sorry to say.

FIRST MERCHANT:
Greater than Pompey
Rome would have been lost without him.
Enormous victories.

SECOND MERCHANT:
Mostly luck.

FIRST WOMAN:
My Reus
Perished in Asia.
All this fuss won't bring him back to me.

FIRST MERCHANT:
Thanks to this man
Many a man made a fortune.

SECOND WOMAN:
My brother's boy too never came home again.

FIRST MERCHANT:
Everyone knows what Rome reaped, thanks to him
In fame alone.

FIRST WOMAN:
Without their lies

Nobody would walk into the trap.

FIRST MERCHANT:
Heroism, alas
Is dying out.

FIRST PLEBEIAN:
When
Will they spare us this twaddle about fame?

SECOND PLEBEIAN:
Three legions in Cappadocia
Not one left to tell the tale.

A DRIVER:
Can
I get through here?

SECOND WOMAN:
No, it's closed off.

FIRST PLEBEIAN:
When we bury our generals
Oxcarts must have patience.

SECOND WOMAN:
They dragged my Pulcher before the judge:
Taxes due.

FIRST MERCHANT:
We can say
Except for him Asia would not be ours today.

FIRST WOMAN:
Has tunnyfish jumped in price again?

SECOND WOMAN:
Cheese too.
*The noise of the crowd increases.*

FIRST HERALD:
Now
They pass through the arch of triumph
Which the city has built for her great son.
The women hold their children high. The mounted men
Press back the ranks of the spectators.
The street behind the procession lies deserted.
For the last time
The great Lucullus has passed through it.

SECOND HERALD:
The procession has disappeared. Now
The street is full again. From the obstructed side-alleys
The carters drive out with their oxcarts. The crowd
Returns to its business, chattering. Busy Rome
Goes back to work.

2

THE BURIAL

CHORUS:
　Outside, on the Appian Way
　Stands a little structure, built ten years before
　Meant to shelter the great man
　In death.
　Before it, the crowd of slaves that drags the triumphal frieze
　Turns in.
　Then the little rotunda with the boxtree hedge receives it.
　*The catafalque and the frieze are carried in by soldiers and slaves.*
　*After the catafalque has been set down the vast frieze is placed*
　*outside the tomb. The soldiers are given the command 'Fall out!'*
　*and move away.*

3

DEPARTURE OF THE LIVING

CHORUS OF SOLDIERS:
　So long, Lakalles.
　Now we're quits, old goat.
　Out of the boneyard
　Up with the glass!
　Fame isn't everything
　You've got to live too.
　Who'll come along?
　Down by the dock
　There's wine and song. You weren't in step.
　I'll come along.
　Be sure of that.
　Who'll pay the bill?
　They'll chalk it up.
　Look at his grin!
　I'm off to the cattle market.
　To the little brunette? Hey, we'll come along.
　No, three's a crowd.
　You'll put her off.

Then
We're for the dog races.
Man
That costs money. Not if they know you.
I'll come along.
Attention! Break ranks!
March.


4

IN THE SCHOOLBOOKS


A VOICE:
From then on teachers would show the schoolchildren
The great conqueror's tomb.
CHILDREN'S CHORUS:
In the schoolbooks
Are written the names of great conquerors.
Whoever wants to emulate them
Learns their battles by heart
Studies their wonderful lives.
To emulate them
To rise above the crowd
Is our task. Our city
Is eager to write our names some day
On the tablets of immortality.
THE TEACHER:
Sextus conquers Pontus.
And you, Flaccus, conquer the three regions of Gaul.
But you, Quintilian
Cross over the Alps.


5

THE RECEPTION


CHORUS:
Ever since the newcomer has entered
He has stood near the door, motionless, his helmet under his arm
Like his own statue.
The other dead who are newly arrived
Crouch on the bench and wait as they have often waited

For good fortune and for death
Waited in the tavern until they got their wine
Waited at the well until the lover came
Waited in the wood, in battle, for the word of command.
But the newcomer
Does not seem to have learned how to wait.

LUCULLUS:

By Jupiter
What does this mean? I stand and wait here.
The greatest city on the globe still rings
With lamentations for me, and here
There is no one to receive me. Outside my war tent
Seven kings once waited for me.
Is there no order here?
Where, at least, can Lasus my cook be?
A man always able to whip up a little titbit
Out of nothing at all!
If, for example, they had sent him to meet me –
For he is down here too –
I should feel more at home. Oh, Lasus!
Your lamb with the bayleaves and dill!
Cappadocian roast game! Your lobsters from Pontus!
And your Phrygian cakes with bitter berries!
And the endless variety of your flavourings
Sage and olives
Thyme, nutmeg and pressed cinnamon.
Such sauces, such salads, O Lasus!
*Pause.*
I demand to be conducted from this place.
*Pause.*
Must I stand here among these people?
*Pause.*
I object. Two hundred armoured ships, five legions
Used to advance at the crook of my little finger.
I object.
*Pause.*

TERTULLIA:

Sit down, newcomer.
All that metal you haul, the heavy helmet
And the breastplate must be tiring.
So sit down.
*Lucullus is silent.*
Don't be arrogant. You can't stand the whole time

You must wait here. My turn comes before yours.
No one can say how long the hearing inside will last.
There's no doubt that each one will be strictly examined
To determined whether he shall be sentenced to go
Down into dark Hades
Or into the Elysian Fields. Sometimes
The trial is quite short. One glance is enough for the judges.
This one here, they say
Has led a blameless life and he was able
To be of use to his fellow men.
With them a person's usefulness counts the most.
They say to him go take your rest.
Of course with others
The hearing may last for whole days, especially
With those who have sent someone down here to the Realm of the
    Shadows
Before the appointed span of his life was over.
It won't take long with the one who went in just now.
He's a harmless little baker. As for my affair
I'm a little anxious, but put my faith in this –
Among the jury within, they tell me
There are little people who know well enough
How hard life is for those of us in times of war.
My advice to you, newcomer . . .

VOICES OF THE THREE WOMEN HERALDS:
Tertullia!

TERTULLIA:
They are calling me.
You must see how it goes
Newcomer – Sit down!

CHORUS:
The newcomer stands stubbornly on the sill
But the burden of his decorations
His own roaring
And the friendly words of the old woman have changed him.
He looks around to see if he is really alone.
Now he goes to the bench after all. But before he can sit down
He'll be called. A glance at the old woman
Was enough for the judge.

VOICES OF THE THREE WOMEN HERALDS:
Lakalles!

LUCULLUS:
My name is Lucullus! Isn't my name known here?

I come from a distinguished family
Of statesmen and generals. Only in the slums
In the docks and soldiers' taverns, in the unwashed
Jaws of the vulgar, the scum
Is my name Lakalles.

VOICES OF THE THREE WOMEN HERALDS:
Lakalles!

CHORUS:
And so yet again called
In the despised language of the slums
Lucullus, the general
Who conquered the East
Who overthrew seven kings
And filled the city of Rome with riches.
At nightfall, when Rome sits down to the funeral feast
Lucullus presents himself before the highest tribunal of the Realm
of the Shadows.


6

CHOICE OF A SPONSOR

THE COURT CRIER:
Before the highest tribunal of the Realm of the Shadows appears
General Lakalles, who calls himself Lucullus.
Presided over by the Judge of the Dead
Five jurors pursue the examination:
One, formerly a farmer
One, formerly a slave who was a teacher
One, formerly a fishwife
One, formerly a baker
And one, formerly a courtesan.
They sit upon a high bench
Without hands to take and without mouths to eat
Insensible to magnificence, these long-extinguished eyes
Incorruptible, these ancestors of the world-to-come.
The Judge of the Dead begins the hearing.

THE JUDGE OF THE DEAD:
Shadow, you shall be heard.
You must account for your life among men.
Whether you have served them or harmed them
Whether we wish to see your face

In the Elysian Fields.
You need a sponsor.
Have you a sponsor in the Elysian Fields?

LUCULLUS:

I propose the great Alexander of Macedon be called.
Let him speak to you as an expert
On deeds like mine.

VOICES OF THE THREE WOMEN HERALDS *call out in the Elysian
Fields*:

Alexander of Macedon!
*Silence.*

VOICES OF THE THREE WOMEN HERALDS:

In the Elysian Fields
There is no Alexander of Macedon.

THE COURT CRIER:

The person called does not answer.

THE JUDGE OF THE DEAD:

Shadow, your expert is unknown
In the Fields of the Blessed.

LUCULLUS:

What? He who conquered from Asia to India
The never-to-be-forgotten one
Who so indelibly pressed his footprint in the globe of the earth
The mighty Alexander . . .

THE JUDGE OF THE DEAD:

Is unknown here.
Unhappy man! Great names
No longer arouse terror down here.
Here
They can threaten no more. Their utterances
Are counted as lies. Their deeds
Are not recorded. And their fame
To us is like smoke showing
That a fire has once raged.
Shadow, your attitude reveals
That mighty enterprises
Are connected with your name.
The enterprises
Are unknown here.

LUCULLUS:

Then I propose
That the frieze from my memorial
On which my triumphal procession is set forth, be fetched.

But how can it be fetched? Slaves haul it. Surely
Entrance is forbidden here
To the living.

THE JUDGE OF THE DEAD:

Not to slaves. So little divides them
From the dead that one can say
They scarcely live. The step from the world above
Down to the Realm of the Shadows
Is to them a short one.
The frieze shall be brought.

VOICES OF THE THREE WOMEN HERALDS:

The frieze shall be brought.


7

THE FRIEZE IS PRODUCED

CHORUS OF SLAVES:

Out of life into death
Without protest, we haul the burden.
Long ago our time ceased to be ours
And the goal of our journey unknown.
And so we follow the new voice
Like the old. Why question it?
We leave nothing behind; we expect nothing.

LUCULLUS:

You jurymen of the dead, look upon my frieze:
A captured king, Tigranes of Pontus
His strange-eyed queen with provocative thighs
A man with a cherry tree, eating a cherry
Two girls with a tablet, upon it the names of fifty-three cities
A dying legionary, greeting his general
My cook with a fish.

CHORUS:

O see, this is how they build themselves monuments
With stony figures of vain sacrifice
To speak or keep silence above.
Lifeless witnesses, those who have been conquered
Robbed of breath, silenced, forgotten
Must face the daylight for their conqueror's sake
Willing to keep silent and willing to speak.

THE COURT CRIER:
  Shadow, the jury take
  Note of your triumphal frieze.
  They wish to know more about your
  Triumphs than your frieze can tell.
  They suggest that all those should
  Be called who have been portrayed by you
  On your frieze.
THE JUDGE OF THE DEAD:
  Let them be called.
  Always
  The victor writes the history of the vanquished.
  He who beats
  Distorts the faces of the beaten. The weaker
  Depart from this world and
  The lies remain. Down here we
  Have no need of your stones. So many
  Of those who crossed your path, General, are with us
  Down here – Instead of the portrayal
  We call those portrayed. We reject the stones
  For the shadows themselves.
LUCULLUS:
  I object.
  I wish not to see them.
VOICES OF THE THREE WOMEN HERALDS:
  The victims of General Lucullus
  And his Asiatic campaigns!
  *The shadows of those portrayed on the triumphal frieze emerge
  from the background and stand opposite the frieze.*

8

THE HEARING

THE COURT CRIER:
  Bow, shadow
  These are your witnesses.
LUCULLUS:
  I object.
THE COURT CRIER:
  These are your witnesses.
LUCULLUS:
  But they are enemies!

Here you see one whom I vanquished.
In these few days between new and full moon
I defeated his army with all its
Battle waggons and armoured cavalry.
In these few days
His empire crumbled like a hut struck by lightning.
He began to fly when I appeared on his frontier
And the first few days of the war
Were scarcely enough for us both
To reach the other frontier of his realm.
So short was the campaign that a ham
My cook had hung up to smoke
Was not yet thoroughly cured when I returned.
And of seven I struck down he was but one.

THE JUDGE OF THE DEAD:
   Is that true, O King?

THE KING:
   It is true.

THE JUDGE OF THE DEAD:
   Your questions, jurors.

THE COURT CRIER:
   At which the shadow
   Who was once a teacher puts a question.

THE TEACHER:
   How did it happen?

THE KING:
   As he says. We were attacked
   As the farmer loading hay
   Stood with raised fork
   His half-filled waggon was taken from him
   And strange hands seized the baker's breadloaf
   Before it was fully baked. All that he says
   Concerning the lightning that strikes a hut is true.
   The hut is destroyed. Here
   Is the lightning.

THE TEACHER:
   And of seven you were . . .

THE KING:
   But one.

THE COURT CRIER:
   Jurymen of the dead
   Consider the testimony of the king.
   *Silence.*

And the shadow who was once a courtesan
Puts a question.

THE COURTESAN:
You there, O Queen
How did you get here?

THE QUEEN:
One day by the Taurion I
Went to bathe there early
From among the olive trees
Down came fifty strangers.
Those men were my conquerors.

Had no weapon but a sponge
In the limpid water.
And their armour shielded me
Only for a moment.
Quickly I was conquered.

Fearfully I looked around
Shrieking for my maidens
While the maidens fearfully
Shrieked from out the bushes.
We were all assaulted.

THE COURTESAN:
And why do you walk here in the procession?

THE QUEEN:
Oh, as a proof of the victory.

THE COURTESAN:
What victory, the one over you?

THE QUEEN:
And the lovely Taurion.

THE COURTESAN:
And what does he call a triumph?

THE QUEEN:
That the king, my husband
Could not with his whole army
Protect his property
From prodigious Rome.

THE COURTESAN:
Sister, then our fates are the same.
For I too
Found prodigious Rome
No shield against prodigious Rome.
When I was on the love market –

Which I was from sixteen on –
I got curses and beatings daily
All for a drop of oil and lousy pasta.
Makes me know how you'll have suffered
On that frightful day
And I feel with you, poor lady.

THE COURT CRIER:

Jurymen of the dead
Consider the testimony of the queen.
*Pause.*

THE JUDGE OF THE DEAD:

Shadow, do you wish to proceed?

LUCULLUS:

Yes, I mark well how the conquered
Have a sweet voice. However
Once it was rougher. This king here
Who captures your sympathy, when he was in power
Was especially ruthless. In taxes and tribute
He took no less than I.
The silver whose production he favoured
Did not pass through him to the people.

THE TEACHER *to the king*:

Why then
Are you here amongst us, King?

THE KING:

Because I built cities
Because I defended them when you
Romans demanded them from us.

THE TEACHER:

Not we, him!

THE KING:

Because, to defend my country, I summoned
Man, wife and child
In hedgerow and waterhole
With axe, billhook and ploughshare
By day, by night
By their speech, by their silence
Free or captive
In face of the enemy
In face of death.

THE TEACHER:

I propose that we all
Rise to our feet before this witness

And in honour of those
Who defended their cities.
*The jurors rise.*

LUCULLUS:

What sort of Romans are you?
Your enemy gets your plaudits!
I did not act for myself
I acted on orders
I was sent by
Rome.

THE TEACHER:

Rome! Rome! Rome!
Who is Rome?
Were you sent by the masons who built her?
Were you sent by the bakers and fishermen
And the peasants and the carters
And the gardeners who feed her?
Was it the tailors and the furriers
And the weavers and the sheepshearers who clothe her?
Were you sent by the marble-polishers
And the wool-dyers who beautify her?
Or were you sent by the tax-farmers
And the silver merchants and the slave dealers
And the bankers of the Forum who plunder her?
*Silence.*

LUCULLUS:

Whoever sent me:
Rome won
Fifty-three cities, thanks to me.

THE TEACHER:

And where are they?
Jurors, let us question the cities.

TWO CHILDREN WITH A TABLET:

With streets and people and houses
Temples and waterworks
They stood in the landscape.
Today only their names remain on this tablet.

THE BAKER:

Why so?

TWO CHILDREN:

One day at noon an uproar broke loose.
Into the streets swept a flood
Whose waves were men, and carried

Our goods away. In the evening
Only a foul smoke marked the spot
That was once a city.

THE BAKER:

Tell us more.

TWO CHILDREN:

And in those cities there were
Two hundred and fifty thousand children –
They are no longer. Mighty Lucullus
Came on us in his iron battle-waggon
And conquered us all.

LUCULLUS:

Yes, I smashed their impertinent cities!
And took their gold and all kinds of riches
And I took away their people to be our slaves.
Because they paid tribute to false gods.
But I overthrew them
So that the whole earth might see our gods
Were greater than all other gods.

THE COURT CRIER:

Whereupon the shadowy juryman
Who was once a baker
In Marsilia, the city by the sea
Makes a proposal.

THE BAKER:

Then we write to your credit, shadow
Simply this: Brought gold to Rome.

THE COURT CRIER:

You jurymen of the dead
Consider the testimony of the cities.
*Pause.*

THE JUDGE OF THE DEAD:

The accused seems tired.
I declare a recess.


9

ROME

THE COURT CRIER:

The accused sits down.
He is exhausted, but he overhears

Talk behind the door
Where new shadows have appeared.
FIRST SHADOW:
  I came to grief through an oxcart.
LUCULLUS *softly*:
  Oxcart.
FIRST SHADOW:
  It brought a load of sand to a building site.
LUCULLUS *softly*:
  Building site. Sand.
SECOND SHADOW:
  Isn't it meal time now?
LUCULLUS *softly*:
  Meal time?
FIRST SHADOW:
  I had my bread and onions
  With me. I haven't a room any more.
  The horde of slaves
  They herd in from every spot under heaven
  Has ruined the shoemaking business.
SECOND SHADOW:
  I too am a slave.
  Say rather, the lucky
  Catch the unlucky's bad luck.
LUCULLUS:
  You there, is there wind still up above?
SECOND SHADOW:
  Hark, someone's asking a question.
FIRST SHADOW:
  Whether there's wind up above? Perhaps.
  There may be in the gardens.
  In the suffocating alleys
  You don't notice it.


10


THE HEARING IS CONTINUED


THE COURT CRIER:
  Now the shadow that was once a fishwife
  Has a question.

THE FISHWIFE:
> There was talk of gold.
> I too lived in Rome.
> Yet I never noticed any gold where I lived.
> I'd like to know where it went.

LUCULLUS:
> What a question!
> Should I and my legions set out
> To capture a new stool for a fishwife?

THE FISHWIFE:
> Though you brought nothing to us in the fish market
> Still you took something from us in the fish market:
> Our sons.
> Tell me, what happened to you in the two Asias?

FIRST LEGIONARY:
> I ran away.

SECOND LEGIONARY:
> And I was wounded.

FIRST LEGIONARY:
> I dragged him along.

SECOND LEGIONARY:
> So then he fell too.

THE FISHWIFE:
> Why did you leave Rome?

FIRST LEGIONARY:
> I was hungry.

THE FISHWIFE:
> And what did you get there?

SECOND LEGIONARY:
> I got nothing.

THE FISHWIFE:
> You stretch out your hand.
> Is that to greet your general?

SECOND LEGIONARY:
> It was to show him
> It was still empty.

LUCULLUS:
> I protest.
> I rewarded the legionaries
> After each campaign.

THE FISHWIFE:
> But not the dead ones.

LUCULLUS:
> I protest.

How can war be judged
By those who do not understand it?

THE FISHWIFE:

I understand it. My son
Fell in the war.
I was a fishwife in the market at the Forum.
One day it was reported that the ships
Returning from the Asian war
Had docked. I ran from the market place
And I stood by the Tiber for many hours
Where they were being unloaded and in the evening
All the ships were empty and my son
Came down none of the gangplanks.
Since it was chilly by the harbour at night
I fell into a fever, and in the fever sought my son
And ever seeking him more deeply
I grew more chilled, died, came here
Into the Realm of Shadows, and still sought him.
Faber, I cried, for that was his name.
And I ran and ran through shadows
And from shadow to shadow
Crying Faber, until a gatekeeper over there
In the camp of fallen warriors
Caught me by the sleeve and said:
Old woman, there are many Fabers here, many
Mothers' sons, many, deeply mourned
But they have forgotten their names
Which only served to line them up in the army
And are no longer needed here. And their mothers
They do not wish to meet again
Because they let them go to the bloody war.
Faber, my son, Faber
Whom I carried, whom I brought up
My son, Faber!
And I stood, held by my sleeve
And my cries died out in my mouth.
Silently I turned away, for I desired no longer
To look upon my son's face.

THE JUDGE OF THE DEAD:

The court recognises that the mother of the fallen
Understands war.

THE COURT CRIER:

Jurymen of the dead

Consider the testimony of the warriors!
*Silence.*

THE JUDGE OF THE DEAD:
But the jurywoman is moved
And in her trembling hands
The scales may tip. To regain her composure
She needs
A recess.


11

THE HEARING IS CONTINUED


CHORUS:
The jurywoman has recovered.

THE COURT CRIER:
Accused, step forward!

THE JUDGE OF THE DEAD:
Lakalles! Our time runs out. You do not make use of it.
Anger us no more with your triumphs!
Have you no witnesses
To any of your weak points, mortal?
Your business goes badly. Your virtues
Seem to be of little use.
Perhaps your weaknesses will leave some loopholes
In the chain of violent deeds.
I counsel you, shadow
Recollect your weaknesses.

THE COURT CRIER:
And the juryman who was once a baker
Puts a question.

THE BAKER:
Yonder I see a cook with a fish.
He seems cheerful. Cook
Tell us how you came to be in the triumphal procession.

THE COOK:
Only to show
That even while waging war
He found time to discover a recipe for cooking fish.
I was his cook. Often
I think of the beautiful meat
The gamefowl and the black venison

Which he made me roast.
And he not only sat at table
But gave me a word of praise
Stood over the pots with me
And himself mixed a dish.
Lamb *à la* Lucullus
Made our kitchen famous.
From Syria to Pontus
They spoke of Lucullus's cook.

THE COURT CRIER:
And the juror who was once a teacher says:

THE TEACHER:
What is it to us that he liked to eat?

THE COOK:
But he let me cook
To my heart's content. I thank him for it.

THE BAKER:
I understand him, I who was a baker.
How often I had to mix bran with the dough
Because my customers were poor. This fellow here
Could be an artist.

THE COOK:
Thanks to him!
That is why I call him human.

THE COURT CRIER:
Jurors of the dead, consider
The testimony of the cook.
*Silence.*

THE COURT CRIER:
And the juryman who was once a farmer
Puts a question.

THE FARMER:
Over there, is someone who carries a fruit tree.

THE TREE BEARER:
This is a cherry tree.
We brought it from Asia. In the triumphal procession
We carried it along. And we planted it
On the slopes of the Apennines.

THE FARMER:
Oh, so it was you, Lakalles, who brought it?
I once planted it too, but I did not know
That you introduced it.

THE COURT CRIER:
And with a friendly smile
The juryman who was once a farmer
Discusses with the shadow
Who was once a general
The cherry tree.

THE FARMER:
It needs little soil.

LUCULLUS:
But it doesn't like the wind.

THE FARMER:
The red cherries have more meat.

LUCULLUS:
And the black are sweeter.

THE FARMER:
My friends, this of all the detestable souvenirs
Conquered in bloody battle
I call the best. For this sapling lives.
It is a new and friendly companion
To the vine and the abundant berrybush
And growing with the growing generations
Bears fruit for them. And I congratulate you
Who brought it to us. When all the booty of conquest
From both Asias has long mouldered away
This finest of all your trophies
Renewed each year for the living
Shall in spring flutter its white-flowered branches
In the wind from the hills.


12

THE JUDGEMENT

CHORUS:
Up jumps the jurywoman, formerly a fishwife in the market.

THE FISHWIFE:
And did you still find
A penny in those bloody hands? Does the murderer
Bribe the court with the booty?

THE TEACHER:
A cherry tree! That conquest
Could have been made

With just one man
But he sent eighty thousand down here.

THE BAKER:
How much
Must they pay up there
For a glass of wine and a bun?

THE COURTESAN:
Must they always put their skins
On sale in order to sleep with a woman?

THE FISHWIFE:
Yes, into oblivion with him!

THE TEACHER:
Yes, into oblivion with him!

THE BAKER:
Yes, into oblivion with him!

CHORUS:
And they look at the farmer
Who praised the cherry tree:
Farmer, what do you say?
*Silence.*

THE FARMER:
Eighty thousand for a cherry tree!
Yes, into oblivion with him!

THE JUDGE OF THE DEAD:
Yes, into oblivion with him! For
With all this violence and conquest
Only one realm is extended:
The Realm of the Shadows.

THE JURORS:
And already
Our grey underworld
Is full of half-lived lives.

THE FARMER:
Yet here
We have no ploughs for strong arms.

THE JURORS:
Nor
Hungry mouths, when above
You have so many of both. What except dust
Can we heap over the
Slaughtered eighty thousand? And you up there
Need houses! How often still
Shall we meet them on our paths which lead nowhere
And hear their terribly eager questions – what

Is the summer like this year, and the autumn
And the winter?
CHORUS:
Now hear the report
Of the Asiatic legions!
*Roman legionaries appear in formation.*
THE LEGIONARIES:
In the murderer's tunic
In the ravager's plunder gang
We fell
The sons of the people.
Yes, into oblivion with him!
Like the wolf
Who breaks into the herd
And has to be destroyed
We were destroyed
In his service.
Yes, into oblivion with him!
Had we but
Left the aggressor's service!
Had we but
Joined with the defenders!
CHORUS:
And the slaves who bore the frieze
Cried out:
THE SLAVES:
Yes, into oblivion with him! How long
Shall he and his kind sit
Inhumanly above other humans and raise
Lazy hands and fling peoples
Against each other in bloody warfare?
How long shall we
And our kind endure them?
ALL:
Yes, into oblivion with him and into oblivion
With all like him!
THE COURT CRIER:
And from the high bench they rise up
The spokesmen of the world-to-be
Of those with many hands, to take
Of those with many mouths, to eat
Eagerly gathering
Avidly living world-to-be.